eBay® Timesaving Techniques For Dummies®

Cheat Sheet

Readers' Picks

I get many questions from my Web site (at www.coolebaytools.com) and when I'm teaching seminars. I try to answer as many as I can, so here are the answers to the top queries (and where to find them in this book):

To Save Time or Money By	Find the Info In	To Save Time or Money By	Find the Info In
Finding merchandise to sell on eBay	Techniques 5 and 6	Making your own auction templates	Techniques 20 and 21
Finding good auction management vendors	Techniques 23 and 60	Finding out what licenses are required for your city and state	Technique 46
Keeping professional accounting records	Technique 47	Producing six-month merchandise plans	Technique 52
Finding the hot-ticket items on eBay	Technique 8	Knowing who makes the claim for a damaged shipment	Technique 40
Setting reasonable shipping costs	Technique 10	Using cost-per-click advertising to promote your listings	Techniques 55 and 57
Starting the bidding at the right price	Technique 9	Getting better pictures for your auctions	Techniques 15 through 19
Understanding your financial reports	Technique 48	Spotting a fraudulent e-mail	Technique 62

Making Google Work for You!

Google is a search engine all right, but it's more than that — it's a business tool, too. The Google Toolbar that you download from toolbar.google.com gives you a Google search window right on your browser along with a pop-up blocker and lots of other handy tools! This table shows some useful stuff you can do with Google.

Quick Business Results with Google Searches

To Find	Type In	You Get
Phone numbers	phonebook:firstname,lastname followed by a space and a two-letter state abbreviation, such as phonebook:pierre,omidyar ca	Gee, no phone for Omidyar listed in California? (That's strange.) But you can find lots of other phone numbers this way.
Tracking numbers	Any tracking number from FedEx, UPS, or USPS	A link to the tracking information
Telephone area codes	Area code (as it appears in Caller ID when you're deciding whether to take the call)	Links to maps and city information that match the area code
Street maps	Street address with city and state 1600 Pennsylvania Ave Washington DC	A link to a map for that address (very helpful f...
Items by UPC or ISBN numbers	UPS or ISBN number you find just below the barcode	L...
Definitions	Define "barbeque" or define barbecue (for example)	A...
Calculations	Any math formula or conversion for units of measure, for example: 133 inches in meters	...

For Dummies: Bestselling Book Series for Beginners

eBay® Timesaving Techniques For Dummies®

Cheat Sheet

Fun Web Sites to Help Your eBay Business

Craigslist online free classifieds at www.craigslist.org is a great place to source merchandise for eBay — or to sell your *too-big* stuff. Broken down by cities, Craigslist currently covers 35 metropolitan areas with many more planned. You can also find part- or full-time help here.

eBay Auction Count Charts at www.medved.net/cgi-bin/cal.exe?EIND monitors eBay's auctions 24/7 and updates every 1.5 hours. Here you can find the total number of listings in chart format for any day back to 1999.

eBay Top 500 Sellers at www.nortica.com/UserArea/ebay500_2.asp gives the top eBay sellers as of June 2003. Each seller has a link to his or her current eBay feedback page. (It's interesting to see where these people are now.)

Strange items on eBay at www.disturbingauctions.com is a fun Web site that's been around since 1999 to chronicle the strange and tacky items people have sold (or tried to sell) on eBay. It might not help your business, but it'll sure bring a smile to your face (unless one of *your* items is featured as disturbing)!

U.S. Department of the Treasury Seized Property Auctions at www.treas.gov/auctions/customs offers you a chance to own property seized by the United States Customs Service for possible resale on eBay. You can often find pallets of apparel sandwiched in between the boats and vehicles. Although the auctions are held in only a few cities, the scope may be expanding.

Cool eBay Tools at www.coolebaytools.com is my Web site where I post updates to my books and send out my free newsletter.

Early eBay History

Labor Day 1995	AuctionWeb (pre-eBay) hits the Internet.		**January 2000**	GMS (Gross Merchandise Sales) surpasses $1 billion.
February 1996	Feedback system introduced and AuctionWeb began charging for listings. For the next two years, sellers could list a limited number of items per day (or the servers couldn't handle the strain).		**March 2000**	eBay Motors launches as a separate site.
			August 2001	A Gulfstream II jet sells on eBay for $4.9 million (still the highest selling price for any item on the site).
May 1997	One-millionth item sold — a Big Bird Sesame Street Jack-in-the-box. The site received a million page hits per week.		**Fall 2001**	Over 100,000,000 items listed
			March 2002	48 million users
			December 2002	Nearly 69 million users and close to 4 billion hits per week
Fall 1997	AuctionWeb changed its name to eBay.		**December 2003**	94.9 million registered users
March 1998	Meg Whitman takes over as eBay's CEO.			

Apparel Size Facts

When buying clothing to resell on eBay, realize that the average American woman's dress size is a 14 — the size where *plus-size* clothing begins — and not an 8. The average American man wears a 40 Regular. Also, ignore the standard "1 Small, 3 Medium, and 2 Large" lot and, instead, stock 1 Small, 2 Medium, 1 Large, and 1 Extra Large for resale.

For Dummies: Bestselling Book Series for Beginners

eBay® Timesaving Techniques

FOR DUMMIES®

eBay® Timesaving Techniques
FOR DUMMIES®

by Marsha Collier

WILEY

Wiley Publishing, Inc.

eBay® Timesaving Techniques For Dummies®

Published by
Wiley Publishing, Inc.
111 River Street
Hoboken, NJ 07030-5774

Copyright © 2004 by Wiley Publishing, Inc., Indianapolis, Indiana

Published by Wiley Publishing, Inc., Indianapolis, Indiana

Published simultaneously in Canada

For general information on our other products and services or to obtain technical support, please contact our Customer Care Department within the U.S. at 800-762-2974, outside the U.S. at 317-572-3993, or fax 317-572-4002.

Wiley also publishes its books in a variety of electronic formats. Some content that appears in print may not be available in electronic books.

Library of Congress Control Number: 2004102342

ISBN: 0-7645-5991-5

Manufactured in the United States of America

10 9 8 7 6 5 4 3 2

1V/SR/QV/QU/IN

WILEY

About the Author

Marsha Collier spends most of her time on eBay. She loves buying and selling — she's a PowerSeller — as well as meeting eBay users from around the world. As columnist, author of four best-selling books on eBay, television and radio expert, and lecturer, she shares her knowledge of eBay with millions of online shoppers. Thousands of eBay fans also read her monthly newsletter, *Cool eBay Tools,* to keep up with the changes on the site.

Out of college, Marsha worked in Fashion Advertising for the *Miami Herald* and then as Special Projects Manager for the *Los Angeles Daily News*. Upon the birth of her daughter, she founded a home-based advertising and marketing business. Her successful business, the Collier Company, Inc., was featured by *Entrepreneur* magazine in 1985, and in 1990, Marsha's company received the Small Business of the Year award from her California State Assemblyman and the Northridge Chamber of Commerce.

More than anything, Marsha loves a great deal. That's what drew her to eBay in 1996, and that's what keeps her busy on the site now. She buys everything from light bulbs to parts for her vintage Corvette to designer dresses. Marsha knows how to apply her business acumen to eBay, and in this book, she shares that knowledge with you.

Dedication

To all the amazing eBay sellers and shoppers I've met over the years. Your questions and dedication to eBay have spurred me on to research your queries and answer them for you in my books. You inspire me to work harder and do my best to help all of you.

Author's Acknowledgments

This book was a challenge due to the many subjects I had to cover. Everyone who worked on this book went over and above the call of duty to be sure we covered the tips, secrets, and business-smarts needed to build a successful eBay business.

I must first thank my husband and daughter, who put up with my 7-day workweeks and long hours at the computer while writing this book.

Then, of course, I thank the gang at Wiley. My publisher, Andy Cummings, without whose continued personal and business support, I don't think I could have ever succeeded. My acquisitions editor, Steven Hayes, is tops. He's a charming, intuitive, and humorous guy with great ideas who holds my hand when things get squirrely and steps up to help me in times of trouble. Steve pulls out all the stops when there's a job to be done, and he always goes the extra mile to make a project number one.

I was lucky enough to have some of the best at Wiley to put together this book. If you're ever lucky enough to work with this brilliant woman, Leah Cameron, you'll know the true meaning of commitment. Sharp as a tack, she's always there to lend an ear or make a comment that will enormously improve the project at hand. I also must thank the editors who worked with her: Kyle Looper and Nancy Stevenson. Without their help, we might have gone crazy, and this book would have never made it to the printer on time.

Barry Childs-Helton is the bestest copy editor a writer could have. His command of the language is immense, and his devotion to the project at hand is unswerving. Plus, he's really funny, and his edits bring a smile to my face at the most stressful of times.

Louise (eBay ID: aunt*patti) Ruby is still my friend (even after acting as tech editor for three of my books). She takes my calls at all hours and snaps me back to reality when I go off on some bizarre tangent. Louise's devotion and knowledge of eBay really helped me center my focus and helped make this book (what I consider to be) the best book for advanced eBay sellers.

Publisher's Acknowledgments

We're proud of this book; please send us your comments through our online registration form located at www.dummies.com/register/.

Some of the people who helped bring this book to market include the following:

Acquisitions, Editorial, and Media Development

Editors: Leah Cameron, Barry Childs-Helton, Kyle Looper, Nancy Stevenson

Senior Acquisitions Editor: Steven Hayes

Technical Editor: Patti Louise Ruby

Editorial Assistant: Amanda Foxworth

Cartoons: Rich Tennant, www.the5thwave.com

Production

Project Coordinator: Adrienne Martinez

Layout and Graphics: Andrea Dahl, Lauren Goddard, Denny Hager, Stephanie D. Jumper, Michael Kruzil, Kristin McMullan, Julie Trippetti, Melanee Wolven

Proofreader: Brian H. Walls

Indexer: Tom Dinse

Publishing and Editorial for Technology Dummies

Richard Swadley, Vice President and Executive Group Publisher

Andy Cummings, Vice President and Publisher

Mary Bednarek, Executive Editorial Director

Mary C. Corder, Editorial Director

Publishing for Consumer Dummies

Diane Graves Steele, Vice President and Publisher

Joyce Pepple, Acquisitions Director

Composition Services

Gerry Fahey, Vice President of Production Services

Debbie Stailey, Director of Composition Services

Contents at a Glance

Table of Contents

Introduction

Thank you for taking the time to look over eBay *Timesaving Techniques For Dummies,* my latest *For Dummies* book about eBay. This book is loaded with advanced tricks, effective methods, and clever tidbits of information aimed at helping you take better advantage of your time and potential on eBay. When you started out on eBay, you may have had the inkling that perhaps you could actually *earn a living* on the site. Then reality set in, and you recognized how all the facets of buying and selling on eBay take a bit more work than you previously expected. Of course they do!

Remember, an eBay business is e-commerce. Many people who start selling on eBay with the idea of creating a successful home-based business have no background in running their own business — and no background in retailing. Understanding how a business works takes some study and practice (some people even spend four years at college to learn about running a business). So don't be disappointed if (at first) all your eBay activities don't just fall into place. There's a definite learning curve, and that's why I write my books. I pull from my years of marketing and advertising work and my current full-time occupation — writing and teaching about eBay — to offer insights and help you through the rough spots.

By buying this book, you've invested two things I truly respect: your money and your time. In return, this book gives you lots of information for your money, and the time you spend reading it and putting this information into practice will be invaluable.

Saving Time with This Book

There are over 100 million registered eBay users. Luckily for us, the majority of them are buyers. But there are a growing number of sellers, too. The simple fact is, to be a success on eBay, you need to know more than the competition.

My entry into the *Timesaving Techniques For Dummies* series focuses on some high-payoff eBay techniques that save you time, either on the spot or somewhere down the road. I've written this book so you can get to the meat of the subject in a hurry, with step-by-step instructions when necessary, without the fluff (or sales pitches) you don't want.

I've identified more than 60 techniques that eBay users need to know to make the most of their time. Many of the ideas may be new to you, but they *all* will help your business take care of its bottom line. Decide for yourself how to use this book: Read it cover to cover if you like or skip right to the techniques that interest you the most.

In *eBay Timesaving Techniques For Dummies,* you find out how to:

- ✔ **Take your eBay business up a notch.** Discover how top online retailers know what goods to buy for resale and when to buy them. I've included in these pages the straight goods — the information that all those *get-rich-quick* e-mails claim to give you — except here you get the real facts. Check the techniques that will help you customize these theories for your own mercantile transactions.

- ✔ **Customize your eBay business to suit you.** Learn about the third-party tools that can work as an adjunct to the best (I'll let you know which ones) of the excellent tools that eBay supplies.

- ✔ **Tame time-draining tedious tasks:** I try to demystify the inner workings of running an e-business and let you in on more than 60 tips and tricks along the way. When you've got a handle on the tedious tasks, you can spend more time creating great results and less time fiddling with a feature to make it work correctly.

Foolish Assumptions

I assume you've been trading on eBay for a while. You may be selling on eBay part time and feel that you've become successful enough to take your business up a notch. Perhaps you are running a business on eBay, and know how to use the site to your advantage; but there are still certain things that escape you. I've unearthed some of those unknown features for you in this book.

Everyone out there — especially eBay — has some advice on how to best sell on eBay. I assume you've seen past some of the propaganda and want to quickly weed through the rest to find out what's best for you.

I also assume you want to know some solid retailing and marketing techniques for your business. I've made a point to put those in this book, too.

From what I've heard from the eBay community, you're probably comfortable with the site, but want to make more of it. That's the basis of this book. Making more of eBay without wasting time and money.

What's in This Book

To save time, this book is separated into techniques. (This really confused me at first — since I'm used to writing full-on chapters.) A technique tackles just one subject and lays it out succinctly and swiftly. It's a way to get your answer quickly, without a lot of extraneous information — or too many of my editorial comments. (Hey, focus is good, too!)

Some of the techniques go into advanced ideas about selling on eBay. If they're not relevant for the work you do now, just skip 'em and come back when you need those nuggets later.

This book follows in the tradition of the *Timesaving Techniques* series. There are lots of visual cues that make it easier for you to enter a technique at the placing giving the information you need. No need to read this book cover to cover — jump in wherever you see something interesting. It just may answer a question you've had for a while.

When I come to an idea that cross-references another, I'll give you a technique number to flip to and check out if you want. Also, if an idea comes to you while reading, check out the index in the back of the book. It helps you zoom directly to your question's answer.

Part I: Buying for Successful Selling

I know you're going to love this part. Aside from refreshing you about the updated nuances of buying product on eBay, I bring you the straight truth on sourcing merchandise for your eBay auctions. Read this part, and you'll have the information you need to be buying at wholesale and below. After you put this information into play for your business, you'll be hip to those hokey "wholesale list" e-books and other gimmicks — and harder for them to tempt!

I've also included some information on saving yourself from buyers who waste your time. Everyone seems out to protect the buyer — and that's fine — but here's where I show you how to protect yourself as seller, too!

Part II: Selling Shortcuts

In the Selling Shortcuts part, you get more information from the brick-and-mortar retail world to adapt to your eBay auctions. I show you how the pros set their product price points, as well as how to make your shipping expense into a profitable cost center (rather than the losing proposition that it often is).

You're also going to get the scoop on what I call the eBay seller's "killer app," Sellathon. Never before have eBay sellers had access to the type of information this program supplies — used with some savvy, this product can help all sellers improve the bottom line.

I also show you how to use some handy eBay tools — such as Turbo Lister — that offer an effective, inexpensive help with organizing sales.

Part III: Prettying Up Your Auctions

Here it is — in-depth discussion of photographing the goods for eBay *and* handling your own image hosting. I take you step-by-step through professional (but doable) photography methods for getting quality images. You also get an HTML tutorial that answers your questions about setting up your listings to foster good, clean, high-bidding auctions.

With the techniques in this part, you find out how to save a mound of money by setting up attractive item pages yourself and not having to pay for "services" at every turn.

Part IV: Finishing Off Your Auctions

"Finishing off" sounds sort of morbid, but it's what auctions are all about. Think of this part as the place where you find out the best ways of tying up loose ends at the end of your transactions. Figure out (finally) which mode of leaving feedback (who leaves it first?) works the best.

Also, when transactions do go south, check out Technique 27 and find out how to keep track of them and get your appropriate credits from eBay.

Part V: Operating Efficiently with PayPal

PayPal's got a lot more going for it than merely accepting your payments for you. It has some truly robust tools that can help you increase the bottom line for your online business. This part explains the tools and shows you the simple way to use them.

Before you leave this part, don't forget to read the technique about setting up your PayPal Shop. Its free — so why not have another connection to your online enterprise?

Part VI: Shipping Made Simple

Finally! I did buckets of research so you wouldn't have to. With this part, you'll be ready to figure out the best shipper for you. Discover the strengths and weaknesses of UPS, FedEx, and the Postal Service.

I also give you the inside story on the hows and whys of carrying your own package insurance for your eBay shipments (the way the big guys do!).

When things go bad — you'll still be ready. I've checked out the claims process for all the major shippers and here is where I let you know which claims process involves the most hassle.

Part VII: Working the eBay Community

Okay, it's a community. So what — what can it do for you? In this part, I give you the lowdown on the community and some ways it can boost your bottom line. For instance — how to make the most from your eBay store (cross-promote your little heart out!), and why you should keep up your reputation as a Power Seller.

I also describe working with SquareTrade and show you how to really become a Trading Assistant (with suggested contract ideas).

Part VIII: Running an Efficient Back Office

Back office is what its all about. Here's where I explain the full-on information on running your own business successfully. Business has certain standards, and in order for a business to succeed, you need to follow the rules. (Just ask the tax man!)

Why reinvent the wheel? In this technique, you find out the professional and easy way to handle your bookkeeping and office feng shui. (Okay, maybe no feng shui — at least not yet — but you will find out some important things you need to do in your business to protect the most important asset of your business — *you*.)

I've also included a technique to help those with disability issues. Many of these tips may help you even if a disability isn't an issue. (For example, enlarging your screen after a long day's work can sometimes be a blessing for tired eyes!)

Part IX: Acting Like a CEO

CEO? Who me? Yes, *you*. You are the Big Louie for your eBay enterprise. Part IX has some great information that you can hand over to your head of marketing. Of course, that's probably you, too — so why not read this information on how to target your audience?

If big business can apply marketing principles to generating online sales, so can you. The information is really going to be an eye-opener — it's there to make you think about your customers.

Also (finally), I've found a viable alternative to escrow. Escrow's reputation has taken quite a hit in the media — that, plus you have to wait for your money. Now there is a clean way to put your customers at ease when you're selling high-dollar items.

Part X: The Scary (or Fun) Stuff

Scary? Fun? I'm not sure which, but this part gives you some good ideas that can help you expand your business. Also, I go into depth on how to keep your online security up to snuff.

Conventions Used in This Book

Conventions? Wow — funny hats, late cocktail parties, free samples! I love conventions. But this isn't what the publisher has in mind (at least not yet). Here *conventions* means the varied ways we've used typefaces to make things stand out for you while you read this book.

- ✔ The online experience has lots of abbreviations: GMS, NWT, URLs. If I come across an abbreviation you need to know, I give you the definition and the abbreviation together. That way, if you see the abbreviation again, you know what it means.

- ✔ To show you things you have to type, I put them in **boldface** text. That way, you can type the commands exactly as needed.

✔ If I show you Web site or e-mail addresses, they're set in `monospace` text. For example, my Web site can be found at `www.coolebaytools.com`.

Icons Used in This Book

One thing I love about *Dummies* books is that authors can use icons to draw your attention to things the author wants to point out. I've noticed that other recently published books on eBay have incorporated the icon philosophy — but I want you to know who started the standard — the *Dummies* crew, laying it out for the smartest readers anywhere (but you knew that, right?).

You'll see the ones I use:

 This is when my mind goes astray and there's something I really want you to know, but it doesn't fit into the text at that point. Think of it as a little note from me.

 When you see this icon, I've interjected an idea that is something you need to keep in mind while proceeding with the task at hand or applying the technique down the road.

 Yikes! When you see a Warning icon, know that you're treading in some delicate territory. Many of the warnings represent situations that can come back to bite you in the rear. Please note the warnings and stay safe!

 You see the little clock, when there's a time-saving tip at hand. It might represent a quicker way to do something — or perhaps just a *better* way. Heed the ticking clock!

Where to Go from Here

As you read each technique, I'd love for you to go directly to the referenced resources on the Web and give 'em a whirl. Of course, you may already know about a lot of those — but they may be worth revisiting to get some more ideas. Check out the links when you find them in the book, and you may find some up-to-date information.

I'd love to give you a super fast way to contact eBay, but the site is so big and changes so fast, that's not practical yet. For now, this book gives you all the links I know. If you have any better contacts, please let *me* know.

You can reach me at my e-mail address, `mcollier@coolebaytools.com`. Please realize that I'm a one-woman-show and often the number of e-mails can be overwhelming. I promise you that I'll read every one and will answer when I can. When lots of readers have the same question, I will address it in my newsletter, which you can sign up for on my Web site, `www.coolebaytools.com`. (I promise you'll never get spam, and I will not sell or giveaway your e-mail address to *anyone*.) It comes out *about* every 6 weeks — and I use the word *about* on purpose. But hey, it's free.

My publisher also has a very sharp Web site, `www.dummies.com`. You'll be able to visit the site and get tips on all sorts of *Dummies* subjects, including tips from me on eBay.

At this point, why not give Technique 1 a shot and just start reading? If you have a particular question, check the Table of Contents and visit the technique that tickles your fancy. From there, just hop around. Enjoy this book. I wrote it for you, and I hope it gives you some new insights into running your eBay business.

Part I

Buying for Successful Selling

The 5th Wave   By Rich Tennant

"Nope, apoplexy. Musta been that last-minute snipe that did it. Won himself a hand-decorated funeral urn, though. Just goes to show—timing is everything."

Technique

Efficient Searching to Find the Best Deals

Save Time By

- Making eBay search for value-priced items
- Finding eBay Search shortcuts
- Letting Favorite Searches do the work for you
- Using outside research to find your items

Do you have a friend who always seems to get incredible deals in the brick-and-mortar world, as well as online? Or someone who sells on eBay, buys most of his or her merchandise on eBay, and resells it for a considerably higher price? You can bet that both your friends know the ins and outs of working the eBay search system. This technique shows how you, too, can master the art of finding the golden nuggets on eBay.

Remember: When you're looking to purchase an item, eBay isn't always your only option. (Check out Technique 2 for other worthwhile places to search online.) But eBay's search engine is a technological wonder. It can search for your request in over 14 million auctions in a fraction of a second. Using this technique, you can take advantage of this amazing feature when you're pricing your items.

 Most search techniques given here also work with other search engines on the Internet. For example, these methods can be extremely useful for getting the most out of your searches through Google or Yahoo!.

Finding Deals with eBay Search

When bidding on an auction, anyone can easily be carried away with the moment. Ego (or is it greed?) urges us not to be outbid by a few cents, then by a quarter, fifty cents, a few dollars, and sometimes more! The bidding war commences, the item sells for much more than it should, and nobody really ends up a winner. So when you see an auction marching off to the bidding war, you have alternatives to joining the fight. Before you jump into the frantic bidding, consider using eBay Search to see how many more of that item are for sale on the site. It's never the last of its breed to be on eBay. That is, unless the item is a high-dollar rarity, (in which case, stop raising the bid by repeat bidding and read Technique 3 on sniping). There will always be another item like it — sooner or later.

Before placing your bids, be sure to set limits on how much you will spend.

Taking the eBay price-comparison shortcut

Whether you're looking to purchase a *stock commodity* (an item that you could also buy in a retail store) or a collectible, you can always benefit by doing some research. First, try searching for your item on eBay, as I did when I wanted to purchase a Hewlett-Packard DVD recorder: Quite a few sellers on eBay were selling my item. But before checking out specific sales (and sellers' feedback ratings), I looked into just how much my item sold for previously.

Follow these steps to quickly avail yourself of the price-comparison options on eBay:

1. **Type your item description's keywords in the basic Search box that appears on most pages on the eBay site and click Search.**

 For the best search results, be specific with your item keywords. Because I also knew which model of DVD recorder I was interested in, I searched by typing the term HP DVD and the model number, too.

2. **After eBay returns the current sales search results, scroll down the page to find the options boxes on the left.**

3. **In the Display option box, as shown in Figure 1-1, click the Completed Items link.**

4. **Click the Price column heading in the resulting list of completed items to sort the list by price.**

To see the results as I wanted, I sorted the items by price from low to high. (See Figure 1-2.)

 The method described in this step list, is the most efficient way to view pricing and availability information. While making your search, you also get to see how many of the item are currently for sale on eBay — a valuable added piece of information when comparing prices.

Display

- Gifts view
- Completed items
- Gallery view
- Items near me
- PayPal items
- Show all prices in $
- View ending times (Ends PST)

• **Figure 1-1:** The Display option box on the Search results page.

Picture	Item Title	Price ▲	Bids	Ends
	HP DVD Movie Writer DC3000	$199.99	1	Dec-21 21:52
	HP DVD MOVIE WRITER DC3000 +R +RW CDRW CD	$227.50	21	Dec-27 07:11
	HP DVD Movie Writer DC3000 New "Buy it Now"	$245.00	-	Dec-28 05:20
	HP DC3000 External DVD Burner (NEW)	$250.00	1	Dec-16 12:29
	HP DC3000 External DVD Burner (NEW)	$250.00	1	Dec-17 08:52
	HP DVD Movie Writer dc3000 - Brand New! Free Shipping within Canada!	C $340.00	8	Dec-20 03:29
	HP DVD MOVIE WRITER DC3000 +R +RW CDRW CD	$270.90	13	Dec-16 20:04

• **Figure 1-2:** A completed item search on eBay, sorted by lowest price first.

 You can also perform a Completed Item search directly from eBay's Advanced Search feature, which is accessible from the Search tab in the Navigation bar.

By knowing an item's current high and low price on eBay, you can estimate how much you'll have to pay when you buy. If you're trying for an item in an auction, a quick Completed Item search can give you an idea of how much to place in your proxy bid.

• **Figure 1-3: The innocent-looking (but powerful) white box for searching.**

 Always factor in the amount that the seller is charging for shipping before bidding or buying! Many sellers charge large "handling" fees disguised as shipping that can add beaucoups bucks to the amount of your item.

Refining your search without missing important data

Using eBay's search engine from the white-box page — a one-stop shop for searching that's shown in Figure 1-3 — is most efficient.

In the olden days of secretarial duties, secretaries took dictation from their bosses. Because the secretaries couldn't possibly write as fast as their bosses spoke, they used a writing method called *shorthand* to help them record the important points without writing down every word. eBay's search engine also responds to a sort-of shorthand. To get the most out of your white-box searches, use the tricks in Table 1-1 to shorten search time!

TABLE 1-1: TIMESAVING SHORTHAND FOR RAPID SEARCHES

Symbol	Impact on Search	Example
Multiple words	Returns auctions with all included words in the title	**reagan letter** might return an auction for a mailed message from the former U.S. president, or it might return an auction for a mailed message from Jane Wyman to Ronald Reagan.
Quotes ""	Limits the search to items with the exact phrase inside the quotes	**"case of"** returns items that come in a case quantity. Quotes don't make the search term case sensitive. You may use either upper- or lowercase to get the same results.
Asterisk *	Serves as a wild card and is especially useful when you're not sure of spelling	**budd*** returns items that start with budd, such as Beanie Buddy, Beanie Buddies, or Buddy Holly — *any* word beginning with budd.
Separating comma without spaces (a,b)	Finds items related to either the item before or after the comma	**(macys,macy's)** returns all Macy's items, no matter in which way the seller listed them.
Minus sign –	Excludes results with the word after the –	Type in **box –lunch**, and you'd better not be hungry because you may find the box, but lunch won't be included.
Minus symbol and parentheses	Searches for auctions with words before the parentheses but excludes words inside the parentheses	**midge –(skipper,barbie)** means that auctions with the Midge doll won't have to compete for Ken's attention.
Parentheses	Searches for both versions of the word in parentheses	**diamond (pin,pins)** searches for both diamond pin or diamond pins.

You can type an auction number into any search box on the white-box page and go directly to the item's page.

Once you get to the Search Results page (as I show you in the preceding section) you have lots more options to refine your search. The left side of the Web page is chock-full of options — with these you can define, redefine, and weed out your searches. I recommend this approach so you don't miss anything. If you predefine your search at the beginning (from eBay's Advanced Search), you may miss some desirable information that may not show up in your "advanced" pre-defined parameters.

You have great tools to further define your search in the Display option box, as pictured in Figure 1-1. To narrow the search, click one of the links you find in the Display options. Here's what they all do:

- **Gifts View:** Narrows your search to sellers who have listed the item and paid eBay 25 cents for the privilege of showing the Gifts View icon. These sellers will guarantee to offer the options of express shipping, card inclusion, gift wrapping and/or shipping to a recipient other than the buyer. (Note that many eBay sellers do this anyway.) If you want a gift sent to someone else or gift-wrapped — just e-mail the seller prior to bidding. eBay sellers will more than likely help you out; they can be a most accommodating crew.

- **Completed Items:** Searches for items that have sold in the past 14 days — giving you a history of whether the item is very popular (How many bids did it get? Did the item go unsold?), and at what price it has sold for. (More about this specific search option in the preceding section.)

- **Gallery View:** Shows you *only* the sellers who have used a Gallery image to give you a better look at their listings. You can also see the Gallery pictures (if you don't see them in your search) by clicking the Show Picture link in the Picture column next to the item title. This is a much more efficient way to view Galley pictured items among the other listings — you won't miss out on any of the other hundreds of deals from sellers who don't use the Gallery!

- **Items Near Me:** Takes you to a page where you can select from over 50 regions of the United States. It's a very handy feature if you need something fast or might want to pick it up from the seller.

- **PayPal Items:** If you want to pay via PayPal, this is a great way to isolate the type of sales you need.

- **Show All Prices in $:** If you want to purchase from overseas sellers, but have a problem mentally converting from United Kingdom pounds or Euros to dollars, click this option. When you click this option, prices from sellers selling in other currencies will appear in the search results in U.S. dollars and in *italics*.

- **View Time Left** or **View Ending Times:** This is my favorite. Without clicking View Time Left, all you'll see is results with the date and time they end. That's in eBay (or Military Pacific) time. Unless you're a math whiz (or you have my Web site page with the eBay time chart printed out next to you — and you can get it at `www.coolebay tools.com`), clicking here makes life easier. It converts search results to how many days, hours, and minutes are left in the auction. If you want, you can toggle back and forth between the two viewing methods till you figure which one works best for you.

 When you choose View Time Left as a search display option, listings ending within an hour show up in red. The number of minutes left in the listing is followed by the abbreviation *m*. If there is less than a minute left, there will be a "less than" symbol and the number 1: <1.

Finding Your Item in eBay Stores

A little known fact about eBay is that when you search the eBay site for an item, your search will not extend to eBay Stores. Many eBay sellers have eBay stores chock-full of merchandise that's often cheaper than the items you'll find on the regular eBay site. (The listing fees are considerably cheaper in the stores.) If you want to search eBay Stores only, you *can* go to eBay's search page and search on the Stores tab, as shown in Figure 1-4.

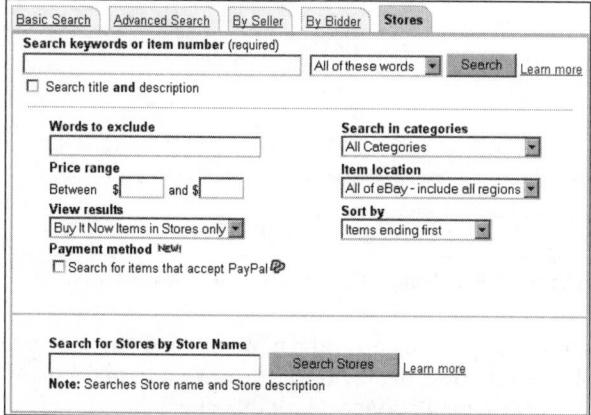

• **Figure 1-4:** eBay's main search, showing the tab that searches Stores only.

A quicker way to get to the stores is to use the white-box search method and scroll down the page to those handy links on the left. Near the bottom of the page, you find the More on eBay box, as in Figure 1-5.

• **Figure 1-5:** Click a link here to go directly to a store or to find *all* stores that match your item.

 If you find yourself in an eBay Store you particularly like, look for a Save this Store in Favorites link at the top of the store's home page. Click this link to save the store in your My eBay Favorites area.

Saving Time with Favorite Searches

eBay's My eBay page has a tab called Favorite Searches. This button shows up in the sub-navigation bar when you click Search on any eBay page, as shown in Figure 1-6. You can access your favorites directly from your My eBay page or by clicking the pictured Favorite Searches sub-navigation button.

 Saving a search as a Favorite is a real time-saver. If you manage to keep your regular eBay searches down to a measly 100, you can store them in one convenient, highly clickable space that's available (through the Favorite Searches tab) from any Search page on eBay. Click the Add to My Favorite Searches link at the top of any Search Results page to turn your regular searches into favorite ones.

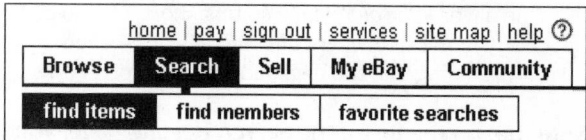

• **Figure 1-6:** The eBay navigation bar with the Favorite Searches tab.

Because aluminum Christmas trees are coming into vogue again, I might want to get one for my office for the next holiday season. Unfortunately, all my Internet searches find them at prices over $300, so eBay is the perfect place to look for my tree. I'm hoping to find one (in good condition) that someone would rather sell than store for another year.

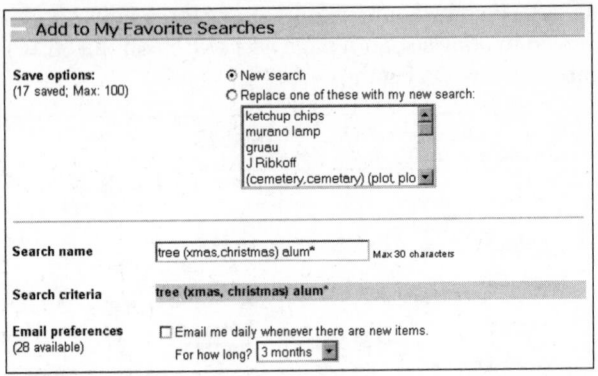

All Categories			Add to My Favorite Searches

111 items found for **tree (xmas,christmas) alum***
Sort by items: **ending first** | newly listed | lowest priced | highest priced

Show picture	Item Title	Price	Bids	Ends
E.S. Swirl Aluminum Taper Christmas Tree Vint 🔴		$46.00	4	in 5 mins
26" vintage table top aluminum Christmas tree 🔴		$56.00	-	in 24 mins
Vintage 6' Aluminum Christmas Tree 🔴		$172.50	31	in 34 mins
Aluminum Sparkler 6 Foot Christmas Tree NR 🔴		$20.50	3	in 54 mins
Peco 6 Ft. Aluminum Pom Pom Christmas Tree 🗃 🔴		$48.56	7	Jan-02 16:15
VINTAGE 6 FT. ALUMINUM CHRISTMAS TREE 🗃 🔴		$24.95	1	Jan-02 16:56

• **Figure 1-7:** A search for the very elusive *cheap* aluminum Christmas tree.

In Figure 1-7, I've performed a search using some eBay search shortcuts (see Table 1-1): `tree alum*` helps me accomplish several things:

- ✔ `tree`: Because I'm looking for a tree, not a stand.

- ✔ `(xmas,Christmas)`: Searches on alternate spellings so that I find *Christmas* even if the seller has spelled it *Xmas*.

- ✔ `alum*`: Correct spelling can be difficult, especially in a word like *aluminum*, so this shortcut also finds any item listed where *aluminum* is misspelled (assuming that the beginning *alum* is correct!).

Note that on the top of the Search Results page, you find a link called Add to My Favorite Searches. Clicking this link takes you to the page shown in Figure 1-8, where you can add the search to your My eBay Favorite Searches area.

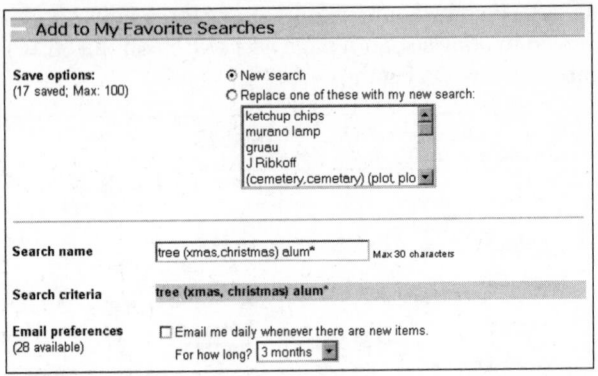

Add to My Favorite Searches	

Save options:
(17 saved; Max: 100)

⦿ New search
○ Replace one of these with my new search:

ketchup chips
murano lamp
gruau
J Ribkoff
(cemetery,cemetary) (plot, plo ▾

Search name: `tree (xmas,christmas) alum*` Max 30 characters

Search criteria: **tree (xmas, christmas) alum***

Email preferences
(28 available)

☐ Email me daily whenever there are new items.
For how long? `3 months ▾`

• **Figure 1-8:** Adding a Favorite Search to My eBay.

On this page, you can add a new search or replace an old search. Best of all, notice the option to make use of eBay's e-mail service. Mark this check box if you want eBay to notify you via e-mail daily for up to 30 searches as matching items are listed on the site. You can set the search — and the e-mail notifications — to go on for as long as a year. I've been successful with that option, especially when I'm looking for a rare item that doesn't show up on eBay regularly. Figure 1-9 shows an e-mail message I received, notifying me of new listings that matched a saved favorite search.

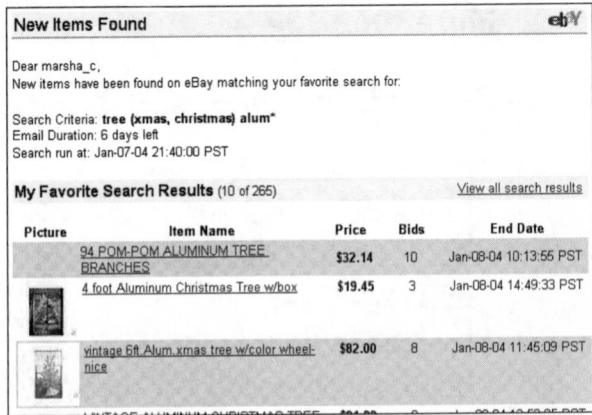

New Items Found				ebY

Dear marsha_c,
New items have been found on eBay matching your favorite search for:

Search Criteria: **tree (xmas, christmas) alum***
Email Duration: 6 days left
Search run at: Jan-07-04 21:40:00 PST

My Favorite Search Results (10 of 265)   View all search results

Picture	Item Name	Price	Bids	End Date
	94 POM-POM ALUMINUM TREE BRANCHES	$32.14	10	Jan-08-04 10:13:55 PST
🖼	4 foot Aluminum Christmas Tree w/box	$19.45	3	Jan-08-04 14:49:33 PST
🖼	vintage 6ft Alum xmas tree w/color wheel-nice	$82.00	8	Jan-08-04 11:45:09 PST

• **Figure 1-9:** An eBay e-mail notifying me of new listings!

Figure 1-10 shows you my personal My eBay Favorites tab. (No laughing when you see the favorite searches — if you ever meet me, just ask me about them.) This tab is where your favorite search shows up after you've recorded one. You can also record a search from this page by clicking the Add New Search link in the top bar.

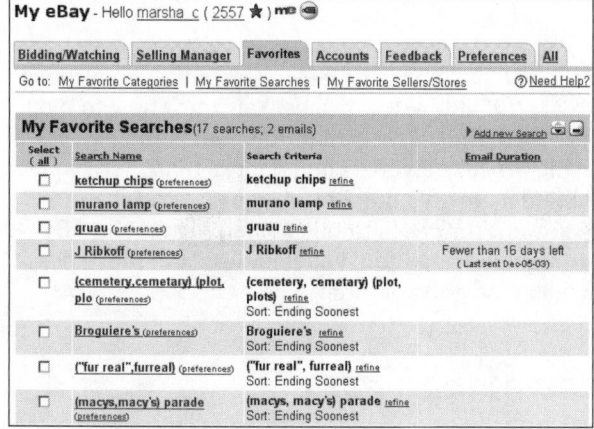

• **Figure 1-10:** My eBay Favorite Searches.

Marking Favorite Sellers for Speedy Return Visits

After I've had a successful transaction with particular sellers and find that they carry the types of merchandise that I'm interested in, I like to go back and check their items for sale from time to time. I'm in

luck! The My eBay Favorites tab also has a place where I can add my favorite sellers!

Anytime you're on the eBay site and find a seller whose items you'd like to visit again, follow these simple steps:

1. Go to your My eBay Favorites area.

2. Click the My Favorite Sellers/Stores link and then the link to ad a new seller.

3. On the resulting page (as shown in Figure 1-11), fill in the Seller's User ID or Store Name text box.

4. Click the Save Favorite button to add this new favorite seller.

You can save up to 30 sellers or stores on this page.

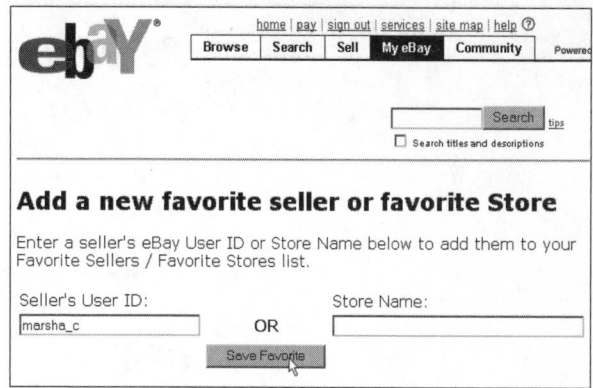

• **Figure 1-11:** Adding a new favorite seller.

Technique 2

Gearing Up for Savvy eBay Buying

Save Time By

✔ Breezing through the different types of eBay transactions

✔ Solving the shipping mystery

✔ Paying quickly and securely through PayPal

When we all initially joined eBay, it's fair to say our main purpose was to find great stuff at low, low prices. You know how to bid, you say? You're no dummy! (Or is that dumm*ie*?) Either way, you're not. But the buying process involves much more than merely placing bids on eBay. You'll find a growing number of transaction types and tools available when you want (or *need*) to buy something on eBay. By the time you finish reading this technique, you'll understand those permutations and how to make the most of them.

Recognizing the Many Faces of eBay Transactions

eBay has grown into this massive mega-marketplace that even the best of eBay-expert buyers can find daunting from time to time. This section looks at the available types of eBay transactions and gives you the goods on how they work.

 For any transaction type, you find the key information at the top of each item page.

 All bidding on eBay is based on the proxy system — if you'd like to bid more than the minimum, eBay will hold you to your high bid, outbidding anyone else who bids against you, until your high bid is met (or until you win when the auction ends).

Scanning through traditional auctions

Single-item auctions are the mainstay of eBay; they're also the easiest to recognize. Looking at Figure 2-1, you can see that the current high bid is listed at the top of the item's information area. You can also see a button to click if you want to place a bid. Simple. Although clicking the Place Bid button at this point would be a bit preemptive (unless you're putting in a snipe — in which case, see Technique 3 for more on sniping techniques).

Before placing your bid, save yourself some time and aggravation by scrolling down the item page to study the description, shipping terms, and shipping costs involved with the transaction.

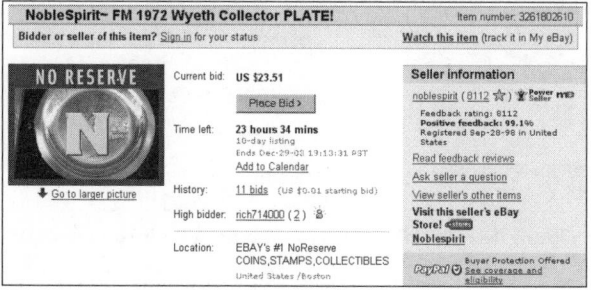

• **Figure 2-1: The auction information area.**

Just below the Place Bid box, you can find the amount of time left in the auction and (below that) how many bids have been placed. This information helps you evaluate the auction for how much time you have left to do your research about the sale, and how strong your competition is for winning the item.

At the bottom of the page, you see an area entitled *Ready to bid?*, as in Figure 2-2. Now you can place your bid by typing the highest amount you wish to bid and clicking the Place Bid button. (In Technique 3, I tell you about bidding strategies that can help you win.)

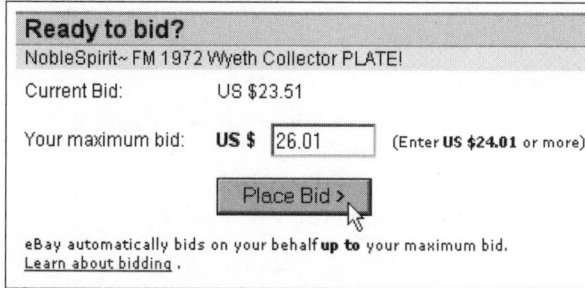

• **Figure 2-2: Placing a bid on an auction.**

Homing in on Multiple Item (Dutch) auctions

Multiple Item (or *Dutch*) auctions offer more than one of the same item in an auction-style format. Although Dutch auctions seem to be a dying breed on eBay, you occasionally still come across them while browsing, and they can be a bit confusing. Normally you see a quantity of available items (more than one), as in Figure 2-3.

• **Figure 2-3: A Dutch auction with 5 items up for auction.**

Even an experienced buyer can find it hard to tell Dutch auctions from Buy It Now, multiple-item listings. The clue that identifies a listing as Dutch: Look for a Starting Bid and the Place Bid button. Multiple-item, single-sale listings have only a Buy It Now button.

In a Dutch auction, bidding progresses just as in normal eBay auctions. You may bid on one or more of the items available, and the highest bidders win (based on the quantity bid for and won). The only trick to this type of auction is that more than one bidder can win — so all bidders win their items at the *lowest* successful bid — *not* the highest!

Before bidding on a Dutch auction, click the High Bidders link to see where the bidding stands and how many of the items are currently bid upon. This way you can gauge how much you want to bid. For Dutch-auction bidding strategies, please read Technique 3.

To place a bid in a Multiple Item (Dutch) auction, follow these steps:

1. Scroll to the Ready To Bid area at the bottom of the page, as shown in Figure 2-4.

2. Type the amount you want to bid in the Your Maximum Bid box.

3. Type the number of items you want to bid on in the Quantity box.

4. Click the Place Bid button.

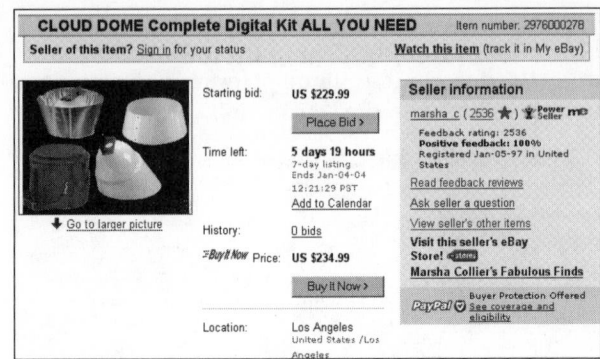

• **Figure 2-5: An eBay auction with the Buy It Now option.**

Ready to bid?

1961 Proof Franklin Halves***DUTCH SALE***

Starting bid: US $11.00

Your maximum bid: **US $** [   ]   (Enter **US $11.00** or more)

Quantity: **x** [1   ]

[Place Bid >]

Unlike a regular eBay auction, Multiple Item Auctions can have many winners.
Learn about Multiple Item Auctions.

• **Figure 2-4: Bidding on one or many items in a Multiple Item (Dutch) auction.**

After you place your bid, eBay shows you a confirmation page where you can verify that what you bid on is what you want. Confirm your bid and you're in the fray.

With Multiple Item auctions, the trick is to *keep the winning price low.* Find out how to do this with the handy bidding strategies I describe in Technique 3.

Saving time at auctions with the Buy It Now option

Often you'll come across auctions where the seller offers a Buy It Now option, as shown in Figure 2-5.

 By clicking the Buy It Now button, any interested party can close the sale at the listed Buy It Now price and end the auction immediately. Buy It Now is your fastest choice if you're certain that you can't live without the auctioned item and you're also okay with the price.

If you don't want to use the Buy It Now option and you think you can get the item for a lower price (that is, you *hope* no one else will see your chosen item), you can place a bid and hope for the best.

The *Ready to bid or buy?* area for this type of sale is pictured in Figure 2-6. And this choice — bid or buy — is truly an "or" proposition. As soon as anyone chooses to bid in the auction (rather than using Buy It Now), the Buy It Now option disappears forever — and bidding proceeds as usual until the last second of the auction.

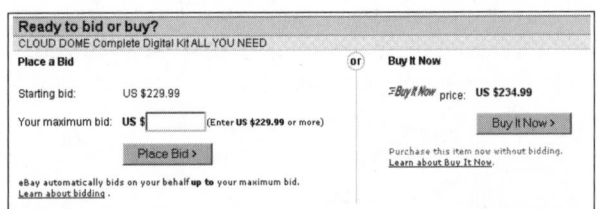

• **Figure 2-6: Ready to bid or buy? (shown in a Buy It Now transaction).**

Buy it quickly with Fixed Price sales

Buying on eBay offers yet another timesaving way to get the goods you want. Items can be purchased quickly and easily on the eBay site as Fixed Price sales or directly in eBay Stores. You can easily recognize these sales because they have no Place Bid option. And you can quickly find these sales by using the eBay search engine and following these steps:

1. Type the key words that describe the item you're looking for (using any of the eBay search boxes), and then click Search.

2. On your results page, click the yellow Buy It Now tab above the listings to re-sort the search results so they show only items you can buy immediately. (See Figure 2-7.)

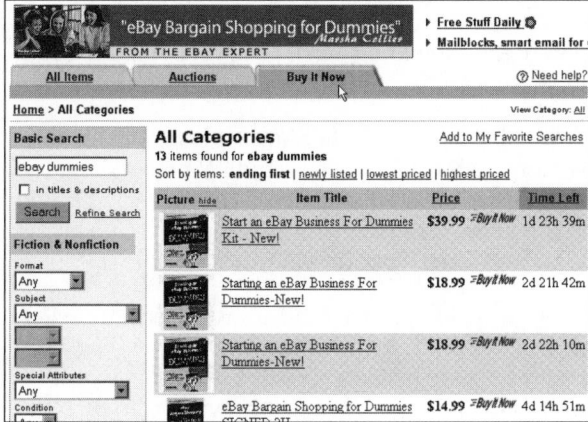

• **Figure 2-7:** Sorting an eBay search to view only Buy It Now items.

3. To find more of your item that you can buy immediately, scroll down the results page until you come to the yellow More on eBay box on the left side of the page, as shown in Figure 2-8.

4. Click links in the More on eBay box to visit eBay Stores that carry items that match your search.

• **Figure 2-8:** More Buy It Now items in eBay Stores.

Making a purchase in a fixed-price sale is as simple as clicking the Buy It Now button, as shown in Figure 2-9. Indicate the quantity you want to buy (if more than one is up for sale).

• **Figure 2-9:** A multiple-item Fixed Price sale.

 Some eBay sellers require immediate payment thru PayPal for their sales. If so, clicking Buy It Now shows you a screen (similar to the one in Figure 2-10) to notify you in case you missed this requirement on the item page.

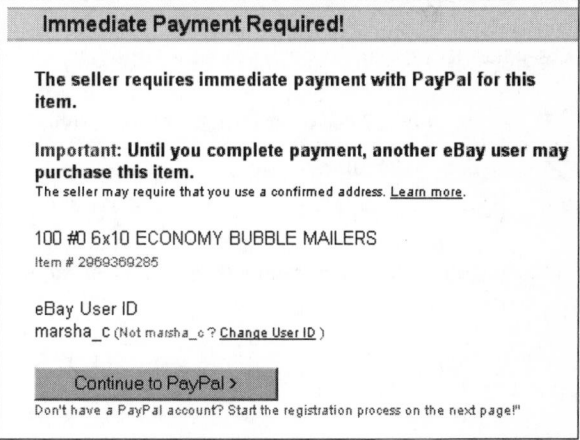

• **Figure 2-10:** This seller requires immediate payment with PayPal.

 Once you click that Buy It Now button for the final time, there's no backing out!

Making eBay's Shipping Calculator Figure Your Shipping Costs

Since the cost of shipping items varies by the distance between the buyer and the shipper, and by the weight of the item, many savvy eBay sellers take advantage of the eBay Shipping Calculator. As the buyer, you find this tool toward the bottom of the item page, just below the description and to the right of the *Shipping and payment details* box, as pictured in Figure 2-11.

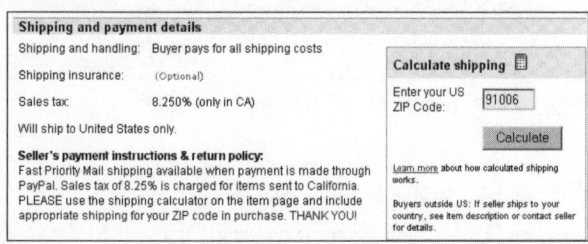

• **Figure 2-11:** The eBay Shipping Calculator on the item page.

To use the shipping calculator to quickly assess your shipping costs for an item, follow these steps:

1. **Type your ZIP code into the text box provided.**

2. **Click the Calculate button.**

A window opens (as in Figure 2-12) with the shipping information (including the method of shipping) and the full costs involved in the transaction (including any handling charges that apply).

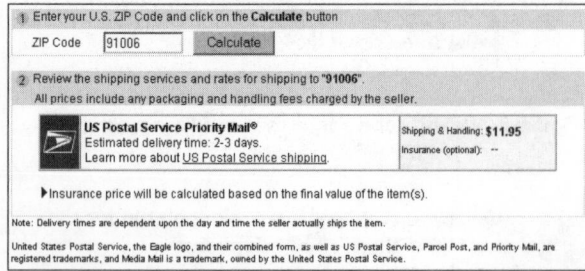

• **Figure 2-12:** Shipping Costs window for the item.

Paying Quickly and Seamlessly through PayPal

Some people in the eBay world have actually accused me of being a bit opinionated. Shocking — but, yeah, okay, sometimes true regarding eBay practices where I have experience. Certain ways of doing business on eBay just *work*; others don't. Why waste time and money experimenting when I can give you the direction you need?

Bottom line: PayPal is the safest way for buyers to pay for an eBay purchase — and it's one of the most economical ways for a business (the seller) to accept credit cards. (See Part V for more information on how PayPal can work for your business.)

Before you bid in an auction, always check the sellers' payment options. If you're comfortable sending a money order to a mailbox somewhere, that's your business. But my advice is to always look to be sure the seller accepts PayPal payments for eBay items.

Look for the PayPal logo under *Payment methods accepted* (as in Figure 2-13) at the bottom of the item description or at the bottom of the Seller Information box.

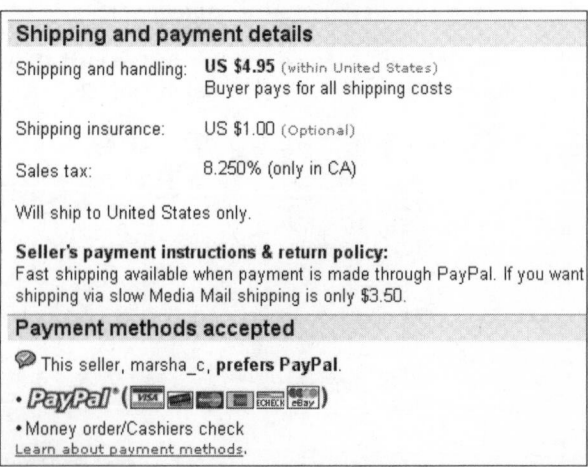

• **Figure 2-13:** Payment Methods Accepted area of the item page.

You can also find the PayPal Buyer Protection Offered logo at the bottom of the Seller Information box.

Winning and paying

After you buy an item on eBay, either through Buy It Now or by winning an auction, you see a button that says Pay Now. Click the button, and you'll be taken to a review page.

 If you aren't on the item page, you can click the word *Pay* that appears above the eBay navigation bar (its on every page of the site). Once you click, you'll see a list of items you won, and by clicking Pay Now next to an item, you will land at the Review Your Purchase page.

Figure 2-14 shows the review page. Here you can make any adjustments to shipping if you've received other information from the seller.

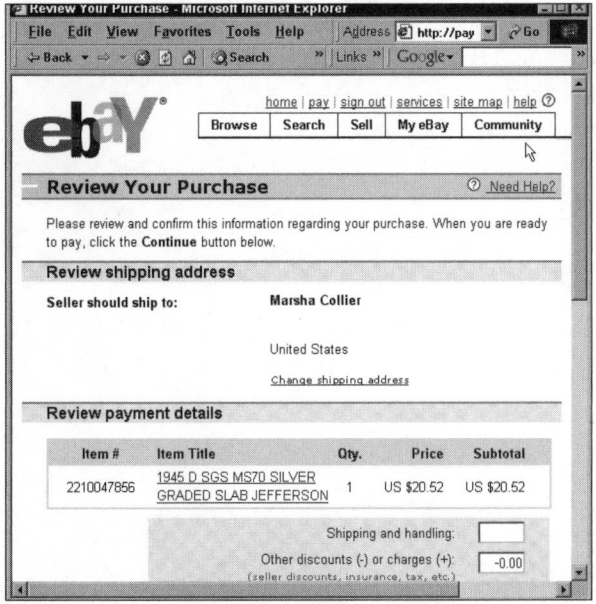

• **Figure 2-14:** Time to Review Your Purchase.

Paying for multiple wins from the same seller

The shortest route to pay for one or a multiple of items is to go directly to the PayPal site, log in to your account, and click the "eBay Items Won" link at the top of your account summary. Figure 2-15 shows you where to click.

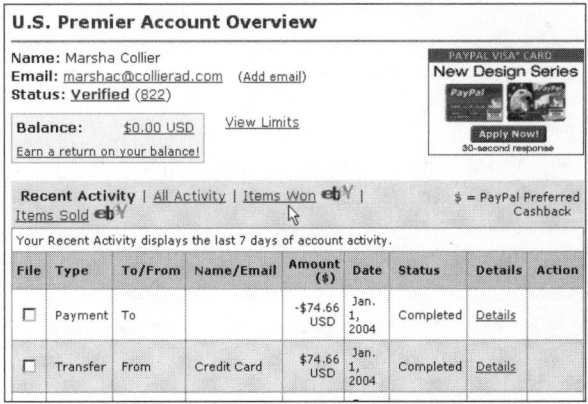

• **Figure 2-15:** Handy Links on your PayPal account summary page.

The next page presents you with a list of items you've won on eBay. If you've purchased more than one item from a seller, just click To Pay once. PayPal combines all the purchases you've made from the seller and presents you with an invoice (as in Figure 2-16). Just verify the totals and follow the prompts.

 If you have a balance in your PayPal account, that amount will be immediately applied to the payment. Be sure to withdraw your PayPal balance first if you prefer to put your purchase on a credit card. Also, the PayPal default is to remove the balance due from your registered checking account. Don't just blast through this part of the payment process; be sure your payment is being paid using the method you intend — and adjust the form accordingly.

Review payment details

Select	Item #	Item Title	Qty.	Price	Subtotal
☑	2212752790	PCGS 1978-S JEFFERSON NICKEL PROOF-69 DeepCam	1	US $10.50	US $10.50
☑	2212752763	PCGS 1976-S WASHINGTON QUARTER PR-69 Deep Cam	1	US $22.27	US $22.27
☑	2212752779	PCGS 1977-S LINCOLN CENT PROOF-69 Deep Cameo!	1	US $16.03	US $16.03
☑	2212752788	PCGS 1977-S WASHINGTON QUARTER PR-69 Deep Cam	1	US $16.01	US $16.01

Don't see an item you purchased from this seller? <u>Learn more</u>.

Subtotal:	US $64.81
Shipping and handling:	US $15.40
Shipping insurance (Optional US $5.20):	Add
Other discounts (-) or charges (+): (seller discounts, services, etc.)	-5.55
Total:	**US $74.66**
	recalculate

Please make sure the amounts above are correct.

• **Figure 2-16:** Reviewing your payment details prior to paying.

Paying for items from your My eBay page

If you've placed some snipes (the fine eBay art of placing bids at the very last second) and weren't around when you won your item, another easy way to pay is from your My eBay, Bidding/Watching tab.

Just scroll down to the area entitled Items I've Won and any items that haven't yet been paid for will display a Pay Now button (as in Figure 2-17).

• **Figure 2-17:** My Items I've Won area after a spending spree.

From here, just click the Pay Now button and (with any luck) things will progress as in the examples given here.

Technique 3

Bidding to Win

Save Time By

- Sniping bids with the best of them
- Following bidding strategies

The heart of eBay is the traditional auction (and the eBay enhanced varieties). Bidding to win is the game, but often our dreams of acquisitions fall at the very last few seconds of the listing. Someone else has bid faster and higher. Winning at eBay can become an art form. The highest bids always win, no matter when they're placed, but we all want to get that elusive bargain. That's where the "art" part comes in.

I always feel as if I've achieved some great victory when I buy a popular item on eBay considerably below retail. An even better triumph is when I can buy something at below *wholesale.* That's cause for celebration! There is an art to this. Working at eBay as much as I do helps — I look for errors made by sellers and misposted listings. I follow tried-and-true strategies. That's what this technique is all about. If you're not getting the deals now, the information put forth here will help guide your eBay Bargain shopping. By the way, (insert shameless plug here) I recently wrote that book too — *eBay Bargain Shopping For Dummies,* also published by Wiley.

One of the most popular strategies is sniping (described in the section "Sniping Your Bids in the 21st Century"). Although sniping is a familiar bidding strategy on eBay, it continues to evolve in practice. Do you think you're a master at sniping? I thought I was too. But with the advent of sniping software and Web sites, casual sniping practices have become passé. Read through this technique for ways to refine the fine art (sport?) of sniping. And while you're here, discover other helpful bidding strategies as well.

Sniping Your Bids in the 21st Century

Sniping, the elegant art of bidding at the last possible second, has been a favorite way for buyers to get great deals on eBay since the site began. Subsequent technological progress made it harder for the dialup user to snipe. That is, an eBay member with a high-speed connection had a distinct advantage — unless the dialup user's bid was *very* high.

Sniping by hand — the 3-window way

Manual sniping means zeroing in on your item during the last few minutes of the auction. Take a look at Figure 3-1: I have two small windows open on an item I'm interested in. I constantly click Refresh on the item page to catch any last-minute bidding.

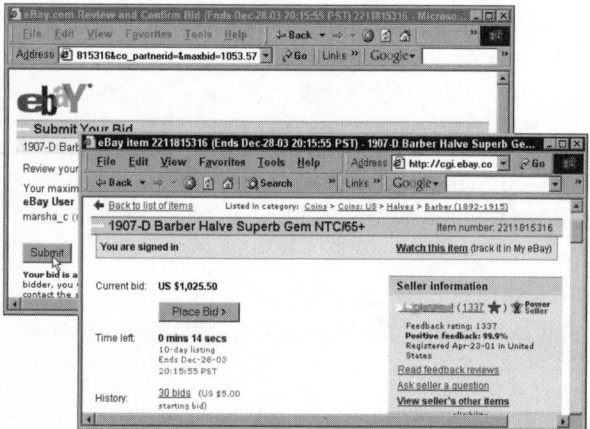

• **Figure 3-1:** Basic sniping in action.

I've checked out how fast my pages can reload, so I know how many seconds I can shave off my bidding — and I have my bid prepared in the second window. (To open a new window with your selected item, press Ctrl+N on your keyboard.) During the final minutes of the auction, I repeatedly refresh the main item page to see how many seconds are left to bid. When the very last second — the final bidding moment — appears, I switch to the smaller bidding page and click the Submit button.

What happens if a sniper swoops in and outbids you at the same second? Have a *third* bidding window (Ctrl+N again) open, ready to submit a prepared higher bid! Often I've used this three-window plan to outbid even some sniping services. Check out the times the bids were placed in the bidding results in Figure 3-2. (That auction closed at 20:55:26.)

User ID	Bid Amount	Date of Bid
marsha_c (2536 ★) me stores	US $84.00	Dec-18-03 20:55:23 PST
(1403 ★) stores	US $83.00	Dec-18-03 20:55:13 PST
marsha_c (2536 ★) me stores	US $82.01	Dec-18-03 20:55:16 PST
marsha_c (2536 ★) me stores	US $82.01	Dec-18-03 20:55:17 PST
(1160 ★)	US $42.54	Dec-18-03 20:17:05 PST
(135 ★)	US $30.00	Dec-18-03 16:14:13 PST

• **Figure 3-2:** A close call, multiple-sniping win — boy, was my heart pumping!

 Of course, the best way to win an auction without straining your nerves is to place your snipe at the highest amount you'd be comfortable paying so you outbid all comers except maybe your local billionaire.

Sniping with an online service

Surprisingly (or not), some people just can't sit around twiddling their thumbs at their computers, waiting for an auction to close. To the rescue come *online sniping services* that place your snipe bids for you when you're otherwise engaged. You can even find sniping software that runs from your computer.

 Here's a word (or two) of warning about using sniping software. You must leave your computer online for sniping software to work, but leaving your computer online while you're away can leave it vulnerable to hackers. Be sure that you have security measures (such as a secure firewall) in place if you decide to use sniping software.

Most folks would rather not leave their computers humming along gaily waiting to place a snipe. They prefer to shut down their home systems for the night, and restart them the next morning. Makes sense — if the kids or the better half should happen to monkey around with your stuff just because they walk by and see a computer on and waiting, bidding disaster could occur. The better solution (for the more security conscious) is an online sniping service.

Two very popular online services among eBay users — BidRobot and eSnipe — accomplish the same thing (placing your last-minute bids), but charge differently for his or her services:

- **BidRobot.com** offers an all-you-can-eat fee structure for your bidding pleasure. I like this one because, when I'm in the mood to shop, I can cast out perhaps 40 snipes at a time. Granted, I pray I get outbid on some; if I won them all, I'd blow my budget! Luckily, I usually win only a few.

  The fees are based on membership time. If you're just doing some serious shopping, you can purchase 3 weeks' worth of all the snipes you can place for $3.95. A full year costs only $34.95 — no matter how many items you win.

- **eSnipe.com** bidding is simple, too, and the company has a unique way of placing your snipes. Not only can you place them from the eSnipe Web site, you can install a small program called SnipeIt! that becomes part of your Internet browser toolbar. When you find an auction that you'd like to snipe, just click the SnipeIt! button — you're logged in to the eSnipe service, and your snipe will be placed on their system automatically.

  eSnipe's fees are based on the final value of eBay winnings secured by the site for you. You pay 1 percent of the winning auction price as your fee for using the service (a minimum of 25 cents per item and a maximum of $10.00). Dutch-auction wins of any quantity are charged $1.00 each. You pay ahead of your snipes with BidPoints (the eSnipe currency) and can buy as little as 500 BidPoints ($5.00 worth) at a time.

Bidding to Win at Traditional Auctions

All bidding on eBay is done in standard increments (Table 3-1 shows how the bidding increases). An excellent way to beat the system and win more auctions is to place your proxy bids with added, almost-random amounts that fall somewhere between the standard eBay bid increments. For example, if you put in a proxy bid for $15.58, and the competition jumps in at the last moment with a bid of $15.50, you win because you had a prior bid of eight cents more. (See an example of this in Figure 3-3.)

Bidding History (Highest bids first)	
User ID	**Bid Amount**
marsha_c (2536 ★) me stores	US $22.03
(537 ★)	US $22.01
(78 ★)	US $20.02
(47 ★)	US $14.69
(67 ★)	US $10.00

• **Figure 3-3: Pocket-change-added bid amounts can win by a few pennies!**

TABLE 3-1: EBAY BID INCREMENTS

Current Price	Bid Increment
$.01 – 0.99	$0.05
$1.00 – $4.99	$0.25
$5.00 – $24.99	$0.50
$25.00 – $99.99	$1.00
$100.00 – $249.99	$2.50
$250.00 – $499.99	$5.00
$500.00 – $999.99	$10.00
$1000.00 – $2499.99	$25.00
$2500.00 – $4999.99	$50.00
$5000.00 and up	$100.00

If you snipe at the very last second, without any wiggle room to put in a second snipe, be sure to bid high. If you have enough time, examine the current high bidder's bidding history (through eBay's Bidder search) — has this person bid on this item before? For how much?

If you must bid early (without the help of any sniping) be sure to bid high — no matter who snipes an auction, the highest bid always wins.

Bidding to Win at Multiple Item (Dutch) Auctions

In a Multiple Item (Dutch) auction, bidders can bid on one or more of the items up for sale — and at the end of the auction, all winners win their items for the lowest successful bid price. So your primary goal for winning Dutch-auction items is to place your bid just right — so you're not the highest bidder (raising the final winning price to a ridiculous amount) — and not the lowest bidder (it's way too easy to be shut out by another bidder at the very last minute).

In Figure 3-4, you can see the results of a Dutch auction that had six items for sale: The high bidder won five of the items at the lowest bid (in this case, $19.52). If the high bidder had bid on *all six* items instead of only one, it would have knocked out the lower price and the winner would have to pay $20.02 apiece for all six items.

Dutch Auction High Bidders (View Bid History)			
User ID	Item Price	Quantity	Date of Bid
(161 ★)	US $20.02	1	Dec-28-03 06:58:48 PST
(627 ★) me	US $19.52	5	Dec-27-03 19:56:45 PST

• **Figure 3-4:** The savvy high bidder gets one item for the underbidder's price!

Before bidding on a Dutch auction, be sure to click the link at the top of the page to see the Winning Bidders list. Check out how many possible winners are hovering around the low bid price and how many are in the high area. To get the best chance of winning, you're usually safe if you place your bid around the high-middle price — unless a sniper swoops up the entire inventory in the last seconds of the auction.

Technique 4

Researching to Save Time and Money

Save Time By

✔ Checking out the seller on eBay

✔ Getting additional information and protection from a SquareTrade Seal

✔ Using Outside Web sites for eBay research

Research. Boring, you say? Just want to get in there and buy? The Internet — especially eBay — is a great place to buy things. But responsible consumerism is just as important online as it is in brick-and-mortar world — maybe even more so. As an enthusiastic participant in online commerce, your twofold task is to

✔ **Know from whom you're buying:** Getting your goods from reputable, reliable sellers is dually important: A professional seller (1) will strive to give you good service, and (2) is more than likely to be selling quality goods. Either way, they don't want to ruin their reputations by disappointing a customer. A lot of hard work goes into building a good reputation — why would they want to ruin it just to snag a couple of extra dollars?

✔ **Know when you're getting the best prices:** In the mega-marketplace that is eBay, you find all sorts of sellers selling similar items at different prices, why not pay less for the same thing?

Especially when you're buying items to resell or making purchases from a *drop-shipper* (a seller from whom you order items to resell on eBay) research helps ensure that you're paying the lowest possible prices. Many online sites may have items for sale that are as close to wholesale as you can get — but you have to find them first.

 The deals are out there, but doing research is how you sniff them out.

In this Technique, I show you how to use research to find a seller who's going to follow through with all the terms of the sale — and I spell out how research helps you undercut the competition when it comes to finding those gems just waiting to be unearthed.

Assessing the Seller Before You Shop

You can save a lot of time when you deal with a reliable seller. The grief and misery of waiting and waiting for a slow-to-arrive package not only takes time but also taxes your good humor. If the item arrives "not as advertised," you're better off dealing with a seller of good repute who cares enough to make it right. Otherwise you may waste weeks (maybe months) waiting for a resolution. A superior eBay e-tailer's goal is to make the customers happy so they return to buy more — and to preserve a positive feedback ranking to attract new customers. So even if you're bent on simplifying your bidding, you *simply shouldn't* bid on eBay without checking out the seller.

 On planet eBay, checking the seller's feedback reviews is a definite *must*.

Finding out how the eBay feedback-and-reputation system works is a real time saver. Staring at an auction or sale and scratching your head because you don't know jack about the seller can be a real waste of time. Check out Table 4-1 for what to look for when you quickly evaluate your seller.

 Maybe not a "must" — but certainly a help — is to see whether the seller is eligible to offer PayPal's additional Buyer Protection so your purchase is fully protected. See Figure 4-1 for the Seller's Information box, and check out the PayPal Protected logo at the bottom.

Examining the Seller's Box

There's a great deal of information in the eBay Seller Information box, as pictured in Figure 4-1. This box appears on every item page and is the condensed version of the seller's online business reputation. But that's all it is. Because this condensed version is just a snapshot, it can also be misleading. That said, I present Table 4-1 to reveal the handiest secrets of the Seller Information box.

• **Figure 4-1:** eBay's Seller Information box that appears at the top of each item page. Take a look here before bidding.

A Quick Way to Evaluate Feedback

In the Seller Information box, click the feedback number next to the seller's name. Above the resulting lengthy listings, you see two areas of information: the Feedback Summary and the Recent Ratings summary.

The Feedback Summary (as in Figure 4-2) sums up the reviews that the feedback percentage is based on.

Member Profile: marsha_c (2693 ⭐	
Feedback Score:	**2693**
Positive Feedback:	**100%**
Members who left a positive:	2693
Members who left a negative:	0
All positive feedback received:	3199

• **Figure 4-2:** The seller's Feedback Summary.

TABLE 4-1: INSPECTING THE SELLER INFORMATION BOX

Entry	Where You Find It	Links to	How Important Is It?
Seller ID (link)	Top line, on the left	Feedback reviews as below	Very. (See Feedback rating link below — so important they linked it twice!)
Feedback rating (link)	Top line, in parentheses after the Seller ID	The seller's feedback reviews	Very. A star (in a variety of colors) following the rating tells you that this seller has earned more than 10 positive feedback comments. To see what the color means, visit `pages.ebay.com/help/feedback/reputation-stars.html`. Colorful? Yes! Useful? Maybe.
Power Seller (icon)	Top line, following feedback rating	Nothing	Very. Tells you that this seller has sales over $1000 per month and maintains a positive feedback percentage of 98 percent. Dealing with someone who consistently meets eBay's highest requirements generally leads to a smooth transaction.
Me (icon)	Top line, following feedback rating	Information about the seller from the seller	Important. It tells you the seller cares enough to spend the half hour or so that it takes to put up the page, ensuring that when you click the icon, you'll know more about that particular eBay business.
Seller statistics (text)	Indented under the top line	Nothing	Very. At a glance, you can get the surface scan about the seller. The Positive feedback percentage is shown; the percentage is derived from dividing the positive feedback rating by the positive feedback rating plus any negative comments. You'll also see how long the seller has been trading on eBay (and in what country they are registered) — the longer they've been on eBay, the better.

TABLE 4-1 *(continued)*

Entry	Where You Find It	Links to	How Important Is It?
Read Feedback Reviews (link)	Second line	The seller's feedback reviews	Gets you the same information as clicking the seller feedback number on the top line. (Somebody at eBay must think this info is very important — I know I do!)
Ask Seller a Question (link)	Third line	An e-mail form that will whisk your question or comment to the seller.	Very important. This is your direct line to the seller. A link to *Ask the seller a question* through eBay's internal e-mail service. This protects everyone's e-mail addresses by not exposing them to pubic view. Before bidding or buying, be sure to clear up any mysteries. Understand everything you need to know about the item. (Who wants to pay $15 shipping on a $7 item?)
View Seller's Other Items (link)	Fourth line	All listings (including Gallery pictures) of items for sale by the seller.	When you've decided to buy from a seller, it never hurts to see what else they have for sale. Most sellers will combine shipping to save you money. (Be sure to click the link to ask the question first if it's not mentioned in the item description.
Seller's eBay Store (link)	Fifth line	To the Seller's eBay Store	Important. If the list you find in the link above is too long, go directly to the seller's store and his or her items will (most likely) be organized in custom categories for easier browsing.
PayPal Buyer Protection Offered	Bottom line	Information on the PayPal Buyer Protection plan	Important. If the seller qualifies, it's an added assurance that you're dealing with a pro. Your purchase will be additionally covered by PayPal Buyer Protection, which protects your purchase up to $500 against fraud. eBay offers protection up to $200, but qualified sellers' items are protected even further if the item is purchased through PayPal.

If the Feedback Summary shows more positive comments than the total number that appears in the feedback rating, it's because the seller has had repeat business. Good sign!

 Only one comment from a unique eBay member counts toward the feedback rating (by one point in either direction), no matter how many times a buyer and seller do business together. Positive feedback comments count as a +1, negative comments count as a −1 and neutral comments are, well, neither here nor there (0).

On the case of two transactions between the buyer and a seller, if one gleans a negative, and the other is a positive, the two comments wash each other out — not affecting the total at all.

Checking Out Current Transactions in the Seller's Recent Ratings

The seller's recent ratings, which appear to the right of the Feedback Summary, give you a look at the results of the seller's feedback received over the last six months. Since a leopard rarely changes its spots, a seller with a high feedback rating will generally stay that way. By checking out the ID Card (as in Figure 4-3) with the calendar registered history, you can easily see whether a seller has changed his spots and gone over to the dark side by accumulating recent negative reviews.

Recent Ratings:

		Past Month	Past 6 Months	Past 12 Months
⊕	positive	69	395	744
◎	neutral	0	0	0
⊖	negative	0	0	0

Bid Retractions (Past 6 months): 0

• **Figure 4-3: My eBay ID card.**

Saving Time with Free GutCheck™ Software

I am also concerned with negative or positive feedbacks to see whether others have purchased an item — and whether they like it. I use feedback as a reference on the item I'm interested in as well. I click through the item numbers on a seller's past feedback to see whether others bought the item. Are previous buyers happy with his or her purchases? Or is the price on this item so low because chimps put it together with crazy glue?

Yeah, I get frustrated if I'm examining a high-volume seller's feedback comments and can't find any negatives. When a seller is listing thousands of auctions a week, it really takes a while to trudge through the hundreds of comments to even make it through 30 days' worth. If only one or two negative feedbacks show up among hundreds of positives, odds are I'll have no problem with the seller.

To solve my problem of finding the negatives, I found wonderful free software from the people at www.team redline.com. They developed GutCheck™ software as a service to the eBay buying and selling community. Quick to download and install, GutCheck resides within Internet Explorer and is available from a pop-up menu (which you call up by right-clicking in any Internet Explorer window). Follow these steps to have GutCheck sniff out negative feedback reviews:

1. **Right-click any eBay member's name or feedback link.**

2. **Choose Get GutCheck from the resulting pop-up menu, as shown in Figure 4-4.**

3. **Sit and wait while GutCheck automatically scans through all feedback posted for the seller.**

The software allows you to stop the scan at any time with a click of the mouse. That means you can limit your examination to a range of feedback comments. When a seller has thousands, I often limit my search to the past couple of months (as in Figure 4-5).

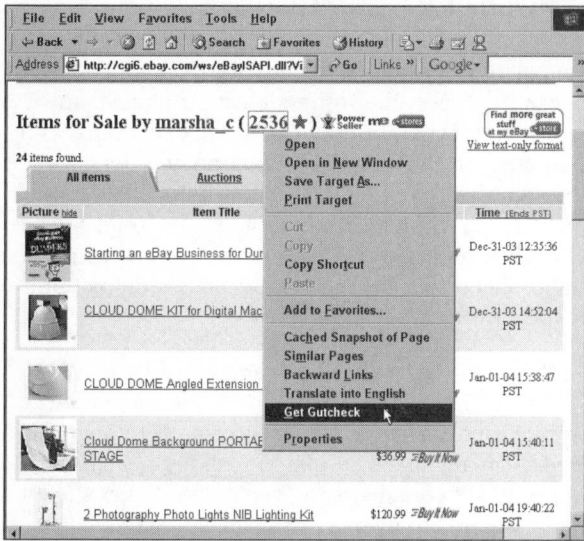

• **Figure 4-4:** Getting ready to get a GutCheck on an eBay seller.

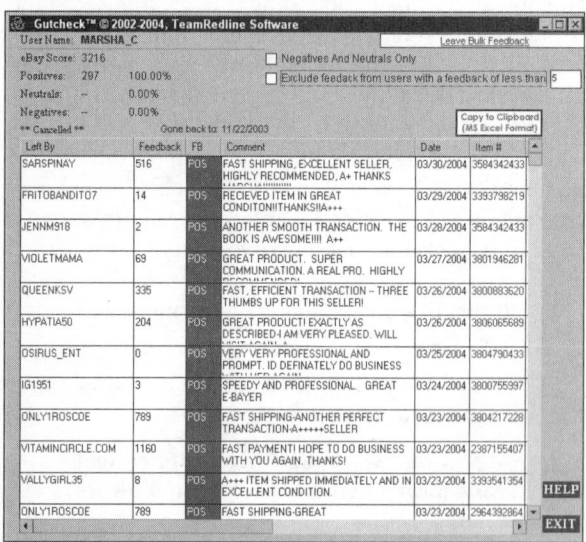

• **Figure 4-5:** Running a GutCheck on feedback.

4. If you've found the negative you're looking for, scroll the program to the sight to see the item number, click the number to open the item page in a second window.

5. To see only the negatives and neutrals that have been left for the seller, just click the box that says *Negatives and Neutrals only* to see these comments on their own, as in Figure 4-6.

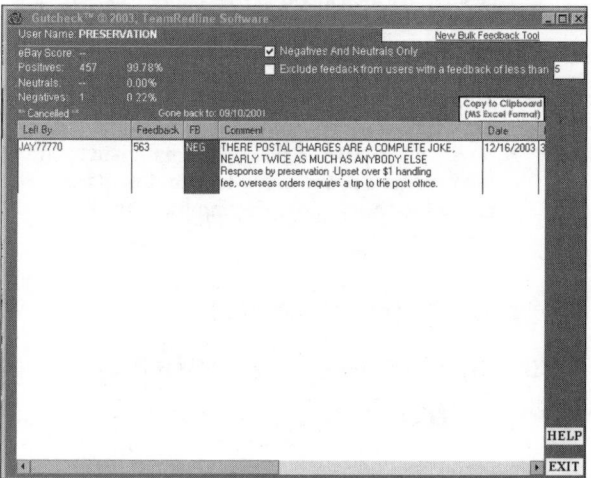

• **Figure 4-6:** Isolating the negatives and neutrals.

Conveniently, the program also picks up the seller's response to the feedback, which can give you a look at what went wrong with the transaction. And there's a first-rate feature that allows you to exclude any feedback left for the user by other users whose feedback rating is less than x (you can fill in the amount — 5 is a good number). Inexperienced eBay users are infamous for leaving spurious, unwarranted feedback instead of contacting a seller to legitimately sort out an issue.

 You can also export the feedback information to Microsoft Excel, if you'd like to keep a permanent record of such things. Best of all, the software is free. Thank you, teamredline!

Using a SquareTrade Seal for More Information

Somewhat along the lines of the *Good Housekeeping* seal of the 1950s and '60s, eBay has set a standard for sellers that works like a stamp of approval. The SquareTrade seal shown in Figure 4-7 is posted on qualified sellers' eBay auctions. True, the seller must subscribe to the service. But many vendors pay to display such seals — including the Better Business Bureau seal.

• **Figure 4-7: My SquareTrade Seal.**

Here are some good-to-know facts about the SquareTrade seal:

✔ A seller must apply for the seal, and SquareTrade does some vigorous investigating. To be accepted for the Seal, SquareTrade inspects the seller's contact information using various services, including Equifax. For businesses, they also require a business Dun and Bradstreet number (or Federal ID number).

✔ On a daily basis, every SquareTrade Seal member's eBay business is scanned to make sure everybody's performing in a professional manner. That's why all SquareTrade seals show the current day's date.

 The SquareTrade seal states: "SquareTrade *cannot* guarantee a transaction or seal member's performance, however SquareTrade's services can substantially lower the risks of buying online."

✔ SquareTrade members also agree to respond to any transaction disputes and to participate in professional mediation through SquareTrade.

A SquareTrade seal also implies an even higher level of fraud protection. SquareTrade's Buyer Protection Program, in addition to eBay's Fraud Protection Program, protects the sealholder's auctions even more. In most instances, SquareTrade provides $250 of protection beyond the $200 provided by eBay, resulting in a total of $450 in coverage.

If available, the actual amount provided by SquareTrade's Buyer Protection Program is shown on the Member Profile Page — accessible by clicking the seller's User ID link on the item-description page, as shown in Figure 4-8. Not all listings necessarily offer the added protection, which limits a seller to offer no more than $5,000 in total added buyer protection at any given time.

Doing business with SquareTrade seal members definitely saves you time and hassle because you have reassurance that you're dealing with a reliable vendor.

 Check out Technique 56 for a way to actually *guarantee* a seller's performance.

• **Figure 4-8: My SquareTrade Member Profile page.**

Finding Discount Pricing on the Web

To find out whether a local brick-and-mortar discounter is selling your selected item closer and cheaper, I check a super-cool Internet site called `SalesCircular.com`, shown in Figure 4-9. This Web site compiles weekly newspaper-insert ads from each state — researching such stores as Best Buy, Circuit City, Kmart, CompUSA, Wal-Mart, and Staples.

 No need to buy the Sunday newspaper just to read the ads — you can go to the SalesCircular site and find the deals. They also have a special area to find items that are *free* after using a rebate coupon. Not too shabby!

• **Figure 4-9:** SalesCircular.com's California hub page for the lowest prices by week.

Another favorite is `pricegrabber.com`. They search the best online prices for everything from high-tech stuff to baby buggies. After you've searched and found sellers for your item on his or her site, you're prompted to type in your ZIP code. This is where `pricegrabber.com` does its magic, calculating the final sale price for you — including shipping. No more being sucked in by cheap product prices and then getting walloped by huge shipping costs.

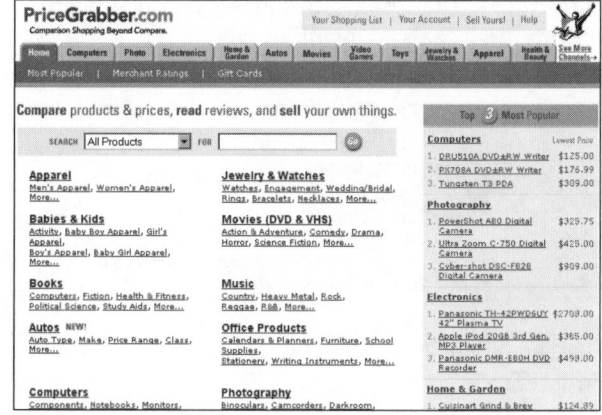

• **Figure 4-10:** PriceGrabber.com.

 When searching for a bargain, I also check the Internet shopping sites like Google's `froogle.com` and Epinions' `shopping.com` for Internet comparisons. You never know when you'll find a cheaper price online.

Technique 5

Real-World Sourcing Strategies for Your eBay Business

Save Time By

- Finding merchandise like a pro
- Visiting marts and trade shows
- Learning the players without a scorecard

The single most-asked question I get, whether in person or in e-mail is: "Where do I find merchandise to sell on eBay?" This, of course, is followed by "What can I sell to make the most money on eBay?" Good questions. But what successful seller has an answer they want to just give to the competition?

As an eBay seller, you find yourself inundated with e-mail — as well as auctions on eBay — offering wholesale source lists. These messages guarantee that you'll find items you *can* sell on eBay very lucratively. Yes, but *will* they sell? More importantly, will they sell at a profit? Not everything on eBay sells like hotcakes.

When profitable eBay PowerSellers have a good, solid source of merchandise, they're not likely to share the name of that source with anyone — nor would any brick-and-mortar retailer. (Think about it a minute.) When I was teaching a class for advanced sellers at eBay Live 2003 in Orlando, Florida, I was asked *the* question in an auditorium-size room filled with PowerSellers. I answered a question with a question: Were there were any PowerSellers in the audience who would like to share their sources with the rest of the group? You could have heard a pin drop. So I upped the ante — "I'll pay anyone $10 for one solid source" — still silence. Business is business.

The bottom line here is that all successful sellers tweak out their own sources. What works for one may not work for another, many types of financial transactions and personal relationships work for many different vendors. Methods for finding goods that I include in this Technique are gleaned from my own research, as well as from interviews with successful online retailers.

Don't make the liquidation mistake

I once also got an e-mail from a young couple planning to borrow money to purchase a pallet of liquidation goods to start an eBay business. I immediately wrote back to try to dissuade these young people. They had no idea of what *liquidation merchandise* meant — and the challenges involved in making a profit with it. They just thought they were buying a load of top-quality merchandise for pennies on the

(continued)

dollar. Don't make that mistake. If a deal seems too good, it usually isn't worth what you're paying for it. (Be sure to read Technique 6 for information on how to make informed decisions about liquidation merchandise.)

Always exercise some caution (and a little healthy skepticism) when someone sells (along with his or her "wholesale" merchandise) tips or newsletters on how to "get rich quick" or "make big money" on eBay. Legitimate wholesalers are there to move goods quickly from their warehouses to retailers. Their business is not to teach you how to "make it big" on eBay. And before you stock up on *anything*, consider this bit of wisdom from Danny Goodman (the guy in charge of merchandise for Dodger Stadium): When a vendor told him that an item would "sell like hotcakes," Danny replied, "Hotcakes don't sell at all in stadiums."

Finding Out Where Stores Buy Their Merchandise

Okay, you want to set up shop on eBay. You kind of know what type of merchandise you want to sell, but you don't know where to turn. Anyone in the brick-and-mortar world who plans to open a new store faces the same quandary: Find merchandise that will sell quickly at a profit.

Merchandise that sits around doesn't give you cash flow — which is the name of the game in *any* business. (*Cash flow* = profit = money to buy better, or more, merchandise.) I spoke to several successful retailers and they all gave me the same answers about where they began their quest. The upcoming sections give you a look at the answers these retailers shared.

To gain access to legitimate wholesale sources, you must be a licensed business in your city or county. You also usually have to have a resale permit and tax ID number from your state.

Finding merchandise locally

Always remember that the cost of shipping the merchandise to you adds a great deal of expense. The higher your expense, the lower your return may be. The more you buy locally to resell, the more profit you can make.

The first place most potential retailers go is to their local wholesale district. You can find yours in your yellow pages (remember that giant brick of a book they drop in your driveway once a year) under the name of your item. For example, you want to sell women's apparel. Look up *Women's Apparel* in the yellow pages and find the subcategory of *Wholesale*, as in Figure 5-1. Bingo! Immediate merchandise sources, within driving distance of your home! Also be sure to check the directories in neighboring communities as well. The value of this printed (and usually overlooked) resource is immeasurable when you're starting up a business.

• **Figure 5-1: A quick flip through the local phone directory finds several wholesale sources for my category of merchandise.**

Newspaper auction listings

Another excellent source of merchandise for resale is your daily newspaper — in particular, the listings of major liquidation and estate auctions (usually on

Saturday). Check out your daily newspaper each day and look for this page or section.

You may want to sell women's apparel, but if you can get a great deal on office or pet supplies, paying cents on the dollar, you just may bend your way of thinking!

Don't miss the daily classified section — look for ads that announce local business liquidations. Do not confuse any of this with garage sales or flea-market sales (run by individuals and often a great source for one-of-a kind items). Liquidation or estate sales are professionally run, usually by licensed liquidators or auctioneers and involve merchandise that may be new but is always sold in *lots* (in a quantity). Figure 5-2 shows a quick way to find some.

• **Figure 5-2:** A Google search for *newspaper classified Los Angeles* brings up plenty of hits to peruse online.

 If your local newspaper has a Web site, use their online search to view the classifieds for major liquidations, estate auctions, or other similar deals. Right there online, you can often find just what you are looking for locally.

Regional merchandise marts

Your next stop, should you be lucky enough to live in a regional area, is to find out if there is a merchandise or fashion mart near you. These are giant complexes that hold as many as several thousand lines of merchandise in one area.

Merchandise marts are hubs for wholesale buyers, distributors, manufacturers, and independent sales representatives. They have showrooms within the property for manufacturers or their representatives to display their current merchandise. Under one roof, you may find both fashion and gift merchandise for your eBay business.

See Table 5-1 for a representative sprinkling of the many marts across the country. Realize this is not a comprehensive list, just one to get your mind moving. You can contact the individual marts for tenant lists and more information. If you are a legitimate business, they will be more than happy to teach you the ropes and get you started.

My very favorite, the California Market Center (the Web site pictured in Figure 5-3) even has a special program for new buyers, offering tons of useful information to help newbies get going.

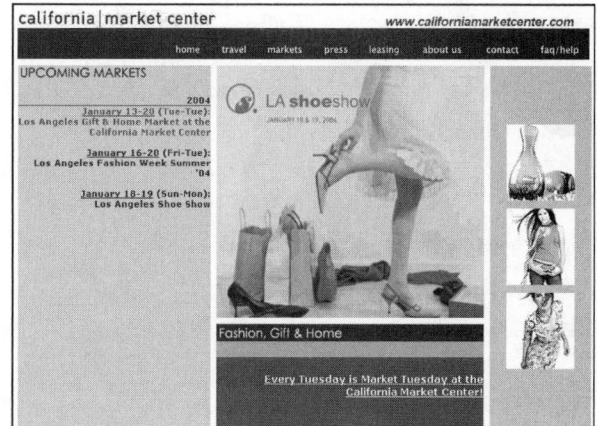

• **Figure 5-3:** The California Market Center Web site.

 When you go to each mart's Web site, you find hundreds of links to wholesale sources. Many marts also send you a directory of the manufacturers represented in the mart.

TABLE 5-1: WHOLESALE MERCHANDISE SOURCE MARTS

Name	Location	Web Site Address	Trade Shows
Americas Mart	Atlanta, Georgia	www.americasmart.com	Gift, Home furnishings, fashion
The Gift Center	Bedford, Mass	www.thegiftcenter.com	Gifts and decorative accessories
California Market Center	Los Angeles, CA	www.californiamarket center.com	Apparel, accessories, toys, gifts, furniture & décor, garden accessories, stationery, personal-care products
Chicago Merchandise Mart	Chicago, IL	www.giftandhome.com	Apparel, Home Furnishings, Antiques, Gifts, Bridal
Columbus Gift mart	Columbus, OH	www.columbusgiftmart.com	Gifts, garden, home furnishings, décor
Dallas Market Center	Dallas, TX	www.dallasmarketcenter.com	Apparel, gift products, decorative accessories, home furnishings, lighting, garden accessories, floral, and gourmet
Denver Merchandise Mart	Denver, CO	www.denvermart.com	Apparel, gifts, souvenirs, gourmet, collectibles, home décor
International Home Furnishings	High Point, NC	www.ihfc.com	Home furnishings and décor of all types
Kansas City Gift Mart	Kansas City, MO	www.kcgiftmart.com	Gifts, gourmet, design, home décor
The L.A. Mart	Los Angeles, CA	www.lamart.com	Gifts, home décor, furnishings
Miami Merchandise Mart	Miami, FL	www.miamimart.net	Apparel, gifts, accessories, home décor
Michigan Gift Mart	Northville, MI	www.michigangiftmart.com	Gifts, home décor, accessories
Minneapolis Gift Mart	Minneapolis, MN	www.mplsgiftmart.com	Gifts, home décor, accessories
New York Merchandise Mart	New York, NY	www.41madison.com	Gifts, home décor, accessories
225 Fifth Avenue	New York, NY	www.225-fifth.com	Gifts, home décor, accessories, stationery
San Francisco Gift Center	San Francisco, CA	www.gcjm.com	Apparel, home furnishings, gifts, jewelry, stationery
Seattle Gift Center	Seattle, WA	www.seattlegiftcenter.com	Gifts, home décor, accessories
Charlotte Merchandise Mart	Charlotte NC	www.charlottemerchmart.com	Apparel, gifts, jewelry, home décor, accessories
The New Mart	Los Angeles, Ca	www.newmart.net	Contemporary clothing and accessories

Wholesale trade shows

By checking out the links to the marts listed in Table 5-1, you'll also end up with links to the thousands of wholesale trade shows that go on across the country each year.

Trade shows are commonly held in convention centers, hotels, and at the local merchandise marts.

 When visiting a show or a mart, view all merchandise before you place an order. Bring a notebook with you to make copious notes of items you find interesting and where you find them.

These trade shows are gargantuan bourses of hundreds of wholesale vendors all lined up and ready to take your orders. The vendors have samples of the merchandise in the lines they carry, and are delighted to answer all your questions about their products, credit applications, and minimum orders. These shows are designed to move product to retailers like you!

Necessary identification for trade shows and marts

When you attend one of the professional trade shows or marts in the country, they want to be sure that you really represent a business. These shows are not open to the general public, and they want to keep it that way.

Below is a list of items that you may be asked to bring with you as identification as a retailer. Check ahead of time with the sponsoring organization for an exact list.

- ✔ Business cards
- ✔ A copy of your current Resale Tax Certificate or State Tax Permit
- ✔ Current Occupational or Business Tax License
- ✔ Proof of a Business checking account or a Letter of Credit from your bank (if applying for credit)
- ✔ Financial Statement
- ✔ Cash and checks

You may have to bring less than the items on this list. Be sure to check with the organization sponsoring the trade show or mart prior to attending so that you'll have everything you need. Don't let this list scare you — wholesale marts are fun and the organizers and vendors will do everything they can to help you make your retailing venture a success!

Very few trade shows are more exciting than the Consumer Electronics Show (CES), sponsored by the Consumer Electronics Association and shown in Figure 5-4. If you buy breakthrough technologies to sell online, this show is a must! You'll find the latest in everything high-tech including digital imaging, electronic gaming, home electronics, car audio, home theater, satellite systems and much, much more. It takes days to see this show. You'll see what's new, but more importantly, you'll see what will be passé in a hurry — great merchandise to sell on eBay!

• **Figure 5-4: The show floor of the 2004 CES show in Las Vegas.**

CES draws over 100,000 buyers each year and the vendors are there to sell their goods to *you*. Visit the CES Web site at www.cesweb.org to get an idea of the excitement that the show generates.

See if the item is selling on eBay before you make your purchase. Bring a laptop with a wireless connection (if there is a hot spot at the show) or make notes for purchases on another day. Getting a good deal is one thing — selling it on eBay is another.

Figuring Out Who's Who in the Industry

It would be very simple if you just bought merchandise from a manufacturer. But that's rarely the case. A full team of players participate in the wholesale game, and each player performs a different task. So you'll understand how to follow the plays without a program, here's a brief rundown:

- **Manufacturers.** Buying directly from a manufacturer may get you great prices, but may not be a place for a beginner to start. Manufacturers usually require large minimum orders from retailers. Unless you have a group of other sellers (perhaps a friend who owns a retail store?) to split your order with, you may have to make your purchase from a middleman.

 An exception to the large-quantity requirement may be in the apparel industry. Because apparel has distinct, rapidly changing fashion seasons, a quick turnover in merchandise is a must. Apparel manufacturers may allow you to make small purchases towards the end-of-season to outfit your eBay store. It never hurts to ask.

- **Wholesalers:** Here's your first step to finding your "middleman." Wholesalers purchase direct from the manufacturer in large quantities. They sell the merchandise to smaller retailers who cannot take advantage of the discounts from manufacturers for large orders.

The important thing is to find a wholesaler who is familiar with (or better yet, specializes in) the type of merchandise you want to sell. Obviously, someone who specializes in prerecorded DVDs and videos will not have a clue about the fashion market and vice versa.

 Don't forget to check local wholesalers (as described in " Finding merchandise locally," earlier in this Technique) to find some good sources.

- **Manufacturer's reps:** These are generally the type of people you'll meet at trade shows or marts. They are the traditional Willy Loman kind of salesman, representing one or many non-competing manufacturers and selling their merchandise to retailers for a commission.

- **Jobbers or brokers:** Jobbers and brokers are independent businesspeople who buy merchandise from anywhere they can at distressed prices. They mostly deal in liquidation or salvage merchandise. (Learn more about this source in Technique 6.)

 Don't forget to negotiate. Almost everything in the wholesale merchandise world is negotiable. Although merchandise may have a set price, you may be able to get a discount if you offer to pay on delivery, or within ten days. Ask whether your sources can help you out with shipping costs (and perhaps promotions). You just may get a discount if you promote their products through banner ads. Ask, ask, ask. The worst they can say is no.

Technique 6

Qualifying Your Merchandise and Methods

You're likely to find various levels of quality when you look for merchandise to resell on eBay. If you take time to evaluate the condition of the merchandise you're getting, you save time (and money) in the long run. Receiving a box of ripped or stained goods when you expected first-quality merchandise can be pretty disheartening. Know what the industry language tells you about the quality of the merchandise you're looking to buy. And ask, ask, *ask* — about the condition of the merchandise, that is. Before you put down your money for goods, qualify 'em.

In addition to qualifying the goods you buy, take the time to qualify the processes and partners you use. For example, *drop-shipping* (shipping goods straight from the stockpile to the consumer) is ever more popular as a method to move the merchandise sold on eBay — but it comes with many caveats. For example, eBay has a policy about pre-selling items, so be sure to check it out — and make sure your drop-shipper has the merchandise ready to go when you place your order. Read on to get the goods on what to check out *before* you get the goods from a drop-shipper.

Use this technique to become a savvy buyer (of goods to resell) *and* an effective mover (of those same goods). To help ensure that industry jargon won't trip you up, I outline the lingo you need to know and offer pointers on making the right decisions about your merchandise and methods.

Know the Lingo of Merchandisers

Yes, you know that *apparel* is clothing, but did you know it's also a whole vocabulary? Here are some terms you're likely to run across:

- **Job lots:** The word *job* appears randomly throughout the wholesale industry. A manufacturer may want to "job out" some merchandise that's off-season. In this use, a *job lot* simply refers to a bunch of merchandise sold at once. The goods may consist of unusual sizes, odd colors, or even some hideous stuff that wouldn't blow out of your eBay store if a hurricane came in. Some of the merchandise (usually no more than 15 percent) may be damaged.

A good way to find a *jobber* (someone who wants to sell you job lots) on the Internet is to run a Google search on *wholesale jobber*. Another great place to find them is the phone book or industry newsletter classifieds.

There are super discounts to be had on job lots — and if the lot contains brand names from major stores, you may be able to make an excellent profit.

✔ **Off-price lots:** If you can get hold of top-quality, brand-name items in off-price lots, you can do very well on eBay. These items are end-of-season *overruns* (they made more items then they could sell through their normal retailers). You can generally find this merchandise toward the end of the buying season.

Many eBay sellers, without having the thousands of dollars to buy merchandise, make friends with the salespeople at manufacturers' outlet stores (that's where the merchandise may land first). Others haunt places like TJ Maxx, Marshall's, and Burlington Coat Factory for first-rate deals.

 Search genuine trade publications' classified ads for items to buy in bulk. Publications like *California Apparel News* have classifieds that are accessible online for a small fee. Visit their Web site, shown in Figure 6-1, www.apparel news.net and click classifieds. You can pay to view current classified ads via PayPal, and as of this writing, the cost is only $2.

✔ **Liquidations:** All the eBay sellers think of liquidations as the mother lode of deals. And, yes, they may be the mother lode of deals if you can afford to buy and store an entire truckload (that's an 18-wheeler's container) of merchandise. That takes a great deal of money and a great deal of square footage. Not to mention the staff to go through each and every piece.

You could end up with close to 50 *pallets* (the wooden platforms that measure 4' x 4', stacked as high) of merchandise from a liquidation purchase.

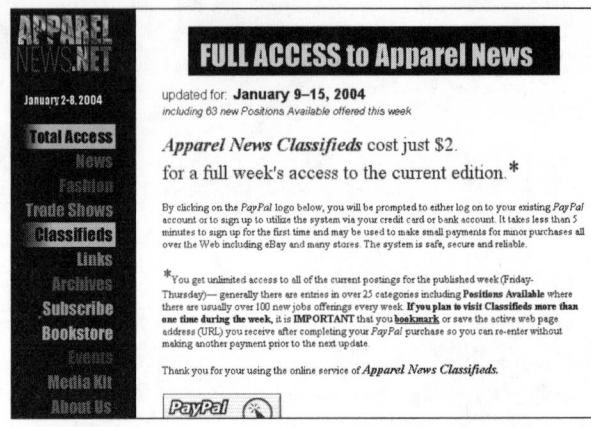

• **Figure 6-1: Access current industry classifieds on the California Apparel News Web site.**

You may be able to buy a single pallet or two from a full load from a liquidator, but a single pallet is even more of a gamble — you won't have the breadth of merchandise to amortize the damaged goods that could be in the load. Check for any of the following when dealing with these wares:

▶ This merchandise can be an assortment of liquidations, store returns, salvage, closeouts, shelf pulls, overstocks, and surplus goods.

▶ As much as 30 percent (if not more) of a truckload may be totally useless.

▶ Some items may be damaged but repairable; others may be perfectly saleable.

Buying liquidation merchandise is a gamble but can have advantages. By buying a full truckload, you have a wide breadth of merchandise, you'll pay the lowest amount for it, and some of it may be good for spare parts.

 Save yourself some money. Don't go on eBay and buy some wholesale "list" for $5. You can get the same names by running a Google search on the term *wholesale*.

Staying Safe when Buying Liquidations

 Nobody offers a quality or fitness guarantee when you buy liquidation merchandise. You could end up with pallets of unsaleable merchandise, and you must steer quickly away from anyone who "guarantees" you'll make money.

Because all liquidation merchandise is sold "as-is," here are a few suggestions for dealing with the uncertainties:

✔ **Get an anonymous free e-mail address** from Yahoo! before signing up for any "mailing lists" or "newsletters." Some Web sites that offer these publications make most of their money by selling your e-mail address to spammers. If you give them an anonymous e-mail address, the buckets of spam will never end up in your real mailbox. (I learned about that the hard way.)

✔ **Raise your shields.** If the "wholesalers" also link their Web sites to miscellaneous make-big-profits-at-eBay Web sites, beware. They may be making most of their money from commissions when the e-book of "road-to-riches" secret tips is sold to you.

✔ **Be sure there is a phone number on the site.** Give them a call and see how you're treated. It's no guarantee of how they'll treat you if you're unhappy with a purchase, but you may get a human being on the phone (rare and precious these days).

✔ **Look for a physical address.** Do they have a place of business or is the company running out of some guy's pocket cell phone? (Often it's not a good sign if there's no place to *hang* a sign.)

✔ **Ask for references.** Seeing the Better Business Bureau Online, TrustE, or SquareTrade logo on the Web site can bolster trust in the company. (They actually have to qualify for those seals.)

✔ **Before you purchase anything, go to eBay and see whether that item will sell — and for how much.** Use the searching approach discussed in Technique 1. Often you find hundreds of listings for an item with no bids. Check completed auctions and be sure that the item is selling for a solid profit over what you expect to pay for it (including shipping).

✔ **Never buy anything just because it's cheap.** That was true in Thomas Jefferson's day and it's still true today. Be sure you can actually *sell* the merchandise. (I also learned this the hard way.)

✔ **Look for the word *FOB*.** That means *freight on board*. You will be charged freight from the location of the merchandise to your door. The shorter the distance, the cheaper your freight costs.

 Before doing business on any Web site, be sure its owners have a Privacy Policy that protects your personal information. Also check for an About Us page. Be sure the About Us page really talks about the business and the people behind it. I hate to be repetitive, but be sure you can reach a human being on a phone or in person (with a street address) if need be.

Internet Shopping for Resale Merchandise

I've come across many legitimate sources of goods on the Internet. There are some really good ones. But as I mentioned in the preceding section, the Internet is loaded with scam artists; it's up to you to check vendors out for yourself before spending your hard-earned money. Even if I mention sellers here, I want you to check them out as if you knew nothing about them. I cannot guarantee a thing; all I know is that at the time of writing, they were reliable sources for eBay merchandise.

You must have a Federal Tax ID number (that's your identification to do business) to even register on many wholesale sites. Finding wholesale Web sites with this restriction is a good thing. It's another way to verify that you're the dealing with a legitimate supplier.

Liquidation.com

If you like auctions (and I *know* you do), check out Liquidation.com. This is a massive all-auction Web site that has incredible deals on all types of merchandise. Figure 6-2 gives you a look at some of the auctions I found with a click from their home page.

• **Figure 6-2:** The Liquidation.com Web site.

One of the things that I love about this site is that when inspecting the individual auctions, many auctioneers provide a link to the *manifest* — a list of every piece of merchandise in the lot. If you click the word *Manifest* at the top of the auction page, you see an exact, piece-by-piece list of the items included in the lot you're bidding on.

Liquidation.com also has a shipping calculator to help you know ahead of time how much your shipping may be.

Wholesale Central

One of the largest sites of wholesalers on the Internet is Wholesalecentral.com. You'll find everything from women's apparel to flea market items — all with their own clickable links and phone numbers. The site is the brainchild of Sumner publications. They have a linked online directory of thousands of wholesale sources selling all types of merchandise. They also publish a monthly magazine called *Web Wholesaler*.

Poke around their pages and check out the ads. Often some good wholesalers offer free shipping on your first order or give you some other introductory discount.

Big Lots Wholesale

If you're familiar with the Big Lots stores scattered around the country, then you have an idea of what you can buy at biglotswholesale.com. A quick click to their Web site showed me they were loaded with great deals on everything from health and beauty items to toys to lawn and garden tools!

 Sites like Big Lots Wholesale change merchandise quickly, so when you find something that piques your interest, research it quickly and buy it. It may not be there when you check back.

Authentic European designer goods from a source for eBay sellers

There are always lots of comments on the "authenticity" of the designer items that are sold on eBay. The bottom line is that if you sell authentic, brand-name luxury items on eBay, the items generally sell for good (read: high) prices. If your item is counterfeit, eBay's VERO trademark police will end your auction or sale.

The VERO team does an excellent job of removing bogus items from the site, when and if the manufacturer reports the listing. For example, the publisher of this book, Wiley Publishing, Inc., is very protective of the *For Dummies* brand and the company is a member of VERO.

Purchasing designer goods from the manufacturers is a rarity. Somehow Burberry or Gucci aren't the least bit interested in the piddly $1,000 I might scrape together to invest in their merchandise. But if you're looking for a legitimate wholesaler of authentic designer goods that sells surplus designer goods in small lots for individual resale on eBay, such a creature does exist: Luxury Brands, LLC has worked out this unique niche in the market. You can find its Web site at www.luxurybrandsllc.com

Dealing with Drop-Shippers

The second-most-asked question I get wants the lowdown on drop-shippers. A *drop-shipper* is a business that stocks merchandise and sells it to you (the reseller) — but ships the merchandise directly to your customer.

By using a drop-shipper, you transfer the risks of buying merchandise, shipping it, and storing it to another party. You become a *stockless* retailer with no inventory hanging around — often an economical, cost-effective way to do business.

The following steps outline the standard way to work with most drop-shippers via eBay:

1. **Sign up on the drop-shipper's Web site to sell their merchandise on eBay or in your Web store.**

   Be sure you've checked out their terms before you sign up — to be sure there's no minimum purchase upon signing up.

2. **Select the items from their inventory that you wish to sell.**

   For this example, say the item you select costs $6.99. The supplier gives you descriptive copy and photographs to help make your sales job easier.

3. **Post the item online and wait (fidgeting with anticipation) for someone to buy it.**

   By the way, you'll be selling this item for $19.99 plus shipping.

4. **As soon as your buyer pays for the item, e-mail the drop-shipper (or fill out a special secure form on their Web site) and pay for the item with your credit card or PayPal.**

5. **Relax while the drop-shipper ships the item to your customer for you.**

6. **If all goes well, the item arrives quickly and safely.**

You make a profit and get some positive feedback.

 The drop-shipper's Web site provides you with descriptions and images. Fine. But you and everybody else who sells that item on eBay will have the same photos and descriptive copy. Do yourself a favor and get a sample of your item, take your own pictures, and write your own description. Then at least you have a chance at beating the competitive "sameness" on eBay.

Drop-shipping works especially well for Web-based retail operations. Web stores can link directly to the drop-shipper to transmit shipping and payment information. When you're selling on eBay, it's another thing. There's more competition and you can't list hundreds of items at no additional cost.

Listing items on eBay costs money and may build up your expenses before you make a profit. (For a complete discussion of fees, go to Technique 9.) You can't just select an item from a drop-shipper and throw hundreds of auctions on eBay without loosing money. That is, unless your item is selling like gangbusters at an enormous profit. If that were the case, believe me there would be another eBay seller buying direct from the manufacturer and undercutting your price.

eBay cutthroat competition

eBay is an extremely competitive, sometimes even cutthroat, marketplace. I recently was in a price war with another eBay seller selling the same item. To compete with me, he cut his price below mine. Then I undercut his price, he undercut me, and profit started to nose-dive.

In this stomach-turning situation, I realized that the other seller was selling drop-shipped goods and had to include hefty ground shipping fees. Immediately, I matched his price and offered free shipping! I had more flexibility in my pricing because I bought the item from the manufacturer in a lot of 12 units.

I switched my product shipping from Priority Mail to FedEx Ground and came out a winner. (I still offered Priority Mail shipping at an additional charge.)

It's one thing to sign up for a free newsletter — or even to register with a particular site — but it's something else to have to pay to see what the drop-shipper intends to offer you. *You should not pay anything in advance to sign up for a drop-shipping service.*

Finding a good drop-shipper

Thousands of Web companies are aching to help you set up your online business. While some of them are good solid companies with legitimate backgrounds, others are out there just trying to get your money. These guys hope you don't know what you're doing; they're betting you'll be desperate enough to send them some cash to help you get your share of the (har-har) "millions to be made online."

Consider the following when you're choosing drop-shippers to work with:

✔ **Skepticism is healthy.** When you come across Web sites that proclaim that they can drop-ship thousands of different products for you, think twice. *Thousands?* I don't know many stores that *carry* "thousands" of items — if they do, they have vast square footage for storage and hundreds of thousands of dollars to invest in merchandise. Most drop-shipping services don't. A much smaller offering of merchandise may indicate that indeed the drop-shipper has the merchandise ready to ship and isn't relying on ordering it from someone for you.

✔ **Look out for long lines of distribution.** Drop-shippers are often middlemen who broker merchandise from several different sources — for example, from other middlemen who buy from brokers (who in turn buy from manufacturers). The line of distribution can get even longer — which means that a whole slew of people are making a profit from your item before you even buy it "wholesale." If even one other reseller gets the product directly from the distributor or (heaven forbid) the manufacturer, that competitor can easily beat your target selling price and make (what should have been) your profit. Verify with the drop-shipper that they stock the merchandise they sell.

Many wholesalers will perform drop-shipping for you.

When you find a drop-shipper who is also a wholesaler (or vise versa), look for one who has a good professional track record. Look for experienced buyers who get in a lot of good merchandise, and can handle pro-level business concerns such as resale permits and sales-tax numbers.

Coping with the inevitable "out-of-stock"

What happens when you sell an item and you go to the distributor's site and find it's sold out? Before your heart completely stops, call the drop-shipper. Perhaps they still have one or two of your items around their warehouse and took the item off the Web site because they're running too low on it to guarantee delivery.

If that isn't the case, you're going to have to contact your buyer and 'fess up that the item is currently out of stock at your supplier. I suggest calling your customers in this situation; they may not be *as* angry as they might if you just e-mailed them. Offer to refund their money immediately. Somebody else's foul-up may net you bad feedback, but that risk goes along with using drop-shipping as a business practice.

Technique 7

Getting Action When Transactions Go Wrong

In the brick-and-mortar world, you go into a store, find your item, pay for it, and take it home. Simple — or maybe not. You bring the item home, try it out — and what if it doesn't work? When you bring an item back to a store, you may get a refund, get an exchange, be told to contact the manufacturer (because that's the only warranty), or have to watch the sales clerk point to a sign that says, "All Sales Final."

Let's translate that sign: You're stuck. Does it really pay to take your chances and buy something clearly marked *All Sales Final*? Whether to take the risk (especially online) is up to you, but it is a risk. Often eBay sellers sell their All-Sales-Final items with a couple of loopholes. Make sure they guarantee the item to be exactly as described. If it isn't, odds are they'll refund your money and make things right if a problem occurs. Before you buy anything online — before you even placing a bid on it on eBay or lock in a Buy-It-Now — give the seller's return policy a careful once-over.

Even if you protect yourself, there's many a slip: Has your item not arrived? Did it arrive broken? The world — especially the online world — always falls short of complete safety. If you end up in trouble, this technique should get you some solid help.

Knowing Fraud When You See It

Here's an obvious transaction trouble spot: You win the auction and pay for your item, but the seller never sends your stuff. Or suppose the item shows up but is totally different from the item you saw or read about online. These situations constitute fraud, and laws exist to protect you (the consumer) from fraud.

In particular, you're protected from

✔ **Untimely shipping:** Did you know that the Federal Trade Commission, in their Prompt Delivery rules, says that your newly purchased item must be shipped within 30 days of the close of the auction or sale? If it isn't, the seller must have your permission to delay shipment further — or they must refund your money.

✔ **Failure to disclose complete and accurate information:** Also, according to the Federal Trade Commission, the seller perpetrates a fraud by failing to disclose all relevant information on an item or by sending you an item that fails to match the description used to sell it.

Find more information about your protection under the law at `www.ftc.gov/bcp/conline/pubs/alerts/intbalrt.htm`.

 Having the FTC watch your back against fraud is great, but you can also actively participate in your own protection. For example, does the picture on eBay show your desired item from only one side? If so, e-mail the seller and ask for a view of all sides!

Meanwhile, beware of these other illegal scams that go on in the eBay world . . .

✔ **Shill bidding:** Confederates of a seller may place ultrahigh bids on an item, thereby forcing you to bid even more if you want the item. This forces you to pay much more than you would in an honest, open marketplace.

✔ **Bid siphoning:** When you are bidding on a legitimate item, an unscrupulous scammer sends you an e-mail offering you the item at a lower price. This usually comes along with a very legitimate-sounding (or not) story about why they're selling this item so cheap. Don't be greedy; the biggest hogs get slaughtered. If you buy the item off-site, you are not protected by any of the eBay fraud protection policies.

Also, you may receive an e-mail from someone other than the seller (from a different e-mail address) in an item you won, asking for payment.

✔ **Bid shielding:** A buyer places a very high bid on an item, and at the very last possible moment, retracts the bid and places another (lower) bid under a different User ID. eBay policy fights this cheat by not allowing retractions when only 12 hours remain in an auction, even if the item is not bid up to the appropriate selling amount before time runs out.

✔ **Online escrow fraud:** The seller puts a high-ticket item up for sale online at a very reasonable price. To protect the buyer (they say), the buyer "must" use a particular online escrow service. After the dupe — guess who — makes the purchase, the seller sends the buyer a link to the "preferred" (fake) online escrow service. The buyer sends the money, the seller keeps the money and disappears, and the buyer never gets the goods. Touch-and-go escrow services are a growing problem; a scammer can set up a bogus "escrow" Web site in a couple of hours and make the whole thing look legit.

 It's safest to use eBay's recommended `www.escrow.com` for escrow transactions, or better yet, read Technique 57 about a new alternative to escrow; *bonding* sales. Bonding can be requested either by the seller or the buyer.

✔ **Money-wire fraud:** Avoid transacting business with a seller who requires you to wire money via Western Union or other sources. The seller can pick up the money anywhere and disappear. You have no further way to find the seller.

Yikes! You've Spotted the Fraud: What Now?

The first feeling that crops up when we know we've been ripped off — right after outrage — is embarrassment. (*Ack! How could I have been so stupid?*) Feeling foolish often triggers an urge to cover up the blunder — just what the scammer is counting on. So head 'em off at the outset: Take a little time to investigate the transaction *before* you buy. If you see a possible violation shaping up before you get sucked in, you do have a few places to turn to. You *can* stop fraud before it occurs.

Reporting questionable items on eBay

Suppose you see an item that perks up your scam-antennae — say, an auction that has lots of bids but all the bidders have no or little feedback. Or you see your bids instantly raised by another bidder, check that bidder's history, and find that person does the same thing in other auctions *but never wins*.

The first thing you must do is report the item in question to eBay. The sooner you report it, the better. If the eBay security folks don't receive notice till a few minutes before the auction is over, they may not be able to protect an eBay member caught in a scam.

1. **Click the Security Center link at the bottom of any eBay page.**

You go directly to the eBay Security Center, as in Figure 7-1. You can also get there by going to `pages.ebay.com/securitycenter`.

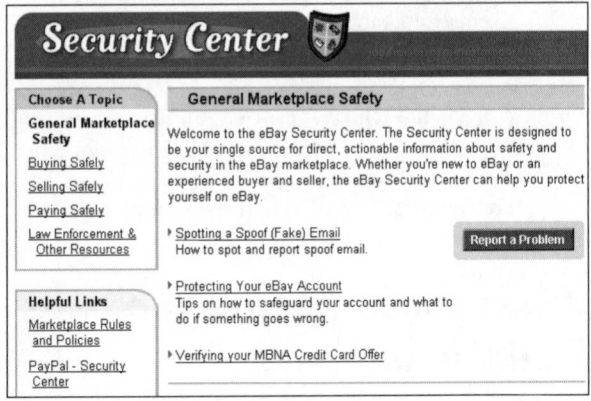

• **Figure 7-1: The eBay Security Center.**

2. **Click the green Report A Problem button.**

You now see a convenient Contact Us online form (as in Figure 7-2).

 You can also reach the Contact Us online form by going directly to `pages.ebay.com/help/contact_inline`.

Notice that the form offers you choices in filmstrip-style lists.

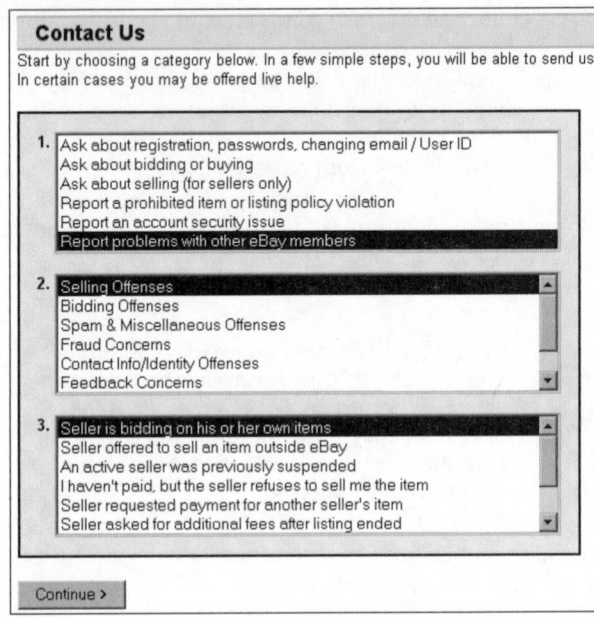

• **Figure 7-2: The Contact Us form on eBay.**

3. **Begin at the top of the form and select the appropriate choices in each box to complete the form.**

When you make a choice in the top box, a corresponding group of responses appears in the second box, and then the third — all based on your choices. In this case, I selected

▶ **Box 1:** Report problems with other eBay members

▶ **Box 2:** Selling Offenses

▶ **Box 3:** Seller is bidding on his or her own items

4. **Click Continue.**

Another Contact Us page appears and offers you several clickable options to read more about eBay's policy on the violations.

5. **Click the E-mail link to send your report to Customer Service.**

6. On the resulting e-mail form, type the item number(s), the Seller's User ID, the User IDs of the suspected shill accounts, and a description of your concerns.

By default, you receive a copy of the e-mail report. If you do not want a copy, deselect the check mark in the appropriate box.

7. Click the Send E-mail button to file your report.

In addition to a copy of your e-mail report, you receive another e-mail with a confirmation that eBay will look into the issue, as in Figure 7-3.

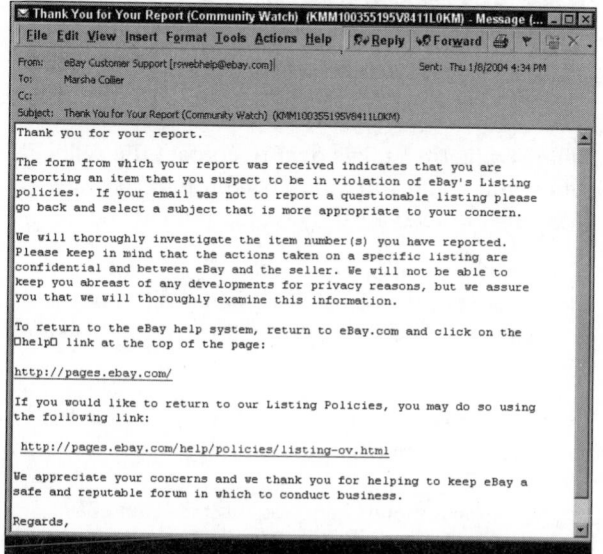

• **Figure 7-3:** An e-mail acknowledgment from eBay that they will investigate your report.

After you file your report and receive your confirmation, don't feel disheartened if eBay doesn't contact you with an update on the investigation. As the confirmation e-mail states, privacy reasons prevent eBay from updating you. The only way you can be sure that the bad-deed-doer was stopped is to revisit the auction in a few hours.

 If you revisit the problem item you reported and the eBay listing police haven't ended the listing, it doesn't mean the investigation is over. As with most crime dramas: eBay has to build a case before going full force after a suspected fraudster.

Taking action if you feel you've been defrauded

Okay, you followed all the rules and paid for your item with PayPal. But ten days have passed, and the item hasn't arrived. Bummer. Or you may have received an item that the seller misrepresented significantly in its item description. Also a bad scene.

 When you win items on eBay, be sure to make note of the day you send your payment. Seven days after that, if the package hasn't arrived, contact your seller by clicking the *Ask the Seller a Question* link on the item page.

Assuming you contacted the seller after a week, and you got no response, it's time to use the telephone. To find the seller's telephone number, follow these steps:

1. Choose Search⇨Find Members from the eBay navigation bar (at the top of every eBay page).

You're now at the Find Members page.

2. Scroll down to the Contact Info area.

3. Type the User ID of the seller and the item number of the transaction in the appropriate text boxes.

You receive an e-mail message with the seller's telephone number. The seller also receives a copy of the e-mail with your phone number.

Hopefully, once you place your phone call, any problems can be worked out.

If the phone number you receive is someone else's number or is disconnected, immediately report the situation to eBay using the Contact Us form, as described in the section "Reporting questionable items on eBay," earlier in this technique. Select *Ask about bidding or buying* in Box 1, *Problems with sellers* in Box 2, and *Seller's e-mail or contact information is not working* in Box 3.

If you get nowhere after a discussion with the seller, and the seller has a good feedback rating to preserve, you can try a last-ditch effort with SquareTrade.

When you go to the SquareTrade Web site at www.squaretrade.com, you arrive at a free online dispute service, as in Figure 7-4.

• **Figure 7-4:** The SquareTrade Web site.

To initiate a dispute resolution, follow these steps:

1. Click the Click here link indicated for eBay Buyers and Sellers involved in a dispute.

This link takes you to the Online Dispute Resolution (ODR) hub page.

2. Click the File a Case link below the headline Trouble with a Purchase or Sales, as shown in Figure 7-5.

You're transferred to a secure connection to file your case.

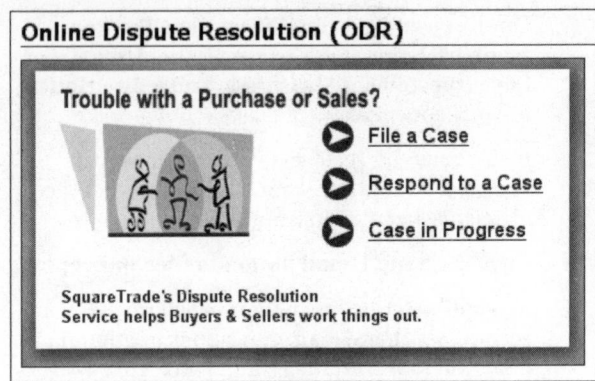

• **Figure 7-5:** Click here to file your case.

3. Follow the on-screen instructions to fill in the details of the transaction.

SquareTrade then takes over to contact the seller about your claim and direct you both to a secure, password protected Direct Negotiation area.

The negations will be transacted over a Web-based communications tool. All discussion will transact over a secure Case Page, accessible by only you and the seller.

If you get nowhere with SquareTrade, it's time to file the eBay Fraud Alert.

 Time is money here. You must file your eBay Fraud alert and/or your PayPal Buyer Protection claim within 30 days of the transaction. Keep watching the clock as you try to get help! After 30 days, no one from eBay or PayPal will help you; you'll have to go to the state and federal government. No refunds likely there.

eBay's Buyer Protection Program

Every transaction completed through the eBay site is covered by the eBay Buyer Protection Program. You are covered for losses resulting from non-delivery or misrepresentation of the item for up to $200, minus $25 (eBay calls it a *processing cost*). If your item was under $25, you do not qualify for a reimbursement under the plan.

If you've paid for the item via PayPal, you may be additionally covered for up to $500. Immediately go to PayPal and file a claim under their Buyer Protection Program (as described in the section "Filing a Claim with PayPal," later in this technique).

If you didn't pay through PayPal, but paid directly through a credit card, contact your credit card company without delay. Most credit card companies offer 100% online protection.

If you paid with a money order or check, follow the upcoming instructions for filing a Fraud Alert with eBay.

Filing a Fraud-Protection Claim with eBay

The first step in reporting fraud (involving a non-PayPal transaction on eBay) and applying for your $200 protection is to file a Fraud Alert.

To initiate your Fraud Alert, you may go to the following Web address: `http://crs.ebay.com/aw-cgi/ebay isapi.dll?crsstartpage`.

You can also find links to the Fraud Alert form in your My eBay Bidding/Watching Buying-Related Links at the bottom of the page (as in Figure 7-6) or in the Security Center's Buying Safely zone.

Buying-Related Links		
Bidding information	**Services**	**Trust & Safety**
New to eBay' tutorial	eBay Toolbar	Safe trading tips
Buyer's Guide	Item authentication	Feedback Forum - how does
Tips for buyers	All about escrow	feedback work
Bidding basics	PayPal	Filing a fraud complaint
Bidding Frequently Asked	Gift Certificates - give the gift of	Reporting trading violations
Questions	eBay	Dispute resolution
Retracting a bid		
What to do after the auction	**Help Boards**	**Finding what you want**
ends	Bidding	Feedback	PayPal		Advanced Search
Use eBay Anything Points to	Search	
pay for your items		**eBay Stores**
		Shop eBay Stores	Learn more

• **Figure 7-6: The very useful Buying-Related Links in the My eBay page's Bidding/Watching tab.**

 When you arrive at the Online Fraud Complaint Reporting form, take a deep breath. You are about to accuse someone of fraud. Be sure you've truly been defrauded;

this program offers no protection for simply buying an item and changing your mind.

To file a Fraud Alert, be sure of the following:

✔ The item was purchased through an eBay auction or fixed-price sale.

✔ You can prove that payment was sent in good faith to the seller. Proof of payment must be documentable.

✔ You have not exceeded three claims in the last six months.

✔ Be sure you have any e-mails sent to you from the seller as well as any other documentation that will prove your fraud case.

 If your fraud claim is approved, the information will be forwarded to the Federal Trade Commission (FTC) for possible further investigation.

After eBay receives your completed Fraud Alert, the crack review team takes over. In short order, you should receive an e-mail with information (and a secure link) so you know how and where to file your Fraud Protection Claim under eBay's Standard Purchase Protection Program.

Filing a Claim with PayPal

When you pay with PayPal, whether you've paid via credit card or bank transfer, PayPal protects your purchase. The PayPal Buyer Protection Program has all the rules of eBay's Fraud program — but kicks it up a notch.

If you paid with PayPal and the listing stated that you would be covered under the PayPal Buyer Protection program (as described in Technique 2), you are covered for up to $500.

To file a claim, you must go to the PayPal Web site and log in to your account. Then follow these steps:

1. **Scroll to the bottom of your PayPal home page and click the link to the PayPal Security Center.**

PayPal Security Center appears, as shown in Figure 7-7.

• **Figure 7-7: The PayPal Security Center.**

2. **Click the File a Claim link under the For Buyers column and follow the on-screen instructions.**

 If you find yourself in a jam with a seller who's item was not covered by the PayPal Buyer Protection program, you can still go to PayPal to get a refund for your payment. Begin this process in the Security Center, and make your claim by clicking on the File a Claim link.

Getting Outside Help

eBay and PayPal will go to the ropes to help you get your claim resolved. But what if you still aren't satisfied? There are others places to turn. These options probably won't get your money back, but at least you'll feel better knowing you've made the seller's sleazy practices harder to get away with.

Federal Bureau of Investigation (FBI)

The G-men — bad-deed-doers fear these guys. The FBI's Internet Fraud Complaint Center Web site receives thousands of complaints per day, but gives each one individual attention. If you've got the goods on someone who didn't deliver the goods, visit www1.ifccfbi.gov/index.asp.

Once there, click File a Complaint.

United States Postal Inspector

The folks in the Postal Inspector's office mean business — and they land hard on people who use the United States mail to defraud others. They do prosecute! Visit the Postal Inspector's home page at www.usps.com/postalinspectors/fraud/ and click the Mail Fraud Complaint form to get things going.

The Federal Trade Commission (FTC)

To file a complaint with the FTC, go to www.ftc.gov/ftc/consumer.htm and click the link that says FILE A COMPLAINT.

The National Fraud Information Center

From what I've heard, the guys at the National Fraud Information Center are like terriers — when they get their teeth into a case, they don't let go. They've even helped people get some refunds. It certainly doesn't hurt to file your report with them. Visit their Web site (www.fraud.org) and click the link for their online complaint form.

 For eBay buyers in the United Kingdom, visit the Department of Trade and Industry at www.dti.gov.uk/ccp/. The Web site lists links to sites where you can make formal complaints.

Part II

Selling Shortcuts

The 5th Wave   By Rich Tennant

"It's an AutoHyperSniper. It puts itself up for auction at eBay, bids itself up for a week, and snipes its own bid at the last nanosecond. Everybody wants one but nobody can get one."

Technique

Building Strategies for Your Sales

Save Time By

✔ Starting your auctions

✔ Timing your auctions

✔ Finding the "hot" items

✔ Using cross-promotions to attract buyers to your store

You can buy the "inside secrets" of eBay from lots of places. Some e-book sellers try to convince you that only *they* have the surreptitious bits of knowledge — gleaned from years (months?) of experience on the site — that reveal what's Really Going On. Truth be told, the eBay market has become an immediate-gratification-shopping arena; the online retail market changes so quickly that eBay can barely keep up with it — the profile of the online shopper changes constantly. How likely is it that anybody has the ultimate answer? Sure, mysterious rumors crop up — do you hear the *Twilight Zone* theme playing too? — magical means to sure-fire auctions. Start an auction at a certain day and time, and you'll automatically make more money? Puh-leez!

I have interviewed many of the eBay high-volume sellers (*Power Sellers*), and they all confirm that, with the exception of a miniscule few, these "theories" are bunk. The sellers do, however, have some practical preferences for when and how they conduct their eBay transactions. This technique gets to the gist of these preferences and the corresponding practices.

 The ideas in this technique come from my discussions with current eBay PowerSellers. These ideas are merely suggestions of methods and starting points that work for others. You definitely need to test them out and find out which practices work — for you *and* for the types of items you sell.

Knowing What Day to End an Auction

Back when eBay counted its listings by the hundreds (then low thousands), it clearly made a difference what day of the week you chose to end an auction. That is, when the number of buyers and sellers on eBay was relatively small, matching your auction time with the bidders' online habits was important.

Now that eBay spawns over 13 million listings a day with countless buyers and looky-loos visiting the site, you find the eBay netizens looking for bargains at virtually all hours of the day and night. So for a traditional auction, you can choose almost any ending time and know that you'll still have some bidders.

 Please realize that there are wildcards in the mix; they are the Buy It Now and Fixed Price transactions. Buy It Now and Fixed Price have become wildly popular on the site. Interestingly, although they don't always follow a daily pattern of sales, they can still follow the preferred auction-ending days you find in this technique.

 The advice in this section encompasses the opinions of many long-time eBay sellers. Do not take the advice as gospel. What works for them may not work for you, so please use these suggestions as a jumping-off point for your own research.

Planning your auction end day by the calendar

To get the timeline of an auction, it's best to look at a calendar. You need to know when to start an auction, in order for you to plan the time it ends. Remember that eBay works by a clock. A seven-day auction lasts 7 days — not seven days and one second, but 7 full days. Figures 8-1, 8-2 and 8-3 show top preferred datelines for running a sale on eBay.

You may notice that all these preferred datelines end on a Sunday. Sunday is the top ranked ending day for auctions by eBay sellers.

Sunday	Monday	Tuesday	Wednesday	Thursday	Friday	Saturday
1	2	3	4	5 **8:00 PM PST**	6	7
8 **8:00 PM PST**	9	10	11	12	13	14
15	16	17	18	19	20	21

• **Figure 8-1: A timeline for a 3-day auction.**

Sunday	Monday	Tuesday	Wednesday	Thursday	Friday	Saturday
				1	2	3
4 **8:00 PM PST**	5	6	7	8	9	10
11 **8:00 PM PST**	12	13	14	15	16	17
18	19	20	21	22	23	24

• **Figure 8-2: Seven days of auction action.**

Sun	Mon	Tue	Wed	Thu	Fri	Sat
	1	2	3	4 **8:00 PM PST**	5	6
7	8	9	10	11	12	13
14 **8:00 PM PST**	15	16	17	18	19	20
21	22	23	24	25	26	27

• **Figure 8-3: A full 10 days of bidding frenzy (if you're lucky).**

 Ending your listing on a major holiday — especially the ones that end on Monday, can have catastrophic results. I actually *like* to shop eBay on those days (especially Thanksgiving). There's lots of deals for buyers.

Since I can't list everyone's opinions on the subject — that would probably confuse you anyway — here are the popular item-ending days, ranked in order:

1. Sunday
2. Monday
3. Thursday
4. Tuesday
5. Wednesday
6. Saturday
7. Friday

Be sure to coordinate these dates with what you sell. Some buyers (say, men who buy golf goods during lunch hour and women who buy collectibles while their husbands are out golfing on weekends) can throw these days a curve.

Deciding how many days to run your auction

Again, here's another little subject with lots of big opinions. Especially now that eBay has introduced the one-day auction. Here's the skinny on the days and suggested uses.

- ✔ **One-day auction.** Did you just get a load of an item that sells as fast as it's put up on the site? Although a buy-it-now feature on any auction can bring great results, that *only* works if the item is *hot! hot! hot!* If people are bidding the item up — and they really gotta have it — you may do best by starting the bidding really low and listing it with a one-day format.

  When you list in a one-day format, your listing goes right to the top of the list. Most people view their searches by auctions ending first. With a one-day format, you can pretty much choose the time of day your item will be at the top.

 If the competition for your item starts their auctions at $.99 with a reasonable Buy It Now price, you'll find bidders foil many of their Buy It Now offers. Retaliate by listing the item with a starting bid just a dollar or so below your Buy It Now (and make your buy it now at least $.50 below the competition) and you'll find your items will be snapped up quickly.

- ✔ **Three-day auction.** A three-day is good, for all the same reasons that a one-day is good — only it's better for the faint of heart and Nervous Nellies (like me) because it gives your item more time to sell.

 Another good use of a three-day auction is when you already have a seven-day auction up on the site, and the bidding is going crazy. You've reached your sales goal by the middle of a seven-day cycle. Once it's in the last couple of days of the listing, throw up a second one on a three-day.

- ✔ **Seven-day auction.** The gold standard for eBay auctions, seven full days of fun, excitement, and (hopefully) bidding. Seven days gives your item plenty of time to be seen on the site and attract bidders.

- ✔ **Ten-day auction.** Okay, say you've got multiples of an item that you stock in your eBay store and want the longest amount of exposure on the auction site. You can put one up for a ten-day auction to draw attention to your items and store.

 Also, a ten-day auction is good for more esoteric items. This can be a special collectible or an expensive item that normally doesn't get listed on the site by the hundred. Putting up a ten-day auction (starting Friday night — so you get *two* weekends' exposure) is a near-perfect way to attract bidders.

Figuring out what time to start your auction

As in our previous example, the only way to figure when to end your auction is by planning when to start it. An auction beginning at 12:00 will end at that same time on the ending day.

Make a photocopy of Table 8-1 and keep it by your computer. (Even after all these years, it still takes too much time to decipher "eBay time" without a printed chart.) eBay Time is military time in the Pacific time zone. The chart converts the eBay clock to real time for your time zone. If you ever need to check your time zone, or want to know exactly what time it is in eBay-land, point your browser to

```
cgi3.ebay.com/aw-cgi/eBayISAPI.
dll?TimeShow
```

and you'll see the map pictured in Figure 8-4.

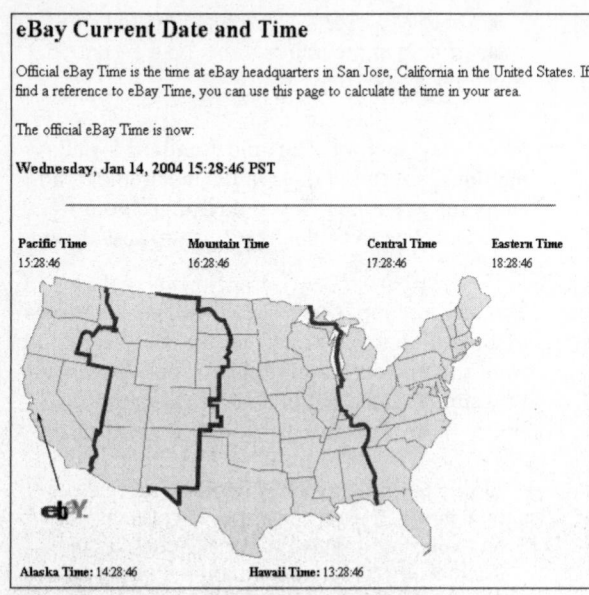

eBay Current Date and Time

Official eBay Time is the time at eBay headquarters in San Jose, California in the United States. If find a reference to eBay Time, you can use this page to calculate the time in your area.

The official eBay Time is now:

Wednesday, Jan 14, 2004 15:28:46 PST

Pacific Time	Mountain Time	Central Time	Eastern Time
15:28:46	16:28:46	17:28:46	18:28:46

Alaska Time: 14:28:46   Hawaii Time: 13:28:46

• **Figure 8-4: eBay Official Time.**

Here's the consensus of some experts in order of ending-time preference (in eBay Time, check the table for a translation):

1. 18:00 to 22:00
2. 21:00 to 0:00
3. 15:00 to 18:00
4. 13:00 to 16:00

Worst times to end an auction (ranked from Worst to Best):

1. 2:00 to 6:00
2. 0:00 to 3:00

This information should give you some good ideas for your own auction sales.

TABLE 8-1: EBAY TIME VERSUS THE CONTINENTAL U.S. ZONES

eBay Time	Pacific	Mountain	Central	Eastern
0:00	12:00 a.m.	1:00 a.m.	2:00 a.m.	3:00 a.m.
1:00	1:00 a.m.	2:00 a.m.	3:00 a.m.	4:00 a.m.
2:00	2:00 a.m.	3:00 a.m.	4:00 a.m.	5:00 a.m.
3:00	3:00 a.m.	4:00 a.m.	5:00 a.m.	6:00 a.m.
4:00	4:00 a.m.	5:00 a.m.	6:00 a.m.	7:00 a.m.
5:00	5:00 a.m.	6:00 a.m.	7:00 a.m.	8:00 a.m.
6:00	6:00 a.m.	7:00 a.m.	8:00 a.m.	9:00 a.m.
7:00	7:00 a.m.	8:00 a.m.	9:00 a.m.	10:00 a.m.
8:00	8:00 a.m.	9:00 a.m.	10:00 a.m.	11:00 a.m.
9:00	9:00 a.m.	10:00 a.m.	11:00 a.m.	12:00 p.m.
10:00	10:00 a.m.	11:00 a.m.	12:00 p.m.	1:00 p.m.
11:00	11:00 a.m.	12:00 p.m.	1:00 p.m.	2:00 p.m.
12:00	12:00 p.m.	1:00 p.m.	2:00 p.m.	3:00 p.m.
13:00	1:00 p.m.	2:00 p.m.	3:00 p.m.	4:00 p.m.
14:00	2:00 p.m.	3:00 p.m.	4:00 p.m.	5:00 p.m.

eBay Time	Pacific	Mountain	Central	Eastern
15:00	3:00 p.m.	4:00 p.m.	5:00 p.m.	6:00 p.m.
16:00	4:00 p.m.	5:00 p.m.	6:00 p.m.	7:00 p.m.
17:00	5:00 p.m.	6:00 p.m.	7:00 p.m.	8:00 p.m.
18:00	6:00 p.m.	7:00 p.m.	8:00 p.m.	9:00 p.m.
19:00	7:00 p.m.	8:00 p.m.	9:00 p.m.	10:00 p.m.
20:00	8:00 p.m.	9:00 p.m.	10:00 p.m.	11:00 p.m.
21:00	9:00 p.m.	10:00 p.m.	11:00 p.m.	12:00 a.m.
22:00	10:00 p.m.	11:00 p.m.	12:00 a.m.	1:00 a.m.
23:00	11:00 p.m.	12:00 a.m.	1:00 a.m.	2:00 a.m.

Finding eBay's Soon-to-Be "Hot" Sellers

Everyone wants to know (the second-most-often-asked question I get) *What's the hot ticket on the eBay site?* How can they find out what's selling best so they can run out, buy it, and *make big money* on eBay? Whoa, there, big fella.

As I've been known to say elsewhere, I am not a believer in the notion that eBay is a "get-rich-quick" program. Nobody can give you secret information that magically transforms you from a garage seller to a warehouse tycoon overnight. You get there by studying the market, learning what works and what doesn't. That's the way the top sellers, who continue to sell on the site, learned eBay. There are no shortcuts.

That said, here's where you can find information on what's hot or what's going to be hot on the site.

Hot on the home page

New shoppers to the site generally enter from the home page at www.eBay.com.

• **Figure 8-5: The eBay Home Page feature promotion.**

In case you haven't noticed, eBay runs promotions smack in the center of the home page (as in Figure 8-5) — immediately drawing the attention of anyone who drops in to browse the site. Each item listed in the feature links to an eBay search for such items.

Now wouldn't you be the smart one if you were to list items that coincided with the eBay promotions? Oh yeah — and I'll tell you where you can find them.

You can go to eBay's Seller Central, or directly to `pages.ebay.com/sellercentral/calendar.html`. Here you'll find a current list of items that will be featured in the next couple of months. Take a look at Figure 8-6 and see how the event from the merchandising calendar carefully matches the headline from the promotion shown in Figure 8-5.

Merchandising Calendar

The following promotions will be highlighted on eBay's home page in the coming months.* Check back often for updates and be sure to stock up by visiting the eBay Wholesale Lots portal.

Event	Month	Featured Categories
Get What You Really Wanted	Jan: Week 1	Entertainment Fashion Collectibles Consumer Electronics Sports
Winter Brand Blowout	Jan: Week 2	Fashion Sports
Winter Sports	Jan: Week 3	Sports
Winter Sale	Jan: Week 4	Consumer Electronics Fashion Entertainment Sports
Valentine's Day	Jan: Week 5	Jewelry Fashion Everything Else
Valentine's Day BIN	Feb: Week 1	Jewelry Fashion Everything Else

• **Figure 8-6:** eBay's Merchandising Calendar in Seller Central.

eBay's monthly hot sellers

eBay has maintained an area that evaluates sales by category, and lets you know which sub-categories are white-hot. That information can be found as a PDF file in Seller Central (`pages.ebay.com/sellercentral`) — look for the "What's Hot" link in the column on the left side of the page. Visit the page directly by going to `pages.ebay.com/sellercentral/whatshot.html` and clicking Hot Items.

You could have knocked me over with a feather when I saw that Beanie Baby sales are on the rise again!

Checking Out the Buzz on Yahoo! and Elsewhere

The eBay site is the world's host for popular culture. If it's hot, people come here to look for it. Aside from following the media (and other sources I point out in *Starting an eBay Business For Dummies,* also from Wiley), you should also look on the Internet to find the buzz.

By *buzz* I mean the latest gossip, rumor, or thing that's talked about at the water cooler at work. It's the thing on everyone's tongues for the current nanosecond in time. Something that's merely buzz can become a trend — and trends are what you look for to follow into the world of eBay.

You can find the beginnings of buzz in any news report or on your Internet provider's home page. It's news.

Yahoo! keeps a page on the site called the Buzz Index. You can find it on `buzz.yahoo.com`. It's a weekly compilation of items that have received the largest number of searches on their system. They show what's new on the list, what's going up, what's going down. Figure 8-7 shows the Buzz List from January 11, 2004.

The Leaderboard			
This Week	Last Week	Subject	Weeks on Chart
1 ▲	3	Britney Spears	146
2 ▼	1	Paris Hilton	9
3 ▲	-	NASA	1
4 ▲	-	Mars	1
5 ▲	6	Kazaa	118
6 ▲	7	Christina Aguilera	60
7 ▲	40	B2K	3
8 ▲	9	Jennifer Lopez	146
9 ▼	5	PlayStation 2	65
10 ▼	8	Beyonce Knowles	31
11 ▼	2	*Lord of the Rings*	9
12 ▼	11	NFL	23
13 ▼	10	Orlando Bloom	3
14 ▼	13	50 Cent	48
15 ▼	14	Linkin Park	39
16 ▲	-	North American International Auto Show	1
17 ▲	32	Hilary Duff	23
18 ▲	19	Kazaa Lite	11
19 ▲	21	Tupac Shakur	61
20 ▲	-	*World Idol*	1

• **Figure 8-7: What's Hot on Yahoo! — a snapshot of the week's pop culture.**

If you're good at prognostication, you may favor the way Yahoo! shows the Buzz as a daily ranking. Figure 8-8 shows January 14, 2004 Daily Buzz.

Leaders				Movers		
Rank	Prev.	Subject (Days on Chart)	Move Score	Rank	Subject	1-Day Move
1	- 1	Britney Spears (672)	-38 291	1	Amber Alert	Breakout!
2	- 2	Paris Hilton (41)	+42 290	2	Lillian Muller	Breakout!
3	- 3	B2K (15)	+8 167	3	Thq	Breakout!
4	- 4	NASA (6)	-91 149	4	Sega Genesis	Breakout!
5	- 5	Mars (6)	-33 118	5	Hubble Space Telescope	3072.12%
6	- 6	Beyonce Knowles (139)	+3 110	6	Calista Flockhart	933.07%
7	- 7	Jessica Simpson (12)	+50 110	7	Alyson Hannigan	560.66%
8	- 8	Jennifer Lopez (201)	+5 106	8	Archos Sa	511.77%
9	- 9	Kazaa (495)	0 97	9	Briefing.com	322.60%
10	- 10	Internal Revenue Service (6)	-4 88	10	Archos	311.41%
11	- 11	Hubble Space Telescope (2)	+82 84	11	Wendy Williams	297.96%
12	- 12	50 Cent (224)	+3 84	12	The Sleeping Dictionary	285.19%
13	- 13	PlayStation 2 (495)	-1 82	13	Ingram Micro	283.52%
14	- 14	Christina Aguilera (166)	-32 81	14	Scarlett Johansson	279.14%
15	- 15	Tupac Shakur (85)	+4 79	15	Tiger	266.93%
16	- 16	Super Bowl (6)	-6 78	16	Steam	240.67%
17	- 17	Linkin Park (185)	+4 77	17	Apprentice	238.36%
18	- 18	Lord of the Rings (44)	-6 74	18	Rhea Durham	231.80%
19	- 19	NFL (107)	-3 72	19	Harrison Ford	226.76%
20	- 20	Orlando Bloom (14)	-7 68	20	Aileen Wuornos	222.57%

• **Figure 8-8: The Yahoo! Daily Buzz.**

Technique 9

Setting Profitable Price Points

Save Time By

- ✔ Knowing where all the pennies go
- ✔ Adding options to up the bottom line
- ✔ Establishing your cost basis
- ✔ Using third-party research tools

Selling on eBay is a grand idea. You clean out your garage, sell things you would have thrown away anyway, and make a profit. What a wonderful marketplace! You can make money in your spare time, enhance your lifestyle and all — with a few clicks on your keyboard and mouse. You get to the challenge — or should I say *challenges* — when you've run out of junk to sell and decide to sell on eBay in earnest.

This is where the novice eBay seller runs into problems. Very few eBay sellers have a background in retailing or marketing, and that's what eBay is all about — retailing and marketing. Universities offer degrees in both areas, so there must be *something* worth learning. In Part I of this book, you find a crash course in buying; this part of the book helps with your selling.

In this technique, I give you tips on pricing strategies — and the first item on the agenda is to understand all the fees involved with running an e-business on eBay.

Keeping an Eye on Where Your Pennies Go

It doesn't seem so much, $.30 to list an item, and a small Final Value fee. Of course, a few cents go to PayPal. One by one, these minute amounts tend to breeze by the seller. You don't really see your eBay fees, because they're not directly deducted from your sales. eBay bills you at the end of the month. It's easy to lose track of your costs unless you are keeping *very* good books (more on that in Technique 45).

 All those nickels, dimes, and quarters build up. The hundreds (thousands?) of sellers who are selling items on the site for $1 can't be making much of a profit — not even enough for a pack of gum! So to avoid this low-profit trap, you must be keenly aware of every penny you spend on eBay listing fees, eBay Final Value fees, listing options, and PayPal fees.

Minimizing eBay Listing Fees

eBay *listing fees* are based on your starting bid price, or your amount for a Fixed Price sale. Although eBay listing fees have remained somewhat stable over the years, in February 2004, eBay raised the rates and changed their pricing levels. For a very long time, the most you would pay to list a regular item on the eBay site was $3.30. Now it's $4.80.

For years, the base listing fee was $.30 for any item priced from $.01 to $9.99. As Table 9-1 shows, the *little guy* (the seller with lower-priced items to sell) takes a minor hit: the percentage of starting price paid in fees. At least it *looks* like a minor hit. But when you work in percentages (and they're what really count in retailing), that's a *16.6-percent increase* over the original fee. Before the rate increase in late January 2004, over 12,000 listings started at $1 and had the word *antique* in the title; sellers these days are moving away from that approach. Here's why . . .

 If you're planning to start your auctions at $1.00, consider starting them at $.99 instead. You save 16.6 percent in listing fees! One seller I know made that change to his auctions and saved $2,400 a month!

Table 9-1 shows you the current listing fees. Notice that the higher your starting price is, the higher your actual fee.

TABLE 9-1: EBAY LISTING FEES

Starting Price	Fee
$0.01 – $0.99	0.30
$1.00 – $9.99	0.35
$10.00 – $24.99	0.60
$25.00 – $49.99	1.20
$50.00 – $199.99	2.40
$200.00 – $499.99	3.60
$500 and up	4.80

Perhaps now you're thinking, *I can use a low listing fee and tack on a reserve price.* (There's fresh news in the reserve area as well — those fees are higher than before, but are refundable if the item sells.) You can always work the reserve to your advantage, but remember: Bidders get edgy when they see a reserve-price auction — they start to wonder whether they should spend their time bidding on the auction or maybe find a better deal elsewhere.

Using Reserve Fees to Save Money

Placing a reserve price on one of your auctions, as pictured in Figure 9-1, means that the item will not sell until the bidding reaches the reserve price. When your reserve-price item does sell, two good things happen: You've sold your item at a profit (let's hear it for optimism!) and eBay refunds your reserve fee. YAY!

Current bid:	**US $2,275.00** (**Reserve not met**)
	Place Bid >
Time left:	**2 days 0 hours** 7-day listing Ends Jan-18-04 19:30:00 PST Add to Calendar
History:	11 bids (US $99.00 starting bid)

• **Figure 9-1: I'll bet this auction has a hefty reserve!**

The reserve fee is based on the reserve price you set, as outlined in Table 9-2.

 Put your reserve price at the top of your listing description. That way there is a good chance the buyer will know what they're in for. You could also offer free shipping in a reserve auction to take the edge off.

TABLE 9-2: eBay Reserve Auction Fees

Reserve Amount	Fee
$0.01 – $49.99	$1.00
$50.00 – $199.99	$2.00
$200 and up	1 percent of reserve price (maximum of $100.00)

The key here is to calculate, *before* you list your auction, whether it costs you more in fees to use a reserve or to list with a higher starting price.

Table 9-3 compares the same item with different listing strategies.

TABLE 9-3: Comparisons of Two Completed Auctions — With and Without Reserve

	Starting at $24.99	Starting at $9.99 with $24.99 Reserve
Listing fee	$.60	$.35
Reserve fee	0	0 (refunded when item sells)
Final Value fee	$1.31	$1.31
Total	$1.91	**$1.66**

If the reserve item in the above table does not sell, listing and reserve fees would total $1.35

Wow! Aren't you surprised? (I was too!)

If your item doesn't sell the first time at the higher starting price, you can always relist it at a lower starting price and *then* use a reserve. If it sells, you'll still get the listing fees waived and you won't have to pay a reserve fee at all.

Second Chance to Sell!

If you have an item up for sale on the site, and the auction goes above your target sales price and you have more of the item in stock, you can offer another of the item to an underbidder.

Figure 9-2 shows you where, at the end of a multiple bidder auction, you can click to offer the item to any of the underbidders for his or her high bid.

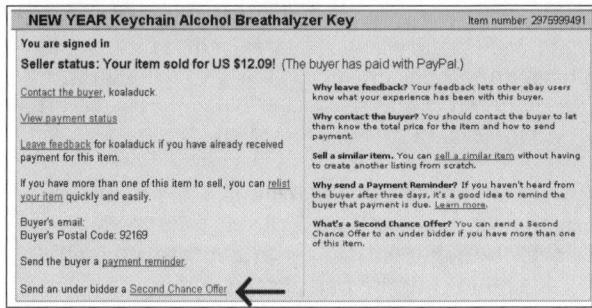

• **Figure 9-2:** It's the underbidder's lucky day.

You will only be charged Final Value fees — not a second relisting fee — if the person purchases the item.

Adding Listing Upgrades

eBay listings, just like anything that comes with extras (your new car, for example), have many options and upgrades. But also like your new car's options, they cost you money. eBay's optional upgrades are almost as fun as heated car seats in the winter — but only if they make you money!

Figure 9-3 shows how even a random search on eBay listings can yield examples of some very popular listing options:

- **Gallery.** This option definitely draws attention to your item. Gallery listings show a small picture next to the item title. The tempting glimpse grabs the gaze of potential buyers right away; a listing with the camera icon simply indicates that a picture of the item is available in the listing description. The gallery option costs 25 cents — and gets a good draw for your money.

- **Buy It Now.** In our immediate-gratification society, the But It Now option is very attractive to savvy eBay shoppers. Of course, those same savvy eBay shoppers know just how much they want to spend, and if your Buy It Now price is too high, they may blast right by your listing. Use Buy It Now for items you have in stock, with a clear target price. For five cents, Buy It Now can move your merchandise quickly.

✔ **Bold.** Applying boldface to your item title really spices it up and pulls it off the page right into the reader's eye. Unfortunately, bold adds an additional $1 to your listing cost, so you better be in a position to make some good profit from the item. Make sure your research shows that it can sell for your target price.

✔ **Item Subtitle.** Notice the subtitle under one of the auctions. This is your opportunity to add additional text to your title, readable by prospective buyers as they scan a search or browse a category. A caveat, this additional text will only be picked up if the searcher is searching both titles *and* descriptions. The additional text does not get pulled up in a title only search. The fee for this is 50 cents. All the text in the world won't help if your starting price is far above your competition.

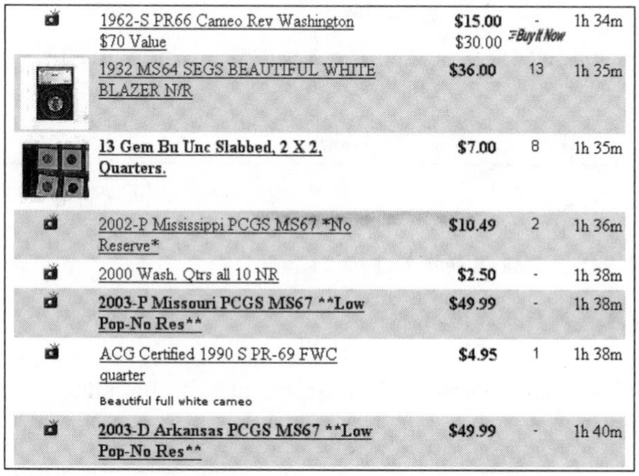

• **Figure 9-3: A piece of a search page including various eBay upgrades.**

Table 9-4 gives you the additional fees involved in the eBay listing upgrades.

TABLE 9-4: EBAY UPGRADES AND THEIR FEES

Listing Upgrade	Listing Upgrade Fee
Home Page Featured (single quantity)	$39.95
Home Page Featured (quantity of 2 or more)	$79.95
Featured Plus!	$19.95
Highlight	$5.00
Item Subtitle	$0.50
Bold	$1.00
Listing Designer	$0.10
Gallery	$0.25
Gallery Featured	$19.95
10-Day Listing Duration	$0.20
Scheduled Listings	$0.10
Buy It Now	$0.05
Gift Services	$0.25

eBay Picture Services

If you are shopping the site or even researching your competitor's auctions, you'll notice that some sellers have a small picture of their item at the top of their auction page as in Figure 9-4.

What a great selling point this is. The prospective buyer can see your item the second they click the page! Best of all there's no additional cost to the seller.

eBay offers the first picture free of cost to all sellers. It's definitely something you should take advantage of. Any additional pictures (easily uploaded to your item page) cost $.15 each. If you want the picture to *supersize* (get bigger) when the buyer clicks it, add an additional $.75 to your fees.

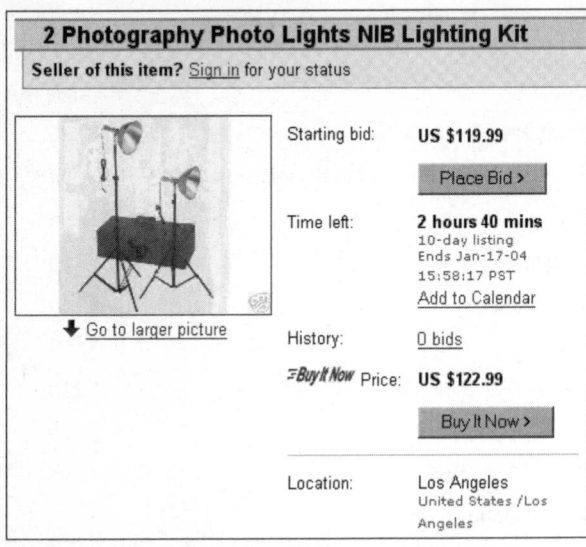

2 Photography Photo Lights NIB Lighting Kit

Seller of this item? <u>Sign in</u> for your status

↓ <u>Go to larger picture</u>	
Starting bid:	**US $119.99**
	Place Bid >
Time left:	**2 hours 40 mins**
	10-day listing
	Ends Jan-17-04
	15:58:17 PST
	<u>Add to Calendar</u>
History:	<u>0 bids</u>
Buy It Now Price:	**US $122.99**
	Buy It Now >
Location:	Los Angeles
	United States / Los
	Angeles

• **Figure 9-4:** Your *free* top-of-the-page picture when you use the free photo from eBay's picture services.

Always use the free picture — after all, it's free! But why not save extra fees by uploading your own additional pictures for your auction? (See Technique 19 for full instructions on how to do this on your own.)

Adding In the Final Value Fees

Final Value fees (FVFs) are charges on the amount that your item sells for — *not* including whatever you charge for shipping. Thank goodness eBay hasn't raised the FVFs lately — they're hard enough to calculate as it is! Table 9-5 shows the basics of the Final Value fee and how it's calculated.

TABLE 9-5: FINAL VALUE FEES

Final Item Price	Final Value Fee
$.01 to $25.00	5.25 percent of the selling price
$25.01 to $1,000.00	5.25 percent on the first $25, plus 2.75 percent on selling prices of $25 to $1,000

Final Item Price	Final Value Fee
$1,000 and up	5.25 percent on the first $25, plus 2.75 percent on selling prices of $25.01 to $1,000, plus another 1.5 percent on selling prices over $1,000

So how do all these percentages translate to real dollars? Take a look at Table 9-6, where I calculated fees for some random closing prices.

TABLE 9-6: SAMPLE PRICES AND COMMISSIONS

Closing Bid Price	Percentage	What You Owe eBay
$10	5.25 percent of $10	$.53
$256	5.25 percent of $25 plus 2.75 percent of $231	$7.66
$1,284.53	5.25 percent of $25 plus 2.75 percent of $975 plus 1.5 percent of $284.53	$32.39
$1,000,000	5.25 percent of $25 plus 2.75 percent of $975 plus 1.5 percent of $999,000	$15,013.12 (whew!)

PayPal Gets Its Cut of the Action

When you've sold your item, you think that's the end of the fees? Nope! If your customer pays via PayPal, you're faced with fess for using the PayPal service.

Having a PayPal Premier or Business account is important to build your commerce for these reasons:

✔ eBay buyers look for the PayPal option because it offers them another level of protection against fraud.

✔ Most customers prefer to pay with a credit card, either to delay the expense or to have complete records of their purchases.

✔ From a seller's point of view, using PayPal can be cheaper than having a direct-merchant credit card account.

✔ PayPal helps with your paperwork by offering downloadable logs of your sales that include all PayPal fees. eBay fees are not included; you're on your own for those.

 The difference between a Premier or a Business account is that a Premier account allows you to do business under your own name. A business account requires the account to be registered in a business name.

PayPal fees are fairly straightforward: Every transaction is charged a $.30 transaction fee, plus a percentage of the total collected — *including* your shipping charges. The percentage collected at the standard rate is 2.9 percent; for a merchant rate, it's 2.2 percent.

The standard rate is charged to all new users of PayPal. After you've been accepting PayPal for a while and have received at least $1,000 a month through PayPal for three months, you have qualified for a Merchant rate.

 Even after you're qualified, you won't get the Merchant Rate automatically. As you attain the needed level of sales, you must e-mail PayPal (once you've logged in to your account) to point out that you've attained it, ask them to put the lower rate into effect, and request that your account be converted to a Merchant account.

Putting All the Fees Together with FeeFinder

I don't have the time (or honestly, even the inclination) to total the applicable fees and expenses for every item I put up on eBay. But I do not recommend such laziness to anyone trying to earn a *living* on eBay.

To combat the laziness that I fear will drastically affect my bottom line, I use a program called FeeFinder, which totals up all the appropriate fees automatically. I use this program to help make better business decisions on pricing my items — and so can you! Here's the drill:

1. **Get and install a copy of FeeFinder.**

For a free trial version (or to purchase it at a discounted rate), visit the Web site at www. hammertap.com/coolebaytools and follow the instructions you find there. After you install the FeeFinder software, follow the remaining steps to calculate your item costs:

2. **Input your price and choose the appropriate settings.**

There are four tabs at the top of the FeeFinder page. First (as in Figure 9-5) is the single item page. Just input the starting price of your auction, whether you have a reserve or not, and click off any options you've used (in the example, I've clicked off Gallery). The second tab performs the same task for a multiple-item sale or "Dutch" auction.

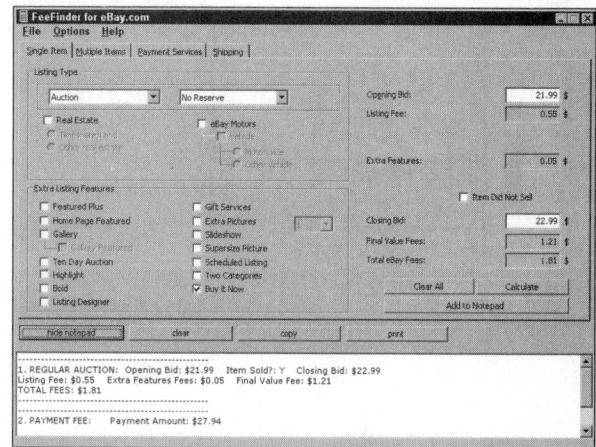

• **Figure 9-5: FeeFinder's Single Item tab.**

3. **Type in your estimate of the closing bid and click Calculate.**

I used my Buy It Now Price (hey, why not?) and Bingo — all figured out to the penny.

The next tab (Figure 9-6) calculates your PayPal fees. Just indicate which level of PayPal account you have and whether the payment is an eCheck or Credit Card. Type in the total amount you'll collect from the buyer — *including* shipping. Press the calculate button and your PayPal fees will show up.

4. **Add the two together and you've got your total expenses for that sale at the prescribed price.**

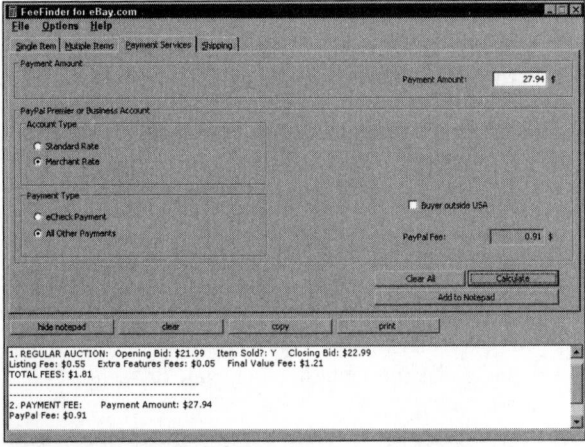

• **Figure 9-6: FeeFinder's PayPal fee-calculating tab.**

There is a fourth tab, called Shipping, which has links to all the shipping calculators for all the major shipping companies in the United States, United Kingdom and Germany. There's even a link to Freight forwarders to get estimates on items too large to ship through the regular resources.

Forewarned Is Smart

Once you know all the fees involved in selling your item, you can play around with the pricing and figure out how much your Buy It Now (or target selling) price should be.

Remember to include all these costs when pricing your items:

✔ How much you paid for the item you want to resell.

✔ The Freight In amount (the cost of shipping the item to you).

✔ The cost of shipping the item to your buyer. (Visit Technique 9 for information on how to calculate the cost involved in your shipping the item out to your buyers.)

Researching with eBay PSP Software

First off, what's a PSP? A PSP is an eBay Preferred Service Provider — a company big enough to make a large technological and financial commitment to eBay. These vendors express that preference by designing software and solutions to enhance procedures for small, medium, or large businesses interested in doing business on eBay. Those products are generally too expensive for a seller who hasn't attained Power Seller status.

A new eBay PSP, HammerTap (the same people who make FeeFinder) have a program called DeepAnalysis — powerful software that can analyze any eBay market sector. You can get current or past sales results by category or search term.

With DeepAnalysis, you can do some serious business:

✔ Research a particular item; see how much it sells for, and see who's selling it.

✔ Examine a category and check out total sales, average sell-through rate, and statistics for Dutch or Reserve auctions.

✔ Find out the most popular, highest-priced items with the average sell price.

✔ Get all kinds of sell-through rates.

That's just a sample of what these higher-end tools can do. When your eBay business gets to Power Seller level, they start to make good sense as an investment.

Setting Sensible Shipping Costs

Buyers who visit the eBay site are bargain shoppers. They want to get their items at the lowest possible prices. They're also becoming more cognizant about the "hidden" expense buried in the item's shipping and handling fees. When you set these fees, you must take into account every expense involved in your packing and shipping. You can't make your shipping area a losing proposition.

Too many eBay sellers — unquestionably out of greed — have increased shipping prices to outrageous amounts. I'll bet those sellers think they've found a cute way to save a couple of cents off their Final Value fees (after all, Final Value fees aren't charged on shipping costs). But when the shipping fee equals a third of the item cost, a prospective bidder may think twice about placing a bid. Of course if the item is big and/or the buyer wants it fast, he or she may feel better about paying higher fees.

Business is business, and when you're on eBay to make a profit, every penny counts. In this technique, I tell you how to evaluate all the costs involved with packing and shipping the items you sell. Also, I show you how to use the tools at your disposal — such as eBay's Shipping Calculator — to make the best decisions about how to charge your buyers for your shipping costs.

Figuring the Hidden Shipping Costs

 When calculating shipping costs, don't assume you have just the cost of your postage. You also have per-item costs for boxes, padded mailers, shipping tape, labels, and pickup or service fees from your carriers. Now and again, you may even pay the college kid across the street five bucks to schlep your boxes for you. Expenses show up in the strangest places.

In addition to adding up the packing and shipping supplies, you need to amortize the monthly fees from any online postage shipping services. When you occasionally pay for a pickup from the carrier, you need to add that expense to the shipping charges, too. The following list runs down some of the expenses involved:

- **Padded mailers.** Select an average-size padded mailer that works for several of the types of items that you sell. Selecting an average size for all your products works well because everything is cheaper when buying in quantity. Even if a few of your items could fit in the next-size-down mailers, buying the bigger size by the case gives you a considerable discount. (For more on standard mailer size, see Technique 34.) Why keep five different sizes of mailers in stock in quantities of 100 if you don't have to? If you don't use all of the bigger ones, you can always sell them. And besides, padded envelopes don't go bad.

 Don't be misled by packaging suppliers' claims that their mailers cost only __¢ each. They *usually* don't include the shipping costs in these price "estimates." Add the shipping that you'll pay to the cost of the packaging supplies you're buying. Then divide by the quantity purchased to get your cost per item.

When you price out your cost-per-piece, be sure to include (as part of your cost) what you have to pay to get the item shipped to you. The prices shown here were taken off the eBay site during this writing. So, if you purchase your mailers — say #4's (9 1/2" x 14 1/2") — by the hundred, they may cost you $.40 each. If you buy a case of 500, they may only cost $.28 each. By buying in quantity, you save $.12 per mailing envelope! The more business you do, the more significant the savings.

- **Packing Peanuts.** I must admit that storing all those packing peanuts is a real drag. (See the upcoming tip for a storage idea.) Here is where buying in bulk also equates to a huge cost savings. The figures below include shipping cost; you can purchase:

    4.5 cubic feet for $11.99 = $2.66 per cu ft

    10 cubic feet for $21.98 = $2.20 per cu ft

    20 cubic feet for $43.96 = $2.20 per cu ft

Actually, 10 cubic feet turns out to be the most economical deal — due to the high amount that shipping adds to the equation. eBay sellers who sell packing peanuts offer them for *half* what they cost when you purchase them from a brick-and-mortar retailer. (That's because a store you can actually walk into has to use up square footage to store these babies, which means a higher cost.)

 In one of my other eBay books, I share my solution to peanut storage, and I've been asked to include it here as well. Here it is (in a nutshell): Take some drawstring-type trash bags. Fill them fully with peanuts, then tie the drawstring. Screw some cup hooks into the rafters of your garage and hang the bags from the rafters. You can store a bunch of peanuts there! *Be sure to recycle!*

- **Packing tape.** Packing tape is free for Priority Mail packages (see Technique 34), but for other uses, you need a stock of clear packing tape. The common size for a roll is 2 inches wide by 110 feet long. The following eBay prices *include* shipping:

    6 rolls = $13.49 = $2.25 per roll

    12 rolls = $20.27 = $1.69 per roll

    36-roll case = $49.85 = $1.38 per roll

Again, compare prices before buying.

- **Boxes.** Price out boxes in quantity orders. I won't take you through the various costs of boxes because *hundreds* of sizes are available. Shop eBay, and check out `www.uline.com` for boxes at reasonable prices. For our example, let's just say a typical box will cost $.38 each.

- **G&A (general and administrative) costs.** For the uninitiated (translation=you never had to do budgets at a large corporation), G&A represents the costs incurred in running a company. But the principle is familiar: Time is money. For example, the time it takes you to research the costs of mailers, tapes, and boxes on eBay is costing you money. The time it takes for you to drive to the Post Office costs you money. We won't actually put a figure on this just now, but it's something you need to think about — especially if you spend half an hour at the Post Office every other day. In effect, that's time wasted. You could be finding new sources of merchandise with the time. It costs you money that you might have earned.

✔ **Online postage service.** If you're paying around $10 a month for the convenience of buying and printing online postage, you have to assume that's an expense too. If you ship 100 packages a month, that amortizes to $.10 per package.

 If you're questioning whether you need an online postage service, here's my two cents: Being able to hand your packages to the postal carrier still beats standing in line at the Post Office.

When you add together expenses from this list, you have the cost for mailing out a padded envelope cushioned with packing peanuts, as in Table 10-1.

TABLE 10-1: SAMPLE SHIPPING COSTS

Item	Estimated Cost per Shipment
Padded mailer	$ .28
Peanuts	.07
Tape	.02
Mailing Label	.04
Postage service	.10
TOTAL	$1.14

Before you even put postage on the package, you could possibly be spending $1.14 — not including your time. (Excuse me while I go to eBay and raise my shipping charges!).

If you're shipping many packages a month, read Technique 47 on how to use QuickBooks to easily and simply see your exact average per package costs.

Using a Shipping Calculator in Your Listings

If you put a flat shipping fee on some larger items, you may be costing yourself money. Make everything fair for the buyer (and for you) — use eBay's free shipping calculator to post clear shipping charges for your items.

When listing an item for sale on eBay, you come to the area where you need to input your payment and shipping information. You have the option of using a flat rate (as in Figure 10-1) where you simply input your flat shipping charges. These appear in a box at the bottom of your item description.

Shipping costs ✱		Click to minimize
Who will pay for shipping costs? ⊙ Buyer ◯ Seller		

Include domestic (United States) shipping rates with my listing:
◯ No, skip section below
⊙ Yes, specify below (faster payment and easier for buyer)

Flat shipping rates Same rate for all buyers	**Calculated shipping rates** Based on buyer address **NEW!**

Shipping & handling (United States)		$ 0.00
Shipping insurance per item	Optional ▾	$ 0.00
Sales tax [hide]	California ▾	8.25 %

☐ Apply sales tax to the total which includes shipping & handling.

• **Figure 10-1: The Flat Shipping Rates form.**

You also have another option for figuring shipping charges on the items you list on eBay. Follow these steps to have eBay calculate the charges for you when your buyer supplies his or her postal ZIP code.

1. **Click the Calculated Shipping Rates link (refer to Figure 10-1).**

The form shown in Figure 10-2 appears.

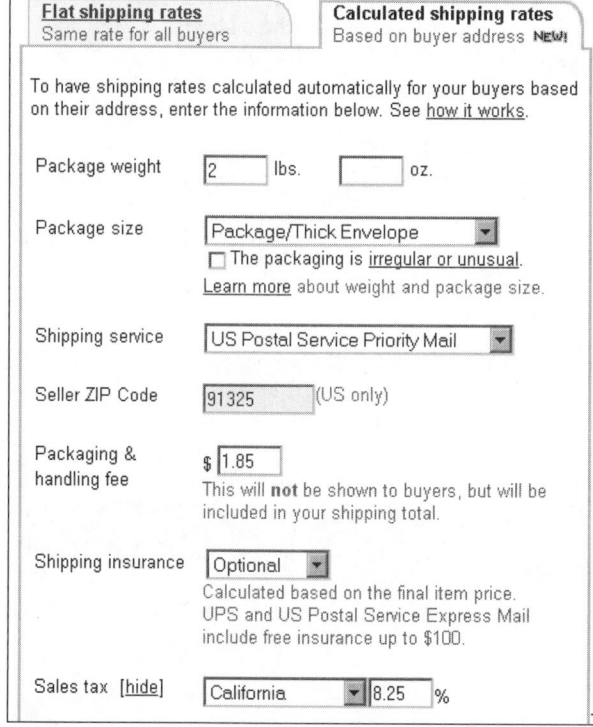

Flat shipping rates
Same rate for all buyers

Calculated shipping rates
Based on buyer address **NEW!**

To have shipping rates calculated automatically for your buyers based on their address, enter the information below. See how it works.

Package weight	`2` lbs. `   ` oz.
Package size	`Package/Thick Envelope ▾` ☐ The packaging is irregular or unusual. Learn more about weight and package size.
Shipping service	`US Postal Service Priority Mail ▾`
Seller ZIP Code	`91325` (US only)
Packaging & handling fee	$ `1.85` This will **not** be shown to buyers, but will be included in your shipping total.
Shipping insurance	`Optional ▾` Calculated based on the final item price. UPS and US Postal Service Express Mail include free insurance up to $100.
Sales tax [hide]	`California ▾` `8.25` %

• **Figure 10-2: Calculated Shipping Rates form.**

2. **Type your Package Weight in the text boxes provided and select a package size from the drop-down list, as shown in Figure 10-3.**

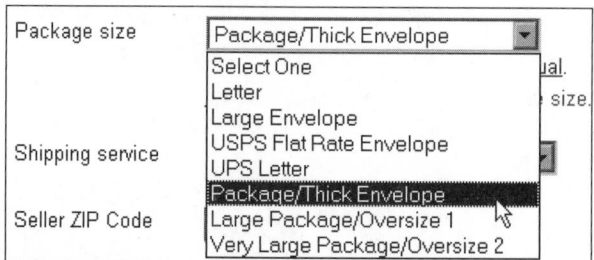

• **Figure 10-3: The package size drop-down menu.**

3. **Select a carrier from the Shipping Service drop-down list.**

Figure 10-4 shows the choices available in Shipping Service drop-down list.

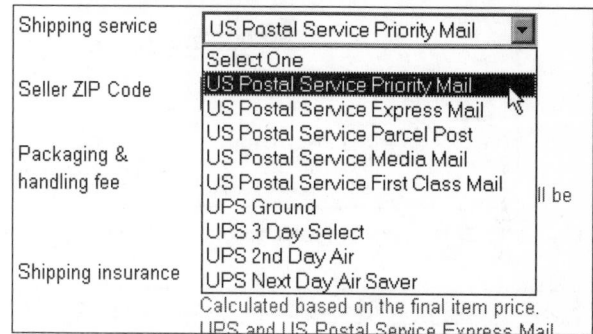

• **Figure 10-4: Selecting the shipping service.**

4. **Type your ZIP code in the Seller ZIP Code box.**

5. **Type your packaging fees in the Packaging & Handling Fee box.**

▶ When adding your packaging and handling charges, don't worry that the buyers will see these individual fees. eBay combines this amount with the actual shipper costs and shows the total as one shipping price.

▶ If you selected the U.S. Postal Service as your carrier, be sure to add the cost of a delivery confirmation (if you use one) when you figure your packing and handling fee.

6. **Select the appropriate options in the Shipping Insurance and Sales Tax drop-down lists.**

If you require the buyer to pay for insurance, or even if it's optional, be sure to indicate it. eBay's calculator will give the buyer the actual insurance cost based on the final bid.

After you've input all your information, you can forget about it; eBay takes over. Figure 10-5 shows you how the calculator looks in your listing, and Figure 10-6 shows the results calculated when a buyer puts a New York ZIP code in the auction's calculator.

• **Figure 10-5: The shipping calculator in my auction.**

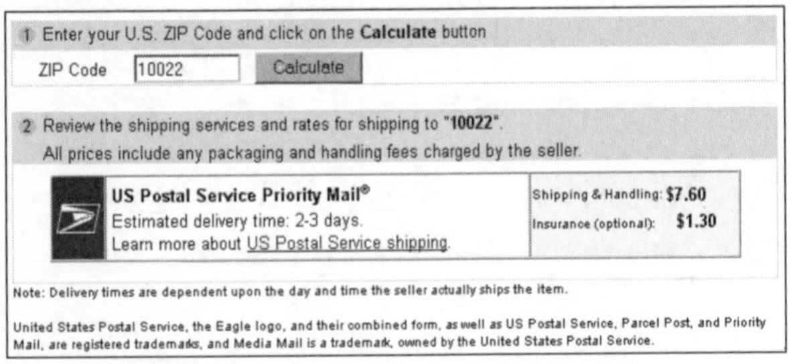

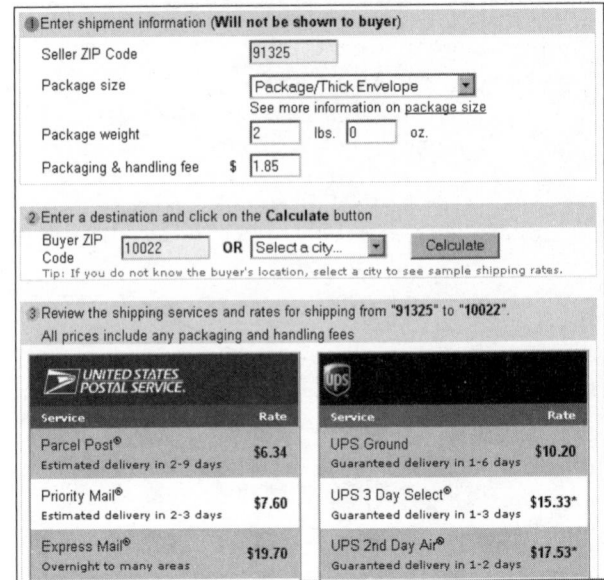

• **Figure 10-6: Shipping to a buyer from New York.**

You can check out the fees for different shipping services by using the full eBay Shipping Calculator located at

```
http://cgi3.ebay.com/aw-cgi/eBayISAPI.
  dll?emitsellershippingcalculator
```

and shown in Figure 10-7. This tool shows you all the shipping costs so that you can decide to ship with either the U.S. Postal Service or UPS.

> I always test my packages from a California ZIP code (because that's where I live) to a ZIP code in New York. Doing this gives me an estimate for Zone 8, which is the most expensive option (by distance) when shipping in the U.S.

• **Figure 10-7: Shipping Calculator's test results for my item.**

Technique 11

Using eBay's Free Listing Tool: Turbo Lister

Save Time By

- Organizing sale items quickly
- Updating automatically to keep current with eBay features
- Using built-in templates to save time when designing a listing

Not much in this world is free, but for now, eBay offers you a free, convenient tool you can use to list your items for sale: Turbo Lister. It's powerful software that provides a professional capability (and look) to the medium-size eBay seller. Turbo Lister helps you organize your items for sale, design their ads, and list them. It also organizes your items for future relisting by saving your initial item input and allowing you to create folders for organized storage. Your items disappear from Turbo Lister only if you delete them.

 Although you get the Turbo Lister program free, you're still responsible for any fees you incur by listing an item on the site.

Turbo Lister is robust software with the following features:

- **Self Updates.** Turbo Lister automatically updates itself regularly from the eBay site, and includes any new eBay enhancements so your listings always take advantage of eBay's latest features.

  Whenever you start the program and it finishes loading, it immediately checks with the eBay server for updates. Waiting for this update can be a bit tedious (especially if the servers are busy), so if you plan on listing items at a particular time, open Turbo Lister with a few minutes to spare.

- **HTML Templates.** Pre-designed HTML templates are built into the program's Listing Designer. If you use one of eBay's multitude of colorful themes or layouts, you'll be charged an additional $.10 on top of your listing fees. You can use these or a template of your own design to jumpstart your ad design (without extra charge) by pasting it into the HTML view. You can even use templates from other sources (such as those in Technique 19), as long as they are in HTML format.

- **WYSIWYG Interface.** If you choose to design your own ads from scratch, you can do it with Turbo Lister's easy-to-use WYSIWYG (What You See Is What You Get) layout designer.

- **Bulk Listing Tool.** Prepare your listings whenever you have the time. When you're ready to launch a group of them, just transfer them to the upload area, and, well, upload them.

✔ **Item Preview.** You can preview your listings to be sure they will look just as you want them to before you upload them to eBay.

✔ **All Item Listing Capabilities** without being online. By using Turbo Lister (with its constant auto-upgrading), you will not sacrifice any of the features available to you when you list on the site using the Sell Your Item form.

In this technique, you'll have an inside look at how Turbo Lister works. Then, when you download the software, you can get up to speed quickly.

Checking the Minimum Requirements

Though this software is definitely useful, you have to decide whether it's really for you. The first thing to check is whether your computer meets Turbo Lister's minimum requirements.

✔ Your computer must be a PC, not a Mac (sorry, Mac users). You have to have the Windows 98, 98 SE, ME, NT 4+SP6, 2000, or XP operating system.

✔ The processor must be at least a Pentium II. The faster your processor, the better.

✔ You must have at least 64MB of RAM (and that's a bare minimum).

 The more RAM you have, the better things work.

✔ You should have at least 20MB of free space on your hard drive to run the installation.

✔ Monitor settings at least 800 x 600 resolution and 256 colors (8-bit). Keep in mind the software interface looks a lot better with 16-bit color and 1024 x 768 resolution. All monitors today have this capability, so you should be just fine here.

✔ Microsoft Internet Explorer should be version 5.01 or later.

 To check your version of Internet Explorer with the browser open, click the Help menu (shown in Figure 11-1). Click the About Internet Explorer command (Figure 11-2); on the top line, your Internet Explorer version number is listed.

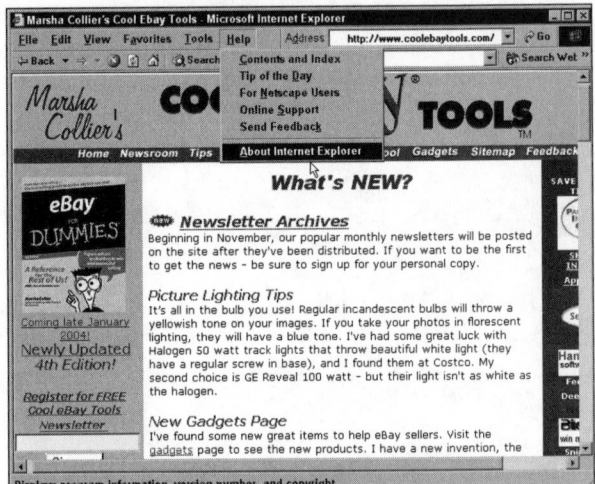

• **Figure 11-1:** Checking your version number.

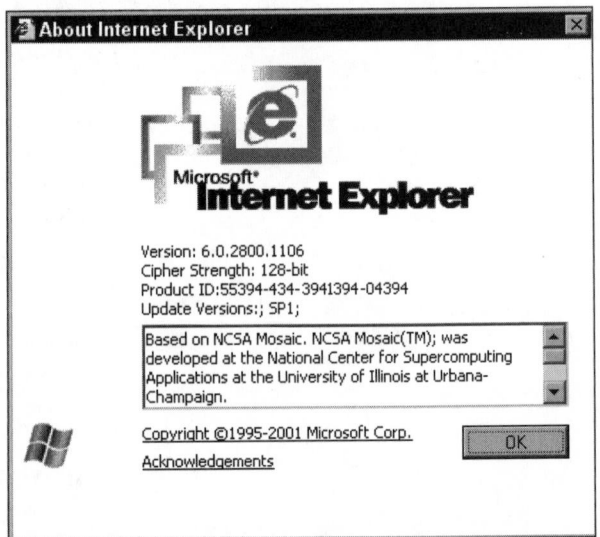

• **Figure 11-2:** Now you know! In this example, I've got version 6.0.2800.1106.

Downloading Turbo Lister

On the bottom of most eBay pages, you'll see a group of links like the ones shown in Figure 11-3. Click the handy eBay Downloads link to display the eBay Downloads page.

> Announcements | Register | Shop eBay-o-rama | Security Center | Policies | Feedback Forum
> About eBay | Home | My eBay | Site Map | eBay Downloads | eBay Gift Certificates
>
> Browse | Sell | Services | Search | Help | Community
> Find Items | Find Members | Favorite Searches

• **Figure 11-3: eBay's navigation links.**

Now, to download Turbo Lister, follow these steps:

1. **Scroll down the eBay Downloads page to locate the Selling Tools area and click on eBay Turbo Lister.**

The Seller Tools, Turbo Lister hub page appears.

2. **Click the Download Now link.**

The requirements for using Turbo Lister appear above the two links for downloading.

3. **Click the Turbo Lister Web Setup link.**

The Windows Security Warning appears (shown in Figure 11-4), cautioning that you're about to download something foreign to your computer.

4. **Click Yes.**

Clicking Yes downloads Turbo Lister. Clicking No doesn't. Just trust me (and eBay) and click Yes.

From this point on, installation is automatic until — voilà! You've got Turbo Lister on your computer!

Note that this procedure first downloads a small setup version of the program that checks your computer for preinstalled files. When that task is done, Turbo Lister checks back with mothership eBay and automatically downloads any files it needs.

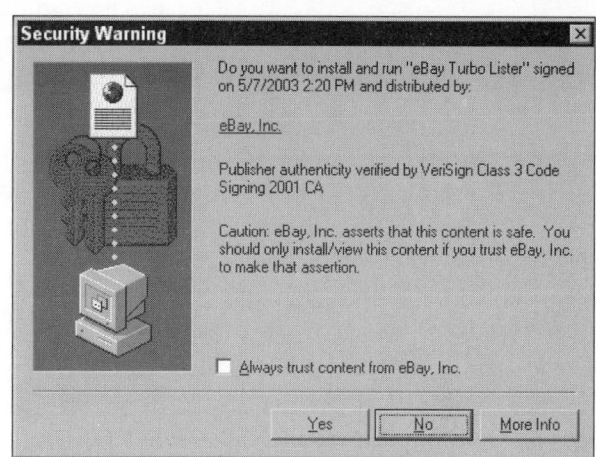

• **Figure 11-4: The Windows Security warning.**

Starting Up Turbo Lister

Once you've installed the program, you'll see a new icon on your desktop; a little green man (don't call Mulder — yet!) juggling magic pixie dust over his head. This is the icon for Turbo Lister. Double-click it and you'll see the Turbo Lister Introduction screen shown in Figure 11-5. This will pop up every time you open the program — which can get annoying. It doesn't really do anything for you and wastes precious seconds of your time. If you want to avoid it, click the check box labeled *Do not show me this screen again*, and then click *Start Here*. The little green man's screen will be forever banished.

When the program is open, the first thing you do is set up a new Turbo Lister file, as follows:

1. **Select that option from the opening splash, and click Next.**

2. **Type your eBay User ID and password in the blanks and click Next.**

Turbo Lister now wants to connect back to eBay to retrieve your eBay account information. Make sure your Internet connection is live.

• **Figure 11-5:** The colorful (though useless) Turbo Lister intro screen.

3. **After you check for a live Internet connection, click the Connect Now button.**

In a minute or so, a small window opens with your eBay registration information (your name, address, and registered e-mail address). The last text block on the page offers you the option of listing locally.

4. **Click the down arrow in the corner of the last text box and choose the eBay region within your metropolitan area, if there is one.**

Your item will be searchable within your region of the United States.

5. **Click Finish, and the program fires up.**

Preparing an eBay Listing

Now that you have the powerful Turbo Lister tool at hand, you can prepare hundreds of eBay listings in advance and, with one click of the mouse, launch them on eBay. You can also select a scheduling format that makes your listings upload and start at a particular time and date. (More on that in the section, "Uploading items to eBay," later in this technique).

This example lists an auction using these steps:

1. **Click the Create New button (the one with the magic-wand symbol) in the upper-left corner.**

The Step One screen appears, as in Figure 11-6. This is where you decide the type of listing you want. You'll notice that most of the information requested is identical to the eBay Sell Your Item form.

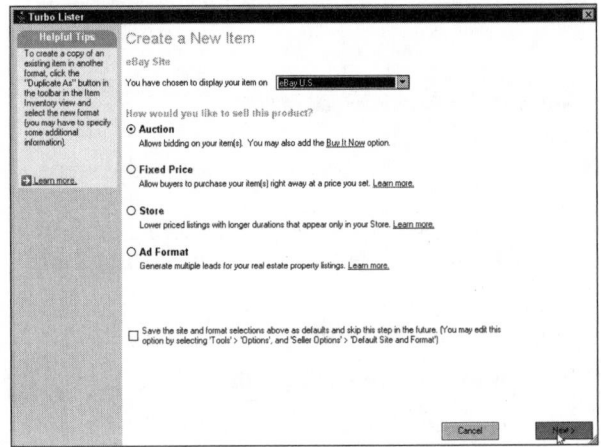

• **Figure 11-6:** Selecting your listing format.

2. **Click the Auction radio button, and then click Next.**

The Create a New Item page appears, ready for you to enter your title and subtitle if you wish.

 You can save bunches of time if you write your titles and descriptions before you go into Turbo Lister. You can type them into Notepad or Word, and then copy and paste them into the listing, adding the HTML tags after the text is inserted.

3. **Enter the title in the Item Title Box.**

If you want to use a subtitle, type that in as well. Subtitles are handy for adding selling points that accompany your title in search results. (Entering a subtitle for your auction adds an additional $.50 charge.)

4. **Select your category by clicking the Find Category button.**

You are presented with a screen that lists all eBay categories in a hierarchal format. The main categories are listed with a plus sign next to them. When you find your main category, click on the plus sign, and subcategories are displayed, as shown in Figure 11-7. To drop even lower into the world of nether-categories, keep clicking plus signs next to subcategories. You know you've hit the bottom rung of the category ladder when you see only a minus sign.

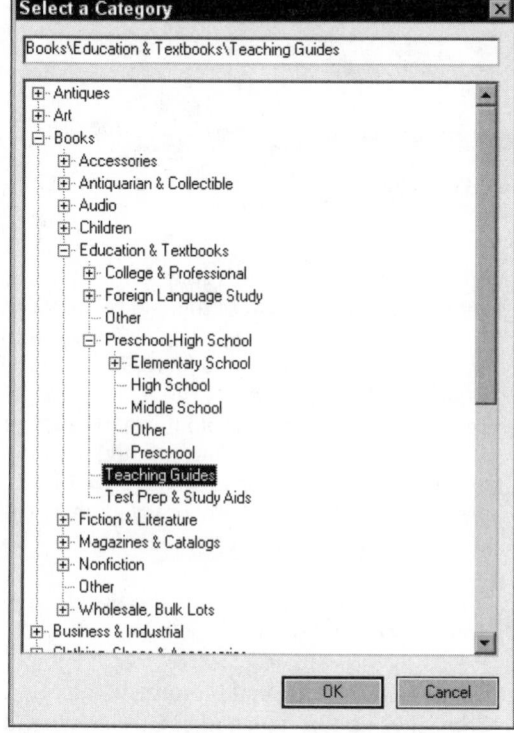

• **Figure 11-7: Select your final category and click OK.**

5. **If you have an eBay Store, select a category for the item in your store from a drop-down menu. Open the drop-down menu (shown in Figure 11-8) by clicking the small arrow on the right. Then click the category you want to use and watch it jump into the selection area.**

This area is automatically populated from your eBay Store when eBay updates your Turbo Lister installation.

6. **After you make all your selections, click Next to continue.**

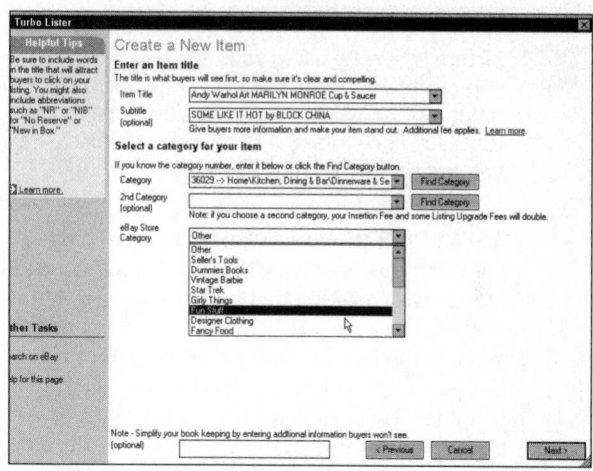

• **Figure 11-8: Select your eBay Store Category from the drop-down list.**

Designing your listing

When it comes to designing your listing, you've got several options. Take a look at the Listing Templates on the left side of the screen. Click on them and be dazzled by their glory. eBay makes it a snap to design your item listing with a few easy features:

✔ **Templates and Themes:** I'm sure you've seen eBay listings with very nice graphics in the borders. These come from eBay's easy-to-use theme templates listed on the left of the screen. You may select any of these colorful templates to doll up your listing. Themes make the listing look pretty, but they may draw attention away from the selling strength of your pictures. Remember, it's your good description and a quality photo that will sell your item. Keep in mind, though, that eBay charges you an additional $.10 to use one of these themes in your listing. You don't have to use any of the themes (just click None when you reach this screen).

✔ **Layout:** You may select from several Layouts: Standard, Photos Left, Photos Right, One Photo

Top, Photos Bottom, or Slide Show if you want to take advantage of eBay's Slide Show option.

 When you use eBay Picture Services, the first picture is free. By using your first free picture, you can have a great-looking header picture at the top of your listing page. Additional pictures are 15 cents and a slide show will cost you the princely sum of 75 cents.

✔ **WYSIWYG HTML Design Form:** You can base your ad on this very easy-to-use design form and come up with a listing that looks similar to the one shown in Figure 11-9. It has a toolbar very similar to the formatting toolbar in Microsoft Word (see Figure 11-10), so the buttons should be familiar. There's even a command to insert a Web link into your description (see Figure 11-11), so you can have the prospective buyer e-mail you with a click of the mouse.

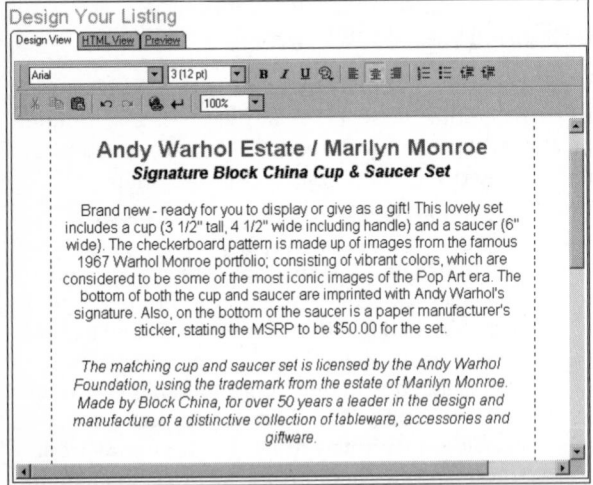

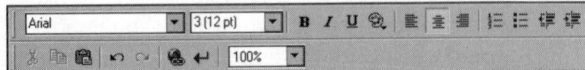

• **Figure 11-9: The Design Your Listing page in Design View.**

• **Figure 11-10: The HTML design toolbar.**

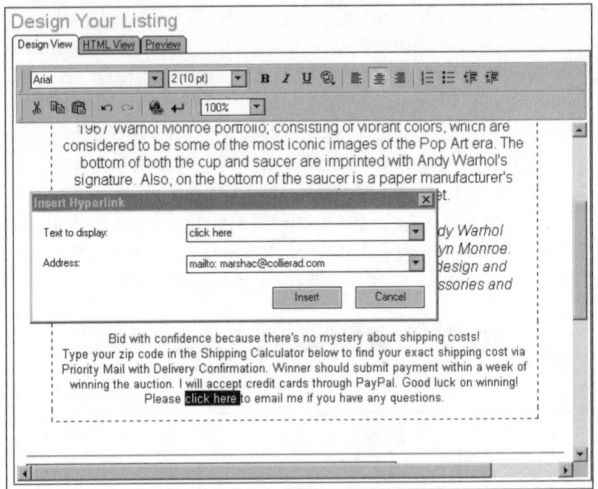

• **Figure 11-11: Inserting an e-mail link in the description area.**

✔ **HTML View:** If you have a smattering of HTML knowledge, you may want to display the HTML view and edit your listing design from there. You can also insert your hosted images by entering supplementary coding into the HTML view. (See Technique 20 for additional information about coding and on inserting your pictures into the description area.) Also, if you have your own predesigned template, just copy and paste the HTML for the template into the HTML view box.

At any time during the design process, click the Preview tab to see what your listing looks like.

Be sure to add any additional pictures using eBay's Picture Services so that you can use the free header picture. Just click on one of the boxes entitled *Click Here to Insert Picture*, select any picture on your computer's hard drive, and it will upload with your listing to eBay. When your picture appears in the Turbo Lister box, click Next.

Getting down to specifics

Now it's time to get all the little details into your listing. How many days do you want the listing to run?

You must add your shipping and payment information, and more. You do all this on the Format Specifics page, your last page as shown in Figure 11-12.

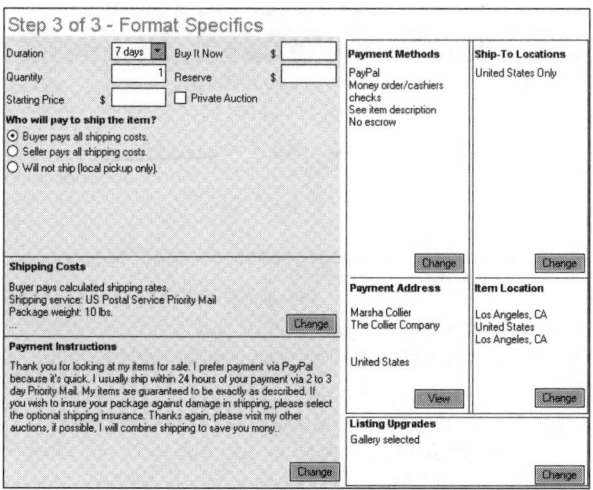

• **Figure 11-12: The Format Specifics page.**

Much of this information is filled in for you by eBay. You can edit the information pertaining to an option such as Payment Methods and Ship To Location by clicking the Change button in the appropriate box. Note that on this page, each format option has a Change button. Clicking the Change button opens a small box where you may add text or change defaults. After you make your changes, click OK. The new information appears in the appropriate Format Specifics box.

 Save time by saving repetitive text as the default. When you come to a box such as Payment Instructions or Payment Methods, and you want this exact information to appear in all your listings, click the Save for Future Listings check box to save this information as your default. You can always change the info on a case-by-case basis when listing another item.

Once you've filled out all the information in each of the Format Specifics areas, click Save.

Organizing your listings

Once you've put together a few listings, your Turbo Lister Item Inventory begins to look something like Figure 11-13.

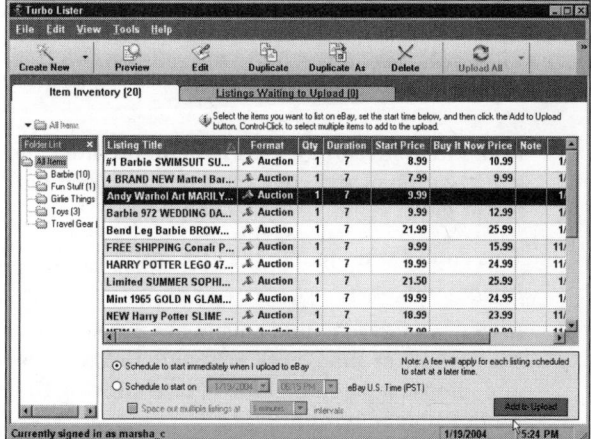

• **Figure 11-13: Turbo Lister Item Inventory.**

Note that you can add folders to the folder list to save inventories for different categories of items.

To create a folder and move items into it:

1. Click the down arrow next to Create New (on the button with the magic wand) and select the command to create a new folder.

2. Give your new folder a name and click OK.

The folder now appears in a folder list on the left side of the screen.

3. Highlight a listing and drag it to your new folder.

 You can save time if you press and hold the Control or the Shift key while selecting multiple items. Then you drag them to the folder all at once.

You now have the option of looking at your items in an All Items view (*All Items* includes those you have inserted into folders), or by double-clicking to open the various folders.

Uploading items to eBay

Here's how you upload the items you see on the Item Inventory tab:

1. **In the Item Inventory list, highlight the item you want to upload and click the Add to Upload button at lower right.**

This copies your item to the Listings Waiting to Upload tab.

2. **If you want to schedule a listing to upload at a later date or time, click Schedule to Start On and choose a date and time before clicking the Add to Upload button.**

 You're charged an additional $.10 fee for any item you choose to schedule for a delayed listing.

When you've populated your Listings Waiting to Upload list, you can view it by clicking the tab, which looks similar to Figure 11-14.

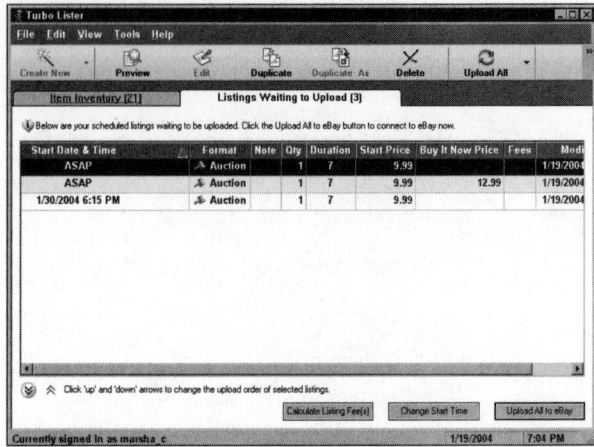

• **Figure 11-14: Just waitin' around is what they're doing.**

3. **On the Listings Waiting to Upload tab, click Upload All to eBay to send your items to eBay immediately.**

eBay calculates your fees before posting the listing; you can approve them before the listing goes live on the site.

Approve the upload, and instantly your items will be live on the site!

Technique 12

Making Multiple Sales without Multiplying Your Work

O ne of the most efficient ways to run an eBay business is to stock the same item in quantity. After getting some eBay experience under your belt, you're bound to find several items that you're comfortable selling. In addition, if you follow my suggestions in Technique 5, you'll buy multiples (dozens? cases? pallets?) of the items at a seriously discounted price. But when you have all these items lying around the garage, your goal is to get them into buyers' hands at a profit.

In Technique 41, I talk about opening an eBay store. But in addition to your own store, you must be running auctions on the eBay site. Why? Auctions are the key to drawing buyers into your store. Stores are not only added potential sales, but they're a distinct marketing tool for your personal eBay brand.

If you don't have an eBay Store and plan to sell the items one at a time through auctions, you don't want to reinvent the wheel for each sale. Relisting your items efficiently will save you time and aggravation.

 I know several sellers who have bought items in such bulk that they're stocked with the item to sell one a week for the next few years! That's a good thing only if the product is a staple item that will always have a market on eBay.

Relisting after a Win

Yeah! Your space-age can opener with built-in DVD player sold! Since you have three dozen more to sell, the quicker you can get that item back up on the site, the sooner you'll connect with the next customer.

When bidders lose an auction on eBay, one of the first things they do is search for somebody offering the same item. The sooner you get an item relisted, the sooner a disappointed underbidder will find your listing. Of course, relisting the item also makes it available to other interested bidders who may not have bid on the item before because the bidding went out of their league.

When you offer an item for bidding and it reaches well beyond your target price, why not offer another one? True, this will slow (or possibly end) further bidding on the first item, but if you've exceeded your target price and there are folks out there hot for your item — sell it to them now! That kind of initiative is what eBay is all about.

If at First You Don't Succeed

Boo! Your Dansk China Maribo dinner plate didn't sell. Don't take it personally. It's not that someone out there doesn't love you. It doesn't mean that your merchandise is trash. It's just that this particular week no one was looking for Maribo plates (go figure).

Often eBay shoppers shop with no discernible pattern. Some weeks no one may want your item at a certain price and then you may sell five or six the next week. It happens to me all the time.

 If you don't have your auctions listed on the eBay site, your goods will stay on your shelves and get dusty. If you list your items regularly, someone will buy them and send you money. Find something that will sell *now*!

 Often, when relisting, you need to make adjustments. For instance, there's always a chance that you're off base on your title. Or perhaps the keywords in your title aren't drawing people to your listing. To help you figure out whether it's you or just the market, try running a search for other, similar items — is anyone buying? If there's just no bidding activity (perhaps you're selling bikinis in January?), then perhaps that item needs to be retired from eBay for a while.

Consider some other variables. Perhaps your starting price is too high? Are other items selling on the site with a lower starting price? If you can comfortably lower your price, do so. If not, wait until other

sellers run out of the item. Then put yours up for auction — you may just get more bidding action if you are one of the few (versus one of the many) sellers offering the same item.

I have quite a few items that I purchased cases of — right along with a bunch of other eBay sellers. They desperately dumped theirs on the site, without paying any attention to the competition. I waited, and got my target price for the item the following season.

 eBay is a supply-and-demand marketplace. If the supply exceeds the demand, prices go down. If you have an item that sells as fast as you can list it, prices go up.

Okay, Time to Relist

eBay gives you so many ways to relist an item, that it's almost dizzying. There are efficient ways and ways that will waste your time. Because this book is all about saving time, let's just concern ourselves with the speedy ways.

Figure 12-1 shows the seller's version of a sold item (only the seller sees this when they are signed in), which includes a link to relist. If you relist all your items using this link on each item's page you'll have to go to the page for every item you want to relist to find the corresponding link. To save time, get off the auction page and go to My eBay page or Selling Manager. These tools were designed to make relisting fast.

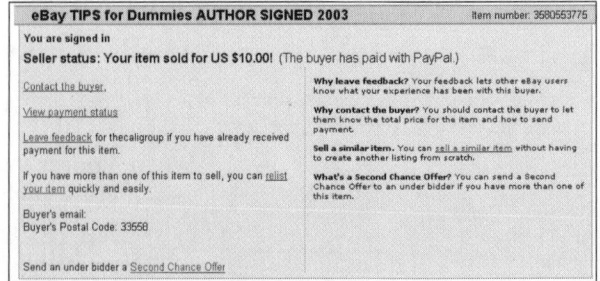

• **Figure 12-1:** Yeah! My item sold!

Relisting from your My eBay page

Your My eBay page has lots of handy features. Best of all, it has all your sold and unsold items in one convenient area. It's so much easier to see *all* your sold or unsold items at once!

Figure 12-2 shows My eBay displaying the Items I've Sold area. The Unsold Items area is further down on the My eBay Selling tab and has similar columns of information.

Items I've Sold (14 Items)										▶ See totals
▶ Show items for past 14 days Go (30 days max) ☐ Save this setting										✓ = Relisted item
Select (all)	Item #	(PST) End Date	Last Sale	End Price	Reserve Price	Qty	High Bidder (s) /Buyer(s)	Next Steps /Status	Payment Reminder	Feedback	Relist	Second Chance hide

Cloud Dome Background PORTABLE PHOTO STAGE

☐ 2979287892 Jan-12 $36.99 n/a 1 Paid Leave Feedback Relist

Starting an Ebay Business for Dummies SIGNED

☐ 3578659417 Jan-14 $21.99 n/a 1 Paid Feedback Left Relist ✓

eBay TIPS for Dummies AUTHOR SIGNED 2003

☐ 3578660928 Jan-14 $5.50 n/a 1 Paid Feedback Left Relist Send Send Offer

• **Figure 12-2: Sample items I've sold.**

Note that the second to the last column is titled Relist. If you click the Relist link for an item, a fully filled in, Sell Your Item page appears. You can then make any changes you want — or not!

What's so very convenient about this method is that all your sold (or unsold) listings appear in one place. You can just go down the list and quickly relist items.

Relisting from Selling Manager

Wouldn't it be better if you could select a whole bunch of items at once and list them all together? Step up to Selling Manager for a one-click option.

I really like Selling Manager as a tool for the midsized eBay seller (even a PowerSeller). One of the many excellent features of the program is that you can relist multiple items in bulk.

You can access items that have sold, logically enough, from the Sold Items area (pictured in Figure 12-3). Relisting is done with a click of the mouse! (On the other hand, if you haven't been so lucky lately, you can look at your unsold items in the Unsold Items area.)

To relist an item through Selling Manager, follow these steps:

1. **Go to the Sold or Unsold Listings by clicking the links in the Manage Listings box on the left of the page.**

2. **Once you're on the page, select an item to relist by clicking the check box next to its record number.**

You may select any or all of the items listed on the page.

3. **Once you have selected all the items that you want to relist, click the Sell Similar button.**

You will be taken to the Relist Multiple Items page.

4. **Review all the items listed (along with the fees being charged) and submit the items by clicking the Submit Listing button.**

Sold Listings
Keep track of sold listings by customizing and sending sales records (🗐) to your buyers.
26 sold listings.

	Mark Paid	Mark Shipped	Mark Paid & Shipped	Sell Similar	Archive

☐ Record #	User ID[Show Buyer Email]		Qty	Sale Price	Total Price	Sale Date▼	☑✉	🖲
☑ 749🗐			1	$10.00	$12.00	Jan-21	1 ☒	🖲
	(3580553775) eBay TIPS for Dummies AUTHOR SIGNED 2003							
☐ 748🗐			1	$4.50	$6.50	Jan-20	0 ☒	🖲
	(2966720670) eBay TIPS for Dummies AUTHOR SIGNED 2003							
☑ 747🗐	(43)		1	$170.99	$170.99	Jan-18	2 ☒	🖲
	(2980166675) FREE SHIP Cloud Dome w 7inch Ext Lighting Kit							
☐ 746🗐	(1)		1	$22.99	$36.19	Jan-16	2 ☒	🖲
	(2978127410) eBay Sellers Steel Rolling Garment Rack NEW							
☐ 745🗐	(149)		1	$4.50	$6.50	Jan-15	1 ☒	🖲

• **Figure 12-3: A portion of my Sold Listings in Selling Manager.**

Figure 12-4 shows a portion of the Relist Multiple Items page that includes a complete review of the details of each of your items. If you proceed, they will be relisted exactly as you had them listed before. On the bottom of this page, eBay gives you a recap of all relisting fees.

Relist Multiple Items: Review & Submit

Step 1: Review your listings

Please review your listings and fees and then click the **Submit Listings** button below. To remove an item, click the "Remove item" link.

▶ **PayPal is now turned on for all your listings.**
You have opted to turn on PayPal for all of your listings. If you would like to turn off this preference, please edit your payment preferences.

Item #2979287892 - Cloud Dome Background PORTABLE PHOTO STAGE   ✕ Remove item

Main Category

Computers & Electronics : Cameras & Photo : Lighting & Studio Equipment : Other Lighting & Studio Items (# **30088**)

Pictures & Details

Duration	7
Quantity	1
Starting Price	$35.99
Buy It Now Price	$36.99
Optional Features	Gallery
Fees	Insertion ($1.10); BIN Fee ($0.05); Gallery ($0.25)	**Total Fees: $1.40**

• **Figure 12-4: Relisting several items at once from Selling Manager.**

Making a Second Chance Offer

When you have multiples of an item and your final bid amount exceeded your target price, you can feel free to make offers to underbidders to buy the same item for their high bid. You can also make a Second Chance offer if the winning bidder does not come through with the payment.

This is a perfectly eBay-legal way to make a second sale. Best of all? eBay doesn't charge you a second listing fee for your offer. You just pay a Final Value fee if the bidder accepts your offer.

Second Chance offers may be offered to underbidders, for a prescribed time period — 1, 3, 5, or 7 days. The underbidder has the opportunity to take you up on the offer or pass. When the underbidder

takes action, that is, buys the item or e-mails you that he is not interested (and you close the Second Chance offer — just like an auction), you can make another offer to a different underbidder. You can follow this process on down the list of underbidders for up to 60 days.

You do not necessarily have to make an offer to an underbidder if you are not comfortable with that person's feedback. It's up to you to which bidder you make offers.

The link to make a Second Chance offer (look at Figure 12-5 to view the link on the My eBay page; a similar link appears in Selling Manager) appears only when an auction has more than one bidder.

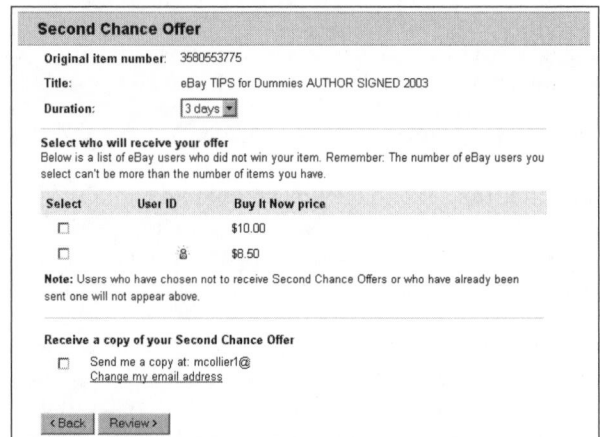

Second Chance Offer

Original item number: 3580553775
Title: eBay TIPS for Dummies AUTHOR SIGNED 2003
Duration: 3 days ▾

Select who will receive your offer
Below is a list of eBay users who did not win your item. Remember: The number of eBay users you select can't be more than the number of items you have.

Select	User ID	Buy It Now price
☐		$10.00
☐	8	$8.50

Note: Users who have chosen not to receive Second Chance Offers or who have already been sent one will not appear above.

Receive a copy of your Second Chance Offer
☐ Send me a copy at: mcollier1@
Change my email address

‹ Back   Review ›

• **Figure 12-5: The decision-making page for making a Second Chance offer.**

Relisting from Your "Item Did Not Sell" Notices

When an item doesn't sell, eBay sends you an e-mail notice, as you can see in Figure 12-6. Whenever I get one, my mind reads it as: *Dear Big Loser, your item didn't sell. Nyah, nyah!*

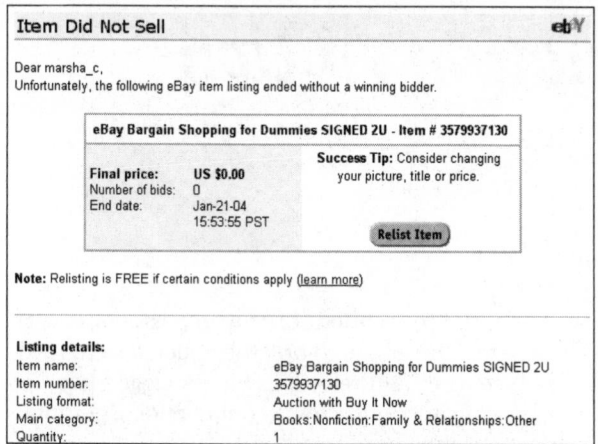

• **Figure 12-6:** eBay's "Your Item Did Not Sell" e-mail.

    That was my reaction, until I noticed that these item-did-not-sell e-mails actually have an excellent purpose. They contain a link that you can click to relist your item instantaneously. It's quick and easy!

Technique 13

Tracking Your Auction Action

Save Time By

- ✔ Keeping track using your My eBay Page
- ✔ Saving time juggling multiple sales with Selling Manager
- ✔ Using Selling Manager's handy links

Sellers who post hundreds (not to mention those who post *thousands*) of auctions each week barely have time to breathe, much less to twiddle around checking to see whether their items have snagged two more bids. They care about listing auctions, closing out auctions, getting paid, and getting the product out the door.

Now that you've heard how the big guys think, let's start small. Many eBay sellers sell part-time. Observing the progress of their auctions is part of the fun, and also serious business when they rely on the money they earn from auctions as a regular form of income. Using eBay's tools — such as the Selling page of My eBay, Selling Manager, and Selling Manager Pro — can help the part-time (and even full-time) seller keep track of all the transactions they're juggling on eBay.

 Selling Manager Pro adds many additional options for post-auction management and inventory.

Using My eBay to Manage Your Listings

Start with baby steps (the best way to start) by visiting the Selling tab of My eBay. For the newbie seller, the tools on the Items I'm Selling page work great. They're simple and get right to the point.

 The small seller can use the Items I'm Selling page in combination with the Sell Your Item form for individual listings and these should be sufficient for managing listings.

For example, Figure 13-1 shows the Items I'm Selling page of My eBay. This feature alone gives you quite a bit of information you can use to track your auctions as they happen.

The Items I'm Selling page uses a color code that helps you quickly see what's going on. If the current price listed for an auction appears in green, a bid has been placed on the item. If it's red, there have been no bids.

• **Figure 13-1:** The Items I'm Selling page.

Active listings

On the Items I'm Selling page, you can view details for your active listings, including:

- ✔ **Links for listings.** Each listing has clickable links you can use to go instantly to an item page.

- ✔ **Item Number.** Just in case you need an item number to contact a bidder or send auction information to a friend, you'll find the item number here.

- ✔ **Current Price.** This may be the starting price of your item (if you have no bids) or the current price based on bids received.

- ✔ **Reserve Price.** This is a very handy feature that reminds you of the reserve price that you've set on an item. There's nowhere else to check this; if you forget to write it down when you're listing the auction, here it is.

- ✔ **Quantity Available.** Here's where you can see how many of this item are still available for purchase on the site. As you can see in Figure 13-1, when a eBay Store item is listed, this feature will show you how many are left and the original quantity you listed.

- ✔ **# of Bids.** When you see that the price is rising on an item, check out this column to see how many bids have been placed to date.

- ✔ **Start Date.** This is the date the listing was posted on eBay.

- ✔ **End Date.** This is the date when the listing will end.

- ✔ **Time Left.** In this column, you can check how much time is left (to the minute) in your listing.

- ✔ **Manage Your Listing.** This is the handiest column of all. Here, you have a link that lets you relist a similar item. This is particularly handy if you use a template and want to use it again for another item. This link brings you to the Sell Your Item form where you can change anything about the listing that you wish and quickly list it.

 In the case of an eBay Store item, the Manage Your Listing feature also permits you to end a Good Till Cancelled (GTC) listing.

On the bottom of your Items I'm Selling listing is a handy recap of all your offerings, as shown in Figure 13-2. The good part about this summary is that the tally gives you the current bottom line of your items for sale.

Totals	Start Price	Current Price	Reserve Price	Total Qty	# of Bids
Auctions					
All items listed	$622.17	$626.92	$0.00	9	5
Items that will sell	$4.25	$9.00	$0.00	1	5
Stores & Fixed Price					
All items listed		$8,745.66		254	
Available to sell		$6,692.17		192	

• **Figure 13-2:** Tote board that summarizes my eBay selling activity.

 If you have an eBay Store, the Items I'm Selling tally won't include revenue for store items that have sold. If you have an eBay Store, I strongly recommend using Selling Manager.

Sold items

There's also an area where your sold items appear, called (coincidentally) Items I've Sold. When the selling cycle is over and someone has purchased an item, it shows up here. I'll cover the tools included here in Part IV, which covers after-the-auction business.

Unsold items

Sob. Sadly, there's an area that lists items that just didn't pique the interest of eBay shoppers — at least this week. (Remember, there's always another selling day on eBay.) Your unsold items appear as in Figure 13-3.

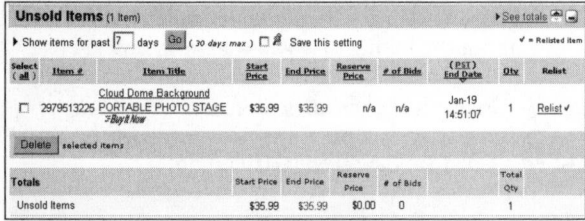

• **Figure 13-3: Your Unsold Items listings.**

From here, for up to 30 days, you can click the Relist link to relist an item on the site.

 If your unsold item sells on the second (repeat) listing, eBay refunds your listing fee for the originally unsold item.

Ramping Up with Selling Manager

Once the selling bug has bitten you, it's a natural transition to go from listing a few items a month to fifty or more. That means, dear reader, that you are now officially running an eBay business. Congratulations!

There's a good and a bad side to this. The good is that you're making considerably more cash than you did before hooking up with eBay. The bad? It's time

to start investing in some tools to keep your business professional.

The first tool that can help smooth your transition makes the process of running eBay auctions and sales consistent — Selling Manager.

Technique 11 gets farther into eBay's *free* Turbo Lister program (it gets your items on the site without having to go through the slow, sometimes-torturous Sell Your Item form). As with Turbo Lister, Selling Manager is a suite of tools for managing your selling business from any computer (as long as it has an Internet connection). eBay gives you 30 days to try out the service for free, thereafter charging you $4.99 per month. (Believe me, the time that Selling Manager will save you is well worth the fee.)

 I've run well over 60 auctions in a single month, successfully managing them with Selling Manager. I use it, along with PayPal's tools and QuickBooks (see Technique 47 for more about this method). This approach provides a professional solution for my medium-size eBay business.

First glimpse of Selling Manager

To download your free Selling Manager trial program, follow these steps:

1. Click the Site Map link in the eBay Navigation Bar at the top of every eBay page.

2. In the first column of the Site Map, under the Sell heading, click the link for "Selling Manager."

3. Read the information on the Selling Manager hub page and click the Subscribe Now link.

You're now subscribed to your 30-day free trial. If you continue using Selling Manager, eBay will add the additional $4.99 fee to your monthly bill. eBay will automatically populate Selling Manager for you with your information from the My eBay Selling tab. The Selling tab will change to Selling Manager when it's all set up.

With Selling Manager, you can click the tab to view a summary of all your auction activities. Figure 13-4 shows my current Selling Manager Summary page.

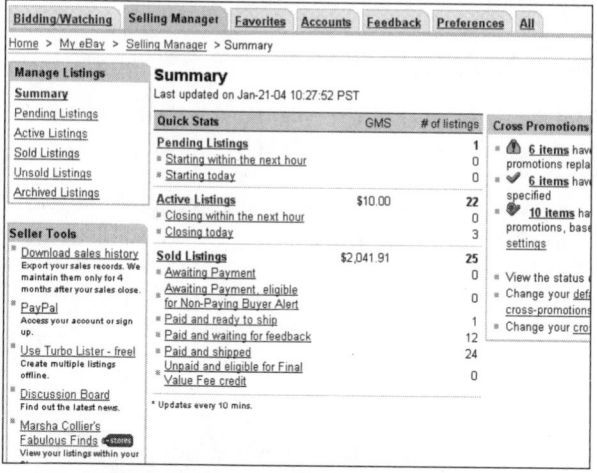

• **Figure 13-4: My Selling Manager Summary page.**

The Summary page lists at-a-glance statistics so I can see what's going on with my sales quickly, at any time — from any computer. Links to other pages in the Selling Manager tool are also included.

 If you plan to exceed 75 transactions a month, consider using Selling Manager Pro; it has bulk feedback and bulk invoice-printing features or a third-party solution. See Technique 60 for information on third-party management tools.

Pending Listings

The Pending Listings link on the Summary page takes you to any auction, fixed-price, or store listing you've sent to eBay through Turbo Lister (or listed on the Sell Your Item page) and scheduled for a later starting date or time. You can also view these pending listings through links on the Summary page that narrow them down to *Listings starting within the next hour* and *Listings starting within the next day*.

When you enter the Pending Listings area by clicking Pending Listings from the Summary page, you can go directly to the listing shown in Figure 13-5. If you want to promote your listing-to-be in a banner ad (or create a link to it from elsewhere on the Internet), you can do so using the URL of the pending listing. See Part IX for more information on promoting your eBay business.

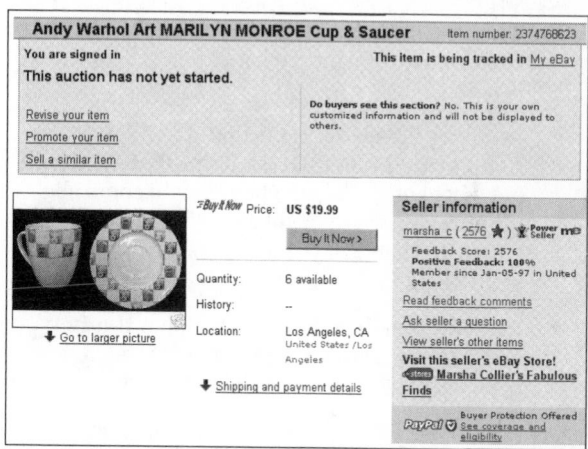

• **Figure 13-5: What an auction looks like before it starts.**

From the Pending Listing page, you can confirm all information about the sale, as well as make any changes to the listing or to the scheduling time.

Active Listings

Click the Active Listings link on the Summary page, and you can observe the bidding action just as you can from the My eBay Selling page. The color-coding that indicates bidding activity is the same as on the My eBay Selling page, and your listings are accessible with a click of your mouse.

You have the option to show only auctions, store listings, or fixed-price items on the Active Listings page. You can also search your own listings by keyword or item number.

 For more about active listings, visit the Summary page, which includes links to items ending within the hour and those ending within the next 24 hours.

Sold Listings

The Sold Listings feature (which you get to by clicking the link on the Summary page) is where Selling Manager really shines. You'll find quite a few links here, including these:

- ✔ **Awaiting Payment:** This is where items that have been won or bought are listed before a payment is made.

- ✔ **Awaiting Payment, Items that Are Eligible for Non-Paying Bidder Alerts:** Items that are awaiting payment are listed when they become eligible for you to file a Non-Paying Bidder Alert. This happens when 7 days have passed without a payment being received.

- ✔ **Paid and Ready to Ship:** If you input the fact that a buyer has sent payment, or if the buyer pays via PayPal, the transaction automatically moves to this category.

- ✔ **Paid and Ready for Feedback:** Once an item is paid for, a reference to it appears here so you can keep track of the feedback you need to leave.

- ✔ **Paid and Shipped:** These are (you guessed it) items for which the buyer has paid, and you've indicated on the transaction record that you shipped the item.

- ✔ **Unpaid and Eligible for Final Value Fee Credit:** This is the sad category where buyers from the Non-Paying Bidder column go if, after all your attempts to get action, they have not responded and sent payment. (If they don't cough up within 10 days after you file a Non-Paying Bidder Alert, the listing moves to this category automatically.)

If you want to see just how useful these links can be, check out Part IV, where I cover the handling end of the auction business.

Archived listings

From this link, you can access completed items that closed within the last three months. You can also download this information to your computer. There are good records here; download them and keep them. See Part VIII for more on what you can do with them.

Seller Tools

The Seller Tools box is on the left side of the Summary page. It's a powerful group of links that allow you to download and export your sales history to your computer. There's also a quick link to PayPal, a link to the Selling Manager Discussion Board, a link to My eBay Store, and a link to the good old My eBay Selling page — in case you get nostalgic for the old, pre-Selling Manager days.

Cross-Promotions

If you have an eBay Store, you may notice that the Cross-Promotions area (which you access from the box to the right of your Summary information) has a great many links. Here is where you can set up a *merchandising bar* that shows selected items you have up for sale on each item page when it's viewed by the prospective buyer.

I have extra links in this area because I have an eBay Store; when you have an eBay Store, you can control which items go into the merchandising bar at the bottom of the description of your items. (You can see a sample merchandising bar in Figure 13-6.)

• **Figure 13-6: Seller's merchandising bar that appears at the bottom of all item listings.**

Technique 14

Boosting Sales through Dynamic Research

Save Time By

- ✔ Using a quality tool to grow sales
- ✔ Finding out when people shop your auctions
- ✔ Seeing what days your items are visited

From my background in advertising, I know that good-quality research can make the difference in whether a business endeavor is a success or a failure. In my books and lectures, I always advocate the necessity of doing at least the minimal research on any item's eBay availably and current selling pricing. (See Technique 4 for how to do this research.)

I also recommend using certain advanced counters (those that break down Web page visits to hours and days, rather than showing only totals), because such tools tell you more than the number of people who click on your page — that number alone doesn't tell you much. Wouldn't it be nice to know, not only how many people visited your listing, but what page sent them there and what city they come from? Wouldn't it be nice to have more data about the people who visit your listings?

The problem with gathering this kind of information is that the coding and programming involved is probably beyond the skill set of even the top-level eBay sellers. After all, they're merchants, not computer programmers. In this technique, I tell you about an online service — ViewTracker — that gives you all the research you can use. And you get the info just by putting a small bit code (which this service supplies) into your listings. Every time someone visits your auctions, the code that you've embedded sends your online account definitive information about your visitor — in real time.

Best of all, this information — while important for your sales efforts — remains noninvasive for your potential customers. For example, you may find out the timeslots and keywords used by your listing visitors, but you find out nothing that compromises their identities.

 The information service presented in this technique doesn't turn your computer into a data-mining robot. It merely gives you the information that is available to every Web site on the Internet. That is, it gives you information such as geographic location, which follows the IP address of all eBay users who visit your listings. This service is not an invasion of privacy (like the data-mining cookies explained in the sidebar "Flushing out the moles").

Flushing out the moles

There's no place to hide on the Internet: Every one of your keystrokes and visits to Web sites can be traced back to you. There's big money in this data as well. If you've ever used a program like *Spybot Search & Destroy* (a program that finds data-mining programs that have been placed on your computer when you visit certain Web sites), you know how much more data sites want about their visitors. My daughter downloaded the free version of Spybot and found 632 data-mining cookies slowing down her computer! Spybot can be downloaded for free from many sites, just google Spybot to find it.

Companies like Mediaplex and DoubleClick make a living by placing cookies on your computer as you browse the Internet. These cookies follow your browsing trail and report your comings and goings to their motherships. Mediaplex and DoubleClick sell that information to the big guys so they can better figure out who their customers are. If you never want Mediaplex to track your Internet browsing, go to

```
http://mediaplex.com/Web-cgi/optout.
    cgi?optOut=1
```

and you will automatically be opted out on the computer you're using. To disengage DoubleClick from your Web roaming, visit the following site to opt out:

```
http://optout.doubleclick.net/cgi-bin/
    dclk/optout.pl
```

Knowing What You Get from Sellathon™ ViewTracker™

If I have ever thought I'd found eBay's "killer app," ViewTracker from Sellathon is *it* — because it answers the most popular questions I'm asked by eBay sellers. Before ViewTracker, when trying to figure out the exact time and day to end an auction, you had to do a considerable amount of research by running test auctions on the eBay site. Now you can follow the "body clocks" of your buyers and find out when they search for your type of item.

You will also find out (I just love this!) which keywords the browser was using when they came to your listing. This information is crucial when writing titles — and planning keyword campaigns (see Part IX for more info on how to build business that way).

Here's a partial list of the type of data you can get by using the ViewTracker system:

- Sequential number of the visitor. Is this the 19th visitor or the 104th — and will this person come back again?

- Date and time the visitor arrived at your auction.

- Visitor's IP address. By clicking the IP address in the Sellathon screen, you can see only those visits originating from this IP address.

- What City, State, and Country your visitor is from.

- Whether the Reserve Price was met when the visitor arrived.

- When the item receives a bid (and how many have been placed to that moment).

- Whether the current visitor is the high bidder, a bidder who has been outbid, or no bidder at all.

- Whether the visitor has chosen to watch this listing in his or her My eBay page.

- Whether the visitor browsed a category, searched a category, searched all of eBay, used eBay's Product Finder Utility, came from "See Seller's Other Items," or some other page.

  ▶ If the visitors were browsing, which category were they browsing when they clicked into your listing?

  ▶ If searching, what search terms did they use to find your item?

  ▶ If they were searching when they came upon your item, did visitor search *Titles Only* or *Titles and Descriptions*?

- Did the user elect to view Auctions Only, Buy It Now, or both?

✔ Did the user refine his or her searches using specific parameters? These include Show/Hide pictures, Sellers that accept PayPal, Price Range, International Availability, Regional Searching, Gallery View, and Show Gift Items.

✔ Was there a preference in the way the user sorted his or her search results? Did they search items from High Price to Low Price?

Amazing stuff, eh? By applying the information from ViewTracker, you can change tactics to help your little business grow into a big one. You'll be able to customize your items to match your very own eBay market.

 Setting up your account is painless. After you give your contact information to Sellathon (and make up a new User ID and password for the site), you will be presented with a small amount of code to add to your listing's description. It's that easy.

Checking Out Your Data

In this section, I show you a portion of the data screens from my ViewTracker account. But keep one thing in mind. I've been busy writing this book, so I haven't had much time to list tons of items on eBay. The few I have listed (I have to keep up my status as a PowerSeller!) will give you a good idea of what you'll see.

When you first log onto ViewTracker, you'll be presented with your General (combined items) page. Here you'll see a couple of statistics. Keep in mind that ViewTracker constantly tracks your items in real time, so the data may change by the minute as you're changing screens within the program!

After you log in to your account, you see a mini-graph at the top of every page, as shown in Figure 14-1. This shows you a quick graphic snapshot of your last 24 hours total up-to-the-minute hit counts.

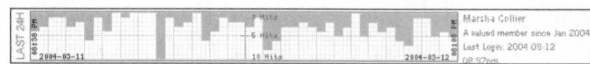

• **Figure 14-1: A 24 Hour snapshot of my hits.**

In the center you see a composite of all your items (as in Figure 14-2) — auctions with bids at the top, and auctions being *watched* by prospective buyers (on their My eBay page) at the bottom.

Here you'll see the total value of all bids placed on your auctions, the number of people watching your items, the average visits per auction, and the total hits on all your items.

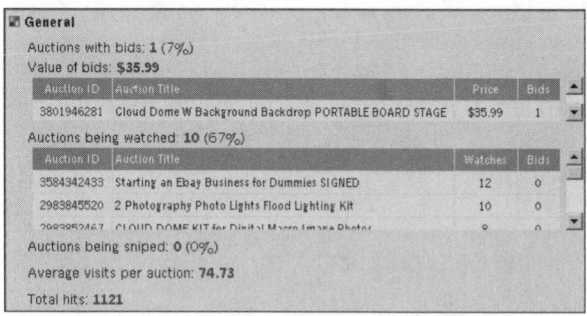

• **Figure 14-2: ViewTracker's General composite screen.**

On the left side of your page, you'll also see some other stats. One will be your Live Auction Stats. Take a look at my instant stats in Figure 14-3.

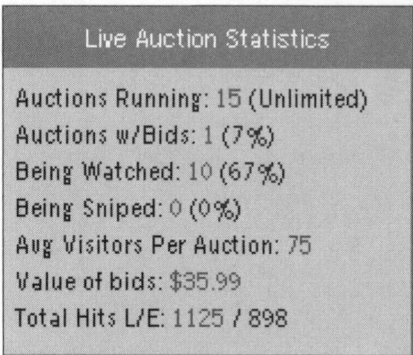

• **Figure 14-3: Live auction stats.**

You'll also have folders on the left, which will have your live and expired auctions. You can click links here to get general information on all your auctions, or click the folder to view information on individual items. You can get data on all your items consolidated together, or individual information for each listing.

Although I don't really want to give away any of my deep dark secrets, I can show you a few screens of data from my expired (closed items) so you know what to look for.

The first shows the most active time of the day for my auctions by hits. I do have to warn you ahead of time that I've been doing a lot of TV and radio these days promoting my books — and if I'm lucky, people log on to eBay and look for my books after they've seen me. That said, realize that the numbers in Figure 14-4 will definitely be skewed.

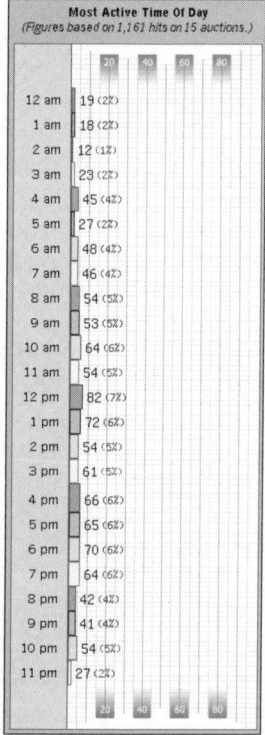

• **Figure 14-4:** My most active hits by the hour.

The next graph you access is the most active day of the week. Figure 14-5 is a portion of the composite report for all my auctions. Think how valuable this data would be when you analyze data from auctions from a similar category. For example, golf equipment, DVD, women's apparel — you get the picture. Remember, this data covers all my listings; this isn't for one particular item (although you can get that data as well).

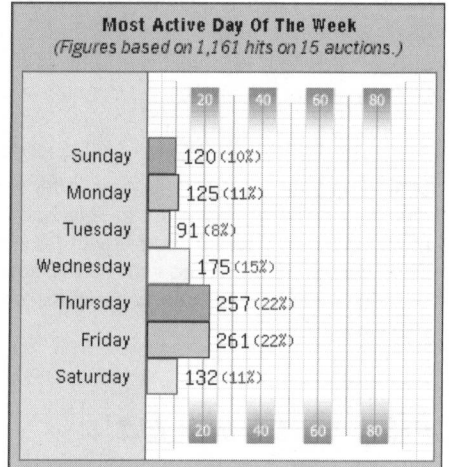

• **Figure 14-5:** Most active days for my items.

I just love this next chart. Figure 14-6 shows you the way people came to my auctions. This is the best way to see whether things you've been doing to boost sales is really working for you. For example, are you taking the best advantage of targeting your cross-promotions? Does your Web site send people to your eBay Listings?

 One sure thing you can glean from viewing the Way Visitors Found Your Auction chart in Figure 14-6: The entries labeled *View Seller's Other Items* and *Cross Promotion* really indicate that cross promoting your merchandise works. See Technique 8 for information on using cross promoting and other selling strategies to your advantage.

This figure is only a portion of the information that appears on the chart. You'll have a complete picture of where all your visitors come from.

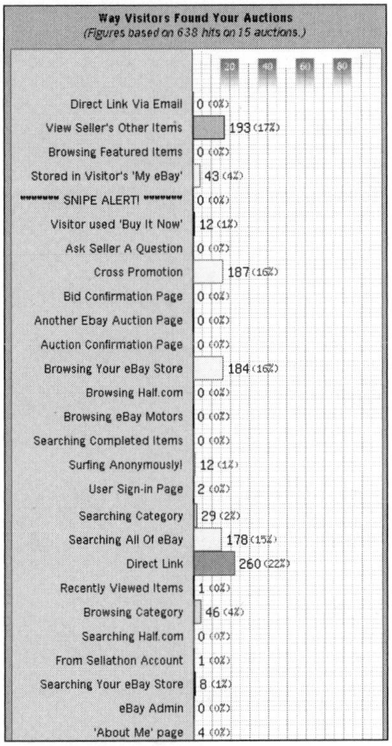

• **Figure 14-6: How people found my items.**

There are other data graphs that you'll see, but the very best is the Top Search Terms Used to find your items. This chart will give you definitive data so you'll know which keywords to include in your titles. (Sorry, I'd *love* to show you my top keywords, but that's a secret! When you work up a list of your own, you'll know exactly where I'm coming from.)

Getting Additional Information from Your Listings

With ViewTracker, you can also view the data for individual listings. Figure 14-7 shows you the data from a very quick auction that ended with a Buy It Now transaction. The data collected and shown here is combined with data from other listings to make up the charts and statistics shown in this technique's other figures.

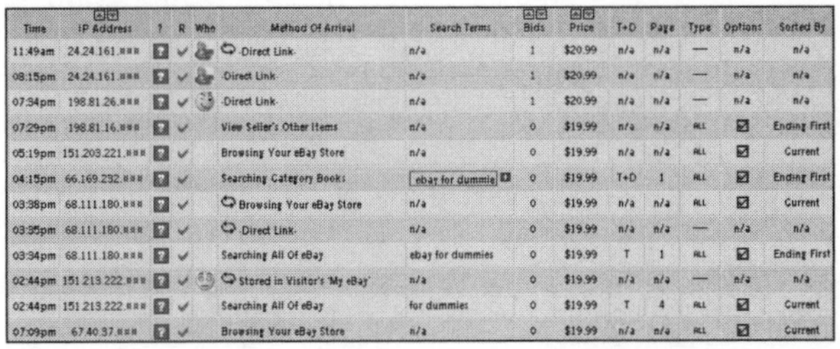

• **Figure 14-7: ViewTracker info for a single listing.**

Note a few things:

✔ **IP Address:** You don't get the complete IP address of the visitor for privacy, but it can show you how many times the same person has visited your listing.

✔ **Question Mark:** If you click the question mark, you will get a pop-up window with the city and state of your visitor.

✔ **Who:** ViewTracker has unique graphic icons to signify different types of visitors. If you click the icon, it will tell you what it signifies. The ones in the figure happen to be: me (so I can see when I go to one of my items), that someone has won the item, and that someone is watching the item in his or her My eBay page.

✔ **Method of arrival:** Here's where you can tell whether your individual promotions are working.

There's a whole lot more to this amazing program. The cost for the program starts at $49.95 a year for a small time eBay seller (like me). For a free trial, go to www.sellathon.com/coolebaytools. Go for the free trial to see what's really happening in your auctions.

Part III

Prettying Up Your Auctions

The 5th Wave   By Rich Tennant

"The divorce was amicable. She got the Jetta, the sailboat, and the recumbent bike. I got to keep the feedback rating on eBay."

Technique 15

Getting Great Images for eBay

Save Time By

- ✔ Finding a camera that works for you
- ✔ Scanning the flat stuff
- ✔ Seeing when a picture goes wrong

Photography has always been a passion for me. The hobby led me (at the age of 10) from developing film in a tiny storage-closet darkroom through my first side-advertising job for a camera store (yes, I was always a moonlighter) to a great professional gig taking photographs of NASCAR auto racing for magazines and newspapers. Although my passion for photography remains unchanged, I learned where to draw the line when exercising my photography skills.

Specifically, when it came to taking pictures for retailer's catalogs, I left that job to an experienced professional. Making merchandise look good is an art. The catalog photographer knows just what it takes to get the lighting perfect, play down flaws in the merchandise, and give everything the right look within a few bracketed snaps.

By working with professional catalog photographers for over ten years, I picked up some tricks for setting up the pictures, buffing up the merchandise, and making everything look picture-perfect. In this technique, I pass on the tips and shortcuts to you. For example, you find out how to select a camera and take pictures that really sell your items. Use these ideas to take great pictures that flatter your merchandise and help you sell!

Choosing Your Digital Camera

The camera you use for eBay is a very personal choice. Would-be big-time sellers, starting out in an eBay business (with no experience on the site) usually go out and buy the most expensive digital camera they can find. Maybe having lots of megapixels is a macho thing, but a camera with a bunch of megapixels is the last thing you need for eBay images. For more information on the importance (or not) of megapixels, see Technique 18.

 Keep these two characteristics in mind when looking for a camera: convenience and optical zoom. Pick a camera that's easy to use and find accessories for. Also, make sure that the optical zoom capabilities will help you capture the level of detail that your merchandise requires.

When shopping for your camera, find one with the highest optical zoom that you can afford. Optical zoom is magnified by the camera's lens — using the camera's internal optics to produce a vivid picture.

Digital zoom is valuable with a camcorder when shooting moving pictures, as the eye can't focus on the fuzzy results as easily. When your camera uses digital zoom, it does the same thing as enlarging a picture in photo editing software. The camera will center the focus over half the focal plane and will use software interpolation to enlarge the picture. This will make your image slightly fuzzy.

Choosing digital media — You can have more than one

After you decide on an easy-to-use camera with the highest optical zoom you can get, think about how to get those pictures from the camera to your computer.

Most cameras can hard-wire connect to your PC with a USB cable, and many sellers are happy with that type of connection, while others don't like a tethered experience. Cameras also have removable media. For some media, you need a media reader attached to your computer — it's like a teeny disk drive for the little cards.

Here's a starter list of the removable storage media currently available:

- **Floppy disks:** Sony has a line of Mavica cameras that save images to a regular 3½-inch floppy disk. After taking your pictures, you just remove the floppy and put it in your A: drive. Voila! The pictures are in your computer. You can then copy the images to a directory on your hard drive for cropping and uploading.

- **CompactFlash memory card:** This is a small medium, slightly smaller than a matchbook. You insert it into a media reader to transfer the data into your computer. You can buy a new USB reader on eBay for as little as $5.00. There are also readers for a laptop's PCMCIA slot. CompactFlash cards come in different sizes and hold from 16MB to 1GB worth of memory capacity.

- **SmartMedia cards:** A SmartMedia card is slightly smaller than a Compact Flash card but is very thin and has no plastic outer case. It is only used in a few brands of digital cameras (such as Olympus). SmartMedia cards come in different data sizes from 8MB to 128MB.

- **Memory Stick:** A tiny media card that is about the size of piece of chewing gum and as long as an AA battery. The Memory Stick is a Sony device and is used in most Sony products. Memory Sticks now hold as much as 2GB of memory. One of the great things about a Memory Stick is that it can be used in numerous devices besides cameras, including PCs and video recorders.

- **Mini CD, CD/RW, and DVD:** These mini optical discs hold tons of pictures for eBay — 185MB worth. You can read them right in your computer's CD or DVD reader. You'll notice that there's a smaller round indentation on the disc platter. This is to hold the mini format.

 You may find that you use more than one type of medium with your digital camera. And because you can record any type of digital data on these removable media, you may find other uses for them. For example, sometimes when I want to back up files or move larger files, I copy them onto one of my 128MB SmartMedia cards in the reader attached to my desktop computer and plug the card into the PCMCIA adapter on my laptop.

Battery life and bargain shopping

When you're picking out your camera, be sure to check into the length of time the camera's battery will hold a charge. The last thing you want to do is run out of juice at the wrong moment. Consider the following:

- Look for a camera battery with at least three hours of photo-taking time.

- Keep a spare battery on hand.

I keep a Lithium CR-V3 battery in my purse so I'll be prepared if my camera battery runs low while I'm on the road — they seem to last forever!

✔ Invest in a charger and rechargeable batteries.

I have a rechargeable backup battery for my Sony Mavica FD92 camera in the office. These batteries last a long time and are worth the cost of investment.

Budget is also a factor. But luckily, as a savvy eBay shopper, you can find deals on lower resolution (3 megapixels or less) cameras on eBay. When the rest of the world is upgrading to mucho megapixels, they sell their perfectly good low-resolution cameras on eBay for about $150. You can be right there to snap up the deals!

Scanning for Images

Do you plan to sell flat items (such as autographs, stamps, books, or documents) on eBay? If so, you can scan your images on a flatbed scanner. Today's scanners are reasonably priced and available as "all-in-ones" that combine copier, fax, printer, *and* scanner.

 When you scan images for eBay, remember to keep the resolution relatively low so the image loads fast. You can set your scanner to the lowest resolution for Web images, no more than 96 dpi.

If you've got three-dimensional items, you can lay them on top of the scanner to get an image. Cover the area around the item with a white T-shirt to get good light reflection without a weird shady background.

Getting Ready to Take Your Best Shot

Aside from setting up a pretty picture, as a professional seller, you have a couple of other things to consider.

✔ **Lighting.** Be sure you have sufficient lighting for your images. If you're photographing small items, you can successfully use an Ott-Lite or the less expensive version made by Cloud Dome as in Figure 15-1. This light is even good enough for jewelry photography as the bulb is a full-spectrum daylight 5000K fluorescent tube. This same light temperature is used where precision is required, such as in diamond grading.

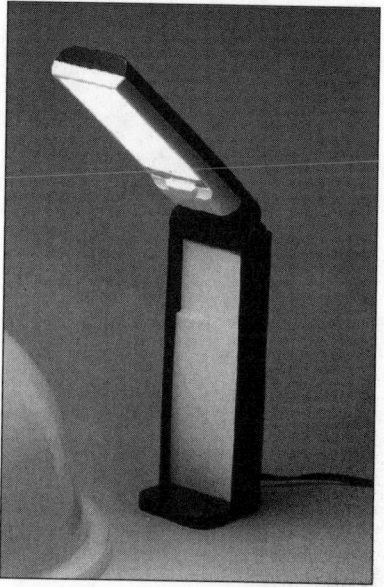

• **Figure 15-1: A folding diamond-grading-quality light.**

 The *color temperature* of a light is the number given to a lighting condition, which ranges from 2500 — 7800K. The K after the number signifies the use of a scale called Kelvin temperature range. Actual daylight color temperature is about 5500K, and it's best to get your lighting as close to that as you can. Using a bulb with a daylight number is important because it's a pure neutral, which means that it throws no blue or yellow cast on your images.

For large-item shots of shelf products, collectibles, big consumer items, and mannequins wearing garments, the least costly high-quality way to get proper lighting is to use a pair of floodlights on adjustable tripod stands. (See Figure 15-2.) I use a pair of those with halogen (white light) bulbs in them. Check my Web site, www.coolebaytools.com for updates on new gadgets for eBay photography.

• **Figure 15-2: Inexpensive floodlights for eBay photography.**

✔ **Macro adjustment:** Most digital cameras have a macro setting for shooting magnified close-ups. Usually, the macro mode can focus (depending on the camera) as close as 1 inch and as far away as 10 inches. A small flower icon in the camera's menu normally signifies the macro setting.

The average camera's *focal length* (focus range) is from 3 feet to infinity. If you have a camera that says the macro focus range is set at 5.1 inches, it means you can't focus it clearly on an object any closer than 5.1 inches.

 Cameras have presets for different focal ranges, and they're usually set in meters. (There's an *m* following the focus range number.) Just so you won't forget, a meter is approximately 3 feet in distance.

✔ **White balance:** This is a pretty tricky feature. Most eBay digital photographers set the camera to Auto (if there is a setting) and hope for the best. If you can adjust the white balance, do so. Manufacturers preset different settings on their cameras. The list of options can include settings for incandescent lights, twilight, fluorescent lights, outdoor, indoor, or shade. All these lighting situations have different "color temperatures."

It's worthwhile to take the time to play with the various white-balance settings of your camera in the different places where you normally photograph eBay merchandise. Make notes on settings that give you the truest colors in your digital images.

Trudging through the eBay Gallery of Horrors

This section shows you a bunch of big-time don'ts. We've seen images like these all over eBay at one time or another. I haven't duplicated it here, but there's the infamous problem of getting your image (with camera in hand) reflected in a mirror, large silver piece, or other reflecting surface. One creative seller said in her auction, "Husband with camera not included." Avoid getting yourself in the photo by shooting your pictures from an angle. If you see your reflection in the item, move and try again.

Mistake #1

Figure 15-3 shows a nice item, but the picture suffers from two major flaws:

✔ **A glare from the camera's flash shows in the cellophane on the item.** This can be avoided by turning the item slightly at an angle so that the flash doesn't give off such a bright glare.

✔ **The price sticker is smack on the front of the item.** Often you'll buy things for resale that have stickers. Be a pro — use a commercial "undo" product to remove stickers. It removes the stickers cleanly and leaves no residue.

• **Figure 15-3:** Glaring errors here.

Mistake #2

What a cute teddy — but what are we selling here? Figure 15-4 shows a common eBay seller mistake. Don't dress your picture with props to decorate the scene. Your photo should be a crisp, clean image of the product you're selling, and only that.

• **Figure 15-4:** And you're selling what?

Mistake #3

I never knew how much colorful upholstery people had in their homes. I could find only a zebra print in mine (see Figure 15-5), but I've seen items photographed on plaid, floral, and striped fabrics. It's distracting from your item. Don't do it.

• **Figure 15-5:** Nice sofa!

Mistake #4

I'm sure the item shown in Figure 15-6 is very desirable, but who can make that judgment without seeing the item? Not to put too fine a point on it: *Take the item out of the box.* If the box is a crucial part of the deal (as in collectibles), be sure to mention that the box is included in the sale.

If you can't open the box without ruining the value of the item, pull in for a macro close-up. When you have a quantity of the item, bite the bullet and open one up. A good picture gets you higher bids, and perhaps that loss of one item will be made up by the higher bids on the sales with good pictures.

• **Figure 15-6:** Peek-a-boo.

Mistake #5

Don't make the mistake shown in Figure 15-7. Can you say *close-up?* Use the zoom on your camera to fill the frame with a full picture of your item. Draw your camera close to the item so the prospective customer can actually see some detail. Don't just rely on cropping the picture in an image-editing program; that only makes the image smaller.

• **Figure 15-7:** Pay no attention to the object on the carpet.

Technique 16

Prepping and Photographing Clothing

Save Time By

- ✔ Making the setting complement the clothes
- ✔ Preparing the clothes to photograph and sell
- ✔ Furnishing your studio

Photographing apparel for eBay is not the *fashionista* type of fashion photography. It's quick and dirty. The (one) rule goes like this: Take the *best picture* you can and move on to the next item so that you can hurry up and list all items for sale on eBay. Period. I hate to admit it, but there were times when we were shooting pictures for major catalogs that we worked in the same way.

Even though I've just said there's only one rule, I also know that taking the *best picture* involves a bit of preparation on your part. Figure 16-1 shows the results of an eBay search for the keyword *dress*. Which of these items for sale look better — the items laid out on the floor or those on a mannequin or model? There's a designer dress in this search that would have probably sold for twice the amount if it had been on a mannequin! When women are searching for dresses, using a gallery picture is *de rigueur* when you want to draw attention to your item and set it apart from thousands of others.

• **Figure 16-1: Random search for Dress on eBay.**

Picture hide	Item Title	Price
	Ann Taylor Dress	$13.17
	NEW GIANFRANCO FERRE DRESS BLACK TOP SHIRT M $175RT NR	$24.99
	Prada Dress Couture Woman womens Dresses NWT	$66.00
	NEW NWT CLAYEUX Wine Colored Velvet Silk Dress 18 Mths	$7.00
	NWT WOMENS VIRGO BLK SLEEVELESS PLUS SIZE DRESS SIZE 22	$14.99
	NWT TO THE MAX BCBG RED MULTI TUBE DRESS M	$44.99
	VERA WANG Casual Chic Tweed Dress sz6 NEW!	$145.00

One of the worst ways to photograph clothing is on a tabletop or folded on the floor. If you've seen eBay auctions featuring clothing folded on a table, you know how you squinted to figure out what you were looking at. Not only does the camera miss essential details in the folded items, but it also misses the opportunity to show off the clothing in all its glory — as worn by a person. To get the highest bids, give your clothing an authentic, lifelike appearance.

Apparel photography can be tricky by all measures, especially when you don't have a model. Using a model is a great idea if you have plenty of time to spare. When you work with a model (even if it's your daughter or girlfriend) you'll have to take many shots of them wearing the same item, because you want the model to look as good as the clothing and vice versa. Not a timesaver.

What's the best way to shoot fashion for eBay? Assembly line. Henry Ford had it right. Have everything assembled in one area and the process can go smoothly and quickly. In this technique, I tell you about how to prepare your studio, your props, and your clothing to get the best picture for the least effort. And best of all, the time you spend preparing the clothes to photograph also makes them customer-ready. Now, _there's_ a timesaver!

Cleaning and Pressing Essentials

Before you photograph your clothing, make sure that the clothing itself imparts the image you want your buyers to see. For example, remove any loose threads and lint that has accumulated on the fabric.

Have the following items handy to help you with the cleaning and pressing chores:

✔ **Garment Rack:** When you unpack your merchandise from the carton they were shipped to you in, they can look pretty ragged. Also, if you've purchased some hanging merchandise and it's in

tip-top shape, you'll want to keep it that way. Hanging the merchandise on a garment rack (as in Figure 16-2) keeps it fresh-looking so it looks great when you're ready to ship.

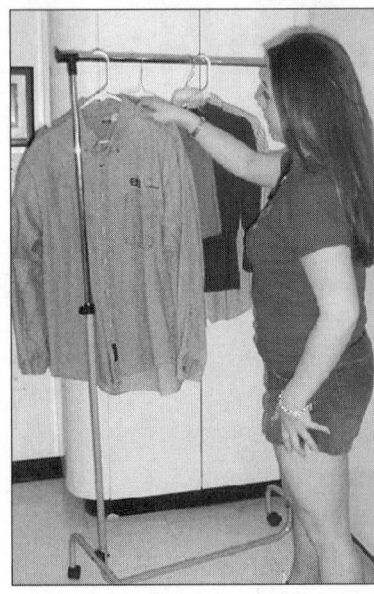

• **Figure 16-2: Garment rack, loaded with clothes to list on eBay.**

✔ **Steamer:** Retail stores, clothing manufacturers, and drycleaners all use steamers. Why? Because steaming the garment with a steam wand is kinder to the fabric and takes out wrinkles in a hurry. Steam penetrates the fabric (not crushing it, as does ironing) and seems to make the fabric look better than before.

 Steaming is also five times _faster_ than ironing (and not as backbreaking) so that's why it's truly the professional's choice. Steaming garments is a breeze; see for yourself in Figure 16-3.

A hand-held travel steamer will work for beginners who sell one or two apparel items a month. While you can steam a garment with a professional-style steamer in a minute or two, you might have to work on a garment with a travel steamer for 15 minutes. If you're thinking about selling a quantity of clothes on eBay, a professional-style, roll-base steamer is what you should look for.

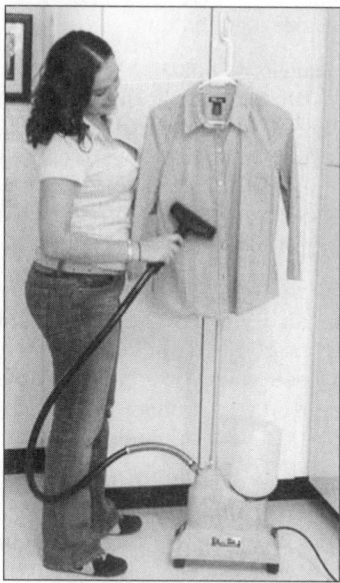

• **Figure 16-3:** Steaming with my Jiffy for eBay!

Steaming hot tips

Or is it *tips for hot steaming?* In either case, keep these few tips in mind when steaming the clothes you sell on eBay:

✔ Always keep the steam head in an upright position so that the condensation inside the hose drains back into the steamer.

✔ Run the steam head lightly down the fabric.

✔ Don't let the steam head come directly in contact with velvet or silk, or it may spot the fabric.

✔ Steam velvet (or any fabric with a pile) from the reverse side.

✔ Hang pants by the cuff when steaming.

✔ Heavy fabrics may do better by steaming from the underside of the fabric.

✔ When you're through steaming your clothes for eBay, try steaming your mattresses and furniture. Steaming has been shown to kill a majority of dust mites and their accompanying nastiness.

I use a Jiffy Steamer that I've had for quite a while. (I even bought it on eBay and got a great deal.) It's the same kind they use in retail stores, only slightly smaller.

✔ **Dryel:** A popular, reasonably priced home dry-cleaning product you use in your dryer. Dryel can be used with *almost* any type of garment (be sure to double-check on the packaging before you use it on an item). After going through a Dryel treatment, the clothes will come out of the dryer sweet and clean. The starter kit even comes with a spot remover. You can buy Dryel at your local supermarket.

According to eBay rules, all used clothing must be cleaned before it is sold on the site. Even if the vintage garment you have up for sale is clean, it can always benefit by a roll around in the dryer with Dryel. New garments, too, benefit; Dryel removes any smells that have clung to the garment during its travels.

✔ **Spot cleaners:** I recommend you have them and use them only if you know what you're doing. There are some really great ones out there that will remove a small spot, but you'd best practice on items that you're *not* selling before using those products.

Assembling Your Fashion Photo Studio

Photographing fashion right takes a little time, but as they say, the right tools make any project easier. Here's a list of some items you need when photographing clothing:

✔ **Mannequin body double.** Since we don't want to deal with supermodels and their requirements for non-fat vanilla lattes, we've got to find someone who will model the garments and not give us any grief. Figure 16-4 pictures my mannequin "Midge" (well I *had* to name her!) who has sold lots of dresses on eBay for me.

• **Figure 16-4:** Midge modeling a vintage fur (photo was cropped prior to listing).

Full-body mannequins can be purchased on eBay for about $200. I bought Midge from a local store that was updating mannequins. Prior to making my purchase, I asked a few stores whether they'd be selling old mannequins, and I struck gold. You can do that too. Major department stores often liquidate their display merchandise in auctions; so keep your eyes peeled for auctions of store fixtures to show up in your local newspaper.

Keep in mind that you needn't spend a mint on a brand-new model. If your mannequin is used and has a few paint chips — so what? Don't we all? The entire purpose of having a mannequin is to display what clothing looks like on a lovely body; a used mannequin works just fine.

Less expensive alternatives to a mannequin are

▶ **Molded body form.** Before you decide to jump in with both feet, you might want to try using a hanging body form. These are molded torsos that have a hanger at the top. You can

find molded styrene forms on eBay for as little as $20. If you decide to stay in the apparel vending business, you can always upgrade to a full-size mannequin.

▶ **Dressmaker's adjustable form.** You can also use a dressmaker's form to model your eBay clothing. The best part about using these is that you can adjust the size of the body to fit your clothing. You can often find new (or — even better — good-condition used) ones on eBay for under $100.

✔ **Vertical photo lights on stands.** To light your merchandise, you'll do best to invest in some floodlights. You don't have to spend a mint, but as you'll see when you start taking pictures, the little flash on your camera isn't accentuating the good parts of your apparel.

You may want to stop the flash on your camera from going off altogether when you take pictures of clothes, because too much light coming from the front will wash out the detail in the fabric.

 Place the clothing to be photographed on the mannequin in the middle of your studio area. Situate each floodlight to either side and closer to the camera than the mannequin. Your setup will be a V-shape, with your mannequin at the point, your floodlights at the top of each V-side, and you holding the camera (or using a tripod) in the middle at the top of the V.

Adjust the distance that you place your lights until you get a good look to the clothes. Be sure to tilt the light heads to pick up extra detail in the clothing.

✔ **Clothespins.** Before you think I'm crazy, I'll have you know that clothespins were used in almost every apparel photo that I've participated in. Think about it, the clothing you're selling will come in different sizes and may not always hang right on your mannequin.

To fit your clothing on the mannequin, use clothespins to take up any slack in the garment (be sure to place the clothespins where the camera won't see them). You'll get a much better look to the outfit. Figure 16-5 shows Midge (a size 6, you know) in a size-10 dress that I sold on eBay. Va-va-voom!

• **Figure 16-5:** My mannequin "Midge," modeling some designer garb.

Technique 17

Photographing the Tuff Stuff: Coins and Jewelry

Save Time By

- Shooting for true color
- Getting the light right
- Avoiding glare and other nasty photo faults

I've been selling on eBay since 1997 — and I thought I was pretty good at showing off and selling my wares, too. But then I purchased a small lot of Morgan silver dollars to resell. I figured, no problem, take my standard digital picture and sell away. Oops, my mistake. My first pictures of the coins bore only the slightest resemblance to the actual coins. The digital pictures made my beautiful silver coins look gold! Eeyow!

Then came my next challenge: photographing some silvertone and goldtone costume jewelry. My setup — with its perfect positioning, beautiful lighting, and black velvet jewelry pads — looked stunning. The pictures should have been perfect. But NO: Silvertone looked gold, and goldtone looked silver. What's the deal?

The deal is lighting — specifically, the need for ambient lighting. I thought back to the days when I worked with catalog photographers who took pictures of jewelry — and I remembered the elaborate setup they used to produce the sparkling images you see in the ads. And although I can't re-create the experts' silk tents, minimalist lighting, and multiple light flashes per exposure, I can still set up for some great-looking images that do justice to my wares. In this technique, I tell you about tools and tricks that can help you with the task of photographing the tuff stuff. You find out how to use Cloud Dome, a great light-diffusing tool, and take advantage of the ambient light you have at home.

Photographing with Ambient Light

Ambient light, light that occurs naturally, is the best light for photographing many types of items (especially shiny items). Problems start when you use flash or flood lighting alone (without a Cloud Dome) for pictures of metallic objects. Common lighting problems that affect the quality of your photographs include shiny spots from reflections (off walls and ceilings), washed-out areas (from the glare of the lights) and loss of proper color.

Enter the Cloud Dome to offer your at-home photos the ability to take advantage of natural, ambient light. The Cloud Dome looks like a giant bowl that you place upside-down over the object you want to photograph. This bowl evenly diffuses ambient room light over the surface area of the object. This way, you can produce quality digital images in average room lighting.

Cloud Dome inventor Cindy Litchfield's father was a meteorologist who invented many varied weather-measuring devices. From her Dad, Cindy was taught how clouds alter the way colors are viewed. She learned that clouds would evenly diffuse light — and that details and a variety of shades could be seen (oddly enough) even better on a cloudy day.

Cindy was in the jewelry business, and she knew the pains of shooting quality images of jewels only too well. To solve the problem, she gathered up her knowledge and got advice from her mad-scientist father (and tools from his well-equipped workshop). After many prototypes, the Cloud Dome was born. Finally, there was a cost-efficient way to photograph delicate objects without hot spots, shadows, and inconsistent lighting.

 A fellow eBay University instructor introduced me to the Cloud Dome, and I've found it an amazing tool. You can purchase the Cloud Dome and accessories at many professional camera shops, from the Web site at `www. clouddome.com`, or (you guessed it) on eBay.

Shooting with the Cloud Dome

The Cloud Dome looks like a giant Tupperware bowl with a camera mount attached. Figure 17-1 shows a Cloud Dome being set up to photograph jewelry. Follow these steps to take a picture with the dome:

1. **Attach your camera to the Cloud Dome's mount with the lens positioned so that it peers into the hole at the top of the dome.**

2. **Place your item on top of a contrasting background.**

See the section "Tips for Taking Cloud Dome Pictures" later in this technique for ideas on choosing a background.

3. **Place the dome with camera attached over your item.**

4. **Check the item's position through your camera's viewfinder or LCD screen.**

If it's not in the center, center it. If you feel you still need added lighting to bring out a highlight, use an added lamp outside the dome.

5. **Focus your camera and shoot the picture.**

• **Figure 17-1:** Taking a picture with the Cloud Dome.

Many items benefit from being photographed through a Cloud Dome, especially:

✔ **Jewelry:** I've found that taking pictures with the Dome keeps the gold color gold and the silver color silver. Also, using the Cloud Dome helps your camera pick up details such as engraving and the metal surrounding cloisonné work. It also gives pearls their unique luster and soft reflection, as in Figure 17-2. Much of the detail that the Cloud Dome helps capture can be washed out when you apply enough light to take the picture without it.

✔ **Gems and stones:** I've seen some beautiful pictures taken of gems and stones with the Cloud Dome. To achieve a special look, you can use a Cloud Dome accessory, a reversible gold and silver reflector, as in Figure 17-3. Especially when you use the silver side, facets of diamonds glisten as if they were in the pinpoint lights at the jeweler's. You may also want to focus a floodlight or lamp on the outside of the dome for extra sparkle.

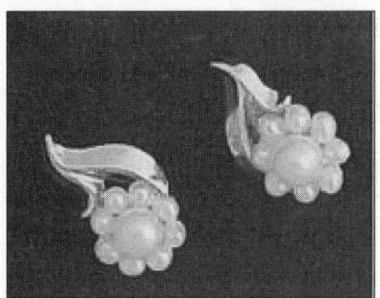

• **Figure 17-2:** A pair of pearl earrings.

• **Figure 17-3:** The facets in the stones of this antique piece are much clearer with ambient light.

✔ **Coins and stamps:** The Cloud Dome allows you to hold the camera steady for extreme close-ups. It also allows you to photograph coins without getting any coloration that is not on the coin. For both coins and stamps, the Cloud Dome helps you achieve sharp focus and true color.

✔ **Holographic or metallic accented items:** If you've ever tried to photograph collector cards, you know that the metal accents glare and holograms are impossible to capture.

Also, the glossy coatings confuse the camera's light sensors, causing over-exposed highlights. Check out the before and after images in

Figure 17-4 and see how clear the hologram on the credit card appears after shooting through the Cloud Dome.

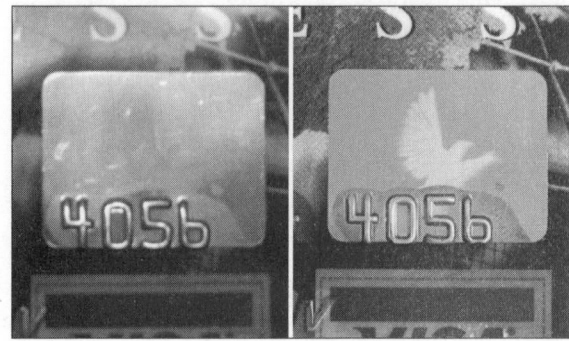

• **Figure 17-4:** A hologram, before and after.

✔ **Reflective objects:** Items like silverware, or even computer chips, reflect a lot of light when lit properly for photos. The Cloud Dome diffuses the light so that the pictures become clear. Check out the before and after in Figure 17-5.

• **Figure 17-5:** Computer chips, before and after shooting with the Cloud Dome.

Tips for Taking Cloud Dome Pictures

Surprisingly, there's very little learning curve to using a Cloud Dome. The simple steps in the preceding section attest to this fact. What may take you more time is discovering the tips and tricks that help you achieve professional-looking results. And reading this section kick-starts your discovery process.

Here are a few things to keep in mind when taking photos with the Cloud Dome.

- **Focus, focus:** Due to the focus limitations of many of today's digital cameras, I found it best to use the Cloud Dome with the extension collar (often sold along with the dome, and shown in Figure 17-6), which allows you to have your camera 17 inches away from the item you're photographing on a flat surface.

- **Close-ups:** When attempting *macro* (extreme close-up) photography, the Cloud Dome holds your camera still while shooting the picture. If you prefer, after you've centered your item, stand away and take the picture using your camera's self-timer.

• Figure 17-6: Cloud Dome with an extension collar attached.

- **Fine upstanding items:** If your item is vertical and doesn't lend itself to being photographed flat, use the angled extension from Cloud Dome, which allows you to shoot the item from an angle versus from the top. An angled collar is also sold separately or in a Cloud Dome package.

- **Keeping background where it belongs:** When selecting a background for your item, choose a contrasting background that reflects the light properly for your item. Make it a solid color; white is always safe, and black can add dramatic highlights.

Technique

18

Touching Up Your Photos for eBay

Save Time By

- ✔ Getting the photo file size right
- ✔ Choosing a handy image-editing tool
- ✔ Discovering why your pictures look crummy
- ✔ Brushing away the crumbs with PaintShop Pro

You may hear all kinds of myths — such as "more is better" — regarding images for eBay, and personally, I refuse to perpetrate any more. Because you already know how to take a reasonable picture of your product (provided, of course, you've read the how-to information from the preceding techniques in this part), I use this technique to show you how fast you can get the photos you take — or the scans you make — spruced up for eBay.

 No eBay seller should spend hours playing with and perfecting images for eBay listings (although some do). One pass through a simple image-editing software program gets any reasonable picture Internet-ready.

The prime concern to have about the pictures you put on eBay is size — that's right, in this case, size *does* matter. You need to limit the picture file size so you don't bog down the prospective buyer's viewing of your item page (especially if you're using multiple pictures in the item description). Why? That's easy — the larger your item's picture files, the longer the browser takes to load the item page. And it's a fact that 4 out of 5 eBay users will click back out of a listing to avoid a long page load. (I'm guessing that you don't want your listings to elicit this behavior.)

The maximum size for your individual photos should be no more than 40KB. That's the *maximum*; less is better. In this technique, I show you how to reduce the file size without destroying your picture quality. Because the size of your picture file is directly related to the picture's resolution, this technique also provides what you need to know about getting the right resolution for an online image.

Viewing Images on a Monitor

To get a better idea of the size for the images you use online, remember (see Technique 15) that no matter which camera setting you choose, your image should be designed to be viewed on a monitor. Low resolution is just fine because the average computer monitor just isn't an HDTV.

The average monitor resolution settings (in pixels) are

- 640 horizontal x 480 vertical (VGA)
- 800 x 600 (Super VGA)
- 1024 x 768 (XVGA)

These settings determine the number of pixels that can be viewed on the screen. No matter how large your monitor is (whether 15, 17, or even 21 inches), it shows only as many pixels as you determine in its settings. On larger screens, the pixels just get larger — and make your pictures fuzzy. That's why most people with larger screens set their monitors for a higher resolution.

 Remember that scanned images are measured in DPI (Dots per Inch). The average monitor displays scanned images at 72 dpi. Do not confuse this with pixel size. See more in Technique 15 about scanned images.

Just keep in mind that when you design pictures for your eBay items, you must design for the lowest common denominator. There are still many people using MSNTV (used to be WebTV), and their screen resolution is fixed at television resolution: 544 x 372. Also consider that over 60 percent of the United States Internet population still hooks up with a dial-up connection; they're not very likely to be using high-end monitors with high resolutions.

 Since the higher resolutions make the screen images smaller, many users prefer their screens at the 800 x 600 size for eye comfort during the time they spend on the computer. They don't want to squint!

The popular viewing resolutions for monitors are:

- 640 x 480 or 800 x 600 pixels for 15-inch monitors
- 800 x 600 or 1024 x 768 pixels for 17-inch monitors
- 1024 x 768 or 1152 x 864 pixels for 19-inch monitors

If you use eBay's Picture Services for all your eBay items, setting your image size is not a big issue. eBay Picture Services apply a compression algorithm that will force your pictures into eBay's pre-prescribed size — and, odds are, they'll look fuzzy as they are forced into high compression (squeezing the pixels to the prescribed size).

Using eBay's Picture Services (for the free image) is a good idea. It's the only way to get a picture of your item at the top of the listing near the title.

 The more compression put into computer images, the less sharp they appear. So why not set your images to a monitor-friendly size in a software program before uploading them?

Choosing an Image-Editing Tool

There are plenty of image-editing programs available these days — everything from simple shareware programs like IrfanView to high-dollar programs like Adobe Photoshop.

Well, okay, I certainly don't expect you to invest hundreds of dollars (and possibly hundreds of hours) in learning the program. But I do suspect you'll spend a few bucks for a program that can give you professional-looking results.

 If you're in business, you need to select software that works well, without too many bells and confusing whistles. Since your images are a lifeline to your sales, I suggest that you plan on paying for a solid program.

I really like the program Paint Shop Pro from JASC. It's so straightforward and easy to use that it may even fully convert me over from PhotoShop, which I learned to use in my graphic-design days. It's reasonably priced and easy to learn. Understandably, JASC Software has become part of the eBay Community — they sell their software on the site and have an eBay Store.

Other popular image-editing programs

There's a wide array of image-editing software used by eBay sellers. As a matter of fact, some listing software has built-in mini-editing capabilities (see Part X for more on third-party software for eBay).

Choosing software for your images is like picking your office chair. What's right for some people is dreadful for others. You might want to ask some of your friends what they use — and take a look at it. Some of the more popular image-editing software used for eBay includes these products:

✔ Ulead Photo Impact

✔ Adobe PhotoShop Elements

✔ Microsoft Picture It

✔ IrfanView (a shareware program)

Getting Your Image eBay-Ready

Suppose you just took a bunch of pictures for your new eBay items, using camera settings between 640 x 480 and 1024 x 768. (Those are common low-resolution digital camera settings.) Now you need to get these pictures snazzed up to give your items the best possible image (and get you the best possible price).

The process for fixing your pictures is twofold: (1) knowing which common edits improve your pictures' appearance on eBay and then (2) doing them. The next two sections show you the quick path through the process.

Knowing what image elements to edit

Surprise. Pictures don't always come out of the camera in perfect form. There are a very few tweaks you can make to bring them into perfection range.

✔ **Cropping.** Sometimes there's a little too much background and not enough product. Don't waste precious bandwidth on extraneous pixels. To crop your image means to cut away the part of the picture that is unnecessary.

✔ **Brightness and Contrast.** These two functions usually work together in most photo programs. By giving your picture more brightness, it (duh) makes the picture look brighter. Raising contrast brings out the detail and lowering it dulls the difference between light and dark.

✔ **Sharpen.** If your camera was not perfectly in focus when you took the picture, applying a photo editing programs *sharpen* feature can help. Be careful not to sharpen too much, or it can destroy the smoothness of the image.

If your images need any more help than the above three alterations, it's probably easier (and faster) just to retake the picture.

Perfecting your picture in Paint Shop Pro

After you evaluate the pictures you've taken for potential improvements, you can get started with the actual editing part of the process. The following steps show you how to take care of the list of common photo edits presented in the previous section.

1. **In the Paint Shop Pro program, choose File➪ Open.**

Figure 18-1 shows the result.

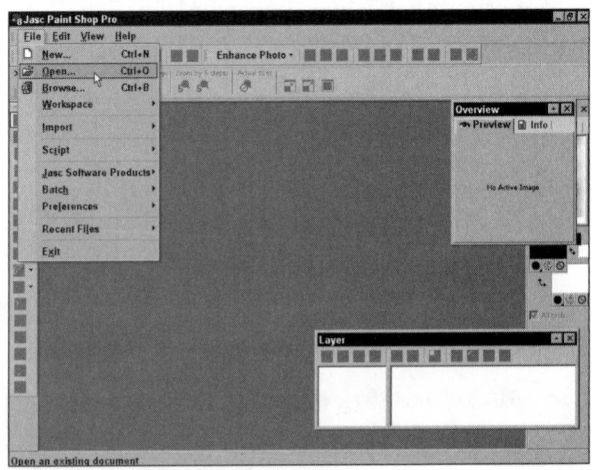

• **Figure 18-1:** Opening your image.

2. Browse to find an image to open on your storage medium.

This can be a floppy disk (such as images from the Sony Mavica FD series), memory stick, compact flash card, or an area on your hard drive where you stored your images.

3. Click to put a check mark in the box that says *Show preview*.

Before you can select the correct image to edit, you have to get a look at it, right?

4. Click the selected image filename so it appears in the File Name box (as in Figure 18-2), and then click Open.

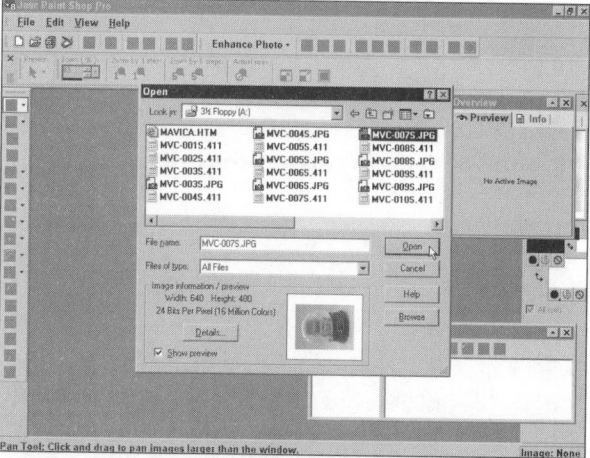

• Figure 18-2: Selecting the image to open.

Your picture opens into the program. Note the Overview palette on the page, the tiny preview of your picture, and the Info Tab.

5. Click the Info Tab to see the specifications of your picture (as in Figure 18-3).

6. If your image is sideways (as they often are), click Image, select the way you want the image rotated, and then click Rotate.

Figure 18-4 shows the list of rotation options you can use to put your picture in the proper perspective. It's so annoying to have sideways pictures on an item page — and so many do! (Hey,

call it an instant advantage when you can reduce annoyance.)

• Figure 18-3: Checking the Image size via the Info Tab.

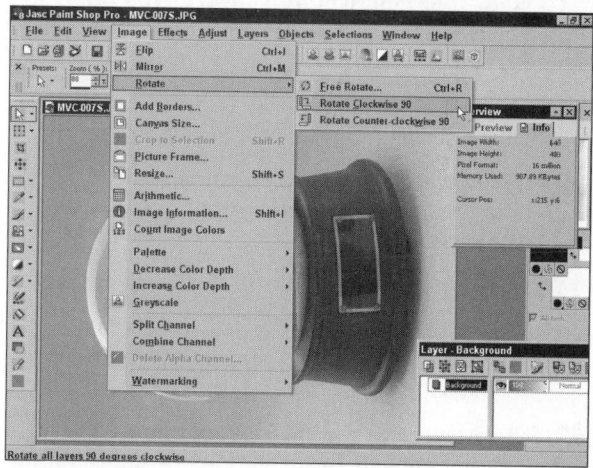

• Figure 18-4: Selecting the rotation parameters.

7. Check your picture for trim size.

When your picture is properly placed, take a good look at it. Does it show any extraneous padding around the subject? There usually is at least some.

8. Point your cursor to the toolbar on the left side of your screen and click the Crop tool, as shown in Figure 18-5.

• **Figure 18-5:** Setting the cropping border.

9. Put your cursor on the approximate place you'd like the new corner of your picture to be, hold your mouse button down as you drag the mouse to the far corner of your selected area.

As you do so, the Crop tool draws a rectangle over the area. Stop when you've reached your desired image size and let go of your mouse button.

10. If you want to adjust your cropping area, click and drag an edge or corner handle to adjust the rectangle's size.

11. When you're satisfied with the terms of your crop, double-click the image.

Poof! It crops itself and appears at your new size, as in Figure 18-6.

12. If you feel that the color of your image isn't vibrant enough, or too dark, click Adjust (at the top of the screen) and go to Brightness and Contrast (as in Figure 18-7).

A window opens with a section of your image repeated twice. There will be Brightness and Contrast boxes in the Window below your image.

13. Click the Brightness arrows that point up (to brighten the picture) or down (to darken the picture). Do the same with the Contrast arrows

until you're happy with the image results. When you are, click OK.

You can view what your image will look like before you go with your choices (see Figure 18-8).

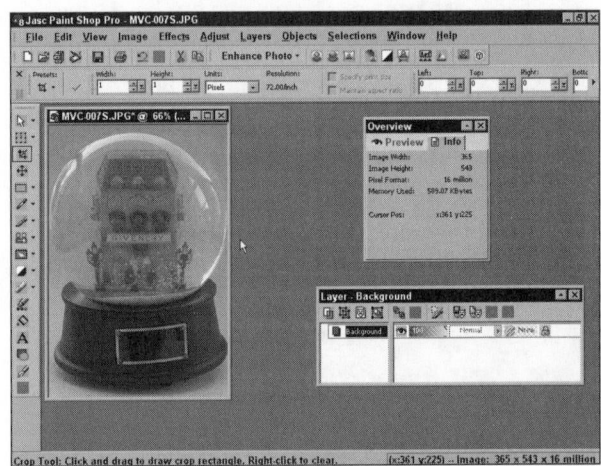

• **Figure 18-6:** Your picture is now cropped to size.

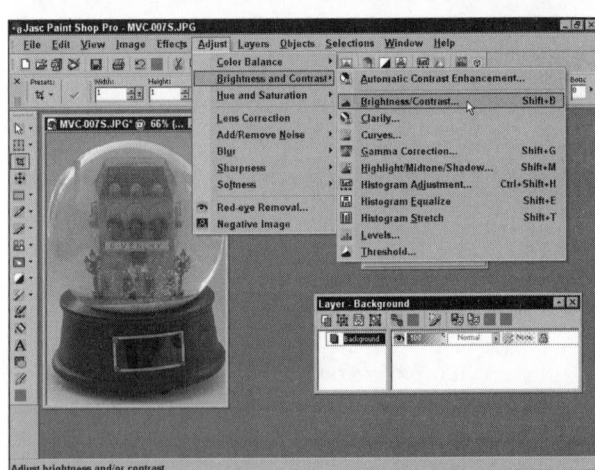

• **Figure 18-7:** Selecting to adjust brightness and contrast.

14. If your picture is too large for your eBay listing, click Image⇨Resize.

A window pops open, as in Figure 18-9.

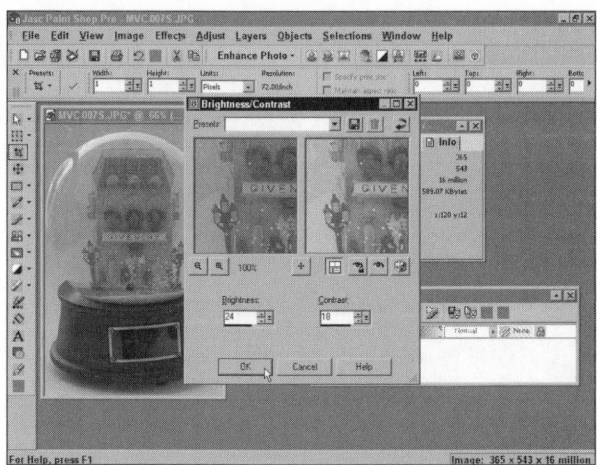

• **Figure 18-8:** Upping the brightness and contrast of my image.

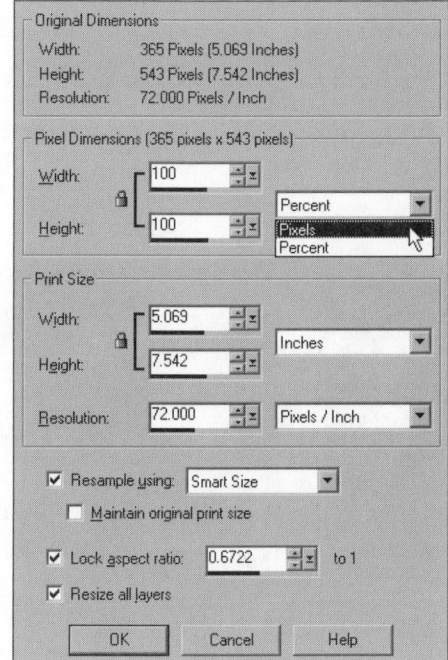

• **Figure 18-9:** The Image Resize tool.

15. In the Pixel Dimensions area, change the drop-down menu from Percent to Pixels, and then type in a pixel size that suits your auctions.

Keep your largest number no higher than approximately 400 pixels. In Figure 18-10, I've selected 350 pixels for my image height.

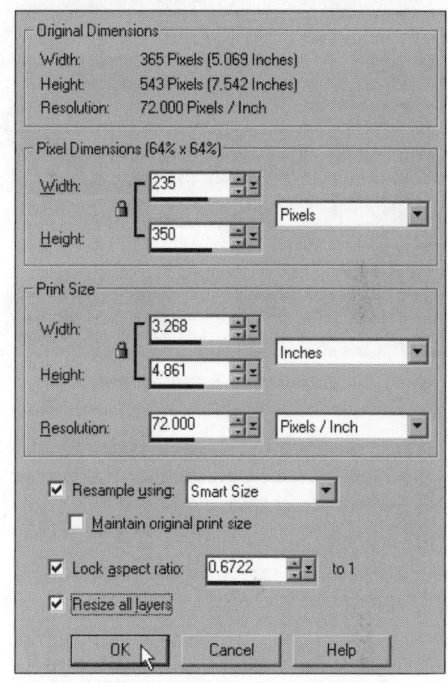

• **Figure 18-10:** Setting the final image size.

16. Click OK.

Your image assumes the desired size.

At this point, it might be nice (though it's not absolutely necessary) to check how your image will look in a Web browser. This isn't necessary with every picture, but I'll show you how you can do it:

1. Click View➪Preview in Web Browser, as pictured in Figure 18-11.

The Preview in Web Browser box asks you to select whether you want to see a GIF or JPG image.

2. Select JPG➪Preview.

The JPEG Optimizer appears.

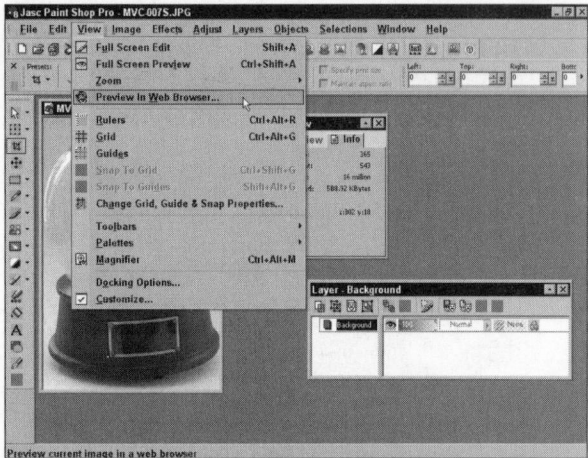

• **Figure 18-11:** Selecting Web Browser view.

 If you don't want to preview your picture in the Web browser, you can also optimize your JPEG when you save the image.

The program shows you both compressed and uncompressed versions of the image file size. You can click a tab to see download times and estimate how long it would take to download at different Internet-connection speeds. In Figure 18-12, it's clear that my image's file size is way to big (and will take too long to load) for use on eBay.

3. Click the Quality tab, to set the Compression Value higher.

A higher number will compress the image file size. You can see how your image is affected by the compression by looking at it in the right view window. Your original image will be on the left for comparison

4. When you're happy that you've compressed the picture all you can without doing too much damage to it, click OK.

You'll see the image in your Web browser with statistics underneath it on loading times as in Figure 18-13.

5. If you're happy with all that you've done, choose File⇨Save As, select the location that you want to save your picture, give it a name, and click Save.

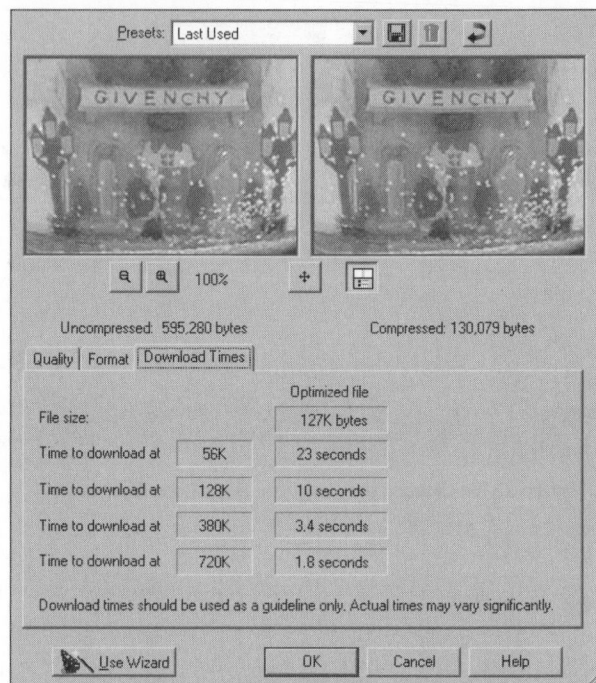

• **Figure 18-12:** Viewing the download times in JPEG Optimizer.

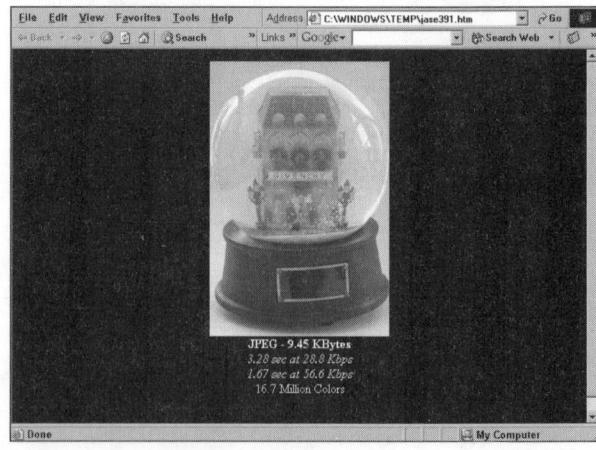

• **Figure 18-13:** Paint Shop Pro previews your image in a Web browser.

Now that I've done this twice, I can do my eBay pictures in this program in about a minute each!

Technique 19

Uploading Your Pictures to a Server

Save Time By

✔ Using your free eBay picture

✔ Uploading to an ISP or Web site server

✔ Uploading to AOL

Everyone eventually seems to figure out how to upload a picture on eBay's Picture Services (but why should you waste time figuring it out when I explain it here?). Still, to most users, uploading their pictures to their own Web space seems to remain a major mystery. Many users are still convinced that they have to pay for an image-hosting service — but that's rarely the case these days.

Higher bids and closed sales go hand in hand with quality images at eBay. The better the quality of your pictures, the more comfortable a prospective buyer feels when perusing your items. At least they know you actually have the item for sale, and they can get a good look at it. Making sales by effectively using images is what this part of the book is all about.

In this technique, I show you some easy ways to upload your pictures to your Web site or to your ISP's Web space. Doing so means you don't incur extra fees from eBay for including multiple pictures in your listings.

I highly recommend that your first move be to take advantage of the one free picture from eBay's Picture Services. First, it's available at no charge, and second, Picture Services offers many other benefits. Read on and I'll show you just a few.

Using eBay's Picture Services

At this point, I'll go back to my basic assumptions about you. I assume you know how to list an item on eBay — or at the very least, you can make your way through the Sell Your Item form and get to the *Add Pictures* step.

When you arrive there, you need to upload a picture to eBay, whether or not you've got pictures in your description. Why? Because the first picture is free — why turn down anything free? — and because your uploaded picture becomes part of the ultraimportant top area of the item page, as shown in Figure 19-1.

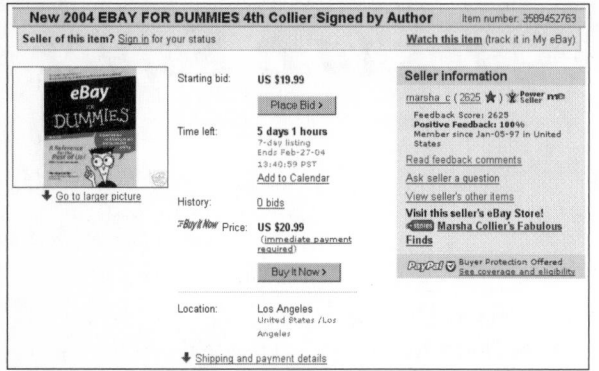

• **Figure 19-1: The item image is often where the prospective buyer looks first.**

Have you ever noticed that some items that you browse on eBay do not have this crucial picture at the top? That's a shame, because these sellers are not availing themselves of eBay's Picture Services and they're losing sales as a result. Having that picture at the top of the page is a first-rate way (and did I mention *free?*) to pull a buyer into your listing.

Uploading your picture

I'm making another assumption here: You've already taken a picture, uploaded or scanned it, and saved it somewhere on your computer's hard drive.

 For organization's sake, you might consider making a subfolder in your *My Pictures* directory called eBay Photos. That way you can always find your eBay pictures quickly, without searching through photos of your family reunion to find the picture of the computer or vase you want to sell on eBay.

When you reach the part of eBay Picture Services that allows you to add pictures, look for the Add Picture button in the First Picture — Free area, as shown in Figure 19-2.

When you reach the part that allows you to add pictures, be sure the area is entitled eBay Picture Services. If, for some reason, your Add Pictures area

shows a tab that says Basic eBay Picture, scroll down and look for the Upgrade to our free full-featured version link. This will send you to eBay's Picture Services as shown in Figure 19-2.

By uploading your picture with eBay Picture Services, you can adjust your pictures by cropping or rotating (in case you shot the picture sideways) online.

• **Figure 19-2: eBay's full-featured Picture Services.**

If you have never used eBay's Advanced Picture Services before, a Windows Security Warning pops up, asking your permission to install a small program on your computer, as shown in Figure 19-3. This is safe (and the only way you can use eBay Picture Service features), so click Yes. Your screen will change to the Advanced Picture Services view.

Then, to upload your picture, follow these steps:

1. **Click the Add Picture button.**

A window pops up, prompting you to open an image file on your computer.

2. **Navigate to the directory that holds your eBay images.**

3. **Select the image you want to upload and click Open.**

Your selected picture appears on the eBay Picture Services screen.

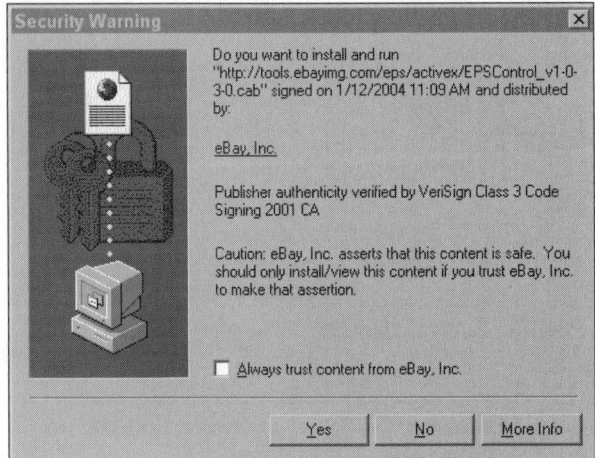

• **Figure 19-3: Windows Security Warning — it's okay.**

 If you've accidentally selected the wrong picture, click the X in the lower-left corner to make the picture disappear so you can select a different one.

Editing a picture on the eBay server

Once your picture appears on the eBay Picture Services page, you can alter its appearance in two ways:

✔ You now may rotate the picture 90 degrees at a time, by clicking the small circle with the arrow in the upper-right corner of the picture.

✔ To crop the picture, place your mouse at the corner or sides of the picture and drag inward. This will produce a small marquee. You can now drag the proportional marquee by placing your mouse in the center and clicking and dragging the square around the picture to select the area you want to use in your listing. Once the picture is uploaded to eBay's server, the picture will be cropped as you indicated.

 If you choose to upload other images, there will be a 15-cent charge per picture. Why not just read on and learn how to use more pictures without paying a fee in the section titled "Using Your Free ISP Space."

On the bottom of the eBay Picture Services page, there is a Gallery option, under the *Increase your item's visibility* headline. (For more on eBay's options check out Technique 8.) If you select the Gallery option, the picture you just uploaded to eBay will become your Gallery picture. I highly recommend the Gallery — for 25 cents. You can't get a better bang for your quarter of a buck.

When you've finished with this page, click Continue. A pop-up window notifies you that your picture is being uploaded to eBay's picture server.

Using Your Free ISP Space

Everyone who connects to the Internet from his or her own computer has an Internet Service Provider or ISP. This is the company that you pay a monthly fee to for the privilege of hooking up to the Internet using their servers. AT&T Worldnet, Earthlink, Road Runner, AOL, or a local provider in your area are examples of ISPs.

Many of these ISPs give you a minimum of 5 MB (that's megabytes) of space to put a personal home page up on the Internet. You can usually store your images for your eBay sales there — unless your provider has some strict rules about not doing that (it's a good idea to check first).

Obtaining an FTP program

Internet providers may supply you with an image upload area, but they may require you to use File Transfer Protocol (FTP) to upload your images. If so, you may want to locate an FTP program to help you manage this process.

You may be able to find a free or shareware (requiring a small fee) FTP program on sites such as

✔ www.tucows.com

✔ www.download.com (formerly cNet)

✔ www.shareware.com

I use a program called CuteFTP. (That name might sound familiar, because I also mention an HTML design program called CuteHTML in Technique 21.) You can purchase CuteFTP in a software bundle with CuteHTML.

 CuteFTP is also available for the Mac.

I've been using both of these products for years because they're easy to use and reliable. They've never given me a whit of a problem, so I highly recommend them. You can find both products at the GlobalScape site at www.globalscape.com/o/912.

 Before you upload a picture, your image must be ready to go and Internet ready. See Technique 18 for details.

Uploading your picture to an ISP server

Now I show you how to upload pictures using CuteFTP. Most FTP software programs work in a similar fashion, but CuteFTP really automates the entire process.

You can download a trial version and install it on your computer to try out for a limited time. After you have installed the program, open it and follow these steps to upload a file to an ISP server:

1. **Select File⇨Connection Wizard.**

   The CuteFTP Connection Wizard shown in Figure 19-4 appears.

2. **Click the arrow on the Choose Your ISP drop-down list to display it, and locate your Internet service provider. Once you've found your ISP, click Next.**

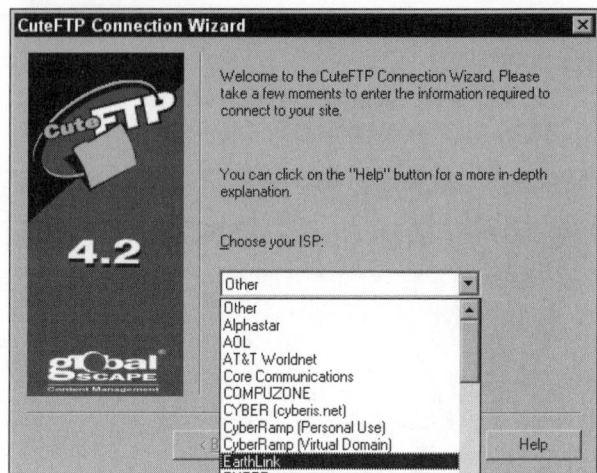

• **Figure 19-4: The CuteFTP Connection Wizard.**

3. **On the next screen (shown in Figure 19-5), type in the user name and password that you use to log in to your Internet account.**

4. **Click Next.**

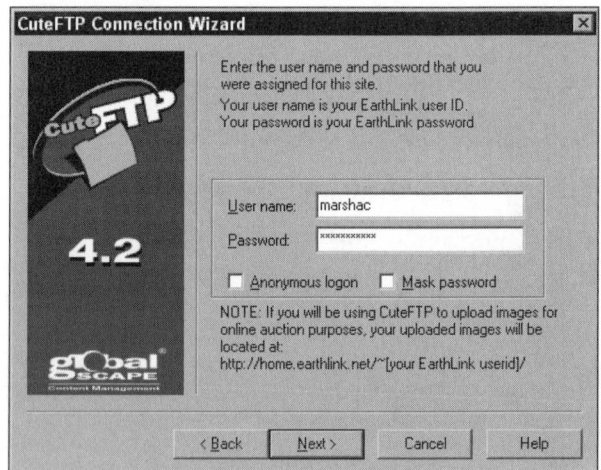

• **Figure 19-5: Entering your login information.**

5. **Click the Browse button (shown in Figure 19-6) to locate the directory on your computer where you store your eBay images.**

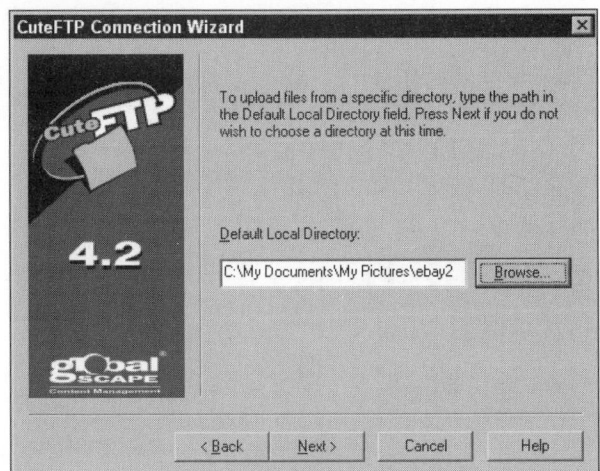

• **Figure 19-6: Selecting your Default Directory.**

6. **Specify the way you want to connect.**

Click the Connect to This Site Automatically check box shown in Figure 19-7 if you want to log in to your FTP space immediately upon opening the CuteFTP program. If not, don't change anything on this screen.

7. **Click Finish.**

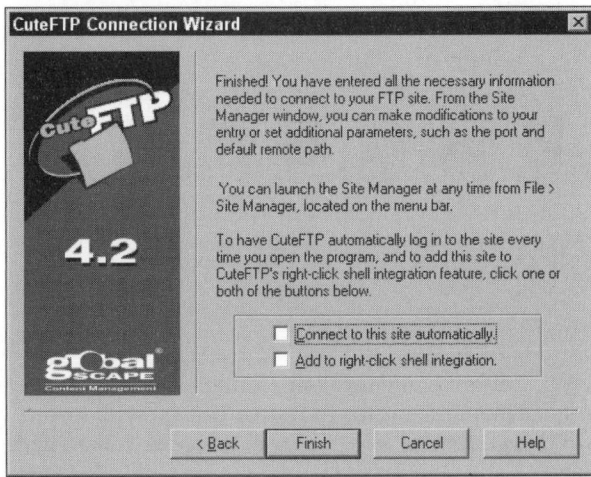

• **Figure 19-7: The last step in the Wizard.**

From this point on, every time you open the program (if you've selected automatic connection in Step 5), CuteFTP logs in to your Web space and displays the screen shown in Figure 19-8. Note that the left side of the program is open to the directory you selected as the default for your eBay images. The box on the right shows what is currently on your ISP-provided home page.

To upload an image, double-click it. Faster than I could take a screen shot (okay, I took it anyway and it's Figure 19-9), it's automatically uploaded to my Web space!

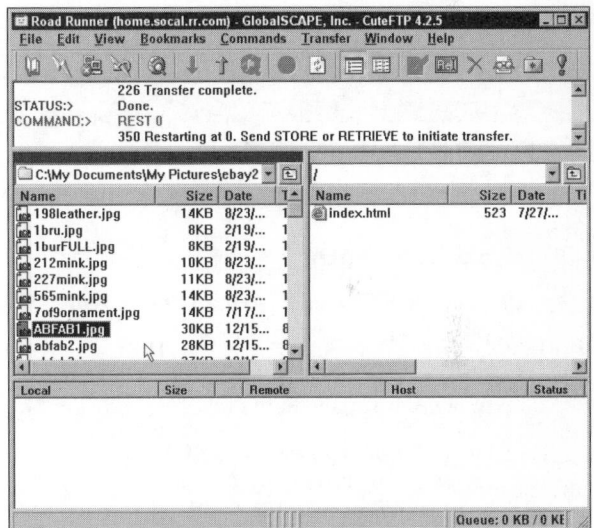

• **Figure 19-8: Signing on to your FTP space.**

Uploading images to AOL

AOL handles image uploads a bit differently from other ISPs. (But those of you on AOL knew that already). Many people love AOL because it provides an easy, step-by-step interface. As you probably imagine, uploading pictures is handled in that same AOL style.

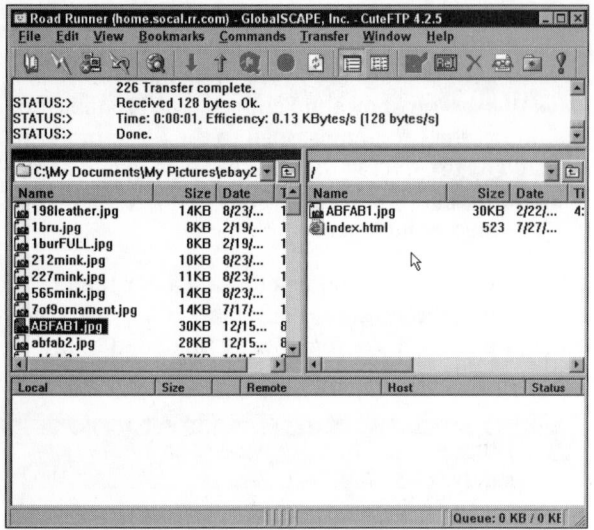

• **Figure 19-9:** Instant image upload!

To upload pictures to AOL, follow these steps:

1. Sign on to your AOL account.

2. Display the FTP area of AOL in one of two ways:

> **For users of AOL 5.0:** Select Keywords and type **my ftp space** in the text line and click Go.

> **For Users of later versions of AOL:** Search Keywords by typing **my ftp space** in the text line (as in Figure 19-10). On the next page, click *members ftp space*. Then double-click *members.aol.com*.

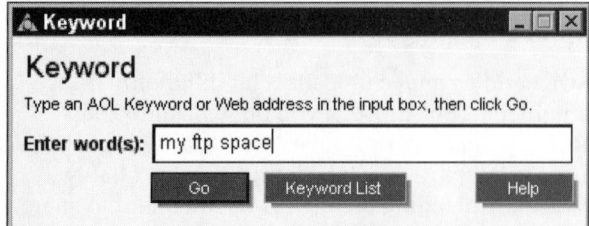

• **Figure 19-10:** Going to your AOL FTP space.

3. Click the bar that says *See My FTP Space*, as in Figure 19-11.

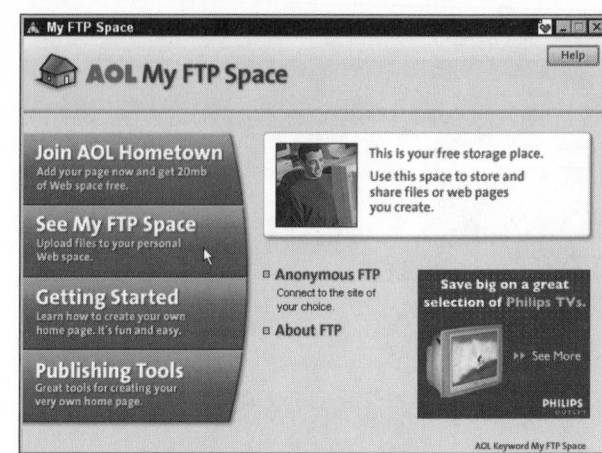

• **Figure 19-11:** Selecting your FTP Space.

Magically you're sent to your AOL storage area.

4. Click the Upload Box to upload a file, as in Figure 19-12.

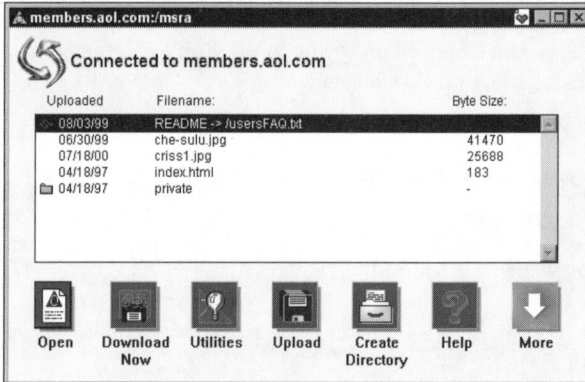

• **Figure 19-12:** Your FTP Control area.

A box appears; it's where you name the file for upload, and it's called *remote file*.

5. Enter a name for your picture in the Remote Filename box (as in Figure 19-13), in all lower-case letters, using no more than eight characters.

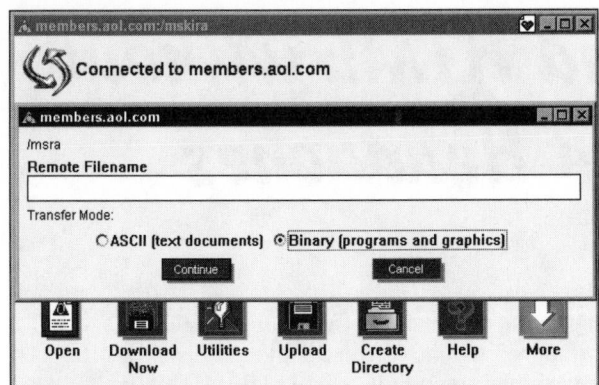

• **Figure 19-13: Giving your file a name for AOL.**

6. **When the name is entered, click Continue.**

A window opens so you can locate the file on your computer, as shown in Figure 19-14.

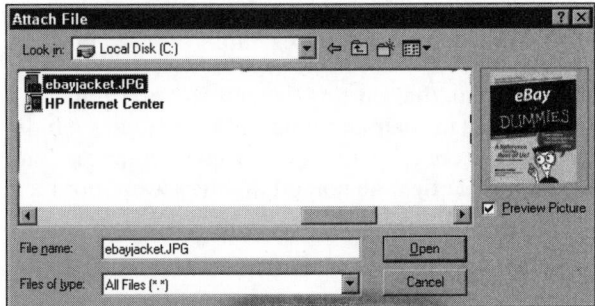

• **Figure 19-14: Finding the file on your computer.**

7. **When you find the file, click its filename and then click Open.**

Your file will now whiz though the wires to the server at AOL, as shown in Figure 19-15.

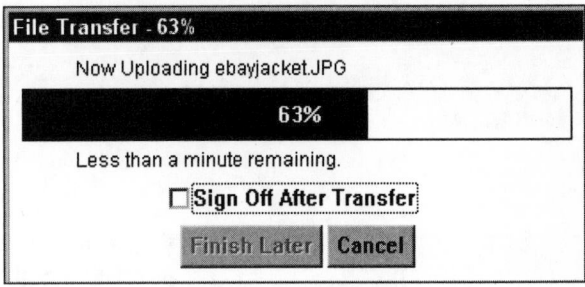

• **Figure 19-15: The file is on its way!**

8. **Double-check to make sure your file arrived safely.**

Type its URL in your browser this way, and then press Enter:

```
http://members.aol.com/yourscreenname/
    picturename.jpg
```

This is also the URL that you use when you insert the picture into your eBay item description, as in

```
<img src= http://members.aol.com/
    yourscreenname/picturename.jpg>
```

See Technique 20 (about HTML) for how to use this coding.

Technique 20

Listing Touchups and HTML without the Headaches

I must admit, the very thought of using HTML in my auctions used to terrify me (pinky swear you won't tell the people at eBay). HTML. Doesn't it sound so very high-tech and geeklike? But HTML isn't all that scary once you realize that it's just a fancy name for Hypertext Markup Language, a pretty easy to use language for creating online content. All you need to know is the markup part. HTML uses tags to mark up pages to include elements such as text and graphics in a way that Web browsers understand. A Web browser sees the tags and knows how to display the document (that is, the Web page). HTML also makes possible the whole work of links. When you click a link, you jump to another place: another Web page, document, or file, for example.

Many eBay sellers somehow think that putting dancing bears, flaming graphics, and background music in their auctions will bring in more bids. Unfortunately, that's pretty far from the truth. People go to your auctions to find information and get a great deal on something they want, not to be entertained. They need to see the facts, placed cleanly and neatly on the page.

 The addition of music to your auction may cause another problem: an extremely s-l-o-o-o-o-w page load for those on dialup connections. If loading your page takes too long, believe me, most people will click back and go to another listing.

So what should you do to attract buyers? I spent most of my career in the advertising business, and the byword of good advertising is, "Keep it simple!" An organized and well-written selling description will outsell dancing bears and pictures of your children every time.

That's why HTML is now my friend — you can create a professional look for your sales through the use of varied typefaces, type sizes, and colors. In Technique 21, I show you how to create templates using an HTML generator. But using the generator without understanding the commands is akin to using a language translator without speaking a word of the language — you're never really sure if what's coming out is correct or how to make minor tweaks yourself. In this technique, I want you to understand what HTML commands are all about.

Writing Your Title and Description

I'm sure most of you are already selling on eBay, so I'm not going to bore you with a beginner's tutorial on writing auction descriptions.

What I'd like to do is to go over some of the glaring mistakes that constantly appear in eBay listings so you can avoid them. Often sales are lost because of obscure titles and overcomplicated selling policies.

All CAPITAL titles

The reason scribes of long ago invented upper- and lowercase letters was that they made phrases and sentences easier to read. When titles appear in all capitals, they are not interpreted as quickly by prospective buyers when their eyes dance over a search result or page.

 Often, when somebody uses all uppercase in auction titles, it looks like a crazed salesman is screaming at the reader. Use upper- and lower-case in bold face type within your *descriptions* instead by using HTML. Read on to learn how.

It is okay to use uppercase letters for a few, *select* words in your title. Take a look at the titles listed here; decide for yourself which ones make effective use of capital letters:

- ✔ NIB Cloud Dome White Photo Background PORTABLE BOARD STAGE
- ✔ Rare LOU GEHRIG Authentic Signed 1934 baseball card NR
- ✔ HIGH RELIEF 1921 PEACE DOLLAR PCGS MS65 NR

- ✔ NEW NFL Bobblehead BRIAN URLACHER Chicago Bears Limited Edition
- ✔ NEW Ladies Black Wool Kenneth Cole Skirt $79 Size 8 NR
- ✔ BEAUTIFUL VINTAGE 23" ARMAND MARSEILLE DOLL

It's easy to see that in a page loaded with hundreds of listings, those in upper- and lowercase combined are easier to read.

Wasted titles

In my research (see Part II), I found that over 65 percent of people searching eBay are searching titles only. To my mind, that makes the 55 characters allowed in an eBay title the most valuable real estate on the site.

Treat your titles with respect. Titles are not advertising, they are tools for the eBay search engine. If your title reflects what prospective buyers want, they'll click your listing to find out more.

 Many eBay sellers use comments in their titles. While teaching classes at eBay University, I've polled the students and have still to find anyone who searches for these words: Nice, LQQK, Must See, Great, WOW, or Cool.

Take a look at some actual item titles and think about how you could improve them:

- ✔ MS65 PCI FULL STRUCK 1921 MORGAN DOLLAR NICE!
- ✔ GARLIQUE, All Natural, 60 Tablets, WOW!!
- ✔ VINTAGE SET PORCELIAN ROSES**LQQK**NR**
- ✔ GREAT Fendi purse Must see!!!!
- ✔ COOL! *BLACK ONYX* silver pendant

There is plenty of room in these titles to list colors, types, sizes, and more descriptive nouns that would make better use of the space. ***Bottom line:*** Use as many keywords as the title will allow.

Negative comments

I'm sure many of us have run across listings that are overrun with negativity. What sells your item (aside from clear and complete information) is a positive tone throughout your description. Here are some examples:

- ✔ DO NOT BID ON MY ITEM UNLESS YOU UNDERSTAND AND FOLLOW MY STRICT POLICIES!

- ✔ If you have a less-than-10 feedback rating, do not bid — it will be cancelled.

- ✔ I will only send one e-mail requesting your information. If you don't respond, the item will be relisted and I will leave negative feedback!

- ✔ If the bidder does not contact me within three days of winning the auction, the item will be relisted and negative feedback will be given.

- ✔ WE WILL FILE NON-PAYING BIDDING ALERTS ON ALL DEADBEAT CUSTOMERS.

I'm sure when you read those comments, you felt a bit queasy. Although there may be a reason for the seller to make those remarks, the way they are phrased makes the reader uncomfortable.

Try to use a nice tone when listing your sales requirements. That way, your verbiage won't set up what could (otherwise) be a positive transaction as an adversarial deal!

 Make your policies in smaller letters — I don't mean teeny-tiny, but smaller. This will get the message across without becoming overbearing.

Getting Friendly with HTML

When you want to dress up your auctions, you *could* use one of eBay's graphic themes. (Remember that will add an additional 10 cents to your listing fee.) You could insert your own graphics into your listing, and it wouldn't cost you a penny more.

But even if you use one of eBay's lovely graphic designs, you would still need to format your text. That's where your HTML coding comes in.

 You can also use HTML to insert multiple pictures in your descriptions to better promote your item. This won't cost you a penny extra, and you can still use eBay's Pictures Services' one free photo for your top-of-listing picture. For information on how to upload your images to a server, see Technique 19.

What HTML can do

Take a look at Figure 20-1; it contains an auction description typed in the Notepad program that you'll find in Windows Accessories.

• **Figure 20-1: Raw auction text in Notepad.**

If I add some appropriate HTML coding from Table 20-1 (at the end of this technique) to the file, the auction page will look a whole lot different, as shown in Figure 20-2.

**Portable Photography Backdrop Stage
from Cloud Dome**

Ebay Sellers! This is for you! Are you tired of trying to find a nice clear spot to take your pictures for eBay sales? Sure you could spend a fortune on backdrops and muslin, but this handy, portable stage works (without glare) flawlessly every time. This is the most versatile product that I've found for tabletop photography.

The Infiniti Board is white textured, washable and scratch proof. It can be used flat or curved; the height and curve are adjustable with the attached locking cords. The total size is 19 inches wide by 28 inches long.

I scour the country looking for new reasonably priced tools for the eBay seller. Check my feedback to see that customer service is the byword of my eBay Business. Winning bidder to pay calculated Priority Mail (2 to 3 day) shipping based on distance. Please use the eBay Shipping Calculator below. Type your zip code in the box below to determine your shipping rate. If time is not of the essence, please email and we will quote a lower FedEx Ground shipping rate. Please submit payment within a week of winning the auction. Credit cards graciously accepted through PayPal.

This item is NOT being drop-shipped by another party. We have these in stock and will ship immediately - directly to you!
GET IT QUICKLY! I ship via 2 - 3 day Priority Mail.

Click below to...
*Visit my ebay Store **for low prices** on handy seller tools and Cloud Dome Products*

• **Figure 20-2: Auction description dolled up with HTML.**

Pretty cool, huh?

How HTML works

HTML uses a series of codes to indicate display specifics to a browser, such as when text should be bold or italic, or when text is actually a link. Brackets are used to indicate commands: What's within them is an instruction rather than actual text that should appear on your page.

In the example that follows, the b and I in brackets indicate that text between them should be formatted **bold** and *italic*. Notice that there is both a start formatting and end formatting indication (`<b>` starts bold formatting and `</b>` ends it). Here's one example:

> ✔ HTML start and end tags:
>
> `<b><I></I></b>`

✔ The same tags with text between them:

`<b><I>eBay tools</I></b>`

✔ The resulting text on your page:

eBay tools

See? Using such commands you can set up text on a page to be formatted in bold, begin a new paragraph, fall into a list format, and so on.

 Table 20-1 lists many of the common HTML tags to get you started.

A few things to keep in mind about HTML:

✔ Don't worry about placing a return at the end of a line. You must use a command to go to the next line so pressing Enter on your keyboard has no effect on what the page looks like.

✔ It's not necessary to put the paragraph command at the beginning and at the end of the paragraph. This is one command that doesn't need a close. Just put the command, `<p>`, where you want the breaking space.

✔ The same principle applies for a horizontal rule, `<hr>`. Just place the command where you want the line and it will appear.

✔ Most HTML coding commands have a beginning and an end. The beginning code is in `< >` and to end the formatting, you must repeat the code — only this time with a slash `</ >`.

✔ Because people have different fonts set up on their computers, they may not have the funky font you want to display. Be sure to list (as in the code shown here) alternate fonts for your text. If you don't, different browsers may substitute other fonts that might look *really* funky on some readers' pages!

If you'd like to see how HTML looks, I've placed an auction description here and put the HTML code in bold so it's easier to spot:

```
<center><font
   face='VERDANA,HELVETICA,ARIAL'
   color='crimson' size=5>
<B>Portable Photography Backdrop
   Stage<BR>from Cloud Dome</B>
</font></center>
<center><font face='verdana,arial,hel-
   vetica,sans serif' color='Black' size=4>
Ebay Sellers! This is for you! Are you
   tired of trying to find a nice clear
   spot to take your pictures for eBay
   sales? Sure you could spend a fortune on
   backdrops and muslin, but this handy,
   portable stage works (without glare)
   flawlessly every time. This is the most
   versatile product that I've found for
   tabletop photography. </font>
<BR><center><font face='verdana,arial,hel-
   vetica,sans serif' color='Black' size=2>
The Infiniti Board is white textured,
   washable and scratch proof. It can be
   used flat or curved; the height and
   curve are adjustable with the attached
   locking cords. The total size is 19
   inches wide by 28 inches long. <P>
<img src="http://www.collierad.com/white-
   board.jpg">
<font face='verdana,arial,helvetica,sans
   serif' color='Black' size=2><center>
I scour the country looking for new rea-
   sonably priced tools for the eBay
   seller. Check my feedback to see that
   customer service is the byword of my
   eBay Business. Winning bidder to pay
   calculated Priority Mail (2 to 3 day)
   shipping based on distance. Please use
   the eBay Shipping Calculator below. Type
   your zip code in the box below to deter-
   mine your shipping rate. If time is not
   of the essence, please e-mail and we
   will quote a lower FedEx Ground shipping
   rate. Please submit payment within a
   week of winning the auction. Credit
   cards graciously accepted through
   PayPal.<br>
```

```
<b>This item is NOT being drop-shipped by
   another party. We have these in stock
   and will ship immediately - directly to
   you!<BR></font>
<font face="verdana,arial,helvetica,sans
   serif" color="crimson" size=2><I>
GET IT QUICKLY! I ship via 2 - 3 day
   Priority Mail.</b> </I></font><P>
<I><font
   face="verdana,arial,helvetica,sans
   serif"color='Black' size=3><p>
Click below to... <BR>
<A HREF=
   http://cgi6.ebay.com/ws/eBayISAPI.dll?Vi
   ewSellersOtherItems&include=0&userid=mar
   sha_c&sort=3&rows=50&since=-1&rd=1
   TARGET=_BLANK>
Visit my eBay Store <B><I>for low prices
   </I></B>on handy seller tools and Cloud
   Dome Products</A></B></FONT></CENTER>
```

 Note that the HTML code shown here is bold-faced to help you spot it, but it's not necessary to bold HTML code when you *use* it.

Using Tables

Have you ever noticed how some people manage to have a photo on the right or left side of their descriptions? It's really not that difficult to do. It just involves a little HTML code added to the listing using something called *tables*, which are thoroughly discussed in Technique 21.

In this example, there is a picture contained in a table on the left side of the description, as shown in Figure 20-3. (By the way, when the full version of this auction ran on eBay, with the kind cooperation of the people on *The View*, we raised over $1,000 for UNICEF!)

"The View"
Cast Autographed
Coffee Mug

Signed by
Joy Behar
Star Jones
Barbara Walters
Meredith Vieira

All you fans of *The View*, this is
your chance to own a coffee cup
autographed by all four stars of
the show. The proceeds from this
auction will be donated to
UNICEF. The winner will be
announced on ABC's *The View* TV
show on Monday. We'll be
checking this auction live on the
show on Wednesday, April 23rd,
2003 with Marsha Collier, the
author of *"eBay for Dummies"*.

Shipping will be via Priority Mail. Credit
cards are accepted through PayPal.

• **Figure 20-3:** An auction using tables with the picture on
the left.

The HTML code for this description goes like this
(the `<tr>` and `<td>` codes make up the table format):

```
<table align=center cellpadding=8
   width='80%' border=7 cellspacing=0
   bgcolor='White'>
<tr><td>
<center><font
   face='VERDANA,HELVETICA,ARIAL'
   color='crimson' size=5>
<B>"The View"<br>Cast
```

```
Autographed<br>Coffee Mug</B></font><P>
<img width=250 src='http://images.auction-
   works.com/viewmug.jpg'>
</td>
<td>
<center><font
   face='VERDANA,HELVETICA,ARIAL'
   color='crimson' size=3>
<b><i>Signed by</i><br><b>Joy
   Behar<br>Star Jones<br>Barbara
   Walters<br>Meredith Vieira</b>
</font><p>
<font face='verdana,arial,helvetica,sans
   serif' color='Black' size=2>
<B>All you fans of <i>The View</i>, this
   is your chance to own a coffee cup auto-
   graphed by all four stars of the show.
   The proceeds from this auction will be
   donated to UNICEF. The winner will be
   announced on ABC's <i>The View</i> TV
   show on Monday. We'll be checking this
   auction live on the show on Wednesday,
   April 23rd, 2003 with Marsha Collier,
   the author of <i>"eBay for
   Dummies"</i></B>.</font><P>
<font face='verdana,arial,helvetica,sans
   serif' color='Black' size=1>
Shipping will be via Priority Mail. Credit
   cards are accepted through PayPal.
   </font>
</CENTER></td></tr></table>
```

TABLE 20-1: BASIC HTML CODES

Text Code	How to Use It	What It Does
`<b></b>`	`<b>eBay tools</b>`	**eBay tools** (bold type)
`<I></I>`	`<I>eBay tools</I>`	*eBay tools* (italic type)
`<b><I></I></b>`	`<b><i>eBay tools</b></i>`	***eBay tools*** (bold and italic type)
`<font color=red></font>`	`<font color=red>ebay tools</font>`	Selected text appears in red. (This book is in black and white so you can't see it.)
`<font size=+1></font>`	`<font size=+3>eBay</font> tools`	eBay tools (font size normal +1 through 4, increases size *x* times)
` `	`eBay tools`	eBay tools (inserts line break)
`<p>`	`eBay<p>tools`	eBay tools (inserts paragraph space)

(continued)

TABLE 20-1 *(continued)*

Text Code	How to Use It	What It Does
`<hr>`	`cool eBay<hr>tools`	cool eBay ——————— tools (inserts horizontal rule)
`<h1><h1>`	`<h1>eBay tools</h1>`	**eBay tools** (converts text to headline size)

Code For Lists	How to Use It	What It Does

`<ul><li>`
`</ul>`
	`<ul><li>I accept`
	`<li>PayPal`
	`<li>Money Orders`
	`<li>Checks</ul>`
		I accept
		· PayPal
		· Money Orders
		· Checks

`<ol><li>`
`<ol>`
	`<ol><li>I accept`
	`<li>PayPal`
	`<li>Money Orders`
	`<li>Checks</ol>`
		I accept
		1. PayPal
		2. Money Orders
		3. Checks

Linking (Hyperlink) Code	How to Use It	What It Does
`<img src>`	`<img src="http://www.yourwebsite.` `com/imagename.jpg">`	Inserts an image from your server into the description text

`<A HREF=  >`	`<A HREF= http://www.yourwebsite.`
	`com/shippinginfo.htm>Click Here`
	`for shipping info</A>`
		When selected text is clicked (in this instance, *Click here for shipping info*), the user's browser goes to the page you indicate in the URL

TARGET=_BLANK	`<A HREF= http://www.yourwebsite.`
	`com/shippinginfo.htm`
	`TARGET=_BLANK>`
		When inserted at the end of a hyperlink, it opens the page in a separate browser window

Table Code	How to Use It	What It Does
`<table border>`	`<table border=4>`	Puts a border around your table at a width of four pixels

`<table>`
`</table>`
	`<table>`
	`sample text`
	`</table>`
		The table command must surround *every* table

`<tr></tr>`
`<td></td>`
	`<tr><td>text</td><td>text</td>`
	`</tr><tr><td>text</td><td>text`
	`</td></tr>`
		Table row `<tr>` must be used with `<td>`
		Table data to end and open new boxes.
		
		text text
		text text

Technique

21

Creating Your Own HTML Templates

When you're ready to take on eBay in earnest, it really helps to have a few auction description templates all set up and ready to go. This is what the big guys, those top sellers on eBay, do (granted, some do a better job than others). Although it's fun to play around with using different graphics as you sell on eBay — and I must admit, I've seem some cute ones — having a standard look to your ads establishes you as a serious, professional seller. After all, how often does eBay change its look? (Okay, maybe that's a bad example.) The answer is *not too often*. The colors and the basic look remain the same because this is eBay's very valuable brand.

What might go into a template? Well, you can insert your logo within your description, or add links to your Me page or your store, for example. Look at it this way: Your template can become your "brand."

Many auction-management services offer predesigned templates for your descriptions, but they often charge a lot of money for their services. Alternatively, you can put together your own template and update it occasionally.

 Keeping your look simple and showing off your product will bring in high bids. Getting carried away with graphics that have nothing to do with your item is distracting (unless you have a cute picture of your dog or cat — doesn't everyone like a fluffy mascot?).

Most HTML generators are often overwhelming and hard to learn. What to do? Here's my secret to good-looking templates: I have been working with easy-to-use software for a long time. In this technique, I show you how to design simple templates in GlobalSCAPE's CuteHTML. I think it's a great tool that grows with you. The more HTML you understand, the more you can do with it.

Also, on my Web site, I offer a quick HTML generator that you can download and use. It will give you an easy template that you can customize with only a little extra HTML knowledge.

Setting Up Your Templates

Few things in this life are absolute necessities, but photos in your eBay listings definitely are! It's a good idea to begin by building a template that includes a space for a photo. You can use a program called CuteHTML to do just that.

 Check out Technique 20 for a sample of a basic layout written in HTML.

Getting CuteHTML

CuteHTML is a wonderful HTML generator from GlobalSCAPE. The software (like me) has been around for many years and over time has added many useful features, though not so many that the program is difficult to use.

You can download a free trial version at

    www.globalscape.com/o/914

After your free trial is over, you can opt to purchase the software for $19.99. It's worth it: The software will be a workhorse for you, as it has been for me, through thousands of auctions.

 CuteHTML is also bundled with another product, CuteFTP. CuteFTP is an extremely easy-to-use program for uploading your eBay pictures to your Web space. Read more about CuteFTP in Technique 19.

Adding text and graphics with CuteHTML

After you've downloaded and installed it, open CuteHTML and you'll see a page with some code on it. Just drag your mouse over this text and delete it.

 The first time you use CuteHTML, choose Tools, then Settings. In the Settings dialog box, select the Word Wrap check box. With Word

Wrap activated, the text you enter will wrap to the next line so you can see all the text on the screen. If Word Wrap is not activated, your text will go off the edge of the screen as you type, wasting valuable time scrolling back and forth to read it.

The first thing to do is to create a table that contains a photo on the right and text on the left.

1. **Click the Table button on the toolbar.**

   A Table palette appears.

2. **Click the top-left corner and drag to the right until the label at the bottom reads 2 by 1 table, as shown in Figure 21-1.**

   This creates a table with two cells side-by-side. When you release your mouse, the table palette disappears, and the HTML coding for 2 cells will appear on-screen, as shown in Figure 21-2.

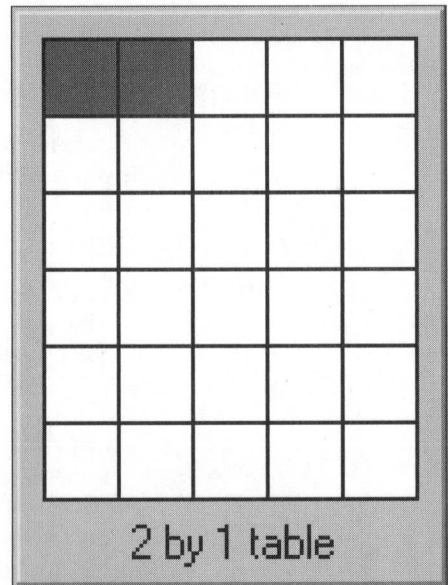

• **Figure 21-1: Creating a table with two cells.**

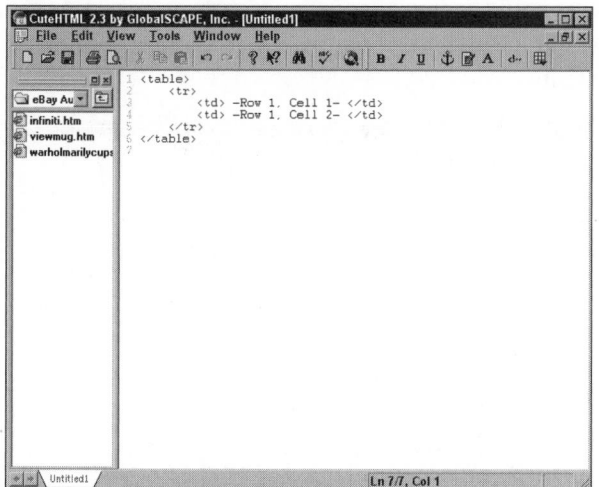

• **Figure 21-2:** Coding for a 2 x 1 table in the CuteHTML screen.

 In CuteHTML, all HTML coding is in blue by default. Words you input into the program are in black. Anchors (which are places you indicated to open another Internet page upon a click by the viewer) appear in green; links to Web pages or images appear in red.

 As an alternative to using the graphic toolbar, you can also click Tools and select most of the tags from *Insert Tag* that you want to insert.

3. Highlight the text Row 1 Cell 1 space between the HTML opening and closing code, and click the Image button in the toolbar. (It looks like a little picture.)

The Image Tag dialog box opens.

4. Type the Internet address (URL) where your image is stored in the Source text box, as shown in Figure 21-3.

If you want to alter the size of your image, you can also type in a numeric pixel width or height (or both) in the appropriate boxes.

5. Click OK, and the HTML code for the image will appear.

6. Highlight the Row 1 Cell 2 text on your screen, and enter the description text you want to appear next to the picture.

For convenience, you can also open an auction description you've already written in the Windows Notepad, and copy and paste it into the cell space.

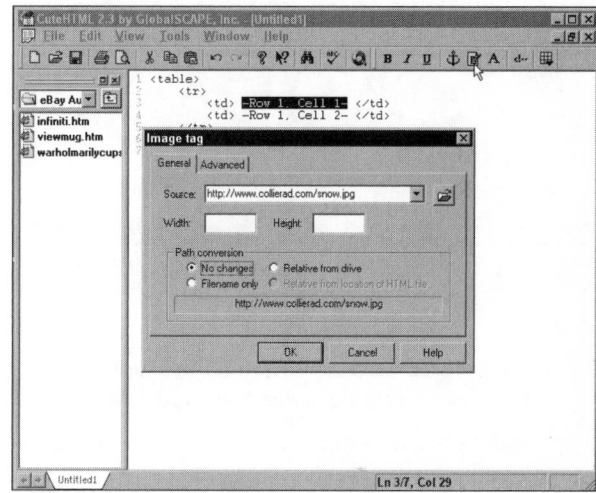

• **Figure 21-3:** Inserting a picture URL.

 If you want to visually check your progress as you go, click the View In Browser button (the teeny magnifying glass over a world globe) on the toolbar. This opens up your work in a browser window, looking as it would appear when viewed on the Internet.

Adding HTML formatting

If you preview your text in an Internet browser at this point, as in Figure 21-4, you notice that all the sentences run together in one mammoth paragraph. Adding HTML text attributes fixes this. You can use buttons on the toolbar to add text attributes or links.

To set text attributes, follow these steps:

1. Highlight the text you want to change.

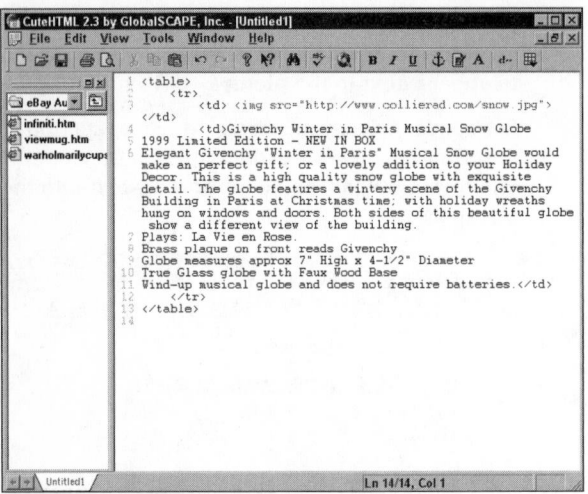

• **Figure 21-4:** A screen filled in with the image URL and straight text.

2. **Click the formatting button on the toolbar for the text formatting styles you want to apply.**

3. **Make your selection, and the attribute coding is automatically inserted.**

 If there are additional commands that you'd like to insert (such as line break, paragraph, list, and so on) and you do not see the corresponding button on the toolbar, type an open HTML command bracket < and the first letter of the command. A list of suggested commands drops down in the next text space; this is the program's "Tag Tips." Click the one you need, and the HTML command is inserted. Then type the closing bracket >. Use the table of HTML tags in Technique 20 for suggestions.

Once you've gone through these steps, the CuteHTML screen will look like the one in Figure 21-5.

Now you can see your final auction description, which will look like Figure 21-6, by clicking the View In Browser button on the toolbar.

Save your HTML when you're happy with the results. When you're ready to use that auction description,

just open the file, copy the code, and paste it into the eBay auction description area for the appropriate item.

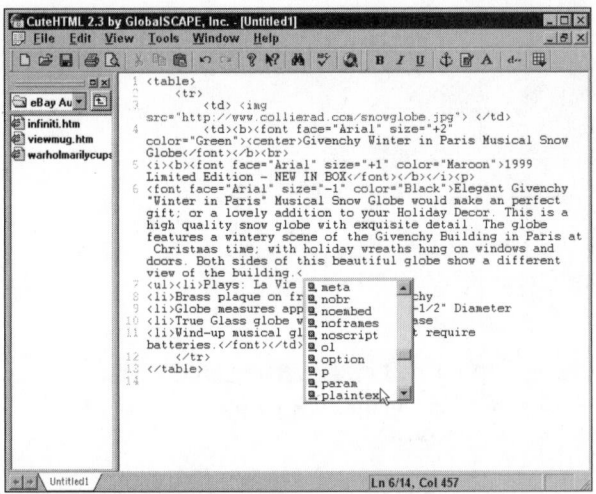

• **Figure 21-5:** Inserting the final paragraph break using CuteHTML's Tag Tips.

• **Figure 21-6:** A beautiful, quickly created template!

CuteHTML has many other features, including custom colors, anchors, and spell check. Once you've learned the basics and can create your own templates, poke around and see how fancy you can get with this small (but powerful) program.

Getting Quick, Basic Templates Online

Because there are times you are in a hurry, and just can't take the time to fool with *anything,* I've put a free ad tool on my Web site at

```
www.coolebaytools.com
```

When you land on my homepage, click the link in the navigation bar labeled `Cool Free Ad Tool`. You jump to my very cool instant template page, shown in Figure 21-7.

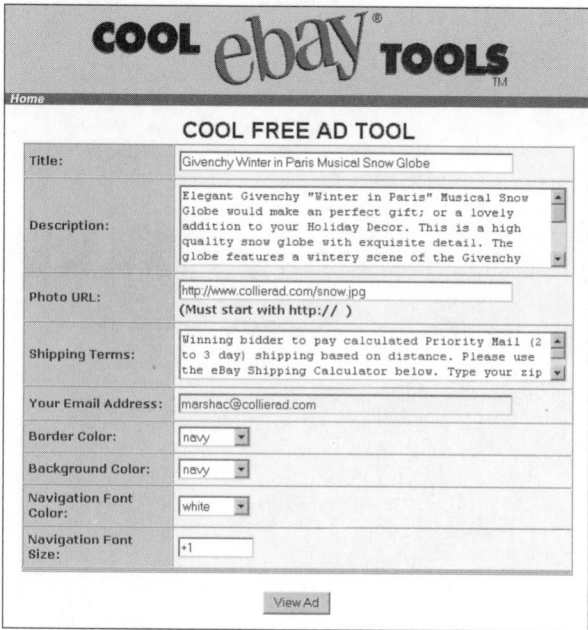

• **Figure 21-7: The Cool eBay Tools ad tool.**

Follow these steps to set up a quick eBay template using this tool:

1. Type in the headline for your description in the Title text box.

2. Enter a description in the Description box. You can copy and paste prewritten text from Notepad or a word-processing program, or just write your copy text as you go along.

3. Enter the URL of your image in the box that asks for it.

4. Enter the e-mail address that you use for eBay. I do not keep your e-mail information; it is used to put code in your description for a Have a Question link.

5. Select the colors and borders from the drop-down menus by clicking the down arrow on the side of each box.

6. Click View Ad.

On the page that appears, you see how your new auction description looks (as in Figure 21-8).

• **Figure 21-8: Your instant eBay ad.**

Scroll down and you see a box containing the auction description HTML code. (See Figure 21-9.)

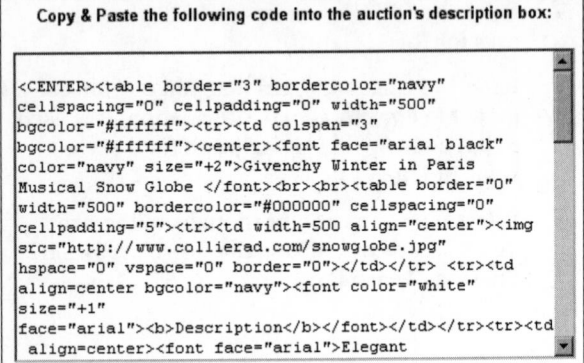

Copy & Paste the following code into the auction's description box:

```
<CENTER><table border="3" bordercolor="navy"
cellspacing="0" cellpadding="0" width="500"
bgcolor="#ffffff"><tr><td colspan="3"
bgcolor="#ffffff"><center><font face="arial black"
color="navy" size="+2">Givenchy Winter in Paris
Musical Snow Globe </font><br><br><table border="0"
width="500" bordercolor="#000000" cellspacing="0"
cellpadding="5"><tr><td width=500 align="center"><img
src="http://www.collierad.com/snowglobe.jpg"
hspace="0" vspace="0" border="0"></td></tr> <tr><td
align=center bgcolor="navy"><font color="white"
size="+1"
face="arial"><b>Description</b></font></td></tr><tr><td
 align=center><font face="arial">Elegant
```

• **Figure 21-9: HTML coding for your auction.**

Your code can be copied and pasted directly into the eBay description area of the Sell Your Item form (or any eBay listing tool). Also, you can add HTML codes to your auction description, or even add another picture.

Part IV

Finishing Off Your Auctions

The 5th Wave   By Rich Tennant

"You gotta see this! One minute left to bid on 100 pounds of celebrity belly-button lint, and we're still the only bidder!"

Technique 22

Notifying Winners and Sending Invoices

Save Time By

- ✔ Thanking your winners
- ✔ Using an e-mail template
- ✔ Getting quicker payments by sending out invoices

Thank goodness, somebody submitted a winning bid on one of your items in an auction. It's a good feeling. When I get those end-of-transaction e-mails from eBay, I whisper a silent YEAH! Then I hold my breath to see if the buyer will go directly to PayPal and make the payment. Usually, that's what happens. More and more buyers are getting savvy and understand about paying immediately after winning an item.

New buyers, and those who buy or win multiple items from you (my favorite kind of buyer!) usually wait to hear from you regarding payment and shipping. Many newbies feel more comfortable hearing from you and knowing who they are doing business with. Also, in the case of multiple purchases, you have to recalculate the postage. The sooner you contact the buyer, the sooner you'll get your payment.

Notifying Winners

eBay sends out an end-of-transaction e-mail to both the buyer and the seller. The e-mail is informative to the seller and, hopefully, a welcome e-mail for the buyer.

Figure 22-1 shows you a typical, "yippee, you won" e-mail. It is brightly colored and joyful, probably designed to evoke some strong level of excitement in the buyer. Note that in the winner's e-mail, there is a link for the buyer to pay via PayPal.

Both e-mails have similar information; the one to the buyer will have the link to pay now. The seller's e-mail will have a link to create an invoice. Either of these linked forms include:

- ✔ Item Title
- ✔ Item Number
- ✔ The Final bid or Buy It Now price
- ✔ Quantity

✔ Seller's/Buyer's User ID

✔ Seller's/Buyer's Details (first initial, last name, city, and state)

✔ Seller/Buyer's e-mail addresses

✔ Ship-to ZIP code

✔ A bunch of links:

▶ For the buyer to confirm his or her ZIP code

▶ To view the item; this link is good for up to 90 days. (Note that this is the only place you get this link, and unless you subscribe to eBay's Selling Manager, you'd better keep hold of it.) Sold items remain on your My eBay page for 30 days, but the items disappear from the eBay search engine within 2 weeks.

▶ A buyer's link to complete checkout to let the seller know the intended payment method

▶ eBay Help

▶ A feedback link

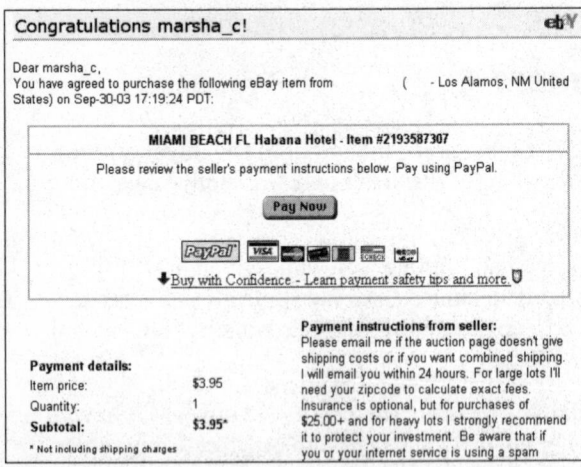

• **Figure 22-1:** Lucky you! You're a winner!

That's a lot of information, and I'll bet the average user just glances over it and either deletes it (bad idea) or files it in a special folder in his or her e-mail program. (Create extra folders in your e-mail program and drag all sold items to an eBay Sales folder,

and all purchased items to an eBay Buy folder — delete the e-mails when the transaction is finished and the feedback is left.)

If you think eBay's notification is good enough, it's time to rethink your customer service policy. An e-mail to the buyer at this point is important. Customer contact is key to a good transaction.

 If the buyer sprints directly to PayPal and sends you some money to pay for a purchase — a different e-mail is required. Thank them for their payment and let them know when the item will ship (see the next section, "Thanking them kindly").

Thanking them kindly

I know you're happy that the customer bought your item, and you know you're happy. Now's the time to let the customer know just how darned tickled you are that this person spent hard-earned money with you.

Time to send out a thank-you e-mail. This is a quasi-invoice and informational note. What should go in it? Well, try to keep in mind what your mother said — always say *please* and *thank you*. After thanking the buyer for purchasing your goods, be sure to cover the following points (this is where the *please* part comes in):

✔ **Item name.** Lest they forget what they purchased from you.

✔ **Payment terms.** Let the buyer know what forms of payment you will accept and how long you intend to wait for your money.

✔ **Payment Address.** Be sure to tell them where you want the money sent.

✔ **PayPal link.** Inserting a PayPal link in your e-mail is a snap and may pay off in some rapid payments; see Technique 33 for instructions.

✔ **Return Policy.** Will you accept returns? Under what circumstances? It's OK if you won't accept returns, but be sure that you had that information in your item description *before* the purchase was made.

✔ **Reminder to print the e-mail and enclose it with payment.** Veteran eBay sellers can all tell you stories about the money order that arrived with no item number, no return address, no e-mail address — basically no clue as to what the payment was for.

✔ **Store pitch.** If you have an eBay Store, mention it here. If not, just be sure to tell the buyer you are happy to have them as a customer and you look forward to serving them again.

✔ **Feedback pitch.** Most PowerSellers that I know include a small pitch at the closing of the e-mail that asks buyers to leave feedback on eBay, which will encourage future sales. Remind the customers to e-mail you immediately if there is a problem when the order arrives. Stress how you want them to be happy with their purchases. That may stave off some of the knee-jerk negatives that beginners tend to leave when an item arrives cracked. (They shoulda bought insurance — and it helps to *require* insurance on very fragile items.)

That ought to do it. Including this information will make your newbie buyer or old-time veteran feel at home doing business with you.

Thanks for the money!

Sometimes you have to beg for payment. On the other hand, when some blessed buyer pays immediately through PayPal, it's time to show your gratitude. Now's the time to send the old thanks-for-the-money e-mail. This doesn't have to be very long. Make it short and sweet and to the point. Be sure to

✔ Thank the customer for the purchase and swift payment.

✔ Let her know when the item will ship.

✔ Let the person know that the business is appreciated.

✔ Let the customer know when feedback will be left. (I leave feedback *only* when the transaction is complete — when the buyer has received the item and is happy with the transaction. You find more about the gentle art of feedback in Technique 25, later in this part.)

Auto-sending invoices from Selling Manager

One of my favorite features of eBay's pay-by-the-month program, Selling Manager, is that I can follow the progress of my sales from the Selling Manager Summary page.

When an item has been won or paid for via PayPal, you can click the appropriate link to see it in the list. Figure 22-2 shows my Sold Listings: Paid & Waiting To Ship area in Selling Manager.

• **Figure 22-2: Sold! And ready to ship.**

Notice that there is a record number next to the winner's e-mail address. To send an e-mail

1. **Click the record number, and you're sent to the Sales Record for that transaction.**

When you get there, you see the items sold to that buyer. (If there have been more than one purchase from the same buyer, you see this notation and can click to combine the purchases in the Sales Record; see Figure 22-3.)

2. **Click the button that says E-Mail Buyer.**

3. **Select the appropriate e-mail to send.**

You can personalize the e-mail further by altering the Selling Manager supplied templates (if you choose) before you send it.

4. **When you're ready for the e-mail to go, click Send.**

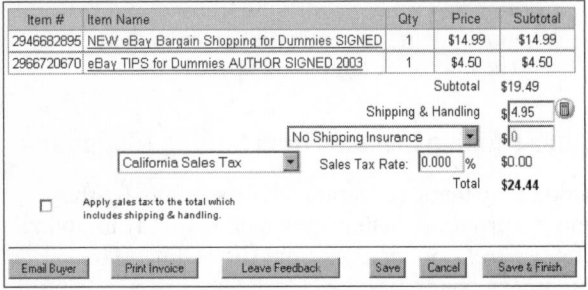

• **Figure 22-3: Item summary and the E-Mail Buyer link.**

Selling Manager's Customizable Templates

Selling Manager has seven e-mail templates that you can quickly and easily customize. As shown in the figure below, these templates allow you to add Auto Text features; eBay's server fills in the proper information for that particular transaction.

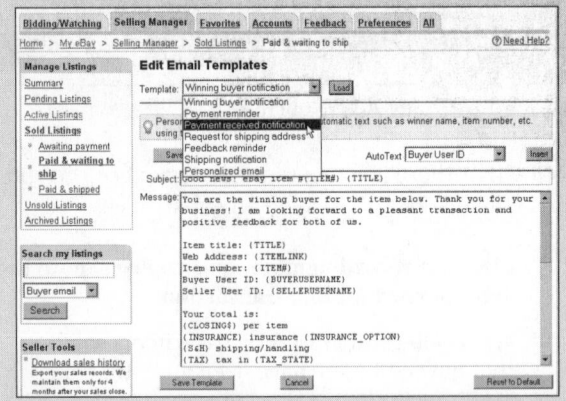

Notice the drop-down menu that provides tools to edit any of the eBay-supplied templates.

When a winner buys an item, I have a preformatted Winning Buyer Notification letter I created from a template; if they pay immediately via PayPal, I also have a payment-received e-mail.

Sending Out Invoices

Invoices look very professional. On the other hand, they can be kind of cold and impersonal. PayPal or eBay will send out invoices automatically for you, but thankfully, you can customize them.

PayPal invoicing

To set up your PayPal account to send out invoices automatically when an item is purchased, follow these steps:

1. **Go to www.PayPal.com and log on to your account.**

2. **Click the Auction Tools tab.**

3. **Scroll down to the heading Invoicing Your Buyer and click the link Winning Buyer Notification.**

The PayPal Winning Buyer Notification Registration page, as pictured in Figure 22-4, is displayed.

• **Figure 22-4: PayPal's invoicing central command.**

4. **Select the eBay User ID you have registered with PayPal from the field labeled Registered User ID.**

If you have more than one eBay User ID registered with PayPal, they will all be listed in a drop-down box in this field.

5. **Customize your message.**

The blank text box allows you to enter up to 2,000 characters of a personal message. There's plenty of room to fill in all the niceties, so lather it on. Remember, this is a cold invoice when it comes to the buyer. It's up to you to make it nice!

6. **If you have a logo you use on your Web site or eBay Store, enter the URL that will display it, so it appears at the top of your invoice.**

You can also select any image that you'd like to appear on your invoice using this method. The image must be 150 x 100 pixels in size, 10 KB or smaller, and in a GIF, JPG, or PNG format.

There's also a link in the logo area that you can click to test whether your logo appears correctly or not. If the logo appears in the pop-up window, everything is fine. If not, double-check the URL.

7. **From your registered e-mail addresses, choose the one you want to appear as the return address on the invoice.**

Again, if you have more than one address registered, you select the correct one from the drop-down list.

8. **Select the Send a Copy to Me check box if you want to receive copies of all the invoices that PayPal sends out for you.**

FYI, getting these copies may get very old fast. But give it a whirl for a while so you can see what your buyers see.

9. **Click the Submit button at the bottom of the page.**

You'll be notified that the invoicing service will commence sometime within the next 24 hours.

eBay invoicing

eBay also allows you to send out invoices for your items, but they're not sent out automatically (as they are by PayPal). For eBay invoices, you have a couple of options:

✔ **From the item page:** Invoices can be sent directly from the item page, as shown in Figure 22-5. You will see the Send Invoice bar only if you are signed into eBay when you visit the auction.

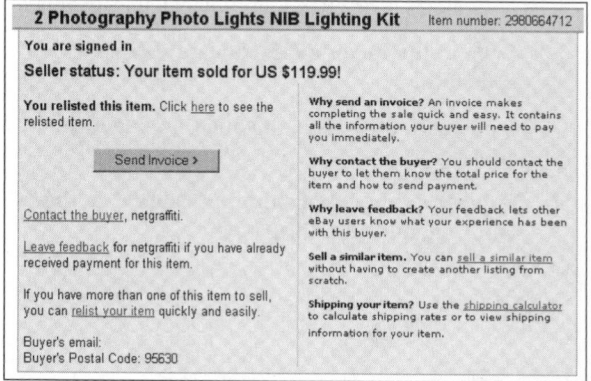

• **Figure 22-5: Click the Send Invoice button in the center of the item page.**

✔ **From My eBay:** Go to My eBay, Items I've Sold page, as shown in Figure 22-6. If the winner did not pay for the item immediately through PayPal, you'll see a Send Invoice button in the Next Step/ Status column.

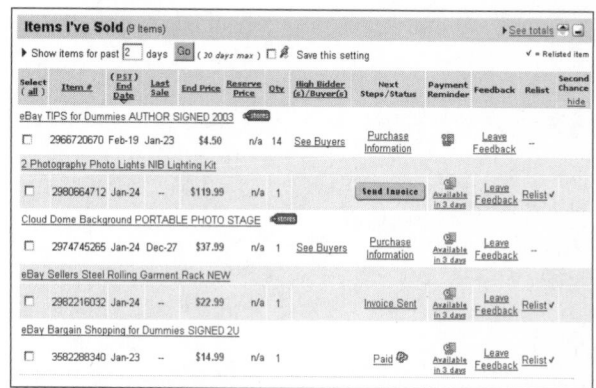

• **Figure 22-6: My eBay status on Items I've Sold.**

After you click the button to send an invoice, you see a page with the auction details, as shown in Figure 22-7. The buyer's User ID, ZIP code, and editable details are displayed.

If the shipping amount hasn't been filled in, due to multiple purchases or calculated shipping, you can calculate it easily enough.

1. Click the teeny calculator button next to the Shipping and Handling box.

A version of the eBay shipping calculator opens.

2. Type in the buyer's ZIP code, and click calculate.

A postal quote based on your shipping location appears.

3. Enter the calculated shipping amount in the Shipping and Handling box.

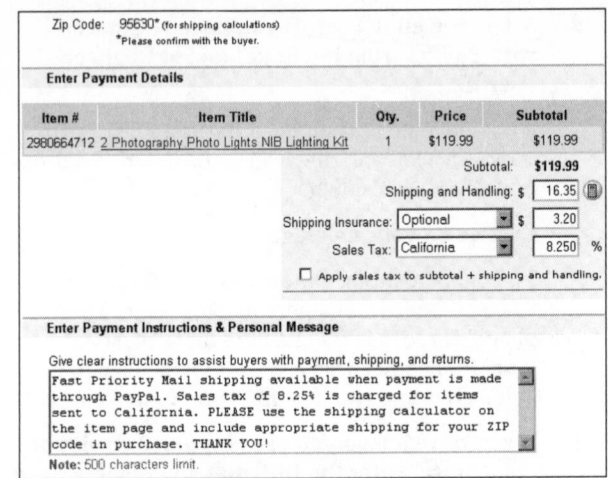

• **Figure 22-7:** Customizing the eBay invoice.

You may also enter a personal message and further payment instructions here. You are allowed up to 500 characters.

Technique 23

Tracking Payments

You've created a winning ad, run a successful auction or sale, notified the winner, and sent off an invoice. Now it's time for the big payoff: getting the money in hand for your item. eBay and PayPal work in concert to offer several tools to notify you when a payment is made.

 The first place to check for payments is your My eBay Items I've Sold page or eBay's subscription-based Selling Manager. If you're expecting payments, be sure to check the page a couple of times a day. When a buyer makes his or her payment, eBay updates your records so that you know — and you can quickly ship the item to the buyer.

PayPal also sends you a Payment Received e-mail — but I have a few caveats about using this form of notification. In this technique, I give you the lowdown on getting paid fast and show you the pitfalls to avoid.

Tracking Payments through My eBay

eBay's selling information tools, the My eBay page (for part-time sellers) and eBay's Selling Manager (for sellers moving up to 100 items a month), give you a plethora of information on each of your transactions. The most important of these features may just be instant notification when a payment for an item has been received.

 If you do not receive any form of notification of a payment received from a buyer, check your PayPal account before taking the time and trouble to send a Non-Paying Bidder notice. A new eBay buyer may have misspelled your e-mail address or applied the payment to an incorrect item number. If this is the case, simply e-mail the buyer and ask that he or she cancel any payment made with the wrong item number or e-mail address and then resubmit payment with the correct information.

Tracking payments on your My eBay page

Once again, the Items I've Sold area of My eBay comes to the rescue if you're a beginning seller. As if by magic, whenever one of your buyers makes a payment on your item through the PayPal service, your My eBay page indicates that the item has been paid. Take a look at Figure 23-1, and notice that the bottom item shows it's been paid for via PayPal.

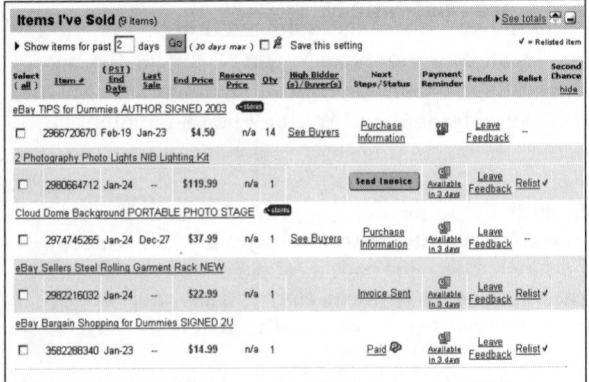

• **Figure 23-1: Items I've Sold reflecting a PayPal payment.**

To confirm the information about a payment shown in the Items I've Sold area of My eBay:

1. **Click the Paid via PayPal link in the item's listing.**

You are taken to a PayPal login page.

2. **Sign in to PayPal with your password and click Continue.**

3. **The PayPal payment details screen appears, giving you all the information on the purchase.**

4. **When you finish reviewing the payment information, click the Return to Log button at the bottom to go to your Account History page.**

From here you can transfer the money to your bank account. (For more information about PayPal banking features, see Technique 28.)

If you don't want to do any other business using your PayPal account, click the Log Out link at the top-right of the page.

Tracking payments from eBay's Selling Manager

Selling Manager makes many selling processes considerably easier. Take a look at Figure 23-2, my Selling Manager Summary page. From here, you can see how many buyers have paid for their purchases — and, sadly, how many haven't.

Here the Paid and Ready to Ship link in Figure 23-2 has the number 3 to the right of it; three items are ready to ship. To see the details on these items, you just click this link.

Summary		
Last updated on Jan-25-04 13:22:50 PST		
Quick Stats	GMS	# of listings
Pending Listings		**0**
▪ Starting within the next hour		0
▪ Starting today		0
Active Listings	$0.00	**22**
▪ Closing within the next hour		0
▪ Closing today		0
Sold Listings	$2,533.83	**35**
▪ Awaiting Payment		3
▪ Awaiting Payment, eligible for Non-Paying Buyer Alert		0
▪ Paid and ready to ship		3
▪ Paid and waiting for feedback		17
▪ Paid and shipped		29
▪ Unpaid and eligible for Final Value Fee credit		0
* Updates every 10 mins.		

• **Figure 23-2: My Selling Manager Summary.**

When you arrive at the Sold Listings, Paid & Waiting to Ship page, each transaction is listed, as in Figure 23-3. The bold dollar-sign icon to the right of a listing confirms that a payment has been made.

After you ship the item, you can access the Sales Status & Memo page shown in Figure 23-4 by clicking the Record Number next to the item on the Sold Listings page. Select the Shipped On check box and enter the shipping date on this page. When you click save, the record moves from the Sold Listings, Paid & Waiting to Ship page to the Paid and Shipped page. This change is also reflected in the numbers on the Summary page (refer to Figure 23-2).

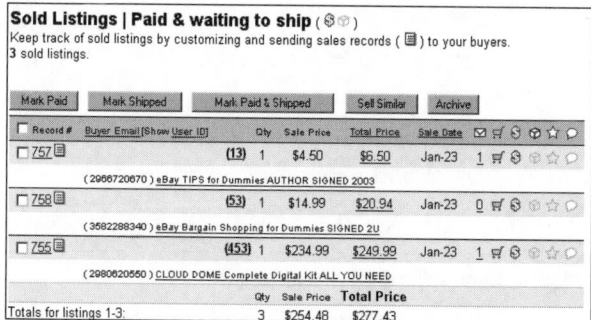

• **Figure 23-3:** Items paid for and waiting to ship.

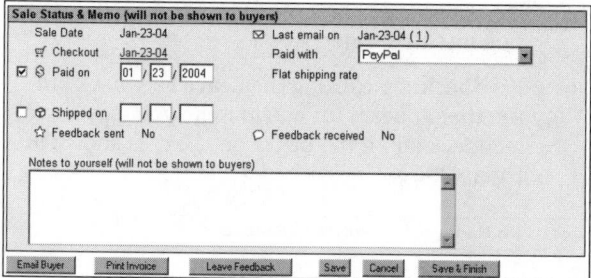

• **Figure 23-4:** Selling Manager's editable sales record information area.

Tracking Payment Info with PayPal

PayPal is the premier tool to use to verify a payment before you panic that it hasn't been made. They have numerous methods of confirming payments, but you need to make the final confirmation, yourself.

Payment notification via e-mail

When you receive a payment through PayPal, PayPal sends you a payment confirmation e-mail. The e-mail is a good tip-off that you've received a payment. Notice I said *good,* but not infallible.

In these days of spoofed e-mail sent by scammers to remove money from hard-working people's wallets, I rarely rely solely on e-mail confirmation. When I receive one of these e-mails, I open my Internet browser and go right to PayPal, www.PayPal.com myself. Once I get to the PayPal Web site, log on, and look at my PayPal Account Overview, I can confirm with certainty that the payment has been made.

PayPal's Post-Sale Manager

Post-Sale Manager is a super tool that just doesn't get enough credit. Unless he's using a tool such as Selling Manager or a third-party management software, the beginning seller need look no further than the PayPal Post-Sale Manager.

To use this tool, follow these steps:

1. **Open your browser and go to** www.PayPal.com.

2. **Log in with your e-mail address and password.**

   The main PayPal Account Overview screen is displayed. Under the line showing your PayPal account balance, you'll see a link labeled eBay Items Sold.

3. **Click the link next to the eBay logo that indicates Items Sold.**

   After a little whirring and grinding on your hard drive's part, you'll see the Post-Sale Manager, shown in Figure 23-5.

This truly useful tool lists all your recent eBay sales. If the item has been paid via PayPal, the payment will be noted here.

There are several columns in the Post-Sale Manager:

- ✔ **Select box:** If you want to invoice a bunch of sales all at once, put a check in this box, and click the Invoice button at the bottom of the page.

- ✔ **Item Number:** This box contains a clickable link to the actual item purchased on eBay. If you click the link, the page opens in a second window, so you still have access to the Post-Sale Manager.

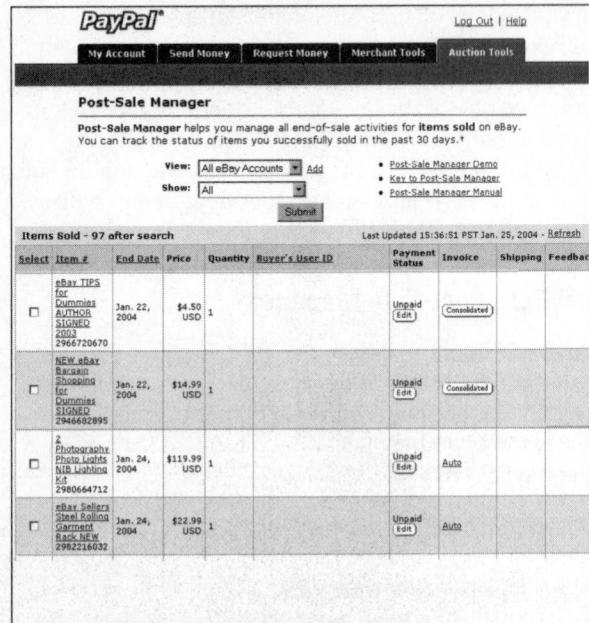

• **Figure 23-5: PayPal's Post-Sale Manager.**

✔ **End Date:** Shows the date the item was purchased on eBay.

✔ **Price:** Lists the final price of the item.

✔ **Quantity:** Shows the number of items purchased.

✔ **Buyer's User ID:** Clicking the User ID in the Post-Sale Manager opens a blank e-mail form (pre-addressed to the buyer) so you can contact the buyer with any questions or comments you may have.

✔ **Payment Status:** Here is where you can see whether the buyer has paid you via PayPal. If you have received payment though the mail, you may click the Edit button and a Post-Sale Manager Payment Status box opens, as shown in Figure 23-6.

✔ **Invoice:** From here you can click to send an invoice (see Technique 22 for more about sending invoices) from PayPal. This column also reflects whether PayPal has automatically sent an invoice for you. Refer to Figure 23-5.

Post-Sale Manager - Payment Status

According to our records, you have not received a completed PayPal payment for this item. If you did receive payment, please specify the payment method and click Mark As Paid.

Item Name:	2 Photography Photo Lights NIB Lighting Kit
Item #:	2980664712
End Date:	Jan. 24, 2004
Price:	$119.99 USD
Payment Method:	○ Personal Check
	○ Cashiers Check/Money Order
	○ PayPal
	PayPal Transaction ID:
	○ Other Method
	Please specify:

[Mark as Paid] [Cancel]

• **Figure 23-6: Editing payment status.**

✔ **Shipping:** If a payment has been made, you can click the Ship button that appears to initiate a UPS shipment. (Technique 37 has more information on this service.)

✔ **Feedback:** By clicking the Leave Feedback button that appears for a paid item, you may leave feedback about the buyer on eBay, as shown in Figure 23-7.

Post-Sale Manager - Leave eBay Feedback

To leave eBay feedback for the buyer, choose a feedback rating, enter your comment and click Leave Feedback. If you have already left feedback for this buyer on eBay, click Mark As Done.

Buyer eBay ID:	fransbargains
Item Name:	eBay Bargain Shopping for Dummies SIGNED 2U
Item #:	3582288340
Rating:	○ Positive
	○ Neutral
	○ Negative
Feedback:	
Characters left:	80

[Leave Feedback] [Mark As Done] [Cancel]

• **Figure 23-7: Leaving eBay feedback through PayPal.**

The PayPal Post-Sale Manager helps you easily keep track of your eBay sales with no need for additional software.

Technique 24

Tracking Your Shipments

Save Time By

✔ Tracking the mailman

✔ Hunting for Brown

✔ Finding FedEx info

Shipping — what a joy! If you think packing the items is a pain, just wait until your shipping company fumbles the ball and delays — or loses — one of your shipments and your buyer gets on your case. Getting the item out the door in a timely manner is your job. But for some unknown reason, eBay buyers seem to think that sellers are responsible for moving the package every inch of the way. You're not. Once the package leaves your hands, either the Post Office, FedEx, or UPS determines its fate.

You often have to lend a hand by tracking an item (often a painful task). The package arrives in the recipient's town and it's on a truck. *What truck,* you say? Who knows? You're waiting for a shipment from your supplier — you ran out of one of your stock items and you have orders coming in. You *have* to know where your stuff is! Getting tracking information for your shipments gives a bit of credence to the element of faith involved in the very act of shipping.

Tracking the Mail

Here's where you get thrown a curve. The United States Postal Service only "tracks" truck-to-truck movements of Express Mail (without extra fees) — that's overnight shipping, government style. eBay buyers and sellers rarely use overnight shipping, as the cost is extremely prohibitive.

The common mode of mailing identification for checking for delivery on eBay packages is fee-based Delivery Confirmation. A bar-coded sticker is either supplied at the Post Office or printed from your printer connected to a USPS enabled site. Delivery Confirmation is available for just about all classes of mail (First Class must be ¾" at its thickest point to qualify), and it lets you know whether a delivery has been attempted or whether the package was delivered. That's the extent of the tracking. The fees vary based on the class of mail and whether you are using online postage (see Technique 36 for how to get these at little or no cost).

Although Delivery Confirmation does not provide actual tracking information, it is accepted by PayPal as reasonable proof of shipment. This is necessary for you as the seller to be protected under PayPal's Seller Protection Policy. (See Part V for more information.)

Tracking with Delivery Confirmation

Individual package information for Delivery Confirmation or Express tracking is available online for 60 days after your shipment at the USPS Web site (shown in Figure 24-1):

`www.usps.com/shipping/trackandconfirm.htm`

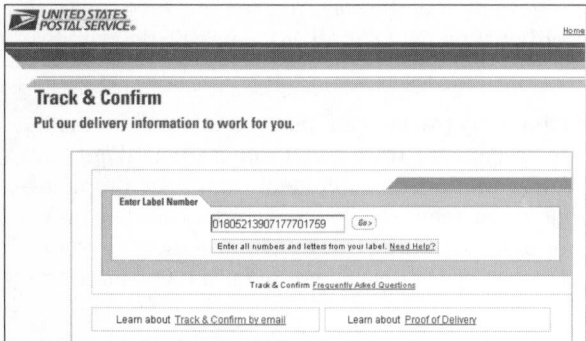

• **Figure 24-1:** Track and confirm your shipments with the U.S. Postal Service.

To look up package information:

1. **Go to the Post Office Web site at**

   `www.usps.com/shipping/trackandconfirm.htm`

2. **Input the (very long) Delivery Confirmation (or Express) tracking number and click Go.**

   The delivery date and time are displayed.

3. **For further information, click the Shipment Details link.**

   You get complete details on your shipment, as in Figure 24-2.

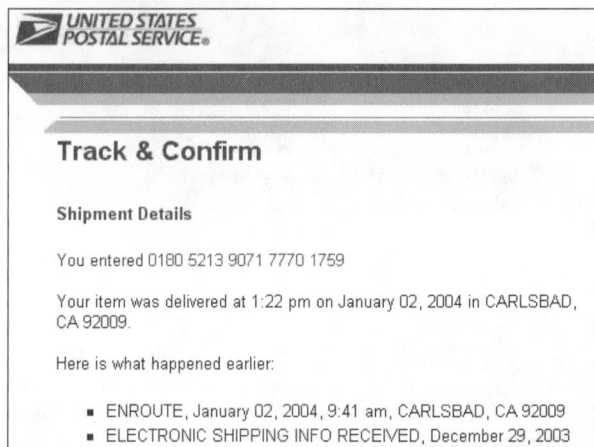

Track & Confirm

Shipment Details

You entered 0180 5213 9071 7770 1759

Your item was delivered at 1:22 pm on January 02, 2004 in CARLSBAD, CA 92009.

Here is what happened earlier:

- ENROUTE, January 02, 2004, 9:41 am, CARLSBAD, CA 92009
- ELECTRONIC SHIPPING INFO RECEIVED, December 29, 2003

• **Figure 24-2:** Full details about your package's journey.

Tracking for users of endicia.com

If you use endicia.com as described in Technique 36 to print your postage and labels, you can access tracking information in a much more efficient manner.

1. **Open the DAZzle software and allow it to log on to the server.**

2. **Open the Endicia Postage Log shown in Figure 24-3.**

3. **Highlight the package you want to track.**

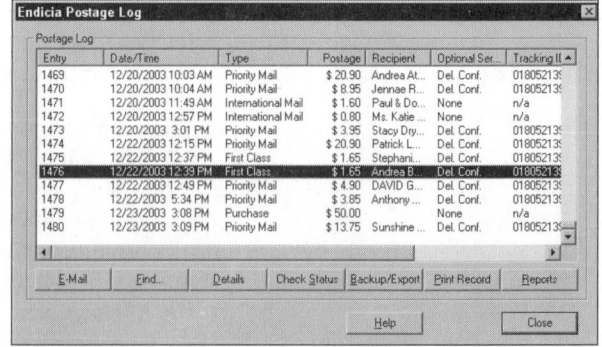

• **Figure 24-3:** Endicia.com's DAZzle Software Postage Log.

4. **Click the Check Status button.**

DAZzle pulls up an instant report directly from the Post Office servers and displays it, as shown in the example in Figure 24-4.

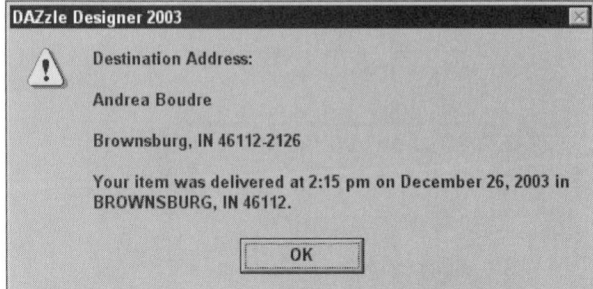

• **Figure 24-4: Your delivery information results.**

You can also get tracking and Delivery Confirmation information by calling the Post Office's toll-free number at 1-800-222-1181.

 Yahoo! can help save time when you're tracking incoming as well as outgoing packages. If you use Yahoo! as your home page, at My Yahoo, you can insert a feature called Package Tracker. It has direct links to the tracking pages of all major carriers.

Also, if you use the Google toolbar, just type any carrier's tracking numbers into the text box and Google will respond with tracking information.

Finding Out Where the Brown Truck Went

All packages sent by United Parcel Service (UPS) are assigned a tracking number. You'll be provided this number when you ship your package with their online service or at the local UPS counter.

If you have a UPS account, you can track a package from your UPS account area online at My UPS. If not, you can track a package in the UPS online package tracking area, as shown in Figure 24-5.

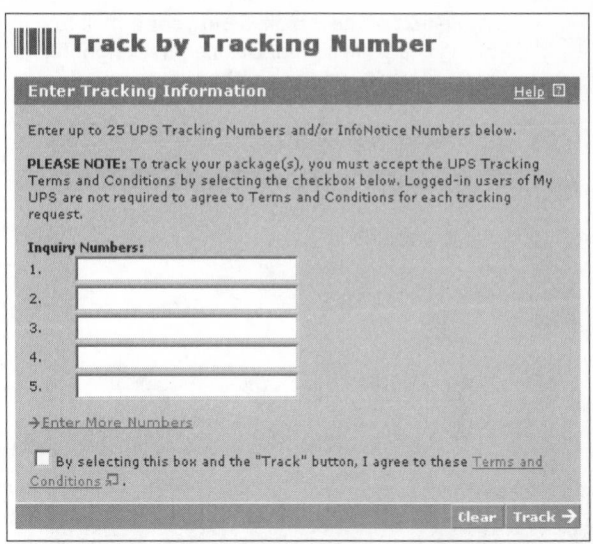

• **Figure 24-5: Tracking a package on the UPS Web site.**

To track a UPS package, just follow these steps:

1. **Open your browser and go to**

`www.ups.com/tracking/tracking.html`

The UPS *Track by Tracking Number* page appears.

2. **Enter the tracking numbers of the packages you want to locate in the text boxes provided.**

You can enter up to 25 different tracking numbers by clicking the Enter More Numbers link.

3. **Click the check box, confirming that you agree to UPS's Terms and Conditions.**

4. **Click Track.**

The delivery information appears.

To see the full transit details, click the Details link, and you'll see where your package stopped every inch of the way, as shown in Figure 24-6.

 UPS also has an e-mail tracking service. For tracking one package, put the tracking number in the subject line of your e-mail. For more than one package, type your tracking numbers in the text of the e-mail. Send your e-mail to totaltrack@ups.com. Detailed tracking information will be sent to you by return e-mail.

Track by Tracking Number

View Details

Status:	Delivered
Delivered on:	Dec 24, 2003 12:42 P.M.
Location:	MC WOMAN
Delivered to:	NORTHRIDGE, CA, US
Shipped or Billed on:	Dec 18, 2003
Tracking Number:	1Z 4E5 378 03 8263 177 8
Service Type:	GROUND
Weight:	4.60 Lbs

Package Progress:

Date	Time	Location	Activity
Dec 24, 2003	12:42 P.M.	VAN NUYS, CA, US	DELIVERY
	4:14 A.M.	VAN NUYS, CA, US	OUT FOR DELIVERY
Dec 23, 2003	11:25 P.M.	VAN NUYS, CA, US	ARRIVAL SCAN
	10:43 P.M.	VERNON, CA, US	DEPARTURE SCAN
	10:50 A.M.	VERNON, CA, US	ARRIVAL SCAN
Dec 19, 2003	12:18 P.M.	HODGKINS, IN, US	DEPARTURE SCAN
	11:51 A.M.	HODGKINS, IN, US	ARRIVAL SCAN
	8:41 A.M.	MAUMEE, OH, US	DEPARTURE SCAN
	12:29 A.M.	MAUMEE, OH, US	ARRIVAL SCAN
Dec 18, 2003	6:38 P.M.	SHARONVILLE, OH, US	DEPARTURE SCAN
	4:31 P.M.	SHARONVILLE, OH, US	ORIGIN SCAN
	9:08 A.M.	US	BILLING INFORMATION RECEIVED

Tracking results provided by UPS: Jan 27, 2004 3:29 P.M. Eastern Time (USA)

• **Figure 24-6:** My package was very well traveled!

Finding Your FedEx Package

FedEx Ground is becoming an increasingly popular, cost-efficient mode of package transport among eBay sellers. Coming from the back of the pack (ground shipping is a comparatively new product of FedEx), this service is becoming more and more reliable.

FedEx's tracking is simple enough. Quickly track packages by following these steps:

1. Go to the FedEx home page at

www.fedex.com/us

In the middle of the home page, you'll see a Track Shipments box (as shown in Figure 24-7).

2. Enter the tracking number *or* a Door Tag number (if supplied by a cranky buyer) in the tracking box.

You can find the door tag number on the tag left at the buyer's door when the FedEx driver attempts a delivery.

• **Figure 24-7:** The handy FedEx tracking box on the home page.

3. You may enter up to 25 numbers, pressing Enter between each number.

4. When you're through entering the numbers you want to track, click the Track It! button.

5. Your full tracking results appear, as in Figure 24-8.

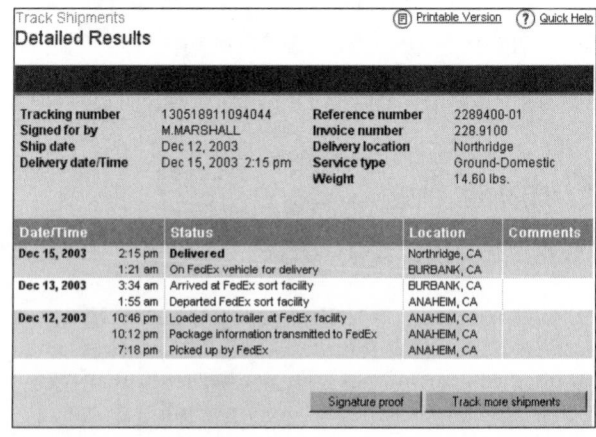

• **Figure 24-8:** Complete tracking information from FedEx.

25 Technique

Leaving Feedback Quickly and Gracefully

Save Time By

- ✔ Going straight to the Feedback Forum
- ✔ Posting feedback from Selling Manager
- ✔ Leaving feedback from an item page

When somebody asks me why eBay has become so popular, I say it is largely due to the community's participation in a feedback system. In February of 1996, eBay's founder, Pierre Omidyar, proposed the feedback system to eBay's 6-month-old community. After personally ending up in the middle of a few member squabbles, he felt that the community could police itself by leaving comments after transactions. "Give praise where it is due; make complaints where appropriate," he posted on the eBay message board — and so it began.

Every eBay member, when participating in a transaction with another, should provide a comment. If you don't leave a comment, you're really not completing your transaction. Leaving feedback on eBay is the last bit of paperwork you do to close a deal.

Here are some guidelines for participating in the feedback system:

1. **You may leave feedback for up to 90 days after a transaction completes.**

2. **After you leave feedback, it cannot be retracted — you are responsible and have to live with its contents for eternity.**

3. **Keep your feedback businesslike and don't make personal comments.**

4. **Do unto others as you would have them do unto you: If you have a problem, try to work it out with the other party via e-mail or phone before leaving negative feedback.**

In Technique 4, I show how to evaluate a community member's feedback ranking. This technique shows how to leave your mark on the eBay system by providing feedback about your transaction partners.

Using the Feedback Forum

At the bottom of almost every eBay page, there is a group of links. Click the one that reads Feedback Forum, and you'll be beamed to eBay's feedback Mecca, as shown in Figure 25-1.

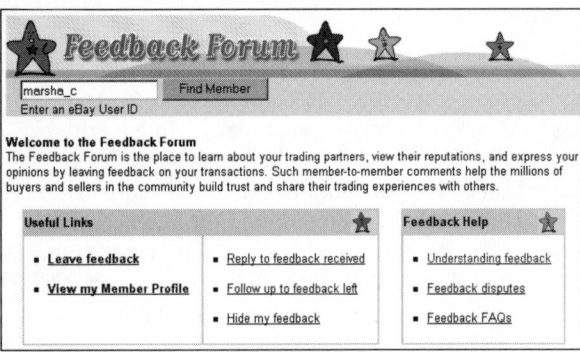

• **Figure 25-1:** eBay's Feedback Forum.

From this page, you can accomplish many feedback related tasks:

- **View a Member's Feedback:** At the top of the page, you can type in another user's ID and you'll be presented with a member profile. (This method is not quite as efficient as clicking the feedback number next to a user's name when you're looking at a transaction.)

- **Leave Feedback:** This is a very handy and efficient tool. If you click the Leave Feedback link, you are taken to a page (or pages) that lists all your outstanding transactions for the past 90 days. You may leave feedback for many transactions at once from this area.

- **View My Member Profile:** Click here to display a page where you enter your User ID to access your own feedback page. It's a lot easier to click the number next to your name when it appears on your transactions or your My eBay page — since you're there a couple of times a day anyway.

- **Reply to Feedback Received:** Here's a link that's worth its weight in gold! You can also find a similar link at the bottom of your Member Profile

feedback page. If you receive feedback that you feel requires a comment from you — especially neutral or negative comments — click here to find the transaction (see the list in Figure 25-2) and leave your side of the story.

Review and Respond to Feedback Comments Left for You

Visit the Feedback Forum for more info on feedback profiles.

Feedback 1-25 of 3065

[1] 2 3 4 5 6 ... 20 ... 40 ... 60 ... 80 ... 100 ... 120 ... 123 (next page)

Left by	Date	Item#	
(307) ☆	Jan-27-04 08:49:12 PST	2976009854	Respond
Praise: Great seller, exactly as described. Fast shipping. A+++++			
(301) ☆ ☺ me	Jan-26-04 20:10:53 PST	3580553775	Respond
Praise: Thnks Maarsha! Great Books! Great Ebayer! A++++++++++			
(45) ☆	Jan-26-04 13:15:52 PST	2980166675	Respond
Praise: What I always wanted, better pictures, and fast shipping			
(190) ☆	Jan-26-04 12:32:44 PST	2979287892	Respond
Praise: Wonderful Seller AAA+++ Great to Work with!! www.prettypartyplace.com			
(43) ☆	Jan-24-04 23:55:20 PST	3582288153	Respond
Praise: Well Packed, Promptly Shipped, Exactly as Described. A+++++++++++			
(55) ★	Jan-24-04 20:23:22 PST	2946682895	Respond
Praise: Great transaction! Highly recommended! Books are very informative!			
(55) ★	Jan-24-04 20:22:28 PST	2966720670	Respond
Praise: Very prompt with communication and shipping! Great to do business with!			

• **Figure 25-2:** Review and respond to feedback here.

To respond to feedback:

1. On your Feedback Forum Review and Respond page, click the link labeled Respond next to the transaction number.

2. On the page that appears, enter your response.

3. Click the Submit button.

You can now see your response in your feedback profile. Figure 25-3 shows sample of a feedback comment with a response.

(55) ★	Jan-24-04 20:23:22 PST	2946682895
Praise: Great transaction! Highly recommended! Books are very informative!		
Response by marsha_c - Thank you for your kind words!		

• **Figure 25-3:** Feedback with a response.

- **Follow Up to Feedback Left:** This link enables you to follow up on comments you have made about a buyer. This is very useful if you have left feedback prior to the completion of the transaction and have a change of heart.

If you've left a neutral or negative comment prematurely, this is a way to smooth things over (but only somewhat — remember your negative feedback becomes part of the other person's permanent record and affects his or her feedback percentage).

If you prematurely left a positive comment and the transaction goes to heck, you can also leave your negative follow-up comment here.

✔ **Hide My Feedback:** From here you make a setting to hide your feedback record from other eBay users. This is *not* a good idea. If people can't see your rating, they may not want to do business with you. Hiding your feedback will generally lower the bids you get on your items. Prospective buyers want to *see* your feedback!

If you're trying to overcome some bad feedback comments by hiding your feedback, you'll be stymied. When you hide feedback, a lousy feedback percentage will haunt you on your transaction pages. A far better idea is to participate in more transactions and get lots more feedback of the positive kind!

Posting Feedback from Selling Manager

As you can tell if you've read any other part of this book, I'm a big fan of Selling Manager. It essentially condenses your eBay business into one command central. Once you've heard from your trading partner that all is well, you can quickly leave feedback from your Selling Manager Summary page (see Figure 25-4).

Here's how to send feedback from Selling Manager:

1. **Click the Sold Listings: Paid and Waiting for Feedback link.**

    You arrive at the transaction listing of items waiting for feedback.

2. **Scroll down to find the transaction you want to leave feedback on.**

Summary
Last updated on Jan-27-04 19:07:39 PST

Quick Stats	GMS	# of listings
Pending Listings		0
▪ Starting within the next hour		0
▪ Starting today		0
Active Listings	$8.52	21
▪ Closing within the next hour		0
▪ Closing today		0
Sold Listings	$3,036.29	39
▪ Awaiting Payment		0
▪ Awaiting Payment, eligible for Non-Paying Buyer Alert		0
▪ Paid and ready to ship		1
▪ Paid and waiting for feedback		15
▪ Paid and shipped		38
▪ Unpaid and eligible for Final Value Fee credit		0

* Updates every 10 mins.

• **Figure 25-4: My Selling Manager Summary page.**

3. **Click the record number next to the listing.**

    The Sales Record page appears.

4. **Scroll down to the action links below the transaction information and click the Leave Feedback button.**

5. **Select an appropriate comment from your stored entries (as shown in Figure 25-5), or feel free to type in a new one.**

6. **Click the Leave Feedback button.**

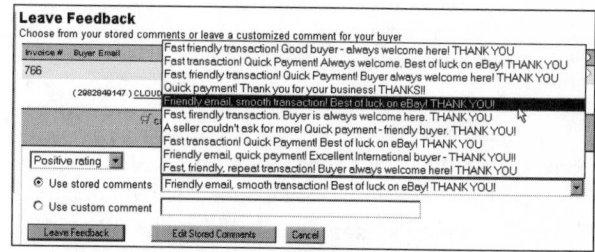

• **Figure 25-5: Selecting an appropriate feedback comment from Selling Manager.**

Entering Feedback from My eBay

On your My eBay Items I've Sold page (as in Figure 25-6), you can see transactions that ended up to 30 days ago. If you are not using Selling Manager, you can easily follow up on your feedback duties here as well.

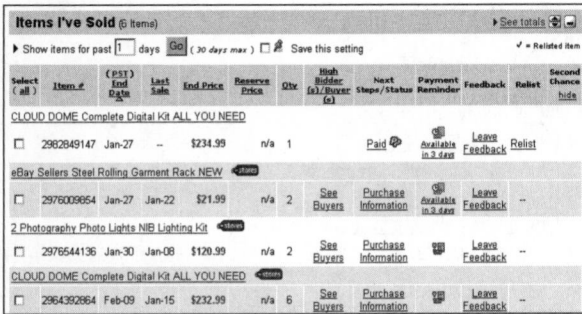

• **Figure 25-6:** My eBay Items I've Sold page, with feedback links.

You can click the Leave Feedback link for the transaction you want to work with. You'll be transported to the official Leave Feedback page, as shown in Figure 25-7.

Feedback Forum: Leave Feedback

⑦ Need Help?
Rating other members by leaving feedback is a very important part of transactions on eBay.

Please note:
- Once left, you cannot edit or retract feedback; you are solely responsible for the content.
- It's always best to keep you feedback factual; avoid making personal remarks.
- Feedback can be left for at least 90 days following a transaction.
- If you have a dispute, contact your trading partner to try and resolve the dispute before leaving feedback.

User ID:			Show all transactions
Item Number:	2982849147		
Rating:	○ Positive ○ Neutral ○ Negative ⦿ I will leave feedback later		
Comment:			80 chars max.

Leave Feedback

• **Figure 25-7:** The Leave Feedback form.

The other person's User ID will already be filled in, as will the transaction number.

To leave feedback (it's as easy as 1, 2, 3!):

1. **Click the radio button next to the Rating you want to leave (Positive, Negative, or Neutral).**

2. **Enter your feedback in the Comment field.**

    Your comment may not exceed 80 characters.

3. **Click the Leave Feedback button.**

Leaving Feedback from an End of Transaction E-mail

You got an e-mail when the transaction ended, and whether you noticed it or not, it contained a link to the item. This link can take you to the item for up to 90 days! Because you save this e-mail until the transaction is complete, you can use it to leave feedback just prior to deleting the e-mail.

Here's how to leave feedback from your e-mail:

1. **Sign into eBay.**

2. **Click the link on the e-mail to go to the transaction page, as pictured in Figure 25-8.**

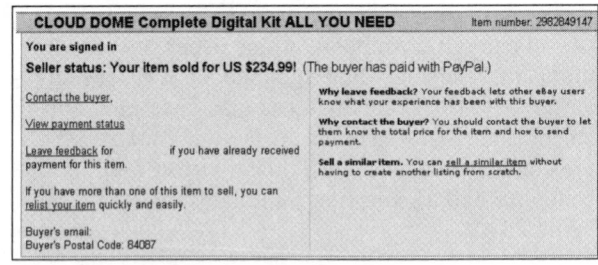

• **Figure 25-8:** The seller information on a closed transaction page.

3. **Click the Leave Feedback link to begin the process of leaving feedback for the other party.**

Technique 26

Downloading Your eBay Sales Reports

Save Time By

✔ Downloading sales info from eBay

✔ Reviewing eBay Store sales reports

✔ Streamlining reports

Reports, reports, reports; when you're active in the eBay selling community, you're deluged with reports. Reports are grand because they give you an idea of where your business is at any point in time. But the key to getting some value out of all these reports is knowing which reports are important to you, based on your levels of online selling.

When you're just starting out, these reports can help you find the direction for your business. But beware; delving into too many reports will make your eyes glaze over and cause you to second-guess everything you do. (*My advice:* Don't make major changes in your selling plan because of something you read in a report until you're sure something isn't working.)

eBay supplies some useful reports that give you a good snapshot of how things are going. Once you've set up your business in earnest, I suggest you graduate to a professional business tool to obtain even more sophisticated reporting features. (See Technique 48 for more on business reports.)

eBay Selling Manager's Reports

I like eBay's Selling Manager because it gives you the opportunity to keep all your selling information in one place. It also gives you downloadable reports that you can archive for your business records.

 You must subscribe to the Selling Manager product to get these reports. There is a $4.99 per month fee. The benefits of the product are mentioned throughout this book; it's an excellent choice for the beginning eBay seller.

Your eBay sales reports include important information about your transactions and download in a spreadsheet format. Here is the information you can expect to find in the reports you download:

✔ **Sales Record Number:** This is the number assigned to the transaction by Selling Manager for identification purposes.

✔ **User ID:** The eBay User ID of the person who purchased the item from you.

- ✔ **Buyer Zip:** The buyer's ZIP code.

- ✔ **State:** The state the buyer resides in.

- ✔ **Buyer Country:** The country your buyer lives in.

- ✔ **Item Number:** The eBay number assigned to the item when you listed it for sale on the site.

- ✔ **Item Title:** The title of the listing as it appeared on eBay.

- ✔ **Quantity:** The number of items purchased in the transaction.

- ✔ **Sale Price:** The final selling price of the item.

- ✔ **Shipping Amount:** The amount you charged for shipping the item.

- ✔ **Insurance:** If the buyer paid insurance, it will be listed next to the sales record.

- ✔ **State Sales Tax:** If you've set up Selling Manager to calculate sales tax for your in-state sales, and sales tax was applied to the item when it was sold, that amount is listed here.

- ✔ **Total Price:** This is the GSA (Gross Sales Amount) for the transaction.

- ✔ **Payment Method:** The method of payment used by the buyer. This is inserted automatically if the item is paid through PayPal or is manually inserted by you if paid by another method.

- ✔ **Sale Date:** The date the sale transaction occurred on eBay.

- ✔ **Checkout:** The date of checkout. This is usually the same as the transaction date.

- ✔ **Paid on Date:** The date the buyer paid for the item.

- ✔ **Shipped on Date:** The ship date you entered in Selling Manager.

- ✔ **Feedback Left:** Indicate whether you left feedback for the buyer with a Yes or No in this column.

- ✔ **Feedback Received:** The feedback rating (Positive, Negative, or Neutral) left for you by the buyer.

- ✔ **Notes to Yourself:** If you input any personal notes regarding the transaction in the Sales Record, they appear here.

 Keep in mind that Selling Manager reports are available on the site for only 3 months. So be sure to download your information regularly.

Notice that there is no column reflecting the eBay fees you paid for listing and selling the item. If you have plenty of time on your hands, you can create another column and input the fees from your eBay invoice for each individual item. Save time by bulk posting the monthly total in your bookkeeping program. (See Technique 47 for more information.)

Now, to get the file from eBay to your computer:

1. **To get to the download area, go to your My eBay page and enter the Selling Manager. The opening page of Selling Manager is your Summary page shown in Figure 26-1.**

• **Figure 26-1: My Selling Manager Summary page.**

2. **Under Seller Tools, click the Download Sales History link.**

You are sent to a Download Sales History page, like the one shown in Figure 26-2.

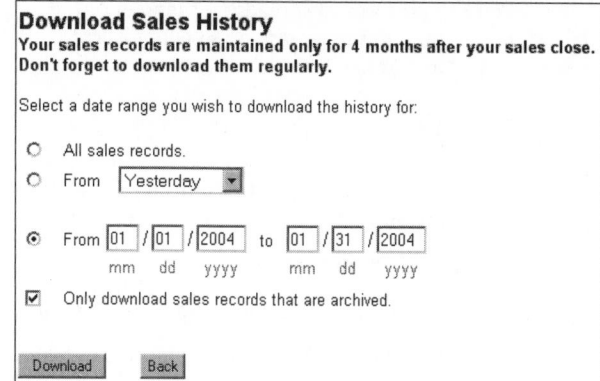

Download Sales History
Your sales records are maintained only for 4 months after your sales close. Don't forget to download them regularly.

Select a date range you wish to download the history for:

○ All sales records.

○ From ▢Yesterday ▾

◉ From ▢01 / ▢01 / ▢2004 to ▢01 / ▢31 / ▢2004
    mm   dd   yyyy   mm   dd   yyyy

☑ Only download sales records that are archived.

[Download] [Back]

• **Figure 26-2:** The Download Sales History page.

3. **Make settings here depending on the time period you'd like to include in your report.**

It's best to generate monthly or quarterly reports, so that your reports coincide with specific tax periods. You can always combine more than one report in your spreadsheet program to show different periods of time.

Be sure to put the dates in the *mm/dd/yyyy* format. Translated, that means: Use a 2-digit number for the month, a 2-digit number for the day, and the full 4-digit year.

4. **Select the check box marked Only Download Sales Records That Are Archived if you don't want pending transactions included.**

If you have some problematic transactions hanging over from another month and you want true figures by month, it's helpful to remove the default checkmark from this box.

5. **Click the Download button.**

Your file may take a minute or two to prepare and download. During this process, you'll be asked if you want to save, open, or cancel the download. Choose Save to save it to your hard drive. The file is downloaded in a format that can be opened in either Microsoft Excel or Microsoft Works spreadsheet programs.

6. **If you like, when the Save As dialog box appears, rename the file to reflect the sales month and year, as pictured in Figure 26-3.**

It's a good idea to create a directory on your computer with a name such as eBay Sales. In this directory, you can store all the reports you download from eBay, PayPal, or any other online service. Be sure to include this directory when you perform regular data backups.

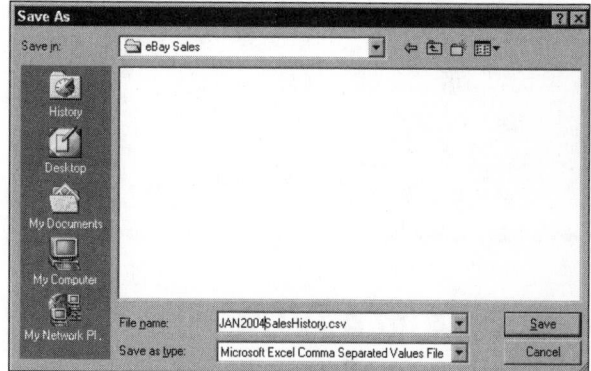

• **Figure 26-3:** Downloading the report to my eBay Sales directory.

Once the file is downloaded, you will see a confirmation with your new filename, as in Figure 26-4.

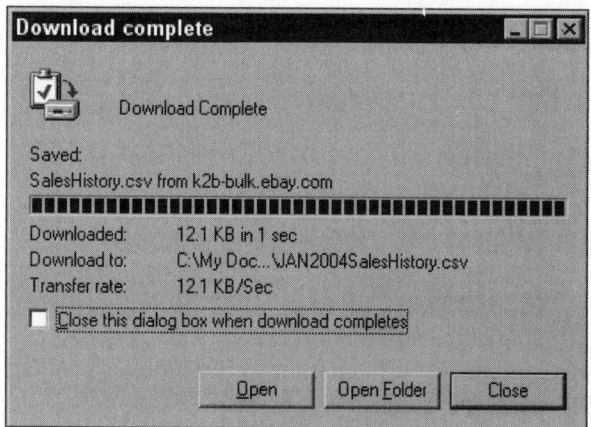

• **Figure 26-4:** Windows confirmation that your file has been successfully downloaded.

Now you can open the new file in your spreadsheet program, and it will look very similar to Figure 26-5.

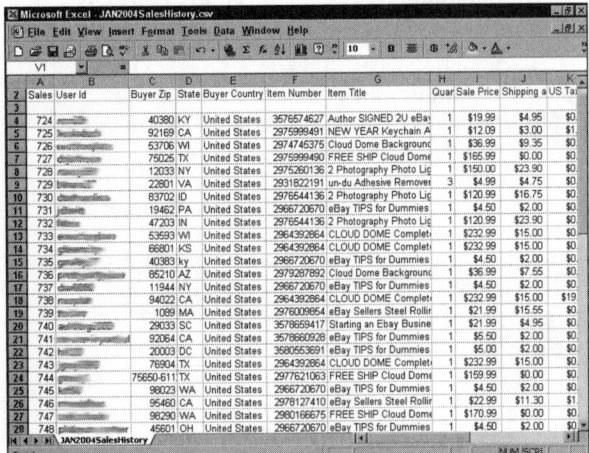

• **Figure 26-5:** My January 2004 eBay sales report.

Customizing a Works or Excel Spreadsheet

With simple spreadsheet commands, you can customize the look of your report. For example, if the column for Buyer Country is unnecessary for your records (you ship only within the United States, so the information is not useful), you can delete the column.

To delete the wasted space:

1. Highlight the column by clicking the column letter.

2. Choose Edit➪Delete.

Voilá! The offending column is no more.

The spreadsheet generated by Selling Manager is much more useful if you total up the columns. That way, you can see your total sales at a glance.

You can perform all spreadsheet tasks mentioned here in similar fashion in either Microsoft Works or Excel.

To total a spreadsheet column:

1. Click in the blank cell at the bottom of the column you want to total.

2. Click the AutoSum button.

3. Click and drag over the cells you want to sum.

But Excel has probably already done this for you.

4. Press Enter, and the total appears.

If you want to total the columns next to the one you just totaled, you don't have to re-input the formula. Just highlight the results box from your last formula and highlight boxes in the same row that you want to contain totals of the columns.

As shown in Figure 26-6, then choose Edit➪Fill➪Right.

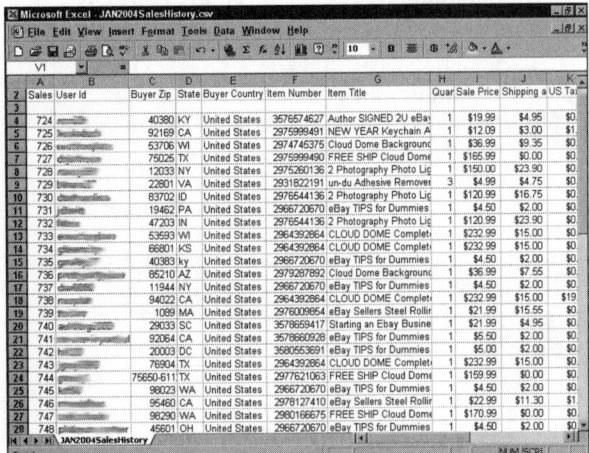

• **Figure 26-6:** Totaling the columns.

This copies the formula to the connecting boxes and all the columns are totaled, as shown in Figure 26-7.

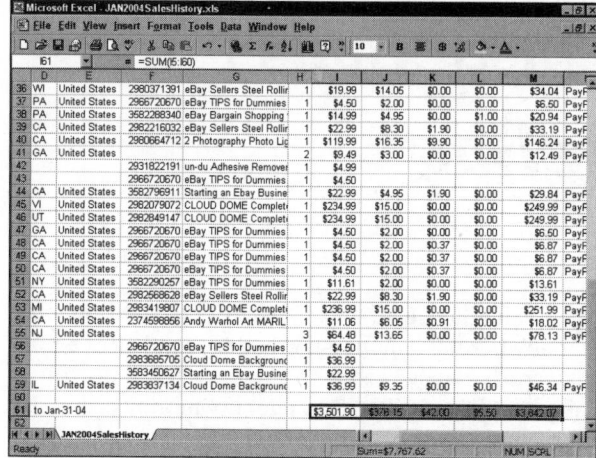

• Figure 26-7: All the totals are automatically filled in!

Your eBay Stores Sales Reports

If you have an eBay Store (if you don't now — you will after reading this book!) you get monthly reports from eBay. The previous month's reports arrive by e-mail around the 15th of the following month. You'll find an ever-popular CSV file included as an attachment. This will handily import into a spreadsheet program.

These reports differ from the Selling Manager reports considerably. While the Selling Manager reports give you accounting data, your eBay Stores reports give you an idea of sales trends by showing you sales ratios and data.

Here's the information you get:

✔ **Total Items Sold**

✔ **Total Sales Amount for the Month:** Pretty self-explanatory, huh?

✔ **Auction Data:** Sales broken down by eBay category including the following data:

  ▶ # of Listings

  ▶ # of Successful Listings

  ▶ Quantity of Items Listed

  ▶ Quantity of Items Sold

  ▶ # of Bids

  ▶ Gross Sales and # of Unique Buyers

✔ **Auction Ratios:** Listings separated into eBay categories, noting each category's ratios:

  ▶ % of Successful Listings

  ▶ % Successful Items

  ▶ Bids per Listing Ratio

  ▶ Bids per Item Ratio

  ▶ Average Selling Price per Item

✔ **Store Inventory:** A quick rundown of the items listed for sale, the quantity sold, gross sales, average selling price per item, and number of unique buyers.

Reporting Failed Transactions to eBay

Save Time By

- ✔ Identifying when your transaction has gone bad
- ✔ Filing a Non-Paying Buyer Alert
- ✔ Getting Final Value Fee refunds

There comes a time in all eBay sellers' lives when a transaction seems to be going nowhere. Payment isn't made, e-mail after e-mail goes either unanswered or answered with excuses: "I'll send you payment next week when I get paid." "You didn't get my money order? I sent it last week." (Sound at all familiar?)

Here's a typical horror story: "I've been having trouble with my bank lately, it's a small bank and I live out in the country — I'm sure the eCheck will clear any day now," a buyer told me recently. For two weeks, I saw a pending, constantly delayed eCheck in my PayPal account. The payment never cleared, and PayPal unceremoniously cancelled the pending payment to my account in a few days, with no reason or explanation. Puzzled, I went back to the transaction and checked the buyer's feedback rating. Boy, had it changed. Eight negative feedbacks in a row, and the sellers didn't hold back:

- ✔ "Paid with a fraudulent account. I lost 18.50 & my fountain pump! JERK!"

- ✔ "STOLEN BANK ACCOUNT! Lost over $100 from this Person! eBay—> Get her off!!"

- ✔ "STOLEN BANK ACCOUNT confirmed by PayPal! LOST Over $25 Bad eBayer, Get her OFF!"

- ✔ "Bad eBayer stolen bank account cheated me out of $32.00 do not trust !!"

- ✔ "Notified by PayPal that she's using a FRAUDULENT bank account, I lost $15.99"

Knowing When a Transaction Has Gone Wrong

The lesson to be learned is that when you're being put off — or are waiting inordinately long for a payment — go to the buyer's feedback. You may just get some hints about how the transaction will go.

A clear tip-off to a possible problem is when a buyer with low feedback has an unconfirmed address with PayPal. Be sure to check these out before you ship. PayPal Seller Protection does not protect you when you ship to an unconfirmed address.

Other times, your buyer may just disappear: no e-mail, no responses to phone calls (should you choose to contact your buyer by phone). It's money out the window.

 You can get the registered telephone number of anyone with whom you are currently involved in a transaction by going to the eBay Search page. Click the link that says Find Members. On the Find Members page, scroll down to the Contact Info section. Type in the item number and the other party's User ID, and eBay will send you an e-mail with the other party's telephone number. Your phone number will also be sent via e-mail to the other party.

Before you completely give up on a transaction, be sure you do the following:

1. Send a payment reminder from your My eBay page or Selling Manager.

2. Try to contact the buyer via e-mail.

3. Try to contact the buyer via phone (if the value of the transaction warrants the additional expense).

Filing a Non-Paying Buyer Alert

If you're caught in a situation with a missing-in-action buyer, eBay will refund a certain amount of your fee. But you must follow the correct procedures.

When you decide to spend no more of your valuable time chasing the buyer, follow these steps:

1. Go to the following Web site:

http://cgi3.ebay.com/aw-cgi/
eBayISAPI.dll?NPBComplaintForm

2. On this page, input the item number and click Send Request.

3. On the following page (shown in Figure 27-1), a drop-down menu appears; use it to select the reason for filing the alert.

4. Click Submit to file the alert.

 If your buyer has given you a good enough sob story that you're willing to forgive the entire transaction (they clicked Buy It Now in your store four times because they didn't think it worked the first three), you can select *Both parties mutually agreed not to complete the transaction.* This way, your buyer's reputation won't get a ding, and you can file for your Final Value Fee refund in 10 days.

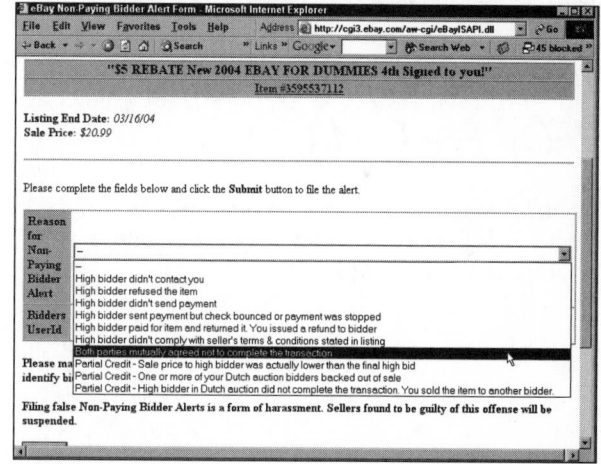

• **Figure 27-1:** Selecting a reason for the Non-Paying Buyer Alert.

After you file the alert, the buyer receives an e-mail something like the one shown in Figure 27-2. A copy of this e-mail is also sent to you. This e-mail will often get the MIA buyer moving — and then again, it might not.

 You must file a Non-Paying Buyer Alert no earlier than 7 days and no later than 45 days after the transaction ends.

```
Congratulations on your winning bid for eBay item 2954836420, CLOUD DOME w 7
inch Ext Digital Macro Photos.  Your seller, marsha_c, has informed eBay that
your payment hasn't been received yet.

If you have already sent payment or intend to pay soon, please contact marsha_c
at              immediately.  Simple misunderstandings are often
resolved through direct communication.

** Do not reply to this email.  All you need to do is contact your seller.**

If you have been unsuccessful contacting the seller via email, you are welcome
to contact them by phone if needed. eBay allows all members involved in a
transaction to request each others' contact information, including phone
numbers. This feature can be accessed through the following URL:

http://cgi3.ebay.com/aw-cgi/eBayISAPI.dll?MemberSearchShow

You and your seller are encouraged to work things out in the next 10 days.  If
this situation is resolved during this time, the matter is dropped and you do
not need to take any further action.

If, however, your seller is still unsatisfied after this period, you may receive
a Non-Paying Bidder (NPB) warning from eBay.  Once you obtain three warnings on
your record your account will be suspended indefinitely.
```

• **Figure 27-2:** An NPB e-mail.

If, after putting this blemish on the buyer's record, you still get nowhere, you can proceed to the next step — applying for the Final Value Fee credit.

The Next Step: Your Final Value Fee Credit

When ten days have elapsed after filing the Non-Paying Buyer Alert, you may file for a refund of your Final Value Fee for that transaction.

Your listing fees are not refunded, but if you relist the item and it sells, eBay gives you a credit for the listing fees.

Alternatively, you can also offer the item to an under-bidder by using the Second Chance Offer (as described in Technique 12).

To file for your Final Value Fee credit, go to

```
http://cgi3.ebay.com/aw-cgi/
    eBayISAPI.dll?CreditRequest
```

where you can fill out and submit the form.

 When a Final Value Fee is credited to you, a Non-Paying Buyer Alert is generated on the buyer's eBay record. eBay takes these Non-Paying Buyer Alerts seriously. When three have been filed against a buyer, that person may be permanently suspended from trading on eBay. If somehow, magically, the buyer contacts you to make amends, you may expunge the alert from his or her permanent eBay record by going to this page:

```
http://cgi3.ebay.com/aw-cgi/
eBayISAPI.dll?RemoveNPBWarningShow
```

Part V

Operating Efficiently with PayPal

The 5th Wave By Rich Tennant

"Me? Lose my head bidding on eBay?
Hah! No way."

Understanding PayPal Accounts and Options

Save Time By

✔ Understanding the ins and outs of the PayPal system

✔ Determining how you're protected

✔ Deciding which account is best for you

I n the early days of eBay, a typical online auction was a scary place. You could send a check to your trading partner, but the wait for the product could be interminable. There was very little feedback in the beginning, so you couldn't separate the good sellers from the bad. The most widely accepted form of payment was a money order. Somehow, we weren't afraid, in our small (but growing) community, to send money orders to strangers. Heck, some sellers even shipped the merchandise *before* the payment was received! Things were a lot simpler, if riskier, in the old days.

Then, rising like a beacon on the horizon came x.com. A brilliant man named Elon came up with the concept of e-mailing money; you could even beam cash to someone's Palm Pilot! There was no charge for using this service, which was even more amazing! The best part about signing up for the new program was that they gave you a $20 credit just to join. If you got friends to join, you got a $10 bonus for each and every friend. (The maximum any x.com user could get in bonuses was $1,000, but hey, that's no small change!)

With numbers like that, the early eBay (née AuctionWeb) crowd signed up quickly. x.com quickly became the most widely used service on the Internet — the first mover-and-shaker in online, person-to-person payments.

Here Comes eBay

The emerging eBay countered, acquiring Billpoint during spring 1999 in hopes of launching its own payment service (in a partnership with Wells Fargo). In a disaster of bad timing, the service was not available to eBay members until the second quarter of 2000. Meanwhile, newcomer PayPal (x.com reborn with a new name) was growing by leaps and bounds — and quietly taking over the market.

PayPal went public in February 2002 to an encouraging Wall Street. The feud between PayPal and Billpoint heated up. The number of customers who signed up with Billpoint couldn't keep pace with the numbers joining PayPal. PayPal posted a profit, while Billpoint was losing millions every year.

In July 2002, eBay bit the bullet and acquired the massive PayPal in a deal valued at $1.5 billion. Billpoint was then simply phased out of the site.

 If you've read any of my books, you know that I've been a huge fan of PayPal from the beginning. PayPal is one of the safest and least expensive ways for a vendor to accept money over the Internet. For a small retailer, PayPal fees can be much more cost effective than a credit card merchant account (as I explain in the next section).

Understanding How PayPal Works

Joining PayPal is just the beginning. No, they don't give $10 bonuses for sign-ups any more, but the benefits far outweigh any fees they charge to sellers. Also, there's no charge to send money to anyone. As of this writing, a seller just starting out can still accept money from eBay sales and not incur any fees at all.

 Before planning on a free ride from PayPal, double-check the PayPal Web site (www. PayPal.com) for any changes in fees and policies.

 You may have up to eight e-mail addresses registered with a PayPal account. Note, however, that you may not register an e-mail address if it's already registered with another PayPal account.

Sending money through PayPal

You can fund the money you send to another party via PayPal in several ways:

- ✔ **Instant Transfer:** Sending money this way means the money will be immediately credited to the recipient's account. That person can then transfer the money to his or her personal bank account

without delay. If you want to send a transfer, you must have a credit or debit card registered with PayPal as a back-up for your funds — just in case your bank denies the transfer. It's like writing a very secure check — without exposing any of your personal information (such as your checking account number) to another party.

- ✔ **eCheck:** Sending an eCheck isn't as "instant" as an Instant Transfer. As with writing a check from your checking account, it can take up to 4 days for the eCheck to clear. You do not need a back-up source of funds when you use eCheck.

- ✔ **PayPal balance:** If someone has sent you money through PayPal, or if you've sold something on eBay and your buyer has paid you through PayPal, you will have an amount deposited to your PayPal account. This balance will first be applied to any purchases, once there is no balance in your account, *then* you can choose to pay by credit card. It's simplest to keep your books balanced if you withdraw any PayPal balance to your business checking account before you make a purchase.

- ✔ **Credit Card:** Charge-it! Putting your PayPal purchases on a credit card is a good idea. Not only are you protected by PayPal, but your credit-card company also backs you up in the case of fraud.

 You can register multiple credit cards on your PayPal account, and select a different one for different types of purchases. That way you can place personal purchases on one account and business purchases on another. It makes end-of-year bookkeeping a whole lot easier!

Figuring out the payment types

PayPal also breaks types of payments into categories based on what you're paying for. You can pay for almost anything in the world on the PayPal system (as long as the recipient has an e-mail address).

After you sign into your PayPal account, you have several ways to send money through PayPal:

✔ **Paying for eBay Items:** When you pay for an eBay item, you input the item number and your eBay User ID so that the payment will integrate directly with eBay's user records.

✔ **Auction Goods (off-eBay):** With this option, you must input the URL for the item you purchased, as well as the auction site. You can even compose a message for the seller.

✔ **Goods (other):** Use this option when you need to send money to anyone in the world for goods purchased anywhere other than in an online auction.

✔ **Service:** You can also make a payment for a service performed for you or your business, such as Web design, bookkeeping, psychic readings, or whatever.

✔ **Quasi-Cash:** Use this when you need to send money to your kid in college (or pay back your roommate for saving you from great embarrassment when you left your wallet at home on a double date).

 When using the Quasi-Cash feature, consider using a payment method other than credit card to avoid possible credit card fees for a cash advance.

PayPal's Protection Plans

Safety — isn't that what paying for things online is all about? Safety for the buyer and safety for the seller are primary concerns in the minds of those dealing on eBay.

So what has PayPal done? They have created protection policies for both parties.

PayPal Buyer Protection

As a buyer who pays for his or her eBay items through PayPal, you can be covered against "fraud" for up to $500. You have to be sure that the seller's item has the PayPal Protection Shield (shown in Figure 28-1) next to the PP PayPal icon to get this Buyer Protection.

Fraud, in this protection program, is loosely defined as non-delivery of items, or receipt of an item that's significantly different from the way it was described. (Sorry — this doesn't cover you when you're merely disappointed with an item when you open the box.)

• **Figure 28-1: The PayPal Protection Shield.**

Notice, when you're browsing eBay, that PayPal icons accompany some listings. Some listings have just the PP PayPal icon, some have the PP icon *and* the Shield, and some have no icon at all. Here's what these mean:

✔ **PP Icon:** The seller accepts PayPal as payment, and you're covered under eBay's Standard Purchase Protection (up to $200 with a $25 deductible).

✔ **PP Icon and Shield:** This means the seller has qualified for his or her listings to be covered under the full Buyer Protection Program (coverage of up to $500).

✔ **No icon:** The seller for the item accepts no PayPal payments, but you are still covered by eBay's Standard Purchase Protection. See Technique 7 for more details.

Figure 28-2 shows a detail of eBay listings with these icons displayed.

	eBay For Dummies, Latest Edition-Brand New!	$15.99
	Starting an Ebay Business for Dummies by M...	$14.00
	eBay Bargain Shopping for Dummies SIGNED 2U	$13.99 $14.99
	Starting an eBay business for Dummies book	$12.00
	Ebay for Dummies 3rd Ed New Never Read	$11.53
	Starting an eBay Business for Dummies	$10.50
	Starting an eBay Business for DUMMIES	c $13.50

• **Figure 28-2:** eBay listings with (and without) PayPal icons.

 Even if PayPal's Buyer Protection does not cover your item, you may still be able to get a refund if you've been defrauded. The PayPal Protection Shield in the Seller Information box (or in the listings) merely tells you that the seller maintains a level of professionalism and safety in his or her sales. Read about seller's qualifications a little later in this technique (under "Getting qualified for a Protection Shield").

There are a few rules for using the protection system and making claims:

✔ **Number of claims:** You may make only one claim per PayPal payment. (If you pay for multiple items at once your total claim may not be over $500.) You also may not file more than two claims per calendar year.

✔ **Timing:** Your claim must be made within 30 days of your PayPal payment.

✔ **Participation:** You must be ready and willing to provide information and documentation to PayPal's Buyer Protection team during the claims process.

PayPal Seller Protection

Don't think that sellers get left out of this protection thing. You do have some protection against unwarranted claims made on your eBay sales. It's called Seller Protection.

To see whether your transaction is covered under Seller Protection, follow these steps:

1. Open your "payment received" e-mail from PayPal and look for the link titled View the Details of the Transaction.

2. Click the link and sign into your PayPal account.

3. Scroll down the Transaction Details page to the buyer's shipping address.

You will see whether the shipping address is confirmed. (PayPal checks to be sure the credit card billing address matches the shipping address to confirm it.) If it is, you must ship to that address to be protected.

When your transaction is protected, should there be any fraud involved (stolen credit card or identity hoax) you will not lose the money. PayPal guarantees the transaction.

 If you receive a PayPal payment that ships to an unconfirmed address, drop the buyer a note and ask about the address. Usually you'll get a reply that makes you feel comfortable, and you'll ship. Remember that you will not be covered under Seller Protection if you ship to an unconfirmed address.

Surprise! There are a few other rules and restrictions. For sellers to be protected, they must meet the following requirements:

✔ **Verified Business or Premier Account.** They must have an upper-level PayPal account.

✔ **Ship to confirmed address.** They must ship to the buyer's address exactly as displayed on the Transaction Details page.

- ✔ **Ship within 7 days.** The item should leave the sellers' place of business within 7 days of receiving payment.

- ✔ **Single payment/single account.** Sellers accept one payment from one PayPal account for the purchase.

- ✔ **Ship tangible goods.** Seller Protection is not available for services, digital goods, and other electronically-delivered items.

- ✔ **Proof of shipping.** Sellers must provide reasonable proof of shipment which can be tracked online. The Transaction Details page must show that the seller shipped to the buyer's address. A Delivery Confirmation will suffice for items valued up to $250.00.

 For items worth $250.00 or more (£150.00 or more for the U.K.), sellers must have a signature from the recipient as proof of receipt.

- ✔ **No surcharges.** Sellers cannot impose a surcharge on the buyer. This is against eBay policy anyway. (Surcharging for any PayPal payment is prohibited outside the U.K.)

- ✔ **Complaint investigation.** If a complaint is filed, sellers must provide complete information about a transaction within 7 days of a request from PayPal.

 If PayPal is required by the buyer's issuing credit card company to respond immediately to resolve a chargeback situation, the seller must provide all information within 3 days.

At this writing, Seller Protection is available only for U.S. or Canadian sellers transacting with U.S. buyers, and for U.K. sellers transacting with U.K. or U.S. buyers. Check back with the PayPal site for any changes in this policy.

Getting qualified for a Protection Shield

What if you want to provide protection for your buyers? It's a way to show them you're professional and have them feel more comfortable making purchases from you.

For a seller to qualify his or her items for Protection Shield status, the seller has to meet a few requirements:

- ✔ Must have a minimum of 50 or more eBay feedback comments.

- ✔ Must have at least 98-percent-positive eBay feedback.

- ✔ Must be a Verified member of PayPal.

- ✔ Must use a Premier or Business PayPal account to accept payments.

- ✔ Must have a U.S. or Canadian PayPal account.

- ✔ Must select PayPal as a payment option when listing items on eBay.

- ✔ Must have a PayPal account that's in good standing.

What's this "PayPal Verified" business all about?

Being PayPal Verified is an important rating for both seller and buyer. It means that someone has checked, and that you really are who you say you are. (Remember when you signed up at the bank? They got information about you to be sure you were you, didn't they?)

Becoming verified isn't a big deal. All you have to do is register your checking account with PayPal. PayPal will make two teeny (under $1) deposits into your checking account. When they've been transferred to your account, you can log back onto your PayPal account and confirm the two amounts. That's it — and you get free pennies too!

If you live outside the United States, you become verified by adding a credit card to your account and enrolling in the Expanded Use Program. (It's a similar confirmation scheme.)

Comprehending PayPal's Accounts

PayPal has three different types of accounts to accommodate everyone from the casual seller to the professional business.

PayPal Personal Account

When you begin your career with PayPal, you may want to sign up for a Personal account. With this basic account from PayPal, you can send and receive money (non–credit card payments) for free.

PayPal Personal accounts are for one person only and not for a business. You cannot have a joint Personal account, either.

Business and Premier Accounts

The PayPal professional seller accounts allow you to accept credit card payments, get a debit card, and participate in PayPal's high-yield money market fund. A Premier Account is held in an individual's name (although it may still be for a business); a Business Account can be held in a business name and allows multiple login names.

Once you reach these account levels, you'll have access to a customer service phone number, and be able to use all the PayPal tools discussed in other techniques in this part.

There is a fee levied on all money you receive through PayPal at this level, but the costs are reasonable. (Just ask anyone with a brick-and-mortar business that accepts credit cards.)

 All U.S. Premier and Business accounts that receive more than $2,000 a month in payments through PayPal have an additional requirement: Holders of such accounts must supply PayPal with additional information about their businesses.

PayPal has two levels of rates, a Merchant Rate and a Standard Rate, as shown in Table 28-1. When you open your account, you will be charged the Standard Rate. When your sales grow and you've been receiving over $1,000 per month through PayPal for three consecutive months, you can apply for a Merchant Rate.

TABLE 28-1: PAYPAL TRANSACTION FEES

Payment Currency	Merchant Rate	Standard Rate
U. S. Dollars	2.2 percent + $.30 US	2.9 percent + $.30 US
Canadian Dollars	2.7 percent + $.55 CA	3.4 percent + $.55 CA
Euros	2.7 percent + €.35	3.4 percent + €0.35
Pounds Sterling	2.7 percent + £.20	3.4 percent + £.20
Yen	2.7 percent + ¥40	3.4 percent + ¥40

Remember: If you receive a payment from a buyer in another country, there is an additional fee — 1 percent for payments in U.S. dollars, and 0.5 percent for Canadian dollars, Euros, Pounds Sterling, and Yen. (This fee is currently waived for Canadian sellers receiving payments from U.S. buyers.)

 If your transaction requires a currency conversion, you are charged an exchange rate. This includes an additional 2.5 percent above the current exchange rate.

Technique

29

Generating Income from Your Web Site with PayPal

Save Time By

- ✔ Offering PayPal on your Web site for non-eBay purchases

- ✔ Letting PayPal do the work by generating your code

- ✔ Selling from AOL

If you think that PayPal is only for your eBay business, think again! Prior to eBay purchasing PayPal, approximately 15 percent of its revenues came from online gaming. (Read: Gambling!) Since eBay took over in late 2002, PayPal no longer draws revenue from this arena. And there's good news for us; today PayPal offers tools that you can use to process PayPal payments on your own personal or business Web sites.

Aside from your eBay Store, you can sell directly from your own Web site or from your AOL Hometown page. In time, as your business grows outside eBay to your own Web site, you'll find that using PayPal as your payment provider is a great deal. You pay the same transaction fees — to PayPal only — for processing your credit card sales.

 Build business by including your Web site URL in your e-mail signature to let the world know you're open for business 24/7. Your My eBay page can also include links to your selling Web site — it's fully in line with the eBay rules!

In this technique, you discover how to make your own Web site an extra revenue builder. I'm going to use my Web site as the example. It's a very basic Web site, but people can (and do) shop there from time to time. Remember, any sale you make from your own Web site involves no eBay fees, which means extra income for you.

Making the PayPal Payment Option Available on Your Site

Once you get a few items in your garage or business location that you stock in quantity, you've got the makings of your own Web store. Don't let the thought of this spook you. You *can* do this!

The first step for having your own online store is to create your Web site. After you have the site up and running, adding Buy Now buttons is the most basic way to enable sales through PayPal from your site. These buttons are easy to insert — you don't have to be a computer whiz to create the links because PayPal makes this almost automatic.

There's no fee to use this service (other than the processing fee when someone buys an item). All you need is a Verified PayPal Premier or Business account.

When someone buys something from your Web site, the procedure is the same as when someone pays for an eBay item. You receive an e-mail from PayPal. The e-mail subject includes the item number you've assigned in your code (it can also be an item name, as in Figure 29-1) and will let you know that it's a Web payment (versus an eBay payment) that has been received.

```
Subject:  Item #INFINITI Board - Notification of Payment Received from

Dear Marsha Collier,

This email confirms that you have received a Payment for $46.50
USD from

View the details of this transaction online at:

https://www.paypal.com/us/vst/id=84U316858W7040358


------------------------------
Payment Details:
------------------------------

Total Amount: $46.50 USD
Currency: U.S. Dollars
Transaction ID: 84U316858W7040358
Total Shipping: $8.00 USD
Quantity: 1
Item Title: INFINITI Board
Item Number: INFINITI Board
Buyer:

------------------------------
                   CONFIRMED Address
```

• **Figure 29-1: PayPal's Web site accepted payment e-mail.**

Creating a button from the PayPal Web site

If you want to save a bunch of time, try to use the sample coding (you can do it — I know you can!) in the section "Coding for Do-It-Yourselfers." Just customize the HTML coding (with your Web site details) and put it into your Web page. If it doesn't work, or you're too nervous to do real coding, read this section with the step-by-step process for placing the PayPal button on your site.

To create a payment button on your Web site, you start by logging on to the PayPal Web site. From there, it takes just four steps:

1. **Click the tab at the top of the page that reads Merchant Tools, as shown in Figure 29-2.**

• **Figure 29-2: The PayPal Merchant Tools tab.**

2. **Scroll down to the Web site Payments area.**

3. **Click the link labeled Create Buy Now Buttons.**

The Selling Single Items page shown in Figure 29-3 appears.

4. **Type your item information, including the item name, ID, price, currency, and default buyer's country.**

Selling Single Items	See Demo

Sell individual items on your website by creating a customized payment button and your buyers will be able to make their purchases quickly and securely on PayPal hosted payment pages.

More Resources
Techniques, examples, demos & more.

Enter the details of the item you wish to sell (optional)

Item Name/Service:

Item ID/Number:

Price of Item/Service you want to sell: ($2,000.00 USD limit for new buyers) ?

Currency: U.S. Dollars ?

If you want your buyer's payment form to default to a specific country, select a country below. Otherwise, do nothing and your buyers can choose for themselves.

Buyer's Country: (Optional) – Choose a Country – ?

Choose a button to put on your website (optional)

⊙ Buy Now   Choose a different button

Or customize your button! Just enter the exact URL of any image on your website.

• **Figure 29-3: Buy Now button factory.**

Here's a list of all the items you are asked to enter on the Selling Single Items page. Remember that many of these are optional.

Refer back to this list when you examine the full sample code shown later in this technique. It will help to explain what goes into each `input type` field.

▶ **Item Name:** Type your item (or service) name.

▶ **ID Number:** Give your item an ID number or Name.

I recommend giving your items both a number and an abbreviated name. When PayPal sends you an e-mail letting you know that someone made a purchase, the item number/name will appear in the subject line. For faster recognition, I recommend that you use an abbreviation. (For the longest time, I'd wonder what Item Number 4 was!)

▶ **Item Price:** Enter the item price here (FYI, there's a $2,000 limit for new buyers).

▶ **Currency:** Decide what currency you're willing to accept for your purchases. (If you're in the U.S. — go for the dollars.)

▶ **International Buyers:** If you accept international orders, specify here whether you want your buyer's payment page to default to a specific country.

If you don't specify a default, buyers can choose for themselves. I select the United States to make it faster for most purchasers.

▶ **Select a Button:** Choose a Buy Now button to insert on your page. If you don't like the one pictured, click the Choose A Different Button link to see more options, as shown in Figure 29-4.

I like the buttons that include the name PayPal, because that may assure new shoppers that their transactions with you will be secure. You also have the opportunity to design your own button, but hey, why make extra work for yourself right now? Just set up a standard button and get fancy later.

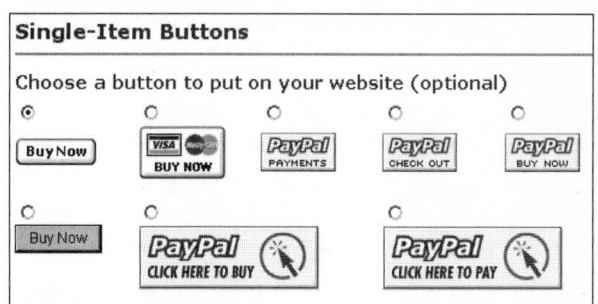

• **Figure 29-4:** Your choices for button selection.

Setting up your payment page

Now it's time to make settings for the payment page people will see when they've clicked your Buy Now button. Follow these steps to do so:

1. **After you make settings in the Selling Single Items page and choose a button to insert, click Continue.**

2. **Make your choices for the following settings:**

▶ **Options:** Click the Add More Options box to enter shipping and sales tax information for your item.

▶ **Shipping and Handling Fee:** On the rest of the form, select a flat shipping and handling charge or one based on a percentage of the item's price.

Unfortunately, PayPal does not supply a cool shipping calculator as eBay does. So you could put a postal shipping chart on your item page and let your buyers insert the proper shipping amount, or you can enter an amount on this page that lands somewhere in the middle of the highest (furthest away) and lowest (closest) shipping zone costs. You'll lose a little on some, but make it up on others.

▶ **Sales Tax:** Select your state and enter the appropriate sales tax to be applied to your in-state purchases.

If you already have a sales tax provision in your PayPal profile, it will automatically be listed here. PayPal will automatically apply the sales tax for sales that are shipped within your state.

▶ **Item Options:** If your item has options (if, for example, it comes in different sizes or colors), you can create a custom drop-down menu for your payment page so the customer can choose; just type the offered options in this box.

▶ **Insert Your Logo:** To add a logo to your payment page, type in the URL where the logo file is stored. PayPal will place the logo on your payment page.

 The logo you use must be sized at 150 x 50 pixels, or PayPal won't accept it.

▶ **Payment Landing Page:** If you want your customers to land on a specific page after they've made a payment — for example, setting up a thank-you page on your Web site is a nice idea — you enter that URL here. Figure 29-5 shows a portion of my Web site's very basic thank-you page. The page also has links to take the buyer back to my Web site.

 *THANK YOU for purchasing my item!*

It will be sent out in a day or so via Priority Mail. Please feel free to email with any questions.

• **Figure 29-5:** Thanks for buying my item!

▶ **Cancel Transaction Page:** If you want to include a page where people are taken if they cancel the transaction before completing it, you can insert that address here. If you don't specify a page, they will land at a PayPal Web page.

▶ **Quantity:** If you'd like your customers to be able to purchase more than one of your item at a time, you may indicate that here. The buyers will then be able to fill in a number in a quantity field.

▶ **Shipping Address:** Click yes if you'd like the customer's shipping address. I guess it would be kind of useless not to ask for a shipping address when you're expected to ship the item somewhere, huh? Including this field *does* kind of take the guesswork out of things!

▶ **Optional Instructions:** If you'd like your buyers to be able to write you a note, click Yes in this field.

That's it for the options.

3. Click Preview to see a sample of the page your customer will see after making a Web payment to you.

4. If the page looks okay, click the Return button to go back to the editing page.

5. Click the Create Button Now button.

Whew. That's all there is to creating your first Buy Now button and the payment page that appears when it's clicked. When you get the hang of it, I'm sure you'd rather code your own. It's really easy (even I can do it) and considerably faster. Read the next section.

Coding for Do-It-Yourselfers

Yes, there's a short way and a proper way to do everything. The easy way may not give you that unerring air of professionalism, but it still works. Since I am unreasonably busy, I did my Web site PayPal buttons the easy way — without a bunch of options.

PayPal coding — the stripped-down version

The items I sell on my Web site can't be combined in one box. Each has to be shipped in individual boxes, and postage must be charged for each item. I therefore don't use the shopping cart method.

Figure 29-6 shows a payment button on one of the pages on my site. When the mouse rolls over the payment button, a PayPal message appears.

• **Figure 29-6:** My PayPal payment button.

When you click the Payment button, you land on my Cool eBay Tools PayPal payment page (shown in Figure 29-7, complete with custom logo). The PayPal payment page is a secure page directly from PayPal. These pages contain a small icon of a lock, which indicates that the site is safe for secure transactions. The URL for the page begins with https; the s at the end indicates that the site is secure.

• **Figure 29-7: The resulting PayPal payment page.**

Here's the actual code I used to create that payment button and link to the resulting page.

```
<form action="https://www.paypal.com/
   cgi-bin/webscr" method="post">
<input type="hidden" name="cmd" value=
   "_xclick">
<input type="hidden" name="business"
   value="marshac@collierad.com">
<input type="hidden" name="undefined_
   quantity" value="1">
<input type="hidden" name="item_name"
   value="INFINITI Board">
<input type="hidden" name="item_number"
   value="INFINITI Board">
<input type="hidden" name="amount" value=
   "38.50">
<input type="hidden" name="shipping"
   value="8.00">
```

```
<input type="hidden" name="image_url"
   value="http:// coolebaytools/images/
   coolT.gif">
<input type="hidden" name="return" value=
   "http:// coolebaytools/thankyou.htm">
<input type="hidden" name="cancel_return"
   value="http:// coolebaytools">
<input type="hidden" name="no_note"
   value="1">
<input type="hidden" name="currency_code"
   value="USD">
<input type="image" src="https://www.
   paypal.com/en_US/i/btn/x-click-but5.gif"
   border="0" name="submit" alt="Make
   payments with PayPal - it's fast, free
   and secure!">
</form>
```

My coding does not contain all the possible options that PayPal offers, but it does get the job done.

PayPal coding with all the bells and whistles

Listed below is the high-octane version of a PayPal button code with sample values filled in. All you have to do is fill in your own values (read the section "Creating a button on the PayPal Web site" for the definitions of corresponding items on the Selling Single Items page) and copy and paste the code into your own Web page.

```
<form action="https://www.paypal.com/cgi-
   bin/webscr" method="post">
<input type="hidden" name="cmd" value=
   "_xclick">
<input type="hidden" name="business"
   value="me@myemailaddress.com">
<input type="hidden" name="return"
value="http://www.mysite.com/thankyou.htm">
<input type="hidden" name="undefined_
   quantity" value="1">
<input type="hidden" name="item_name"
   value="TShirt">
<input type="hidden" name="item_number"
   value="Tshirt01">
<input type="hidden" name="amount" value=
   "9.95">
<input type="hidden" name="shipping"
   value="3.00">
<input type="hidden" name="image_url"
value="https://www.yoursite.com/logo.gif">
```

```
<input type="hidden" name="cancel_return"
value="http://www.mysite.com/cancel.htm">
<input type="hidden" name=" no_note"
    value="0">
<table><tr><td><input type="hidden" name=
    "on0" value="Color?">Color?
<select name="os0">
<option value="Blue">Blue
<option value="Green">Green
<option value="Red">Red</select></td></tr>
    </table>
<input type="hidden" name="cn" value="How
    Did You Hear About Us?">
<input type="image" src="http://images.
    paypal.com/images/x-clickbut01.
gif" name="submit" alt="Make payments with
    PayPal - it's fast,
free and secure!">
</form>
```

Adding a PayPal Buy Now Button to Your AOL Hometown Page

The procedure for adding a payment button for AOL users is pretty easy. And what's better than making money from your own free Web page!

Here's how to insert your button:

1. **Sign in to your AOL Hometown account.**

2. **Click the Edit My Pages link.**

3. **Select the page to which you want to add the Buy Now button.**

4. **Click the Insert button on the toolbar.**

5. **Select Advanced HTML.**

   A dialog box where you put your HTML code appears.

6. **Copy the HTML code generated by the button factory (or your own homemade coding as I show you in the previous section), and paste it in the text box.**

7. **Click Save.**

   You can type the URL in the browser to go test your page.

Technique 30

Downloading Your Payment History from PayPal

Save Time By

- ✔ Understanding the downloadable reports
- ✔ Choosing report options
- ✔ Performing the download

I've been running a home-based business since the mid-1980s. Because I came from a corporate background working in the newspaper business, I've always known that record keeping is important. But record keeping has always been the bane of my existence. The first thing I did, when I began my home-based business, was to hire a lawyer and a CPA to teach me what I had to do.

Record keeping means keeping track of everything: every penny, sou, farthing, or ruble that you spend or take in. Here, in the United States (and in most other countries), we have a little thing called taxes. We all have to turn in tax returns of several sorts when we run a business — and they'd better be correct. There may come a day in the near (or hopefully, far) future when we, as online businesspeople, will receive a letter from a State or Federal tax agency asking to take a look at our books. This is simply a nice way of saying the dreaded word, AUDIT.

 The best defense against an audit is to have backup records. The more records you have proving your business income and expenses, the less painful your audit will be. One excellent piece of information to have at your fingertips is your PayPal history.

Besides meeting tax-reporting requirements, keeping good records keeps you on top of your business dealings. See Techniques 47 and 48 for more about how good record keeping helps your business succeed. PayPal helps you with this all-important record keeping by providing customizable, downloadable reports on your buying and selling activity.

PayPal's Downloadable Reports

PayPal allows you to customize and download your transaction reports at any time. You might want to consider downloading your reports on a monthly or quarterly basis — as well as generating one big report at the end of the year. You may want to download the reports to coincide with your state sales tax payments (for backup documentation) or to keep a record of your monthly totals.

You can download reports in several formats. The most flexible is a comma-delimited file that can be opened and edited in a spreadsheet program, such as Excel or Microsoft Works.

 By using a spreadsheet file as your record of customers, you won't bog down a bookkeeping program with hundreds (and eventually thousands) of records of one-time buyers. Even a robust program like QuickBooks will max out at around 14,000 customers!

Starting the Download from PayPal

To get your reports from PayPal, you need to go to www.PayPal.com and log on to your account with your e-mail address and password. After you're logged on, the top of the page displays various tabs, as shown in Figure 30-1.

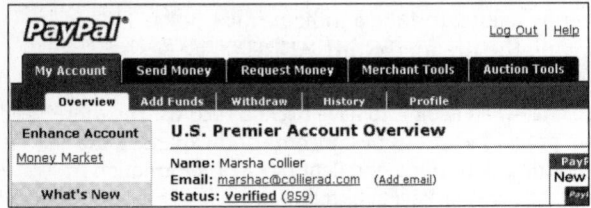

• **Figure 30-1: The PayPal navigation tab bar.**

Now follow these steps:

1. **Click the My Account tab.**

2. **Click the History item on the navigation bar.**

You are now in your account History area; on the right you'll see a box entitled Reporting Tools.

In that area are a few options, including Download My History and Merchant Sales Report. The Merchant Sales Report is a nice tool, but if you're posting your sales regularly to a program such as QuickBooks, you'll have reports out the wazoo that'll give you tons of higher

quality information. (Check out Technique 47 for the timesaving way to post your information without overloading the program.)

3. **Click the Download My History link.**

You now land on the Download History page. But, before you start clicking anything else, you should consider customizing your reports.

4. **If you decide to customize reports (which I recommend), click the link labeled Customize My History Download.**

See the next section for information on your choices.

5. **If you decide not to customize, you can skip ahead to the steps in the section "Doing the Actual Download (Finally!)."**

Customizing Your Download

You may need *all* the information that PayPal gives you. If that's what you want, that's great. But PayPal can give you information overkill. I suggest that you look over the following list of available info so you can pick and choose the fields to download and keep in your permanent records.

All your downloadable PayPal reports can contain the following information by default:

✔ **Date:** The date each PayPal transaction occurred.

✔ **Time:** The time the payment was made.

✔ **Time Zone:** The time zone used for recording transactions in your PayPal account.

✔ **Name:** The name of the person to whom you sent money or from whom you received money.

✔ **Type:** The type of transaction that occurred: Deposit, Withdrawal, ATM Withdrawal, Payment Sent, Payment Received, and so on.

✔ **Status:** The status of the transaction at the time you download the file (Cleared, Completed, Denied, and so on).

✔ **Gross:** The Gross amount involved in the transaction (before any fees are deducted).

✔ **Fee:** Any PayPal fees that are charged to the transaction.

✔ **Net:** The net dollar amount of the transaction. (This is the total received, less any PayPal fees.)

✔ **From e-mail:** The e-mail address of the sender.

✔ **To e-mail:** The e-mail address of the recipient.

 If you use different e-mail addresses to classify different types of sales, this can be a good sorting point for your reports. For example, I receive payments for my personal auctions at one e-mail address and payments for my business at another.

PayPal has lots more data that you can have, too. You can set the options listed here separately for your eBay sales and your Web site sales (where people use your PayPal Buy Now button to make a purchase). If you want more information from one type of sale than from the other, you can set these options appropriately.

✔ **Item ID:** This is that strange combination of letters and numbers that PayPal assigns to each transaction. Decide whether this is important for your own records. (I don't use it.)

✔ **Item Title:** The title of the auction related to the transaction.

✔ **Shipping Amount:** The amount the buyer paid for shipping. It's a good idea to use this field, as it helps you to separate merchandise revenue from shipping revenue.

✔ **Auction Site:** If you're collecting money from other auction sites through PayPal, you might want to include this link so that you can sort your sales by auction site.

✔ **Item URL:** The Internet address of the auction or transaction. (For eBay, the URLs are on the site for up to 90 days — here you can go back a year.)

✔ **Closing Date:** The date the transaction closed. The record will always contain the date the payment posted to your PayPal account, whether you indicate closing date here or not.

✔ **Shipping Address:** The address to which the item was shipped.

✔ **Counter Party Status (Verified versus Unverified):** A record of whether your buyer was PayPal Verified.

✔ **Address Status (Confirmed versus Unconfirmed):** Shows whether the address you shipped to was confirmed.

✔ **Sales Tax:** Information about sales tax you collected.

After you've selected the fields you want to include (by selecting the check box next to the desired data), click Save. You find yourself back at the Download History page, as shown in Figure 30-2. Your customization will be saved for future report downloads.

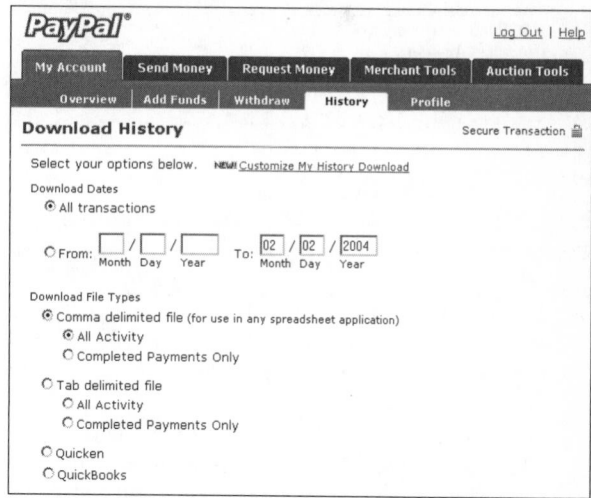

• **Figure 30-2: Downloading your permanent records.**

 If you are a seller in the UK, your Download History page will look slightly different than the one pictured. Your dates will be in the format of DD/MM/YY. U.S. users read their dates with the month first, the day, and then the year; UK users read the day, month, and then the year.

Doing the Actual Download (Finally!)

On the Download History page, follow these steps to download a report:

1. Type in the dates that you'd like to have covered in the downloaded report.

2. Select a format for your download from the following:

> ▶ **Comma-delimited file:** This type of file downloads with the extension .csv. You can open a comma-delimited file easily in Microsoft Excel or Microsoft Works. (Microsoft Works doesn't have a direct .csv importer, but the file will open under the All Files (*.*) option as shown in Figure 30-3.)

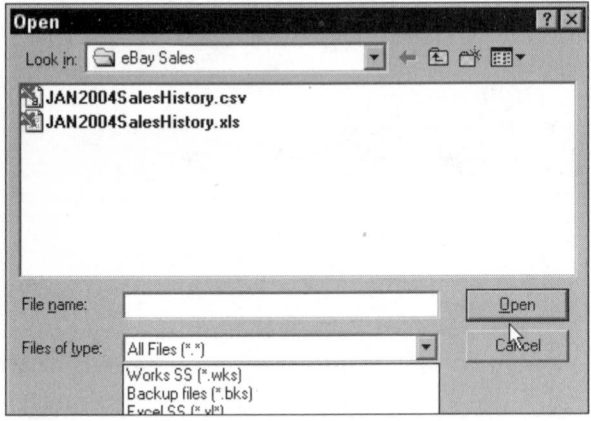

• **Figure 30-3:** Opening a csv file in Works.

> ▶ **Tab-delimited file:** This file downloads with the extension of .txt. You can open it in a spreadsheet program, or as a text file in Windows Notepad or a word-processing program such as Microsoft Word.

> ▶ **Quicken or QuickBooks file:** PayPal reports download in the native format ready to import into these Intuit bookkeeping programs, which I discuss in Technique 47. Just

remember, once these files get imported, they're in your bookkeeping format for good.

 Saving these report files for spreadsheet use will not limit you in the future as to what version of which program will open what. .txt and .csv are universal files and can be opened on any PC with basic spreadsheet capabilities.

3. After you specify dates and format, click the Download History button.

If you've asked for a long timeframe (like a year), get up and make yourself a cup of joe. When you come back, your file will be ready to download.

Saving and Editing Your Reports

When your computer finally is ready to receive the downloaded file (which may take a while — especially if you have a dial-up connection), a window pops up like the one shown in Figure 30-4.

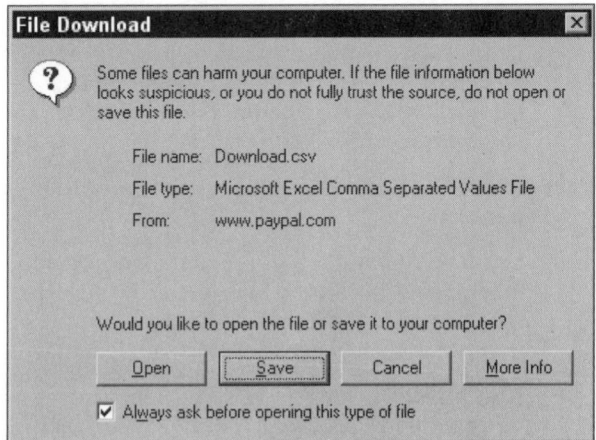

• **Figure 30-4:** The Windows File Download window.

Click the Save button and, in the next screen, select the directory on your computer where you want to save the file. I recommend setting up a directory that contains only Internet and eBay sales files.

After you save the file, you can open it. Figure 30-5 shows a downloaded history file opened in Microsoft Works. You can now work with your sales history to your heart's content — re-sorting the records, totaling up sales, deleting unnecessary columns, and so on.

This file is now part of your eBay business archive, should the day come that you need to produce it. Be sure to back it up, just in case.

 Some CPAs recommend you keep these files for up to 7 years but, to be safe, check with your own tax professional who understands the needs for your particular tax situation.

	A	B	C	D	E	F	G	H	I	J
1	Date	Time	Zone	Name	Type	Status	Gross	Fee	Net	From Ema
2	2/2/2004	11:38:00	PST		Refund	Completed	-13.61	0.6	-13.01	
3	2/1/2004	18:08:28	PST		eBay Payment Receive	Completed	152.1	-3.65	148.45	
4	2/1/2004	13:03:30	PST		eBay Payment Receive	Completed	13.23	-0.59	12.64	
5	1/31/2004	18:23:19	PST		Update to Payment Rec	Completed	46.34			
6	1/31/2004	12:45:31	PST		eBay Payment Receive	Completed	46.34	-1.32	45.02	
7	1/30/2004	19:46:21	PST		Payment Received	Completed	280	-6.46	273.54	
8	1/30/2004	12:36:17	PST		eBay Payment Sent	Completed	-47.15	0	-47.15	
9	1/30/2004	12:36:17	PST	Credit Card	Charge From Credit Car	Completed	22.78	0	22.78	
10	1/30/2004	12:31:53	PST	Bank Account	Withdraw Funds to a Ba	Completed	-1136.44	0	-1136.44	
11	1/30/2004	12:05:00	PST		eBay Payment Receive	Completed	78.13	-2.02	76.11	
12	1/30/2004	9:26:55	PST		Web Accept Payment R	Completed	46.5	-1.32	45.18	
13	1/30/2004	8:56:36	PST		Web Accept Payment R	Completed	179	-4.24	174.76	
14	1/30/2004	8:54:42	PST		Web Accept Payment R	Completed	138.5	-3.35	135.15	
15	1/30/2004	6:43:52	PST		eBay Payment Receive	Completed	18.02	-0.7	17.32	
16	1/29/2004	13:37:16	PST		eBay Payment Receive	Completed	251.99	-5.84	246.15	
17	1/29/2004	12:07:03	PST		eBay Payment Receive	Completed	33.19	-1.03	32.16	
18	1/29/2004	4:34:28	PST		eBay Payment Receive	Refunded	13.61	-0.6	13.01	
19	1/28/2004	23:51:19	PST		Web Accept Payment R	Completed	148.48	-3.57	144.91	
20	1/28/2004	15:29:53	PST		eBay Payment Receive	Completed	6.87	-0.45	6.42	
21	1/28/2004	15:26:27	PST		eBay Payment Receive	Completed	6.87	-0.45	6.42	
22	1/28/2004	15:23:31	PST		eBay Payment Receive	Completed	6.87	-0.45	6.42	
23	1/28/2004	10:59:09	PST		eBay Payment Receive	Completed	6.5	-0.44	6.06	
24	1/27/2004	10:41:38	PST		Update to Payment Rec	Completed	7			
25	1/27/2004	10:35:21	PST		Payment Received	Completed	7	-0.45	6.55	
26	1/27/2004	8:54:43	PST		eBay Payment Receive	Completed	249.99	-5.8	244.19	

Zoom 100%

• **Figure 30-5: The downloaded file opened in a spreadsheet program.**

Technique 31

Arranging Shipping Directly through PayPal

I consider PayPal to be *de rigueur* (a 'must have', to all you non-French speakers) for all eBay sellers. By using PayPal, a seller can streamline the buyer's shopping experience, making it simple to buy, click, and pay. Those out in the eBay world who haven't used PayPal find using the service to be a life-changing experience. Along with all its timesaving tools for the seller, PayPal now offers online shipping services through the United States Postal Service (USPS) or UPS at no extra charge. This technique shows you how to take advantage of this incredibly convenient system. Shipping through PayPal is especially helpful for those who don't ship many packages per week because there's no need to use additional software or sign up with an additional service.

 But (I hate the *buts,* don't you?), the PayPal postage system can make bookkeeping a nightmare for large-scale shippers. That's because PayPal withdraws the postage amounts directly from your PayPal account balance. This is problematic for keeping your books in balance: Your final deposits won't match your posted eBay or Web sales.

 You can make the bookkeeping end of the shipping process work more efficiently by posting your PayPal sales to your bookkeeping program and withdrawing your money (from your PayPal account) prior to processing your shipping. Then, simply charge your shipping to a credit card and make it easier to balance your books at month's end. See Technique 47 for more advice on professional bookkeeping.

Shipping Directly from PayPal

When you get those wonderful e-mails from PayPal letting you know that someone has made a payment, it's a great feeling. But it's also your notice that you've got to ship out our merchandise really soon. When you're ready to deal with shipping, it's very simple to sign on to your PayPal account and handle it right on the site.

In Figure 31-1, you see my PayPal Overview page. It's clear that I have to ship some items pronto.

U.S. Premier Account Overview

Name: Marsha Collier
Email: (Add email)
Status: Verified (885)

Balance: $551.12 USD   View Limits
Earn a return on your balance!

PayPal VISA® CARD
New Design Series
Apply Now!
30-second response

Recent Activity | All Activity | Items Won | Items $ = PayPal Preferred
Sold   Cashback

Your Recent Activity displays the last 7 days of account activity.

File	Type	To/From	Name/Email	Amount ($)	Date	Status	Details	Action
☐	Payment	From		$26.94 USD	Feb. 18, 2004	Uncleared	Details	
☐	Payment	From		$26.94 USD	Feb. 18, 2004	Completed	Details	Ship
☐	Payment	From		$37.49 USD	Feb. 18, 2004	Completed	Details	Ship

• **Figure 31-1: After signing in, you can see which items need shipping.**

To begin the shipping process

1. **Click the Ship button in the item's row.**

You'll arrive at the page shown in Figure 31-2.

2. **Choose which method of shipping you'd like to use: U.S. Postal Service or UPS.**

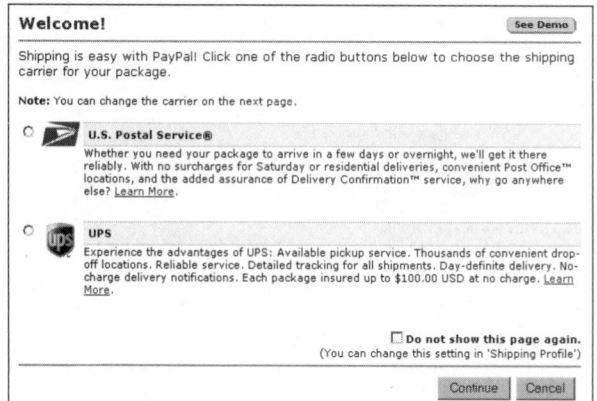

Welcome!   See Demo

Shipping is easy with PayPal! Click one of the radio buttons below to choose the shipping carrier for your package.

Note: You can change the carrier on the next page.

○ **U.S. Postal Service®**
Whether you need your package to arrive in a few days or overnight, we'll get it there reliably. With no surcharges for Saturday or residential deliveries, convenient Post Office™ locations, and the added assurance of Delivery Confirmation™ service, why go anywhere else? Learn More.

○ **UPS**
Experience the advantages of UPS: Available pickup service. Thousands of convenient drop-off locations. Reliable service. Detailed tracking for all shipments. Day-definite delivery. No-charge delivery notifications. Each package insured up to $100.00 USD at no charge. Learn More.

☐ **Do not show this page again.**
(You can change this setting in 'Shipping Profile')

Continue   Cancel

• **Figure 31-2: Choose your shipper!**

I hope that you already decided which shipping method to use prior to coming to PayPal. You had to specify a shipping amount in your auction, and it would be a tad awkward (and possibly costly) to switch shippers now. If you

need help deciding which shipper to use, please check out Part VI of this book.

PayPal Shipping with the USPS

If you plan to use the ever-popular United States Postal Service (USPS), printing your postage and label through PayPal gives you a free Delivery Confirmation with Priority Mail. A Delivery Confirmation is also available for Media Mail, Parcel Post, and First Class Mail for a minimal charge. (For Priority Mail, that's a savings of about $.45 from walk-in post office rates.)

After you've chosen USPS as your shipper, you'll see a confirmation page similar to the one shown in Figure 31-3. At the top of the page (not pictured) your mailing address and the ship to address are listed.

Service Type: Priority Mail® ▼ ?
Choose a different shipper

Package Size: Flat Rate Envelope ▼ Learn More About Package Sizes

Weight: 2 lbs. 0 oz. ?

Delivery Confirmation: FREE ?

Signature Confirmation: ○ Yes ($1.30 USD) ◉ No ?
Note: Signature of receipt is available upon request for Express Mail.

Display Postage Value on Label: ☐ ?

Email message to Buyer: (optional)

Note: U.S. Postal Service Shipping Insurance must be purchased directly from a U.S. Postal Service Post Office. Click here for more information.

Item(s) Being Shipped to Your Buyer

Note: If you have multiple packages for this transaction, you can print multiple labels by clicking **Create Additional Labels** button after creating the current label.

Item #	Item Title	Qty
3587277118	New 2004 EBAY FOR DUMMIES 4th COLLIER Signed	1

Continue   Cancel

• **Figure 31-3: Confirming the details of your shipment.**

After you confirm that this information is correct, fill out the details of the form, including:

✔ **Service Type:** Choose the level of mailing service you want for your package from this drop-down list. Priority Mail is usually the standard.

✔ **Package Size:** From this drop-down menu, select the type of package you're sending. To decide which packaging to select, keep the following in mind:

▶ **Package/Thick Envelope:** Your package or envelope qualifies for this status if the length and girth are no more than 84 inches.

▶ **Large Package:** Your package is a Large Package when it is larger than the previous category, but doesn't exceed 108 inches in combined length and girth.

▶ **USPS Flat Rate Envelope:** These handy Express and Priority Mail envelopes are available free from the USPS. (See Technique 36 for information on how to get them delivered to your door.) You can ship whatever fits into the envelopes at a flat rate, no matter how much the package weighs.

> If you really stuff your flat rate envelopes, you can always reinforce your envelope with clear shipping tape — I do!

✔ **Weight:** Here you enter the weight of your package. (You may use your bathroom scale; or better yet, buy a digital postage scale on eBay.)

✔ **Delivery Confirmation:** Confirmation is free with Priority Mail. Find more info on the DC (Delivery Confirmation) in Technique 36.

✔ **Signature Confirmation:** Signature confirmation provides you a signature and date of delivery, and is available for many levels of service. If you'd like a signature confirmation for your package, it will add $1.30 to the postage cost. You can request Proof of Delivery online or on the phone.

✔ **Display Value of Postage on Label:** If you'd prefer not to show the actual amount of the postage on the label, do not check this box. That way, whatever handling fees you charge your customer are transparent.

✔ **E-mail Message to Buyer:** Customer service to the fore! Type in a nice note letting customers know you appreciate their business. This might also be a good place to ask them to e-mail you immediately if there are any problems with the item when it arrives. (A good defense against knee-jerk negative feedback.)

✔ **Item(s) Being Shipped to Your Buyer:** In this area will be the item number and name of the item you are shipping.

If you've finished filling in the form and everything looks okay, complete the USPS shipping process with these steps:

1. **Click Continue.**

The USPS Shipping Confirmation page appears, as shown in Figure 31-4. On the Shipping Confirmation page, all the information from the previous page is listed.

2. **If you've made a mistake on any entry, click Edit Shipment Details, or cancel the transaction by clicking Cancel.**

• **Figure 31-4:** Your USPS Shipping Confirmation page.

3. **Click Pay and Continue if everything looks okay.**

Your PayPal account is charged for the postage amount and a new window opens to allow you to print postage on your printer. You have the option of printing a sample label, which is a good idea: You can print the sample to make sure that your printer and all the connections are working properly.

4. **After you print the sample and you're happy with the results, print the label by clicking Print Label.**

The label will look similar to the one in Figure 31-5.

• **Figure 31-5: The printed PayPal Priority Mail label.**

You can now request a pickup from the post office by clicking the Request Pickup link that takes you directly to the USPS site.

Shipping with UPS

Shippers such as UPS charge different rates based on how often you use their services (see Technique 37 for this breakdown). If you're shipping many packages a week, it might be best if you printed your labels directly from the UPS site. All PayPal UPS shipments are charged the occasional shipper rate. If you use UPS just once in a while, the PayPal method will work perfectly for you.

If you've selected UPS as your shipper on the PayPal Shipping page, you'll arrive at a page with these choices:

✔ **UPS Account:** You can open a new UPS account immediately online, or, if you have an existing UPS account number, you may type it in this field.

To open a new account you'll have to verify your company data (it's already entered here from your PayPal account information) and let UPS know approximately how many packages you ship per week.

✔ **Shipping Payment Information:** You also have to indicate whether you'd like to pay for your shipping with your PayPal account, or you'd like the shipping billed to your existing UPS account.

When you're through with these choices, finish the shipping process with these steps:

1. **Click Continue.**

2. **If any information on the resulting confirmation page is wrong, press Edit to go back and fix the erroneous entries.**

3. **When all the information on the confirmation page is correct, click Continue.**

4. **Read the UPS Shipping Agreement (if you're opening a new account), and**

▶ If you agree, click I Agree.

▶ If you don't, click I Decline. Then you can go back and ship via the USPS.

Now you're ready to print a label. Fill out the requested information and progress in the same manner as for USPS shipping, which I described in the preceding section.

When your label has printed, you may elect to go back to your PayPal Overview page, as shown in Figure 31-6. The items you've selected to ship will include a Track Package button, and the charges for your shipment will appear in your history log. You may click the Track Package button at any time after you've shipped your item to track the package's progress and confirm delivery.

• **Figure 31-6: Your PayPal Overview page after shipping.**

Expanding Your Business with PayPal Shops and Tools

Save Time By

- ✔ Joining PayPal Shops
- ✔ Shopping the Web securely with a virtual credit card
- ✔ Benefiting from the PayPal referral program

Before PayPal joined eBay, they were pulling out every trick in the book to get members. The company was founded with a real desire to give customers plenty of extras for their loyalty, as I explain throughout this part. They have tons of tools to enhance the seller's online selling experience. The tools and the prices charged by PayPal truly are unmatched by any other online payment service. This technique fills you in on a couple more really cool tools from PayPal.

Joining PayPal Shops

The best part of joining PayPal Shops is that there is no cost to you. A PayPal Shop is really not a separate online store, but a link from the PayPal mall (so to speak) to a unique group of shops. Over 40 million PayPal members may browse this area at any time — so why not avail yourself of this free marketing opportunity? The shop can link to your eBay Store, or you can link to your PayPal-enabled business Web site. Think of it as a way to double your store's visibility on the Web without spending more in fees. Your store will be listed in the PayPal Shops directory, as shown in Figure 32-1.

Notice that the PayPal hub has categories (down the left side of the page) and a shop search. The categories whittle down into subcategories, just like at eBay. Except, unlike at eBay, you won't find any *sub*-subcategories.

I used the search box to find some innocuous, pretty things and came up with the search results shown in Figure 32-2. Notice that there is a number next to each store name. No, it's not the seller's feedback rating; it's the PayPal Seller Reputation number, which I explain in the following section.

Your PayPal Seller Reputation number

Did you ever wonder what that number next to your name on PayPal meant and who sees it? It's the PayPal Reputation number, and it shows how many Verified PayPal members have paid you. Your number increases 30 days after a transaction is complete; the delay ensures that the number reflects only successful transactions.

• **Figure 32-1:** The PayPal Shops hub page.

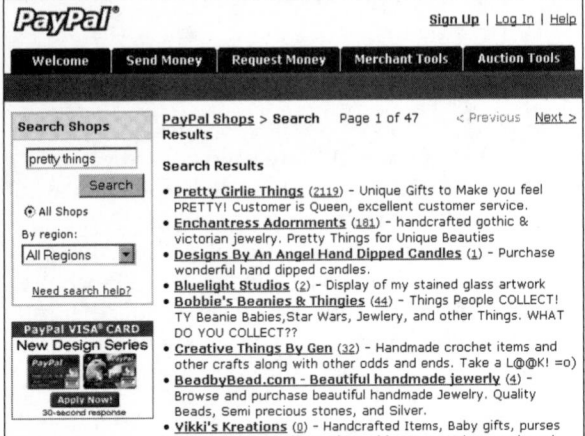

• **Figure 32-2:** The results of a search in PayPal Shops.

Clicking the number will bring up a box reflecting the number of successful transactions and information about the seller, as shown in Figure 32-3.

PayPal Shopping invitations

As a PayPal shops owner, you have an additional benefit. Whenever a customer sends you a payment from an area other than your Web site (hmmmm, like your sales on eBay, for example?), PayPal sends them an invitation to shop at your store! A sample of that invitation is shown in Figure 32-4.

• **Figure 32-3:** PayPal's Member Information box.

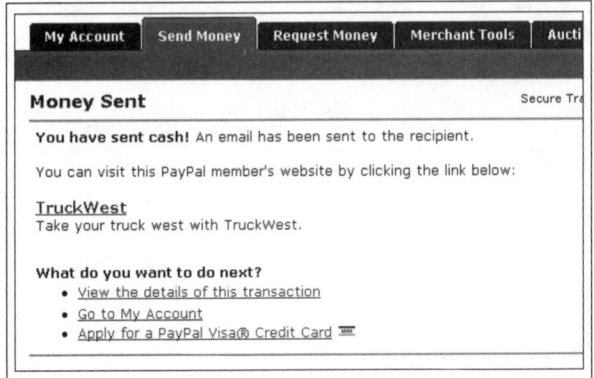

• **Figure 32-4:** An example of the PayPal Shops invitation from the PayPal Web site.

That's a pretty cool deal — don't you think? Who would have figured you'd get help for your outside Web site from an eBay company?

But, as with any really cool deal, there are a few requirements you must meet before you can set up your shop at PayPal.

- ✔ **Verified Premier or Business Account:** You must maintain one of the higher-level PayPal accounts.

- ✔ **Registered credit card:** You must maintain a current credit card registered to your PayPal account.

✔ **Confirmed checking account:** You must have at least one confirmed checking account tied into your PayPal account.

✔ **Money Market Fund:** You are required to sign up for the PayPal Money Market Fund. This means you must supply PayPal with your Social Security number or your business's Federal ID number.

 PayPal does not send out Federal 1099 forms on your PayPal sales. That income is coming from your buyers, and because you're not paid by PayPal, they won't issue a 1099 for your PayPal sales.

PayPal Money Fund

For the initiated, PayPal offers its members an interest-paying Money Fund that is partnered with Barclay Global Investors. By being a part of this fund, you can earn interest on money that you leave in your PayPal account. The money you earn from sales is best transferred ASAP to your own business account at your bank, so many sellers don't leave any money in his or her PayPal account. The membership in the money fund is strictly for PayPal's sake. So they have one more way to verify that you're really you (they have your Social Security number) — or that your business is really real.

 PayPal offers you FDIC pass-through insurance. PayPal deposits your money as part of pooled accounts in several banks: Wells Fargo Bank, N.A., Comerica Bank – California, USA, and Bank of America, N.A. In the very unlikely event that any of these major banks should fail, your money would be covered under the FDIC pass-through deposit insurance, along with any other deposits you have at that bank, up to $100,000. FDIC pass-through deposit insurance protects you only against the failure of the bank at which PayPal places your funds, and does *not* protect you against PayPal's very unlikely insolvency.

After you're committed to the idea that you'd like a PayPal store (and assuming that you're qualified), the application process is easy. Just follow these steps:

1. **Give your PayPal Shop a name.**

The name doesn't really have to match your Web site. Make it a smart marketing name — something that will catch people's eye as they browse the stores.

2. **Give PayPal the URL that you want to link your PayPal shop to.**

This can be your eBay Store or your own e-commerce, PayPal-enabled Web site.

3. **Type a short description of your Web site.**

Be as descriptive as possible and make it interesting!

4. **Select two categories that best describe your store from the PayPal Shop category list.**

5. **List up to 10 keywords to describe your store to search engines.**

Be smart! Learn which are your best keywords with the ViewTracker tool explained in Technique 14.

Featured Shop consideration

After you set up your PayPal Shop, you can apply to be selected as featured — with your logo — on the PayPal logoff page (you know, the page that opens when you sign off of PayPal).

To apply, you must include another brief Web site description, along with all the reasons you'd make a great selection as the Featured Shop. PayPal then selects their shops from the applications according to the quality of each site and how well PayPal is integrated into it. Not a bad deal!

 Before you apply for Featured Shop status, review your site's design and usability. Selection is based on the quality of the site and just how prominently PayPal is integrated into it.

Just think: If just a few of the 40 million PayPal members click onto your Web site when exiting their transactions, you *could* be rolling in orders! In

Figure 32-5, check out the amount of hits one featured store got from that link on PayPal alone.

Site statistics

Every month, PayPal sends statistics on hits to PayPal shopkeepers. Don't worry; these statistics aren't a bunch of useless information — they're all about your Web site hits! Take a look at a sample in Figure 32-5. Remember that this report counts only those hits that come through links from the PayPal Shops area, not any independent hits you get from the Internet.

```
Sent: Tuesday, February 24, 2004 5:51 PM
Subject: Your PayPal Shops Weekly Traffic Report

Dear Pretty Girlie Things TM,
Here are the current PayPal Shops traffic statistics for your website:

This week's visitors to your site:  1649
Total visitors to your site, ever:  3534
Total websites in PayPal Shops:  46664
```

• **Figure 32-5:** Monthly PayPal hit statistics.

Spending Your PayPal Balance with a Virtual MasterCard

Gee, now they've gone and done it. As if I didn't get into enough trouble with my plastic already, now they've invented a *virtual* credit card. This virtual credit card is one that you can't hold or touch. You're supplied with a temporary MasterCard number that allows you to spend your PayPal balance (your credit limit) at non-PayPal retail sites on the Internet.

Most likely, you don't often keep a balance in your PayPal account (so that you can keep your books straight). But occasionally you might just sell something of a personal nature on eBay (like that Zippo lighter that's been in your dresser for years) that's not part of your regular, official business. If the buyer pays for it through your PayPal account, and you don't want to deposit that money into your business banking account, you've got three options.

- ✔ **Withdraw the money to your personal checking account:** The transaction will show up in your monthly PayPal download so that you can isolate that as separate income from your business.

- ✔ **Buy something on eBay:** Pay for it with the money you got for that old Zippo in your PayPal balance after withdrawing your business receipts.

- ✔ **Get a virtual MasterCard:** You can spend it anywhere on the Web that accepts MasterCard payments.

To get a virtual credit card, log onto your PayPal account, and go to PayPal Shops. The link is at the very bottom of the page, as shown in Figure 32-6.

```
Mobile | Mass Pay | Money Market | ATM/Debit Card | BillPay | Referrals | About Us | Accounts | Fees |
Privacy | Security Center | User Agreement | Developers | Shops | Gift Certificates/Points

an eBay Company

Copyright © 1999-2004 PayPal. All rights reserved.
Information about FDIC pass-through insurance
```

• **Figure 32-6: The very handy Shops link at the bottom of every PayPal page.**

After you get to PayPal Shops, look on the right side of the page. There will be a shaded blue vertical box with links to PayPal features. Find the link that reads *Shop Anywhere* and click it.

You'll now arrive at the Shop Anywhere page. From this page you can select a store from the drop-down menu as in Figure 32-7, or you can type in the URL of any store on the Internet that accepts MasterCard payments for their goods.

After you make your selection, a window opens for the selected store, and in a small window at the bottom, you will have your PayPal Debit bar with a virtual credit card number. (See Figure 32-8.) Your Debit bar will have the total amount of your PayPal balance as the credit limit. You can spend only to a limit of $150.00 a day through this method.

Now all that's left is to select an item and, when you check out, indicate that you're paying with Master-Card. Type your virtual account number in the credit card number and your PayPal account will be debited for the amount of your purchase.

 If you change your mind and choose not to spend money with your Debit bar, don't worry. The money will not be debited from your PayPal account unless you actually spend it.

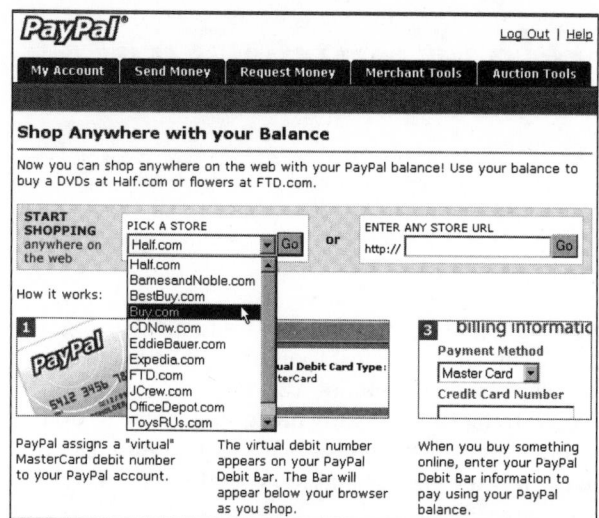

• **Figure 32-7: Going shopping with my virtual credit card! Wheee!**

• **Figure 32-8: The Debit bar appears — and it's off to shop with virtual credit in hand!**

Cashing In on the PayPal Referral Program

And you thought the days of getting money for referring people to PayPal were over? Hah! It's just that now PayPal has set its sights a little higher. Now they want business account referrals rather than personal users.

You can send invitations to use PayPal in your e-mails via a custom link, or you can place a banner on your Web site. You receive $10 the first time a merchant you refer uses any of PayPal's Web site tools, and you can earn more after your referral receives a total of $1,000 in Send Money payments.

It's kind of like multilevel marketing. After the referral posts the initial $1000 in sales, you receive a percentage of your referral's revenue, up to a maximum of $100, for the first six months of his or her PayPal account. The residual payout equals .5 percent of the merchant's net sales.

✋ **No spamming!!!**

To get in on this good deal, go to the little navigation bar at the bottom of the page, and click Referrals. After you arrive at the target page, you're presented with two ways to link, as shown in Figure 32-9. One is a referral link for e-mail, and the other is a big honking PayPal banner that you can put on your Web site. (HTML custom coding is already generated for you — just copy and paste it onto your Web page.)

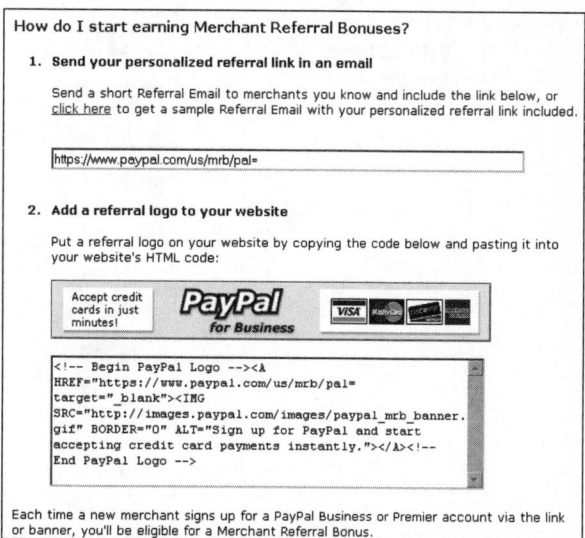

• **Figure 32-9: Two ways to set up PayPal Merchant Referral links.**

Technique 33

Using PayPal's Little-Known Tools

Save Time By

- ✔ Making the payment tools work for you
- ✔ Managing post-sales activities
- ✔ Using the Outlook Payment Wizard

PayPal is constantly adding new, convenient tools to make using the service even easier. Many of the newest tools are for those with their own Web sites, as discussed in Technique 28. PayPal provides so many cool tools that you'd think the company had nothing else to do but come up with these — but, then again, I guess that's its job. And it's my job to keep up with all the newest gizmos and tell you about them.

To find PayPal tools, check out the Merchant Tools section of the PayPal site when you're next depositing your auction receipts into your bank account. Simply sign on to the site, transact all your business, and then click the Merchant Tools button on the PayPal tab, as pictured in Figure 33-1.

• **Figure 33-1: PayPal Merchant Tools page.**

PayPal's Merchant Tools

On the PayPal Merchant Tools page, take a minute to read about what's available. Then, be sure to scroll down to the lowly bottom of the list to the area called *Other PayPal Tools*, as pictured in Figure 33-2.

Other PayPal Tools
Automate inventory management, attract buyers from around the world, let employees use your PayPal account, or expand your business to the eBay Marketplace.
Instant Payment Notification
Multiple Currencies
Multi-User Access
Auction Tools
Payment Request Wizard for Outlook
NEW! Auto Return
NEW! Custom Payment Pages
NEW! New Merchant Tools

• **Figure 33-2: The mysterious "Other" PayPal Tools.**

PayPal has several "secret" tools listed in this area — but be sure to check back regularly; they're always adding new ones. Here's what you'll find:

✔ **Instant Payment Notification:** Here is a super deal for those who have sophisticated Web sites. This is PayPal's interface for handling real-time purchase confirmation and server-to-server communications. It delivers immediate notification and confirmation of PayPal payments that you receive through your Web site, and more. This tool is so *not* for the amateur!

✔ **Multiple Currencies:** This link goes to a page that thoroughly explains PayPal's current policies on international trade and dealing in foreign currencies. If you are doing business in foreign countries and want to accept international currencies, be sure to visit this area.

✔ **Auction Tools:** Clicking here is another way to get to the Auction Tools area, pictured in Figure 33-3.

It seems PayPal acknowledges that their "merchants" are more than likely also sellers on eBay. (Ya think?) In the Auctions Tool hub, you'll find links to all the information you'd ever care to know about some related matters:

▶ **Add PayPal to Your Listing:** This link goes to your PayPal preference settings for your

auction accounts. Here you may select to insert PayPal logos manually or automatically in your eBay sales pages.

To change your auction account preferences click the Automatic Logos link; you'll see a page like the one in Figure 33-4.

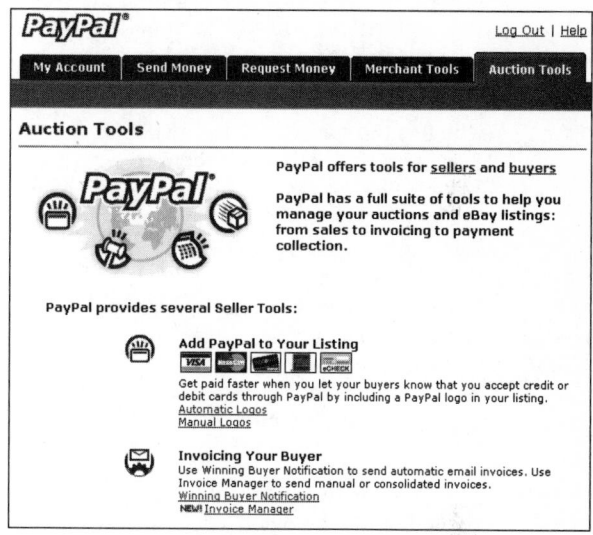

• **Figure 33-3: The PayPal Auction Tools hub.**

Auction Accounts				Back to Profile Summary
Use this page to manage your auction accounts.				
User ID	Site	Automatic Logo Insertion	Winning Buyer Notification	PayPal Preferred on eBay
○ marsha_c	eBay	On	Off	On
○	eBay	Off	Off	On
Edit Password Remove				Add

• **Figure 33-4: Auction account preferences.**

On this page, you see a list of your PayPal registered eBay User IDs. By clicking the On/Off links, you can turn on and off Automatic Logo Insertion, Winning Buyer Notification, and PayPal Preferred.

You may also add another eBay user ID (if you have more than one). To add another User ID, click the Add button. To change any of your eBay passwords, click the Edit Password button.

▶ **Invoicing Your Buyer:** You may click the Winning Buyer Notification link to set your preferences for PayPal's automated invoicing. This service sends a PayPal invoice to your buyer immediately after an eBay transaction is complete.

Visiting this page also allows you to indicate your preferences and add personalized text that will appear on your PayPal invoices.

There's also a link to the Invoice Manager (which is the same thing as the Post-Sale Manager described next, except the Invoice option will be selected). This helps you manage your end of sale tasks for items that closed in the past 30 days.

 In lieu of spending big money on an expensive subscription to an auction management system, you might want to try PayPal's Post-Sale Manager. It certainly gives you some top quality tools to run your eBay business.

▶ **Manage eBay Items Sold:** This links to the PayPal Post-Sale Manager.

▶ **Shipping and Tracking Tools:** If you ship your item through PayPal, here's an additional link you can use to check up on the shipping process. (See Technique 31 for information about how to ship directly from PayPal.)

▶ **Manage Your PayPal Payments:** Here are links to your history log and download records.

✔ **Payment Request Wizard for Outlook:** This links you to an easy-to-use, downloadable program that allows you to turn your Microsoft Outlook program into an invoicing machine. OK, maybe not. But the program does allow you to insert PayPal clickable payment links into your e-mails. For more info, see section "Taking Advantage of the Outlook Payment Request Wizard," later in this technique.

✔ **Auto Return:** This goes to PayPal's Web site Payment preferences for Auto Return. If you have a PayPal Pay Now button on your Web site and haven't indicated a return page on your site in your coding (I show you how to do that in

Technique 29), you can manually set the URL for a page on your Web site where customers return to after making a purchase from your site.

✔ **Custom Payment Page Styles:** This link leads you to a place where you can customize your PayPal payment pages. By default, your customers will see a simple PayPal payment page. By clicking the Add button, you can design a completely custom payment page to match your Web site.

Using the Post-Sale Manager

The powerful Post-Sale Manager can handle a good deal of your auction management business. Because you go to PayPal to check your sales and deposits anyway, why not use its tools to manage your eBay sales? Best of all, Post-Sale Manager is free.

Figure 33-5 shows the Post-Sale Manager, which enables you to manage all your post sale activities.

Post-Sale Manager

Post-Sale Manager helps you manage all end-of-sale activities for **items sold** on eBay. You can track the status of items you successfully sold in the past 30 days.†

| View: | marsha_c | Add |
| Show: | Uninvoiced | Submit |

• Post-Sale Manager Demo
• Key to Post-Sale Manager
• Post-Sale Manager Manual

Items Sold - 61 after search   Last Updated 16:47:29 PST Feb. 17, 2004 - Refresh

Select	Item #	End Date	Price	Quantity	Buyer's User ID	Payment Status	Invoice	Shipping	Feedback
☐	Cloud Dome Background PORTABLE PHOTO STAGE 2982648688	Feb. 16, 2004	$37.99 USD	1		Unpaid (Edit)	Invoice		
☐	2 Photography Photo Lights Flood Lighting Kit 2983845520	Feb. 16, 2004	$120.99 USD	1		Unpaid (Edit)	Invoice		
☐	un-du Adhesive Remover 2931822191	Feb. 15, 2004	$4.99 USD	1		Paid (PayPal)	Consolidated		Leave
☐	eBay Sellers Steel Rolling Garment Rack NEW 2986975807	Feb. 14, 2004	$24.99 USD	1		Unpaid (Edit)	Sent		

• **Figure 33-5: PayPal Post-Sale Manager.**

Every item you have sold on eBay in the past 30 days is displayed in rows with columns of status indicators. You will see:

✔ **Payment Status:** Here you see whether the item has been paid through PayPal. If you click the link on this row next to a paid transaction, you'll be taken to the payment detail page. If the item is unpaid and you receive payment in the mail, you can click the Edit button here and enter information about how you were paid, as shown in Figure 33-6.

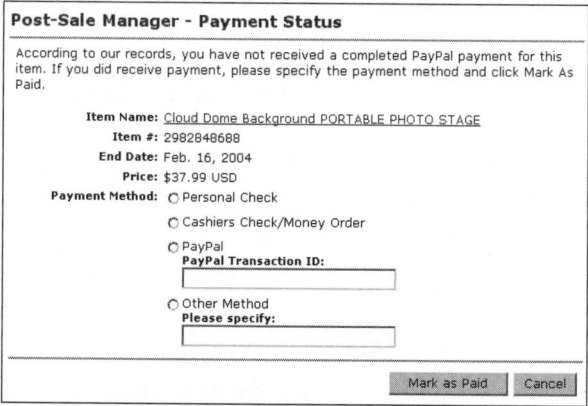

Post-Sale Manager - Payment Status

According to our records, you have not received a completed PayPal payment for this item. If you did receive payment, please specify the payment method and click Mark As Paid.

Item Name:	Cloud Dome Background PORTABLE PHOTO STAGE
Item #:	2982848688
End Date:	Feb. 16, 2004
Price:	$37.99 USD
Payment Method:	○ Personal Check
	○ Cashiers Check/Money Order
	○ PayPal
	PayPal Transaction ID:
	○ Other Method
	Please specify:

[Mark as Paid] [Cancel]

• **Figure 33-6: Updating Payment Status in the Post-Sale Manager.**

✔ **Invoice:** If you do not have PayPal's automatic invoice turned on, you may click the Invoice button for an item to send an invoice.

If you click the item title in the Post-Sale Manager list, the item page opens up in a new window.

When a buyer has purchased several items from you and paid via PayPal, you see a button indicating that the item is Consolidated with another purchase.

If you use PayPal's automatic invoicing, the Invoice column for the item will include the word Auto.

✔ **Shipping:** To print shipping labels and pay for your item's shipping through PayPal, click on this link. Instructions for this process are found in Technique 31.

✔ **Feedback:** Press the Leave button to leave customer feedback for an eBay transaction. You are brought to a PayPal Feedback page (shown in

Figure 33-7). Fill in your feedback here and click Leave Feedback; it will go immediately to eBay. If you have previously left feedback on eBay, and want to update a record, merely click Mark As Done.

Post-Sale Manager - Leave eBay Feedback

To leave eBay feedback for the buyer, choose a feedback rating, enter your comment and click Leave Feedback. If you have already left feedback for this buyer on eBay, click Mark As Done.

Buyer eBay ID:	ctskaty
Item Name:	Cloud Dome Background PORTABLE BOARD STAGE
Item #:	2986310880
Rating:	⦿ Positive
	○ Neutral
	○ Negative
Feedback:	
Characters left:	80

[Leave Feedback] [Mark As Done] [Cancel]

• **Figure 33-7: Leaving eBay feedback through PayPal.**

To send a quick e-mail to the buyer, click the buyer's User ID. An e-mail message window opens, pre-addressed to the buyer.

✔ **Memo:** Click this link to leave a personal memo for yourself.

Updating Payment Status

To record all those great checks piling up in your bank account, update Payment Status with these steps:

1. **On the Payment Status page, select the appropriate payment method.**

If there is an unposted PayPal payment (this happens when a buyer sends you money without indicating the item number, for example), you may enter the transaction ID in the PayPal text box.

2. **Click Mark as Paid.**

When you return to the Post-Sale Manager page, the transaction is marked Paid.

Using search filters

Note that at the top of the Post-Sale Manager there are two drop-down boxes. You use one to filter by eBay User IDs and the other to define your Post-Sale Manager report view.

- ✔ **View:** Select an eBay User ID to apply a filter that lets you view only that buyer's transactions. If you have more than one ID registered with PayPal, you can set this to view all transactions from that user for all your User IDs. Just select from the drop-down box to view All eBay Accounts.

  If you have more than one eBay account, and it isn't shown here, you can add an account by clicking Add. On the following page you'll be prompted for the new User ID and the eBay password. Type it in and press *Add.* You now have an additional eBay User ID attached to your PayPal account.

- ✔ **Show:** Customize your Post-Sale Manager report view to display all items, or break down your report to show one of these categories:

  Unpaid items

      Uninvoiced

      To Consolidate

      Invoiced

  Paid Items

      Needs Feedback

      To Be Shipped

      Shipped

      Done

  Removed

 If you want to sort the entries, click links at the top of the columns to sort by Item #, End Date, or Buyer's User ID. The default is sorted by End Date.

Taking Advantage of the Outlook Payment Request Wizard

Have you ever done business with someone who asks you, "How do I pay by PayPal?" Or how about when someone wants to purchase multiple items from your Web site and you need to send a combined invoice?

The Outlook Payment Request Wizard enables you to give your e-mail response a more professional look by including a custom icon link to a PayPal payment page.

To download the Wizard (it's a 3.9MB file), go to the Merchant Tools tab. Scroll down and click the Payment Request Wizard for Outlook link (under the Other PayPal Tools heading):

1. **Click the Download the Payment Request Wizard Now link on the Payment Wizard page.**

    A window pops-up asking what you'd like to do with the file you're about to download.

2. **Click Save.**

    A new window appears, showing the contents of the hard drive of your computer.

3. **Select the appropriate directory to save the file to and click Save.**

    The file is downloaded and saved to your hard drive.

4. **Open the directory you saved the file to and double-click the filename.**

    The file opens and is installed on your computer.

Now the Wizard is safely installed so that when you open Microsoft Outlook, you will see a new option at the top of the program, as shown in Figure 33-8.

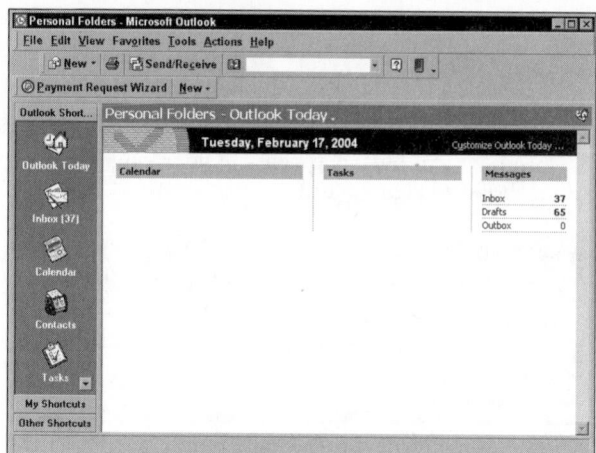

• **Figure 33-8: Outlook with the new Payment Request Wizard button.**

Now, to send a PayPal payment request in an e-mail, open your Outlook program and click the PayPal Payment Request Wizard button to begin the process.

1. **Click Next when the introductory window appears.**

2. **In the next screen, choose the kind of Payment Button you'd like in your e-mail. Your choices are:**

Basic Payment Button

Product Button

Service Button

Auction Payment Button

Donate Button

To include button that allows buyers to pay for an item bought at auction, select the Auction Payment Button.

3. **Click Next, and you see a window like the one shown in Figure 33-9.**

4. **Fill in your e-mail address, the winning bidder's e-mail address, the eBay item number, and a note, if you'd like.**

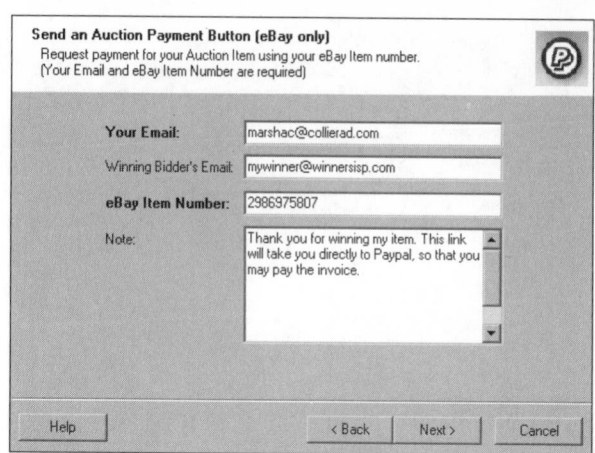

• **Figure 33-9: Filling out the Wizard's form.**

5. **Click Next and select which style of PayPal button you'd like to include in your e-mail, as shown in Figure 33-10.**

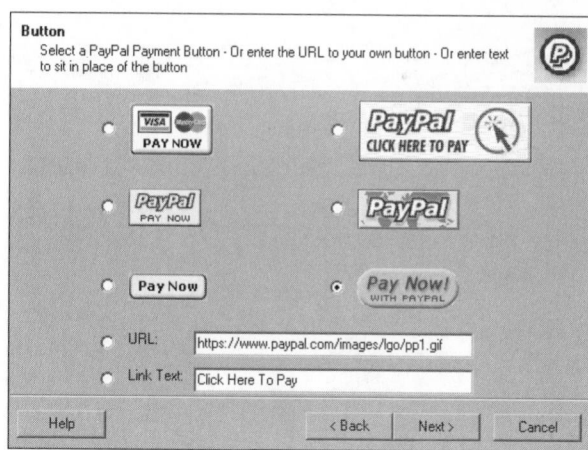

• **Figure 33-10: Selecting your payment button.**

6. **Click Next.**

The next screen is where you confirm your work. Double-check that you've done everything right before previewing the button.

7. **Click Test on the bottom of the confirmation window, as in Figure 33-11.**

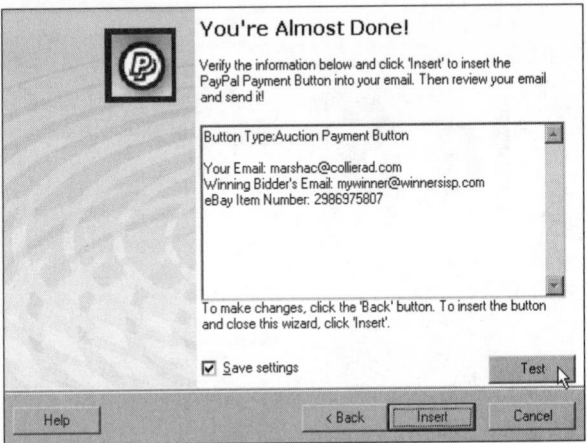

• **Figure 33-11:** You're almost done!

A preview of the PayPal payment window pops up (as in Figure 33-12) so that you can see what your buyer will see when he clicks on the button to make a payment.

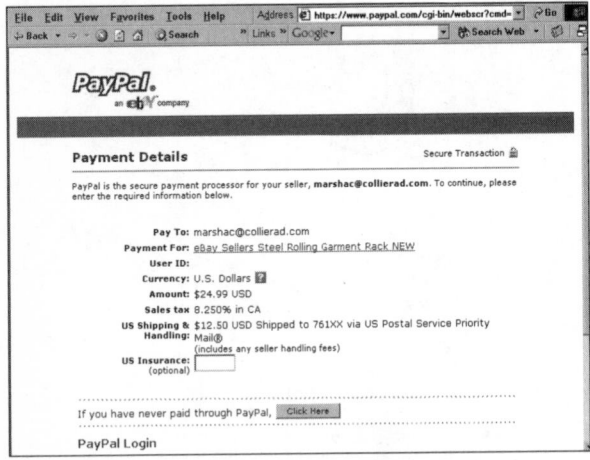

• **Figure 33-12:** PayPal payment window preview.

8. If you're satisfied with the way the payment window looks, click Insert. (If you are not happy with the results, press the Back button to make changes.)

A payment button appears in your e-mail, as shown in Figure 33-13.

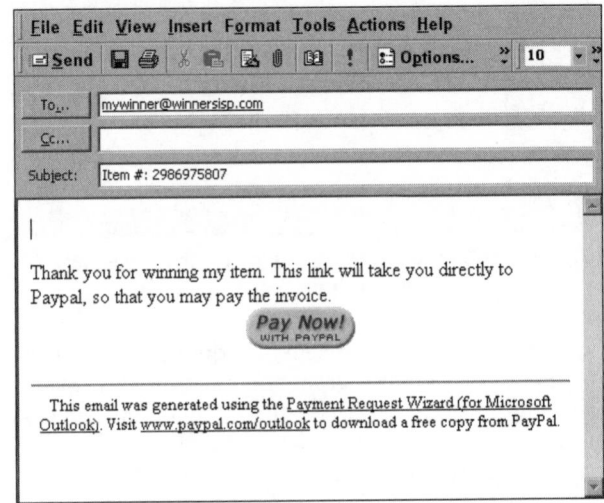

• **Figure 33-13:** The e-mail ready to go, including a payment button.

Now you can enter any additional information in your e-mail (a thank-you would be nice).

9. Click Send to send the e-mail on its merry way to your buyer.

 If you select any button option other than Auction Payment at the beginning of the Wizard, you'll be asked for specific information about the item including price and shipping amount.

Part VI

Shipping Made Simple

The 5th Wave   By Rich Tennant

"The bids are coming in, all right, but where are we gonna find a shipping crate for an attack submarine?"

Technique 34

Selecting the Best Packing Materials

Save Time By

✔ Padding the package safely

✔ Picking the right envelope for your item

✔ Understanding the types of mailing envelopes

✔ Getting deals on boxes

Because saving time and money is what this book is all about, you should know that the most important area where sellers drop the time-and-money ball is in shipping. I buy hundreds of items from eBay and have seen it all when it comes to packing, padding, and shipping.

I've received triple-packed unbreakable plastic items, swathed in yards of plain newsprint sheets. I've seen money thrown out the window by e-tailers who have used incorrect packing materials, which are expensive for the seller and often increase the shipping cost of the package for the buyer due to the final weight.

 The packing materials that you use for your shipments can either make or break your bottom line in the shipping income/expense column of your business reports. (Read more about tracking expenditures in Technique 48.)

Many sellers remark, "The buyer pays shipping, so what do I care what it costs? I pass on all those expenses to my buyers." Well, yes and no. Prudent packing can be a boon to your business because, in the constant competition with other sellers on the site, having lower shipping costs can often make the difference between a sale and a no sale. This is especially true when several people have the same item up for sale, with a minuscule difference in the item's selling price. Reasonable shipping charges can make the difference.

Pay attention to packing. It's only expensive if you don't know what you're doing. You can ship your items in quality packing, keep buyers happy, and still make a dollar or so on each item for your handling fees.

Buying your shipping materials on eBay is trés economical. eBay shipping supply e-tailers make their livings selling online. Their overhead is much lower than any retail outlet. Even after paying shipping to get the bubblewrap to your door, you save money and time. Most of these sellers ship the same day they get your order. It's wise to compare, know where you can save money, and recognize where saving money isn't prudent.

Use only as much packing material as necessary to get the item where it's going intact. This saves time, money, and space.

Using Void Fill

Nope! Void fill is not a new drug to prevent hunger pangs when dieting. *Void fill* is the industry term for the stuff you use to fill up space in shipping boxes to keep items from rolling in transit. (It's really the modern-day term for the old-fashioned word *dunnage.*)

There are many forms of void fill, and the best kind really depends on the item that you're shipping. Here are the most popular types and a description of their plusses and minuses.

Air packing pillows

I first found out about these nifty little pillows when I received books from a major online bookseller. (See Figure 34-1.) When I looked into purchasing the pillows, I was disappointed to find out that they are made on-site in the shipping department by a rather expensive machine that injects air into pre-manufactured continuous tubing and then produces pillows of the desired size. Sadly, my shipping department (a table in the garage) was not big enough for this machine, and my shipping budget couldn't absorb the price of the equipment.

After you have the machine installed (and paid for), producing these pillows is very cost effective. But if you don't want to make that investment, you'll be glad to hear that buying them from sellers on eBay is quite economical, mainly because the manufacturing and shipping costs are low. What these folks are essentially shipping you is 99 percent air (something the Post Office hasn't yet figured out how to charge for).

Air packing pillows are perfect for filling in the area around smaller boxed items that you want to double box. They are also handy if you have breakables that

you've pre-wrapped in bubble wrap; just use the pillows to fill out the box. They're crushproof and can support about 150 pounds of weight without a blowout.

• Figure 34-1: eBay seller XDR2 auctions pre-made packing pillows at reasonable prices.

Plentiful packing peanuts

Every serious eBay seller has to have a stock of packing peanuts. They're handy for padding Tyvek® envelopes, filling boxes so that items don't shift around, and filling collectible milk bottles so they look full when you sell them on eBay.

Peanuts seem to multiply in dark areas. I know, because in all my time on eBay, I've never had to buy any. That's probably because I buy almost everything online, and everything comes in peanut stuffing — so I never run out. (By the way, bags of peanuts make great bumpers in the garage.)

For functionality, foam packing peanuts are the granddaddy of all void filler. When properly placed in a box, they fill every nook and cranny and cushion your shipment to make it virtually indestructible. The key is to not go short in the land of plenty — use plenty of peanuts and make sure there are no vacant air spaces in your box. An extra bonus: They're cheap and if you recycle them, they don't hurt the environment.

Figure 34-2 below shows you how eBay sellers ship packing peanuts in very big bags!

• **Figure 34-2: Gary (eBay seller) Gatorpack waits for his mail pick up.**

Bubble wrapping by the roll

Bubble wrap (or *air cellular packaging material*) is *de rigueur* shipping material. Bubble wrap is made up of air-filled cushions of polyethylene. It's supplied in rolls of different widths and lengths (see Figure 34-3). It really shines for those who wrap very delicate, breakable items.

When wrapping items with bubble wrap, wrap it one way and then the other, then affix some packing tape to make your item an impenetrable ball. Bubble wrap is reasonably priced and adds next to no weight to your packages.

 When you purchase bubble wrap, be sure you buy the perforated, or tear off kind. Cutting a giant roll of bubble wrap with a box cutter can be a dangerous proposition.

• **Figure 34-3: Different sizes of bubble wrap from eBay seller, GraMur Supply.**

Plain old white newsprint

In the right shipping situation, plain white newsprint is fantastic. It's cheap and easy to store. The bad news? It's heavy and sellers often use too many sheets to wrap the items they pack.

eBay sellers dealing in glass, china, and breakable knick-knacks often use newsprint to wrap each piece before placing it in a box full of packing peanuts.

If you really feel you must use newsprint, I suggest you buy it by the roll and use a table mounted roll cutter to cut the exact size you need. (This is the kind of thing you may have seen in old-style butcher shops and delis.) This set up helps you to avoid using too much paper.

Mailing Envelopes

Many eBay sellers miss the boat completely when they ship all their items in boxes, just because they're free from the Post Office (Technique 36 shows you how to get free boxes and envelopes as well). When you get into serious selling, using envelopes will cut your shipping costs and your items will still arrive safe and sound.

 Items sent in envelopes can be sent via First Class mail as long as they weigh 13 ounces or less.

Thankfully, the envelope makers of the world have united to manufacture their envelopes in standard sizes. Figure 34-4 gives you an idea what these look like.

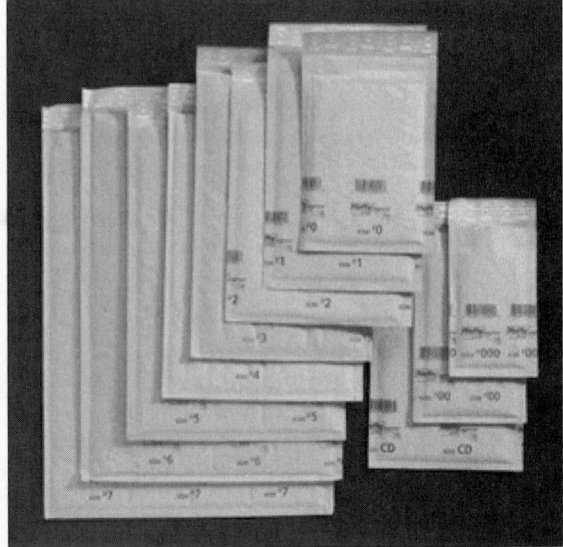

• **Figure 34-4: A variety of bubble envelopes in standard sizes from eBay seller, grasup.**

Not only are there different sizes, but someone actually gave some thought to making these envelopes so that they fit certain items. Take a look at Table 34-1 for a listing of standard envelope sizes and their uses.

TABLE 34-1: STANDARD BUBBLE-PADDED MAILER SIZES

Size	Measurements	Suggested Items
#000	4" x 8"	Collector trading cards, jewelry, computer diskettes, coins
#00	5" x 10"	Postcards, paper ephemera

Size	Measurements	Suggested Items
#0	6" x 10"	CDs, DVDs, Xbox or PS2 games
#1	7¼" x 12"	Cardboard sleeve VHS tapes, jewel-cased CDs and DVDs
#2	8½" x 12"	Clamshell VHS tapes
#3	8½" x 14½"	Toys, clothing, stuffed animals
#4	9½" x 14½"	Small books, trade paperbacks
#5	10½" x 16"	Hardcover books
#6	12½" x 19"	Clothing, soft boxed items
#7	14¼" x 20"	Much larger packaged items, framed items and plaques

Mailing envelopes come made of many types of materials. Some are sturdier than others. Here's what many eBay sellers use:

- ✔ **Poly Vinyl Envelopes:** If you've ever ordered clothing or bedding from any of the television-shopping clubs, this is what they came in. Poly Vinyl envelopes are lightweight, puncture and tear resistant, and light as a feather. They are the most durable envelopes available. Who says you *have* to ship in boxes?

- ✔ **Tyvek Envelopes:** You know those really cool indestructible white envelopes you get from the Post Office or FedEx? They're made of DuPont Tyvek. It isn't made of paper, it's spun-bonded olefin fiber. It's got all the benefits of vinyl envelopes and more. Tyvek breathes (allows air to reach your product) and has a higher strength-to-weight ratio than other envelope materials. (That ratio business means it's very strong, yet feather light.)

- ✔ **Bubble Padded Mailers:** These are the type of envelope most-used by eBay sellers. The envelopes are lined with small bubbles, very similar to bubble wrap. They're great for shipping a variety of items. Bubble lined mailers come in different materials; the pros and cons of each are

  - ▶ Plain paper bubble mailers are the cheapest possible way to go, but can be damaged in the mail if you ship heavy items in them. The perfect way to get around that is to wrap some cheap clear packing tape once around the envelope in each direction.

▶ Vinyl bubble mailers aren't very expensive and are a super protective way to ship. They're 15% lighter than paper bubble mailers and are water resistant.

Getting It Boxed

Boxes come in thousands of sizes.

Buying in bulk

If you've been buying shipping boxes from brick-and-mortar office supply stores, you're paying a lot for the convenience. Yes, they do deliver — but so do the companies who do nothing but manufacture boxes. And these guys offer terrific discounts if you buy 100 at a time.

Check your local phone book and look up Boxes, Manufacturers. If you're a legitimate business, they will be happy to sell to you if you buy in quantity.

Buying boxes on eBay

If you want smaller quantities of boxes, say 25 at a time, look for eBay sellers offering various sizes of boxes on the site. Just use your search tricks and search `shipping (box,boxes)`. (eBay search-engine tricks are in Technique 1.)

Free Priority Mail boxes

Yes, you savvy sellers out there, I know that many of you already know you can get free boxes from the Post Office to ship your Priority Mail packages. But every day I meet more sellers who don't know. So here's the deal . . .

The U.S. Postal Service will ship free boxes, packing tape, labels, and shipping forms for Express Mail, Priority Mail, and Global Priority Mail to your home or business. In the U.S., you can order by phone (800-222-1811) or online (`supplies.usps.gov`). Find out more about this in Technique 36.

 What happens when you put a new item up for sale and someone buys it immediately, but you have no box to ship it in? If the item comes in a sturdy, shippable box, you're somewhat safe. However the Post Office won't always accept boxes that are overprinted with manufacturer's pictures and promotional info. Get some tan color shipping tape, and cover most of the box. It will make the package look somewhat like a plain brown box. You can label it and off it goes.

If the item didn't come in its own box, you can always do some box begging at your local shopping center for a box of appropriate size (just be sure you get it *before* it hits the dumpster — the package smells better that way).

35 Technique

Picking the Right Shipper

Save Time By
- ✔ Knowing your shipping front line
- ✔ Locating service hubs
- ✔ Evaluating costs

One decision about your eBay business that seems easy is selecting the right shipper — but actually it's one of the more difficult choices, at least if you care about your buyers. Shipping can make or break your customer service. Whoever delivers the package to the buyer is a virtual extension of your company.

Professional labels, clean boxes, nifty packing peanuts — those are the things you control. But safe and timely delivery falls into the hands of complete strangers. Once the package leaves your door, it's no longer under your control — yet somehow the buyer blames you for the tardiness or sloppiness of the shipping. Your bottom line isn't the shipper's concern, and no matter how many refunds you get for missed delivery schedules, it won't help when you have one irate customer after another. Simple equation: Irate customers = lousy eBay feedback.

So, what's a seller to do? Do you use the shipper that other sellers rave about? Perhaps opt for convenience over low price? After you decide on a shipper, how often do you re-evaluate its services?

 Did you know that the big two — United Parcel Service and Federal Express — raise their rates every year? The United States Postal Service raises its rates too, but the difference is that the media makes a lot more noise (it's in the newspapers and on the TV news) every time a postage stamp goes up by 1 cent. (Hey, *that's* traditional!)

It's easy to go on the Internet, or talk to friends and hear horror stories about any of the main shippers. The bottom line is, which one works best *for you?*

Meeting the Front Line

Who constitutes your eBay business front line? My shipping front line is Scott, the UPS man; Tim the Post Office carrier, and Jorge who picks up for FedEx Ground. I know the front-line guys because they make my eBay business run smoothly. They don't leave deliveries outside under a bush, and always deliver packages to my neighbor if I'm not home. They pick up my sundry packages with a smile and a lighthearted "They're sure buying things on eBay, aren't they?" I respond with a smile and a bit of friendly chitchat.

Wait, are you telling me that you don't get the same service? Have you ever taken a moment to chat with your delivery person? When you personalize a business relationship, you become more than a street address, you become . . .well . . . a *person*. When you're no longer a number, you become a fellow human being with needs and wants. Believe it or not, people want to make other people happy, even when they feel grumpy. (I'll bet your eBay activities leave you grumpy sometimes too!)

Your front line can help you by watching out for your packages. They can be sure that your packages go into the bin that leaves immediately, versus the one that sits till the end of the day.

I leave a signal when there are packages to be picked up, and every one is picked up. When my thoughtful delivery person delivers a big box, he brings it to the back door near my studio so I don't have to drag it through the front door and across the house.

Of course, your front line can go on vacation — or (heaven forbid) have a sick day. On one day, I was the victim of what I refer to as a "dump and run" from a substitute driver (see Figure 35-1). He dumped stacks of large boxes on my front doorstep — practically blocking access to the door — and didn't even ring the bell!

Try building a relationship with your shipping front line. I've invited them to company holiday parties, and offered them a cool drink on a hot summer day. The result? My shipping is the easiest part of my business.

You can imagine what happens when you have a good front line — and I've got one. On a day when I had a lot coming in, they had to call in the reserves — and I got *two* trucks for the price of one!

• **Figure 35-1:** He dumped, ran, and didn't even ring the bell.

Location, Location, Location

What happens if you have to drop off your packages for shipment? It's important to consider where the closest local drop-off point for your carrier is.

Each of the major carriers has a search feature on its Web site to find the nearest drop-off location. You input your address or ZIP code, and the feature tells you the locations closest to you.

To get the nearest location lowdown quickly, go to the following sites:

- **FedEx:** www.fedex.com/us/dropoff/?link=1
- **USPS:** www.mapsonus.com/db/USPS/
- **UPS:** www.ups.com/dropoff?loc=en_US

Remember that when you go to a drop-off location, it is invariably at the height of rush hour traffic. Take this into consideration and plan your time accordingly. From where I live, a half mile drive can take anywhere from 5 to 20 minutes — depending on the route I take and the amount of traffic at the time.

Be sure to read the details about each location online. There may be different fees involved in dropping off packages. Some locations may accept certain types of packages and not others. Read the fine print.

Take a look at the FedEx locator result in Figure 35-2. It lists times for final drop-off, types of packages accepted, and which days they're open. The devil is in the details!

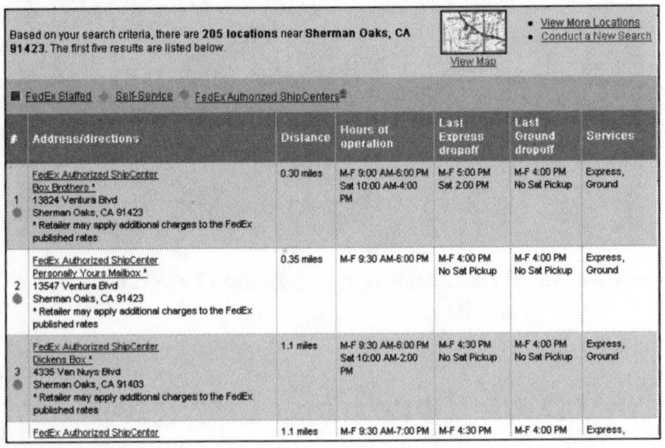

Based on your search criteria, there are **205 locations** near **Sherman Oaks, CA 91423**. The first five results are listed below.

• **Figure 35-2:** Locate your local drop off at the FedEx Web site.

Compare the Costs

The general consensus is that a particular method of shipping is cheaper for large items and another is cheaper for small packages. Each method has its own personal peculiarities.

Take a look at Table 35-1 — compare the pricing for certain types of packages. Know that there are extras to consider for some services, so become familiar with the variations and hidden costs.

TABLE 35-1: SAMPLE COSTS FOR HOME DELIVERY PACKAGES (NEW YORK CITY TO LOS ANGELES)

Weight	FedEx Ground	UPS Ground	USPS Parcel Post
2 pounds	$4.26	8.35	3.45
5 pounds	7.61	10.10	9.43
10 pounds	9.59	12.85	18.14

This table should get you thinking about your carrier. It's very revealing. Even more revealing is when you realize that the USPS charges a fractional amount more for 2-to-3-day Priority Mail.

The upcoming techniques go into more detail on the major shipping carriers. Stay tuned for tales of the tape!

Technique 36

Shipping with the U.S. Postal Service

Save Time By

- Getting free Delivery Confirmation and tracking

- Mechanizing your shipping process with third-party services

- Getting free pickup of your packages

I'm a big fan of the U.S. Postal Service (USPS). Just ask my wonderful letter (or multiple-parcel) carrier, Tim. I use the Post Office for the bulk of my eBay sales because it's convenient. In my eight years selling items on eBay, they've never lost a package.

The Post Office has worked hard to keep up with the competition in the parcel business by offering many online features and custom pickup. USPS also offers many classes of service that top out with a maximum weight of 70 pounds. Table 36-1 shows services that are most popular with eBay sellers.

TABLE 36-1: CLASSES OF USPS SERVICE MOST USED BY eBAY E-TAILERS

Service	Time to Cross the Country	What You Can Ship
First Class	Three days	First Class mail can be used to mail anything, as long as it doesn't weigh much. You can send a letter, large envelope, or a small package. Maximum weight is 13 ounces.
Priority Mail	Two days	Priority Mail is just First Class mail on steroids (for heavier items).
Parcel Post	Eight days	Parcel Post is significantly cheaper (and slower) than Priority Mail.
Media Mail	Eight Days	Media Mail is the least expensive way to mail heavy items. The only caveat is that you can use Media Mail to ship only books, film, manuscripts, printed music, printed test materials, sound recordings, scripts, and computer-recorded media such as CD-ROMs and diskettes.

Before taking any of the transit times I've mentioned (say from Los Angeles to New York) to heart, be sure to get a calculation from the Post Office Web site (which you'll find at `postcalc.usps.gov`). When you calculate postage, the Post Office will indicate expected transit times for your packages.

Understanding the Costs

The Postal Service levies additional charges for some often-used services, including:

✔ **Pickup:** If you have a postal license through an online service (see the section "Print Your Own Postage and Get Free Confirmations," later in this technique), the Post Office offers free pickup. You have to give your packages to your carrier at the time of your regular delivery, or schedule a pickup on the USPS site.

✔ **Insurance:** This guarantees that you're covered if your package doesn't arrive safely and will reimburse you up to the value you declare when purchasing the insurance. There is a maximum of $5,000. If your package gets lost or severely mangled in shipping, the Postal Service will, after a thorough investigation (see Technique 40), pay your claim. Fees start at $1.30 for packages up to $50, and $2.20 for packages up to $100. You can then add $1 for each $100 of insured value. For discounted insurance, read on.

 The Post Office will not compensate you for more than the value of an item. If you have to make a claim, be sure that you have invoices to back up the insured amount.

✔ **Delivery Confirmation:** Delivery Confirmation provides you with proof of delivery or attempted delivery. You can purchase Delivery Confirmations for $.45 or $.55 (for Priority Mail and Parcel Post, respectively) at the Post Office when you mail a package. You get a tracking number that you can check online at `www.usps.com/shipping/trackandconfirm.htm`. You can also verify a package's delivery by calling a toll-free number, 800-222-1811.

 The Post Office now charges for your Parcel Post and Priority Mail package shipping based on miles sent as well as weight. To estimate postage charges for your packages, go to `http://postcalc.usps.gov/Zonecharts`. Just type in your ZIP code and the site will generate a custom zone chart for your mailing location.

Getting Free Delivery Confirmations

If you aren't shipping a great many items each week, you can get free Delivery Confirmations by visiting a secure area of the Post Office Web site at `https://sss-web.usps.com/ds/jsps/index.jsp`. Here you can generate a custom bar code mailing label with an e/Delivery Confirmation number for Priority Mail packages (see Figure 36-1). You can print these labels directly from your inkjet or laser printer, and then simply tape the label to your package.

• **Figure 36-1:** Sample of a free Delivery Confirmation Label generated from the Post Office Web site.

If you're in business and need to keep records of your shipping (dates, weights, and confirmation numbers), this method may be the way to go. The Post Office site, although free, prints out a label only once. If you want keep records, you'll have to enter the information separately into a spreadsheet or a text file.

 You can also get a free Delivery Confirmation (one at a time, without any detailed record) at `www.shippertools.com/standard/label addresses.php`.

And you can get free Delivery Confirmation for Priority Mail packages if you subscribe to an online shipping service, as described in the next section.

Online Delivery Confirmation Services

If you want to ramp up your business a bit and you have more packages than you'd like to take to the fine folks who live behind the counter, why not try a service such as shippertools.com.

shippertools.com is an online delivery confirmation service that's hooked directly into the Post Office API (Application Program Interface, read: the Post Office's computer). For a flat $6.95 a month, you can use as many Delivery Confirmation mailing labels as you wish. If you ship more than 16 Priority Mail packages a month, you'll break even. More than that, and you're in the money!

 It has been proven by top eBay sellers that the use of Delivery Confirmation numbers cuts buyer fraud dramatically.

The site also has a useful and easy-to-use interface that allows you to pre-design e-mails to send to your customers directly from their site. You can also get downloadable and printable records of your mailings with one click tracking. See Figure 36-2 to find out what all these features look like.

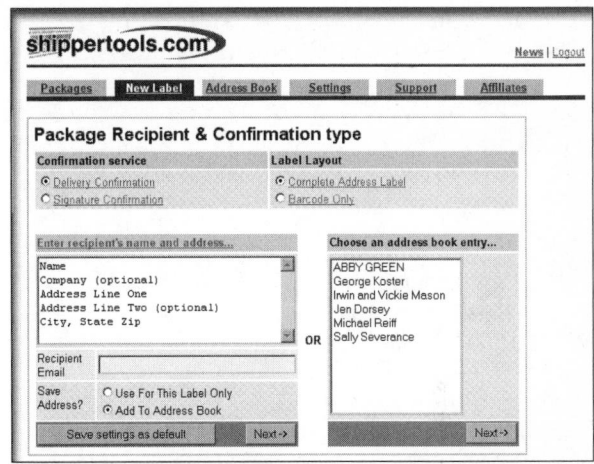

• **Figure 36-2: The shippertools.com Delivery Confirmation service.**

 When using most online services for printing postage or DCs, you get free Priority Mail Confirmations. But, you can also get Delivery Confirmations for First Class, Parcel Post, and Media Mail for an additional 13 cents of postage (a big savings!).

Print Your Own Postage and Get Free Confirmations

I've been printing my postage directly from my computer since the early days of online postage, with the now defunct e-stamp. I like printing my own postage because it's convenient: I never have to go to the Post Office.

There are currently two preeminent vendors of online postage; stamps.com and endicia.com. My favorite is endicia.com, which offers a full online postage service for the eBay seller. Using endicia allows you to use state-of-the-art mailing software (see Figure 36-3) that includes capabilities for custom label design. They offer templates for over 30 label sizes and envelopes. You can even design your mailing label to print on a regular piece of paper.

• **Figure 36-3: Using the downloaded DAZzle design software to customize a mailing label.**

endicia offers two levels of service, and the fees are reasonable. The basic membership is $9.95 a month and the Premium level of service is $15.95. (If you pay for a year in advance, you get a discount.) The Premium service adds additional features, such as customizable e-mail, enhanced online transaction reports and statistics, business reply mail, return shipping labels (prepaid so your customer won't have to pay for the return), and stealth indicia.

What's a stealth indicia?

Have you ever wondered why, when you receive a package from UPS or FedEx, you can't see how much the service charged for the shipping the way you can with postage stamps? Well, that's called a "stealth" indicia.

When you register as a member of endicia.com, you are also signing up for a USPS postal license, which permits you to print your own postage for all classes of mail. It also permits you to print the free Delivery Confirmations and pay the 13-cent discounted rate for Parcel Post, Media Mail, and First Class confirmations. This is charged to your postage account directly.

 For a 60-day free trial of their service, go to www.endicia.com/coolebaytools.

Your credit card information is safely stored with endicia, and whenever you run out of postage, you can just make a purchase using a drop-down menu.

Mechanizing Your Shipping

Okay, I'm not talking about moving giant mailing machines into your home office; I'm just talking about using a label printer. There are several quality brands of label printers on the market. Two of the most popular sold on eBay are the Zebra 2844 and the Dymo LabelWriter 330.

 If you're interested in investing in one, be sure to look for one of these label printers on eBay. You can often get them at a hefty discount off of retail price.

When using an online postage service, you simply cut and paste the address of your buyer from the PayPal payment confirmation e-mail into the postage software. When the address is in the program, you can print the postage and Delivery Confirmation directly to a label that you peel off and place directly on the package. No taping, no muss, or fuss.

I have received packages from several of eBay's largest sellers only to get handwritten mailing labels, or my address cut out from the PayPal payment confirmation e-mail printed on a piece of paper. Wow, real businesslike, huh? This is not a good way to impress your customers with your professionalism.

The investment in a label printer saves you time and money, and pays for itself in short order. When you use a "mechanized" set-up, you'll never want to print labels on plain paper again.

U.S. Postage at a big discount!

I just had to share this with you! Look at the figure in this sidebar. It's a picture of an envelope that I recently received on an eBay purchase. I had to e-mail the seller to find out how and why she used so many stamps.

It seems that the seller is a collector of U.S. postage. She checks out eBay auctions and buys deals on old sheets of mint-state stamps. United States stamps, no matter how old, are always good, so she buys these stamps at discount and uses them on her eBay packages.

Of course, she *also* says that when she brings her packages to the Post Office, all the clerks scatter to take a break!

Getting Free Package Pickup from the Post Office

Because most package services charge for pickup, the Post Office decided to one-up them. If you have a postal license and print your own postage from an online service, the Post Office will pick up your packages free. If you're afraid that you'll miss your regular carrier — visit http://carrierpickup.usps.com/cgi-bin/WebObjects/CarrierPickup.woa to arrange for your packages to be picked up (see Figure 36-4).

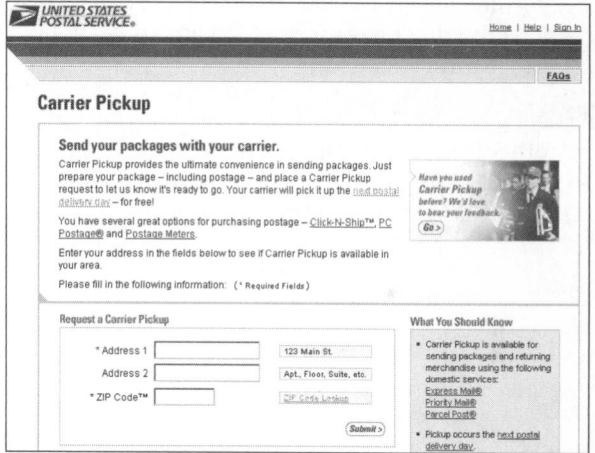

• **Figure 36-4: Just put in your request for pickup the day prior to your pickup day.**

 Be sure to check my Web site, www.coolebay tools.com, for discounts and free trials on many of the services I mention in this book.

Private Postal Package Insurance

If not standing in line at the Post Office waiting for your insured packages to be hand stamped by the clerk sounds like a good idea, and if saving up to 80%

on your package insurance appeals to you, check out Universal Parcel Insurance Coverage (U-PIC). This insurance company automates the whole postal insurance hassle.

 By using U-PIC, you can also insure packages that you send through the USPS, UPS, FedEx, and other major carriers at a major discount off of their standard insurance rates.

When you use the U-PIC service to insure your packages, you can mail them as you usually do. If you print your postage through an online postage service, you can give packages directly to your USPS mail carrier. (You don't have to stand in line to get your insurance form stamped.)

Applying for the U-PIC service is like applying for any other form of insurance. Just fill out a Request To Provide (RTP) form on their Web site at www. u-pic.com. You must answer a few questions about who you are, how many packages you send, how many insurance claims you've filed in the past two years, and your average value per package. When you've applied for coverage, a U-PIC representative will contact you within 48 hours. (For more information, see Technique 39.)

Free Priority Mail shipping supplies from the USPS

Type in the URL for the Post Office Web site at supplies. usps.gov and find yourself in the Postal Store. Under the Browse Store heading, choose Shipping Supplies⊅ Business Use. When you select Priority Mail, you can order boxes in nine different sizes, Priority Mail packing tape, and several sizes of Priority Mail envelopes at no charge. You have to order the boxes in lots of 25, but have no fear. Your regular letter carrier will deliver the boxes to your home! It's free and easy to order.

37
Technique

Getting Brown with United Parcel Service

Around the turn of the previous century (in 1907 to be exact), an enterprising 19-year-old figured he could make some money delivering pizzas for the local Italian restaurant. Just kidding about the pizzas. Actually James (Jim) Casey borrowed $100 from a friend to buy some used bicycles and began the American Messenger Company to run errands, send messages (no fax machines or IM!), deliver packages, and (you guessed it) carry trays of food from local restaurants to off-site patrons in Seattle, Washington. And from American Messenger's 6-foot-by-17-foot headquarters in a basement beneath his uncle's tavern, Jim helped The Little Parcel Service That Could grow into the Jolly Brown Giant we know as UPS.

You can see the sidebar "UPS Evolution" later in this technique for more UPS history, but what you really need to know is how UPS — with its strict policies of customer courtesy, reliability, round-the-clock service, and low rates — can help you deliver the goods for your eBay business. Many eBay sellers just love using UPS. They think of it as the ultimate way to ship their packages. But as I note in Technique 35, the right shipper for one seller may not be the best for another. For example, since the USPS has converted to the cost by mileage/weight formula, you may find (based on your location and the buyer's location) that the U.S. Postal Service may be more economical.

So while you make your shipping decisions, use the handy tables and other information in this technique to make the most of the services that UPS offers.

Using UPS Today

Today's UPS is a $30 billion company focusing on enabling commerce around the world. Every day UPS delivers over 13.3 million packages and documents — I'm sure much of which represents eBay transactions.

UPS (along with the USPS) has hooked up with eBay, and you can access their information through the eBay site. To visit the eBay/UPS Shipping Center, visit `pages.eBay.com/ups/home.html` (as pictured in Figure 37-1).

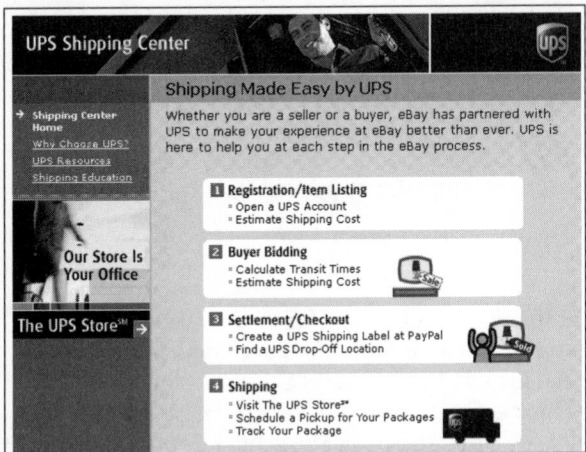

• **Figure 37-1: eBay's UPS shipping-info page.**

UPS Evolution

Realize that it wasn't until 1913 that the United States Postal Service began its Parcel Post deliveries — so this left quite an opening for the young entrepreneurs of the day. There were few automobiles, and department stores used horses and carriages for their deliveries. A bicycle service would be a fast and economical alternative.

This environment set the stage for Jim Casey, his partner Claude Ryan, and a handful of other teenagers to beat out the delivery service competition. They instituted strict policies of customer courtesy, reliability, round-the-clock service, and low rates. They even slept in the office so that they could deliver service 24/7.

In 1915, they changed their company name from American Messenger Company to Merchants Parcel Delivery. The little company grew, and Jim Casey retired as CEO of United Parcel Service in 1962. The now not-so-little parcel service had revenues approaching $14 million. Casey served on the UPS Board of Directors until a month before his death at age 95 in 1983.

Wow. Maybe in 50 years we'll have a story like that about an eBay entrepreneur who worked hard at building an eBay business and became a national institution. Quite a tribute to hard work.

You have choices for how you set up shipping arrangements, and you can pick the way that saves you the most time. If you take a look at Technique 31, you can find out how to ship through USPS or UPS directly from your PayPal account. You can also access shipping information through your My eBay Selling tab, Items I've Sold area as in Figure 37-2. Clicking the Print Shipping Label button in the item's row takes you to the PayPal shipping area.

• **Figure 37-2: My eBay Items I've Sold page with Print Shipping Label buttons.**

Timing your shipments

If you're thinking about using UPS, you'd do yourself a favor by becoming familiar with the company's different classes of service — and what those classes mean to your customers in shipping days — as listed in Table 37-1.

TABLE 37-1: CLASSES OF UPS SERVICE MOST USED BY EBAY E-TAILERS

Service	Time to Cross the Country
UPS 2nd Day Air	Two business days
3 Day Select	Three business days
UPS Ground	Seven business days

UPS considers neither Saturday nor Sunday to be delivery days. So when your package is quoted for a 5-day delivery, and the 5 days cross over a weekend, add two days to the delivery schedule. (The USPS and FedEx Ground deliver on Saturday.)

Comparing the costs

Although we always complain when the USPS raises its rates, you should know that all other shipping carriers religiously raise their rates every year.

 Annual rate increases are why being lulled into complacency can be a dangerous thing; be sure to evaluate your shipping charges (and your shipper's fees) every year to keep up with the increases and possible cuts into your bottom line.

Remember also, that UPS charges a different rate for home delivery than they do for deliveries to a business. Eighty percent of UPS business is commercial, and the home delivery business takes a whole lot more man-hours to deliver fewer packages. In their last rate increase, residential delivery took the biggest hit. The premium for home delivery rose 22 percent; the previous year it rose 4.5 percent. That's an increase from $1.10 to $1.40 in just two years.

While we all *think* that UPS ground is cheaper than the Post Office, it's not true in every case. Take a look at the cross-country rates in Table 37-2.

 Every UPS package is automatically insured for up to $100 (assuming you declare a value). The Post Office charges extra for the service, but you can save money either way by using a private insurance policy for your packages (see Technique 39).

The de-facto standard for eBay shipping is Priority Mail, which I've compared to UPS 3 Day Select. If you ship packages for swift delivery, the clear cost saving winner is Priority Mail.

For heavier packages (those over 6 pounds), UPS is considerably cheaper than Parcel Post. So if you continually ship items over 5 pounds, and time is *not* of the essence, UPS may be the best way to go.

TABLE 37-2: UPS EBAY RATES VERSUS THE POST OFFICE

Weight	USPS Parcel Post	UPS Ground	USPS 2 Day Priority	UPS 3 Day Select
1 lb	3.75	7.35	3.85	11.81
2 lb	4.49	8.35	5.75	13.40
3 lb	6.32	9.10	8.55	15.15
4 lb	7.87	9.60	10.35	16.93
5 lb	9.43	10.10	12.15	18.81
6 lb	11.49	10.40	12.30	20.27
7 lb	12.83	10.80	14.05	22.15
8 lb	15.04	11.45	15.75	23.83
9 lb	17.04	12.10	17.50	25.60
10 lb	18.14	12.85	19.20	27.38

Checking Out UPS Rates

UPS has several different rate levels depending on the type of account you have with them.

 The UPS charges charged through PayPal are based on "occasional" shippers (the "on demand" rate) shipping to home addresses. If you're shipping a lot of merchandise via UPS, you could have your packages picked up, and it might cost you less in the long run.

When you ship via UPS and wonder how to get the best rates, you've got quite a conundrum. UPS basically charges small-time shippers three different rates:

✔ **Retail Rate:** This is the rate you pay when you go to the UPS Customer Center and they create the label for you. It's the most expensive, and with the eBay/PayPal solution, you can save yourself some bucks by printing your own label and dropping the packages at the Customer Center.

✔ **On Demand:** The charges you see on eBay/PayPal shipping are these rates. They are really made for the occasional shipper.

✔ **Daily Rate:** When you have arranged a daily pickup through UPS. This is when you get to make friends with the folks in brown shorts, and as an added benefit, you pay the lowest possible rates. (See Table 37-3 for a comparison.)

Saving Big Money with Package Pickup

If you're anything like me, you are suffering from the delusion that it costs a bundle to have regular UPS package pickup service. Surprise! It doesn't.

If you look at Table 37-3, you can see that if you have daily pickup, you'd net a savings of close to $2 per package by using the daily rate. You could also print

out your labels directly from the UPS Web site and have a preprinted manifest ready for the driver.

You *do* have to pay for that pickup service, but let's do the math. Here are the actual costs of UPS pickup service. The fees are on a sliding scale from $7 to $16, based on the amount of "postage" that you use in a week.

POSTAGE PER WEEK	UPS CHARGES FOR PICKUP
$0 to $14.99	$16
$15.00 to $59.99	$11
$60.00 and more	$7

Shipping seven ten-pound packages or eight five-pound packages coast-to-coast would easily meet the $60 in postage per week minimum. If you're selling heavier items on eBay, UPS service with package pickup wins over the Post Office, hands down!

 You could easily charge customers the familiar UPS eBay/PayPal rate (and use the shipping calculator in your item listings) plus a small handling fee and be strengthening your bottom line on every shipment!

TABLE 37-3: UPS SERVICES COAST-TO-COAST RESIDENTIAL RATE COMPARISON

Service	Weight	UPS Customer Center	eBay/PayPal Rate	Daily UPS Pickup
Residential Ground	2-lbs	9.10	8.35	6.36
Residential Ground	5-lbs	11.05	10.10	7.61
Residential Ground	10-lbs	14.10	12.85	9.59
3 Day Select	2-lbs	15.12	13.48	11.29
3 Day Select	5-lbs	21.09	18.81	15.66
3 Day Select	10-lbs	30.89	27.51	22.58
2nd Day Air	2-lbs	19.06	15.68	14.70
2nd Day Air	5-lbs	26.94	22.05	20.55
2nd Day Air	10-lbs	42.60	34.97	32.38

Absolutely, Positively FedEx

Unlike the warm and fuzzy story of the beginnings of UPS (see Technique 37), where a teenager borrowed $100 to start a business, Federal Express was the brainchild of a rich kid. (Somewhat reminiscent of touching apocryphal stories you hear about a few top-ranked eBay sellers from moneyed backgrounds, who had lots of cash and connections before they ever came to eBay and met with immediate success.)

Yep, in 1965 — while an undergraduate at prestigious Yale University — Frederick Smith wrote a term paper about current air carriers' freight-forwarding side-business. Smith thought this a very uneconomical way to ship freight, and proposed that a freight-only carrier would do a better job for less money. Fast-forward to 1971. After serving in the military, Smith bought controlling interest in Arkansas Aviation Sales. He felt the need for even faster delivery than in days past, and worked to fill the void in the second- and next-day delivery services. Federal Express was born and officially launched in 1973, with 14 planes housed at the Memphis International Airport. On the first night of operation, Federal Express delivered 186 packages to 25 U.S. cities from Rochester, New York, to Miami, Florida.

Although Federal Express spent its first years as an air-delivery service (see the sidebar "The road to FedEx"), the company later expanded into a ground business that now reaches all over the U.S. In Techniques 36 and 37, you found out about the pros and cons of shipping through (respectively) the U.S. Postal Service and UPS. Here in Technique 38, I show you the advantages and potential savings from using FedEx Ground.

The road to FedEx

In its early years of business, Federal Express struggled, but by 1976, the company showed a profit and owned 76 aircraft, including 39 Boeing 727s and four Douglas DC-10s. After officially being in business for only ten years, the company posted revenues of $1 billion — a previously unheard of amount for such a young company. In a deft move, Federal Express merged with the highly successful Tiger International in 1989. Tiger International was known also as the Flying Tiger Line, one of the country's first air freight companies — founded in 1945 by a member of the World War II original Flying Tiger squad. (Google *that* if you want to read a good story!)

Federal Express purchased RPS (Roadway Package Systems) in 1985 to try for a piece of the UPS stronghold on ground delivery. Then in 1994, answering the need to get with the times, the company changed its name to FedEx — using their customer's verbal abbreviation for the company. (As in, "I'll *FedEx* you the papers overnight.")

The FedEx expansion into ground services grew to include home delivery as well as commercial, and by 2002, the company's ground service delivered packages to virtually every address in the United States.

Saving by Shipping with FedEx Ground

"The road to FedEx" sidebar tells an impressive business story. Do you think that FedEx is too expensive for your eBay shipping? Perhaps it's not as convenient as using the PayPal shipping area, but the savings just might be worth your while.

Here are a few time- and money-saving facts about shipping with FedEx that you should know.

- ✔ **Saturday delivery:** FedEx Ground will deliver to residences on Tuesdays through Saturdays at no extra charge.

- ✔ **Delivery until 8:00 p.m.:** If your customers work for a living and can't make it home to babysit deliveries, FedEx Ground will deliver until 8 p.m.

- ✔ **Guaranteed delivery time:** FedEx guarantees one to five delivery days to every address in the United States, and three to seven days to Canada and Puerto Rico.

- ✔ **Printing labels online:** Through the FedEx Web site, you can print bar-coded labels on plain paper and place them in the FedEx-provided clear envelopes that stick to your packages.

- ✔ **Many drop-off locations:** After printing your label, you can drop off your packages at any FedEx counter, many private postal stores, or at your local Kinko's (now owned by FedEx).

- ✔ **Lower pickup costs:** FedEx Ground charges less for their pickup service (read on).

 To find out if there's an ultra-close drop-off location for your FedEx packages, go to www. fedex.com/us/dropoff **and type in your ZIP code.** If you're shipping via ground, be sure to check that your closest location is accepting ground. Also check the cut-off times. To find Kinko's locations, go to www.kinkos.com/locations/index.php.

Signing up with FedEx

You sign up for an account only once; there's no cost and it only takes a few minutes. This is a two-step process. You've first got to sign up for a Web site login, and then sign up for an actual, for-real FedEx account. When you have a fedex.com login and account, you'll be able to ship your items quickly from your own private FedEx Web space.

To get a FedEx account and be able to ship right away:

1. Go to www.fedex.com/us.

2. **On the left side of the screen, click the link to FedEx Ground.**

   The FedEx Ground page appears.

3. **From the FedEx Ground page, click the Ship tab (first tab at the top).**

   You land at the login page. If you've previously signed up for an account with a password and User ID, you can login immediately here.

4. **If you're signing up for a new account, click the link that says "Sign Up Now!"**

5. **On the resulting registration page, type in the following information:**

   ▶ **User ID:** Make up an ID you'll remember. (I tried my eBay User ID and it was already taken — I guess they have lots of customers).

   ▶ **Password:** Come up with a password you'll remember. For tips on selecting safe passwords, see Technique 63.

▶ **Password Reminder:** Input your password reminder question and answer. This way, if you ever forget your password or have to prove your identity to FedEx, you'll have your mind jogger.

▶ **Contact Information:** This includes the usual — your name, (optional) company name, address, city, state, e-mail address, and phone number.

▶ **Agree to Terms of Use:** If you want to ship via FedEx, you must agree to their terms. You may click the link provided if you want some really boring legalese to read. When you've decided to play by their rules, press the bar that says I Accept.

6. **On the next page, there's some more legalese in the form of FedEx's License Agreement.**

7. **When you're through reading that (I'm sure you'll read every word), click Yes, indicating that you accept the Agreement.**

8. **When asked whether you want to set up a FedEx account, follow the prompts and input your credit-card information.**

   You're presented with your very own 9-digit FedEx Account number.

9. **Click Start Using FedEx Ship Manager to ship now, or log in later when you're ready to ship.**

Saving on your shipping costs

I was very impressed when I researched FedEx Ground rates. In their early days, many sellers were leery of using FedEx due to spotty delivery areas and all. But now, they cover all residences in the country and charge less to boot!

 FedEx Ground will deliver on Saturdays at no extra charge.

Check out Table 38-1. The rates quoted are at the time of this writing from Los Angeles to New York (the longest distance — Zone 8 — that you can ship). It's clear that when shipping packages over 3 pounds, you can really save by using FedEx Ground.

 Since eBay doesn't include FedEx on their shipping calculator, I'd say you'd be very safe setting up the online shipping calculator so that buyers can set their shipping costs for UPS Ground rates.

TABLE 38-1: FEDEX, UPS, AND THE POST OFFICE (NEW YORK CITY TO LOS ANGELES)

Weight	UPS Ground	FEDEX Home 4 Day	USPS 2 Day Priority	UPS 3 Day Select
1 lb	7.35	**5.86**	3.85	11.81
2 lb	8.35	**6.36**	5.75	13.40
3 lb	9.10	**6.89**	8.55	15.15
4 lb	9.60	**7.25**	10.35	16.93
5 lb	10.10	**7.61**	12.15	18.81
6 lb	10.40	**7.84**	12.30	20.27
7 lb	10.80	**8.13**	14.05	22.15
8 lb	11.45	**8.59**	15.75	23.83
9 lb	12.10	**9.06**	17.50	25.60
10 lb	12.85	**9.59**	19.20	27.38

Saving more by paying with American Express

If you have an American Express Business Credit Card (which also allows you access to the American Express Open Network), you can save even more on your FedEx shipments!

✔ **Save 5%** of ALL FedEx Ground Shipments when you fill out your forms online.

✔ **Save 10% to 20%** on your FedEx Express shipments.

To be sure your American Express card is officially linked so you get the discount, call the Fedex/Open Network desk at 1-800-231-8636.

As a member of the Open Network, you can also save money on other business needs. See Technique 61 (the fun stuff) for more about those savings.

Shipping Your Packages Online

Perhaps one day we'll actually be able to beam our products to the buyers (kinda like Scotty in *Star Trek*). Meanwhile, shipping online merely means filling out the forms and printing them out.

To ship your item on the FedEx Web site, just go to the online Ship Manager by pressing the Ship tab on the navigation bar. You'll be presented with a simple, all-in-one online waybill, somewhat like the kind you're used to filling out by hand. Figure 38-1 shows you what it looks like.

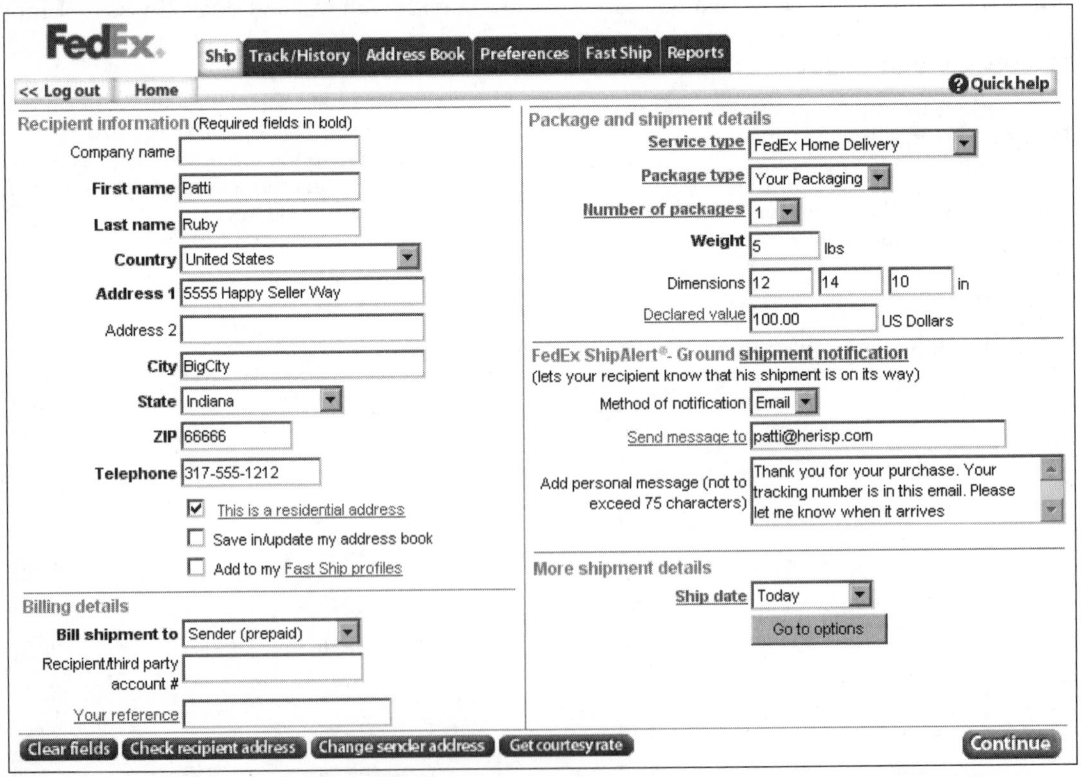

• **Figure 38-1:** FedEx Ship Manager online shipping form.

Copy and paste addresses from your PayPal account by highlighting the text you want to copy and pressing Ctrl + C. Paste in the text by placing your cursor in the area you want to fill and pressing Ctrl + V.

When you're filling out the form, note some important entries:

✔ **Service Type:** Be sure to use the FedEx Home Delivery option from the drop-down menu if you're shipping to a residence.

✔ **Dimensions:** Be sure that you know the proper dimensions for the package you're sending.

 If you sell repeat items in your eBay business, why not measure the boxes ahead of time and keep a list near your computer so you'll know the size? For example: *Light kit 14 x 12 x 26.*

✔ **FedEx ShipAlert®:** Select the e-mail option to send the buyer (and yourself — at up to 3 e-mail addresses) a notice that the package was shipped. Add a personal message so that the e-mail won't have a cold, automated feel to it.

Once you've filled out the form, you can press the button at the bottom to get a courtesy rate. This will give you a rate estimate (not including any special discounts) on your shipment.

 When shipping with FedEx online, if your package is valued over $100 and you use U-PIC for your insurance (a private insurance company, see Technique 39), put $0 in the Declared Value box. Make note of the package on an insurance log and submit it to U-PIC. (FedEx will charge you 50 cents per $100 in value, and U-PIC will charge you only 15 cents per $100.)

39 Technique

Insuring Against the Worst

Save Time By

- ✔ Looking at self-insuring your shipments
- ✔ Using the convenience of major carrier insurance
- ✔ Applying for private package insurance

When you're shipping a large amount of merchandise out on a regular basis, you're going to have to deal with the question of whether you offer your buyers insurance against damage or loss. Bottom line: Whether you offer insurance or not, you (the seller) are ultimately responsible for getting the product to the buyer. The lost-in-the-mail excuse doesn't cut the mustard, and having a delivery confirmation number doesn't guarantee anything either.

 You may *think* that it's the buyer's responsibility to pay for insurance. If they don't, you say, it's their hard luck if the package doesn't arrive. This is far from the truth; a buyer who does not receive an item that she's paid for can legitimately file a fraud report against you. Buyers can also have the payment removed from your PayPal account if you have no physical proof that you've shipped the item, and you have no defense against this.

With all that said, I say this again: You'd best realize that the responsibility for delivering the goods is in the seller's hands. So, offering insurance to your buyers is good business, and including insurance with every shipment is excellent business. This technique tells you about the various ways you can insure your packages — and stay within a reasonable budget.

 Even the best insurance won't protect you against shoddy packing practices. If you end up with a damaged shipment because *somebody* threw a couple of crystal goblets in a box with a few pieces of paper, odds are the shipper won't pay off on the claim. (They do request to see the package before they pay.) Follow safe shipping practices; see Technique 34 for more info.

Self-Insuring Your Items

Some sellers on eBay self-insure their packages. In other words, they take the risks and use money out of their own pockets if they have to pay a claim. These sellers are usually very careful about packing their items to prevent damage. (Check out Technique 34 to find out about choosing and finding packing materials.) They also purchase delivery confirmations when using the Postal Service.

 Savvy self-insurers usually do not self-insure items of high value. If you sell mostly lower-priced items (under $50) and decide to self-insure, consider making an exception when you do occasionally sell an expensive item. Bite the bullet and pay for the shipping insurance; doing so could save you money and hassle in the long run.

How do you afford to self-insure? Here are a couple of the common methods:

✔ Tack an additional $1 onto every item's postage amount as part of your handling fee. The more items you sell and ship, the more that little dollar-per-item profit builds up and gives you a fund that you can use to cover the rare instance of a damaged or missing item.

✔ Offer optional shipping at full USPS prices as part of the sale. Then, rather than pay the Post Office to insure the items, keep the extra fee. Again, if something untoward happens to one of your packages as it gets (or doesn't get) to its destination, you'll have accumulated a small fund to cover any refund to the buyer.

 This second method of building your self-insurance fund may be a risky proposition. But if you sell a lot of items for under $50, you might find that this works for you.

Insuring through the Major Carriers

All the major shippers are in the shipping business (duh), not in the insurance business. Insuring is a dirty, annoying — but necessary — sideline to their package-transit business.

Most carriers, other than the United States Postal Service, cover all shipments automatically (and at no extra charge) for the first $100 of package value. By the way, the *package value* of an item sold on eBay is the final bid (or Buy It Now) amount. Of course, you can always buy additional package insurance for your shipped items. Should a package get lost or damaged, making a claim opens an entirely new can of worms. (Technique 40 gives you the scoop about the procedures for filing insurance claims with the major carriers.)

Table 39-1 shows you what the major carriers charge for their additional insurance.

TABLE 39-1: INSURANCE RATES FOR COMMERCIAL CARRIERS

Shipper	Shipper Rate
USPS	$1.30 for $0.01 to $50.00 value
	$2.20 for $50.01 - $100.00 value
	$1.00 per $100 (for each additional $100 of value)
UPS	$0.35 per $100 (after first $100 of value)
FedEx	$0.50 per $100 (after first $100 of value)
Airborne	$0.70 per $100 (after first $100 of value)
DHL	$0.70 per $100 (after first $100 of value)

Getting Private Shipping Insurance

Some smart person, long, long ago, came up with the idea of privately insuring freight as it traveled over long distances. As early as 1688, Edward Lloyd became known in business circles as the guy who knew all about shipping. His small coffeehouse became the hub where ships' captains, merchants, and rich men went to get the facts about lost ships and salvage cargo.

A merchant wanting to insure cargo being sent out on a ship would show up at Lloyd's coffee shop looking for a broker to get a policy. The broker would solicit many wealthy individuals to pool their resources so that each took just a portion of the risk. Mr. Lloyd ran his business from the coffeehouse until his death in 1713, and the brokers who started with Lloyd formalized the business that is now the famous Lloyd's of London. The company currently insures much more than shipments — movie stars' body parts, singers' voices, and just about anything that one might wish to insure.

 The point of the Lloyd's of London story is that your business can have a separate insurance policy to cover your eBay shipments. Depending on quantity and type of goods you ship, such insurance could ultimately save you thousands of dollars per year.

There is a company, U-PIC, that caters to individual eBay sellers amidst its many big-business clients. Here are some great features of the U-PIC service:

✔ **No time wasted standing in line at the Post Office:** The U-PIC service is integrated into online shipping solutions such as endicia.com (described in Technique 36).

✔ **Quick payments on claims:** When you do have a claim, U-PIC pays it within 7 days of receiving all required documents from the carrier.

 As with any insurance policy, assume that if you have many claims against your packages, you can be dropped from the service. (This thought only gives me more impetus to package my items properly — I never want to be banished to the counter lines again!)

✔ **Blanket approval:** U-PIC is approved by all major carriers. And turnabout is fair play: All carriers covered must be on the U-PIC approved carrier listing.

✔ **Cost savings:** Again, depending on the quantity and type of items you ship, using U-PIC may save you between 65% and 90% on your insurance costs. Table 39-2 shows the company's current rates. International coverage is available for all carriers listed in the table, as well as for approved air carriers.

 To apply for your own U-PIC policy — with no charge to apply and no minimum premium — go directly to the application on their Web site at http://delta.u-pic.com/Apply/rtp. aspx. Tell 'em that Marsha sent ya!

TABLE 39-2: U-PIC STANDARD RATES

Shipper	U-PIC Rate
UPS	$0.14 per $100
FedEx	$0.18 per $100
USPS	$0.50 per $100 with Delivery Confirmation
Airborne	$0.25 per $100
DHL	$0.25 per $100
LTL Freight	$0.40 per $100

Technique 40

Making a Claim When Shipping Goes Bad

Save Time By

- Preventing label mistakes
- Knowing when things go south
- Making a quick claim with your carrier

If you've been selling or buying on eBay for a length of time, odds are you've been involved with making a claim for lost or damaged packages. The process is often grueling — with all the paperwork that's involved — and the decision of the carrier is final. If you don't agree with the carrier, you could try small claims court. But realize that you'll lose around a day of work and, in court, you'll face all the legalese you find in the teeny-tiny print on the carrier's Terms of Service.

I understand the hassles because I've had to make several claims myself. One claim that I actually won several years ago, after much haggling, was for (please don't judge me here) a framed original wardrobe uniform tunic from the *Star Trek* series — autographed by Leonard Nimoy. (Find the rest of the story in the sidebar, "A couple of claim stories," also in this technique.) I'd like to help you avoid similar unpleasant experiences, or at least make them less unpleasant, and that's why I wrote this technique.

As a shipper, you have control over how you label and ship your packages. This technique explains how to accurately label your packages and what you should include in the package to help with identification, in case the package does lose its way. But if you do a lot of shipping, you'll inevitably be faced with making a claim. In this technique, I first present information about the U.S. Postal Service because their claim process is more stringent than that of the other carriers. With any carrier, you need to gather the same type of backup information before making a claim.

Mistyping Addresses Means Losing Parcels

Lost packages are the bane of all carriers since they started accepting packages for delivery. The Post Office has been dealing this problem since it opened the Dead Letter Office in 1825.

The Postal Service's Dead Letter Office employees (I'll call them DLOs) are the only people legally permitted to open lost mail. When an address label gets smooshed, torn, wet, or otherwise illegible enough that the box can't be delivered, it finds its way into the hands of the DLOs, who open the package with the hope of finding enough information to get it to the rightful owner.

 Make sure that you always include a packing slip — like the kind you print from Selling Manager or My eBay — inside your packages. The packing slip should have both your address and the buyer's so that if the label is illegible, the packing slip will identify the owner and the package can be delivered.

Of course, having the buyer's address correct on the label is critical to begin with. The following ideas and practices will help you create accurate shipping labels:

✔ **Cut and paste the buyer's address:** The safest way to correct addressing is to cut and paste the buyer's address information from an e-mail or the PayPal payment confirmation or download. If your buyer's address shows as unconfirmed through PayPal, send a quick e-mail to your buyer to verify. People do make mistakes, even when writing their own addresses.

✔ **Don't depend on the carrier to correct an address:** No carrier is really going to tell you whether the address you have is incorrect. To test my theory, I've deliberately typed nonexistent addresses into the Post Office, UPS, and FedEx forms. The carrier's forms didn't correct a thing. The only time I've had inaccurate addresses corrected is when I used the Dazzle software.

✔ **Use software or online services to check your buyer's address:** It's good business practice to confirm the viability of an address before you send your item. Software like Dazzle (from endicia.com) through Dial-A-ZIP corrects most common addressing errors such as misspelled city or street name. If you have a question about a ZIP code, you can check it at the Post Office Web site www.usps.com/zip4. Notice how it corrected the city (and questioned the street address) in Figure 40-1.

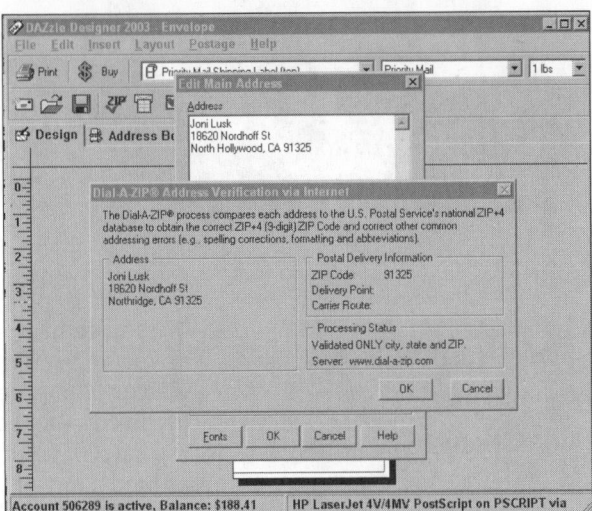

• **Figure 40-1: Address verification in Dazzle's Dial-A-ZIP.**

 If you have the Google toolbar (which I highly recommend in Technique 55 — also find more Google tricks on the Cheat Sheet), or go to www.google.com, you can type in any UPS, Post Office, or FedEx tracking number and find the current tracking information from the carrier's Web site. Just copy and paste the tracking number into the Google search box and start your search. You'll come to a page that presents a link to track packages — with your number and carrier showing. Click the link and you end up at the carrier's site with all the current tracking information! Nice!

A couple of claim stories

Several years ago, I purchased an original wardrobe uniform tunic from the Star Trek series that was framed and autographed by Leonard Nimoy. And I was anxiously awaiting its arrival. When it came, in an appropriately large box surrounded with lots of Styrofoam peanuts and bubble wrap, it also sported a 4" x 4" hole in the side, and it looked like someone had taken a sword to the box! Not only that, but there was a sad sound of glass tinkling when one shook the box. Oh, yes, the deliveryman had dumped the box, rung the bell, and run.

The carrier couldn't really argue about the damage. The claim department tried to give me the line that the item was packed incorrectly. (Does that mean it was sent with a big hole already in the side of the box?) Then they offered me a partial payment. Gee, I really wanted the glass-particle-infested, ripped tunic now. It took a while, but the damages were so obvious that the carrier had to give in and agreed to send a check to the seller. Upon hearing this decision, the seller refunded my payment. (I wonder how long the seller had to wait for *his* payment?)

There was also a dress that I sold and shipped Priority Mail. It never arrived. I had a boiling-hot buyer on the other end, but luckily, I had proof of mailing in the form of a Delivery Confirmation to show her. I nagged the Post Office about the package, but as you'll read in the section, "Making a Claim with the Post Office," you have to wait 30 days for a package to be *officially* declared lost. On the 29th day, the box was returned to me with no explanation or fanfare and just a return-to-sender stamp on the front.

Here's something to keep in mind when you're thinking about filing a claim. When you purchase insurance from a carrier, only the content of the package is insured. The shipping carrier doesn't seem to care whether an item's packaging gets destroyed. I've heard that many a claim for damaged packaging has been denied on collectibles where the packaging in mint condition is just as important as the item being perfect. If a Barbie doll was shipped, only the safe intact arrival of the doll seems to matter, not the special collector's box surrounding it.

Making a Claim with the Post Office

Making a Claim with the Post Office: Oh man, talk about a hassle. But making a claim with any carrier isn't a bowl of cherries on any day! Before making a claim with the USPS, check to make sure your package was actually covered by Postal Insurance, which was purchased at the time of mailing. If you use private insurance instead, you don't make a claim to the Post Office.

If an item arrives at the buyer's door damaged, you may immediately make a claim with the Post Office. When a package is lost in transit, the Post Office puts some time constraints on your making a claim. That is, you must wait a minimum of 30 days after the mailing date before you make the claim.

There's always a question as to who makes the claim:

- **Damaged or loss of contents:** Either the seller or the buyer can make the claim.

- **Complete loss:** When a package never turns up after 30 days and it's officially MIA, the seller must be the one to file a claim.

First, you *must* go to the Post Office to get a copy of *PS Form 1000, Domestic Claim or Registered Mail* inquiry. (The Post Office doesn't have this form currently on the Web site for download.) Fill out the form with all the details required and bring your backup information.

To make a damage claim, you must produce evidence of insurance. This can be either of the following documents:

- **Original Mailing Receipt:** The receipt that was stamped at the Post Office counter when the item was mailed.

- **Original box or wrapper:** This must show the addresses of both the sender and the recipient along with whatever tags or stamps the Post Office put on the package to say it's insured.

If only the box or wrapper is presented as proof of insurance, the Post Office will likely limit the claim to $100.

You must also produce evidence showing the value of the item *when it was mailed*. The list below shows some of the documents accepted by the Post Office for damage claims. Be prepared that they may ask for more thorough proof.

✔ Sales receipt or descriptive invoice.

✔ Copy of your cancelled check or money order receipt.

✔ Picture and description of a similar item from a catalog if your receipt isn't available.

✔ A letter from the seller stating the value of the item.

✔ Your own description of the item. Include date and time the item was purchased and whether it is new or vintage.

For missing packages, you (the seller) need a letter from the buyer (dated 30 days after the package was mailed) stating that they never received the package.

If your buyer is too cranky to cooperate, go to the Post Office where you mailed the package. Ask for a written statement that there is no record of the delivery being made. Postal employees can look up the insurance or Delivery Confirmation numbers to find whether the delivery took place, but the Post Office will charge you $6.60 for their efforts. That amount will be reimbursed if the Post Office pays your claim and doesn't locate your package under a bale of hay in Indiana.

If all goes well and your claim is deemed legit, you should get your payment within 30 days. If you don't hear from the Post Office within 45 days (maybe the payment got lost in the mail?), you have to submit a duplicate claim using the original claim number.

 Note to self (and to you): Always make a copy of any form you give to the government.

Buying lost packages

When the Post Office pays your claim, it will usually ask to keep your item. Your item and thousands of others will end up at one of the Mail Recovery Centers across the country. Here it joins the other lost and salvage mail to be sold, usually at auction.

The Post Office used to run these auctions on eBay under the user ID `usps-mrc-everythingelse`. I used to buy some great case lots from them and turn around and resell the goods on eBay! (You can still find the USPS About Me page at `http://members.ebay.com/ws2/eBayISAPI.dll?ViewUserPage&userid=usps-mrc-everythingelse`.)

Now the Post Office sells the stuff at live auctions. If think you'd like to attend one, check the Post Office site at `www.usps.com/auctions` for dates and times. The Post Office always has good stuff for sale and usually in good quantity (not everything is trashed).

If you're interested in buying Post Office surplus, check it out on eBay under sellers `usps-ne-springfield` and `usps-al-pmsc`.

Filing a Claim with UPS

Whoa! The stories of filing claims with UPS are legendary. Almost any eBay seller can tell you quite a story. I must admit that making a claim with UPS is a good deal easier than making a claim with the Post Office. At least, once your damage claim is filed and accepted, you get a check within five days.

For damaged packages, UPS recently streamlined the process as well, although the buyer must make the claim. You *can* (if you really want to) call 1-800-PICK-UPS (cute, eh?) to file your claim. The better idea is to go directly to the online reporting form at `www.ups.com/content/us/en/resources/service/tracking/claims.html`. Be sure you make your report to UPS within 48 hours of delivery.

On the online claim form, you'll be asked to input all information about the package and the damage. UPS seems to be very familiar with its own handiwork; you get to select a particular type of damage from a menu.

Once you've filled out and submitted the form, just sit on your haunches and wait for the UPS claims department to contact you.

I recommend that you print your form after filling it out so you can keep all reference information for the claim in one place.

After the buyer makes the claim, UPS sends a Damage/Loss Notification Letter form to the seller. The seller must fill out the form to state the item's value and attach supporting documentation. The form can then be faxed back to UPS for final verification.

 Save the damaged item and all the packaging that it came in. UPS may send an inspector out to look at the package before approving a claim.

If a UPS shipment appears to be lost, the seller must call UPS to request a package tracer. If UPS is unable to prove delivery, the claim is paid.

Filing with FedEx

Filing a claim with FedEx is similar to the UPS procedure, except FedEx gives you a little more leeway as to time. Instead of the 48-hours-after-delivery deadline, you have 15 business days to make your claim. (This extra time sure helps out when a package is delivered to your house and you're out of town.) FedEx processes all Concealed Loss and Damage claims within five to seven days after receiving all the paperwork and information.

As with UPS, keep all packaging, including the carton, along with the item in case FedEx wants to come and inspect the damage.

You can make your FedEx claim in a couple of ways:

- ✔ **By fax:** You can download a PDF claim form with instructions at `www.fedex.com/us/customer/claims/Claims.pdf`.

  Fill out the form and fax it to the number on the form.

- ✔ **Online:** Fill out the online claim form on a secure server at `https://www.fedex.com/us/claims online`.

  To file a claim online, you must have a FedEx login to begin your claim. (See Technique 38 on how to get this.) If you file your claim online, you'll still have to mail or fax in your supporting documentation. When you file online, you can also choose to receive e-mail updates from FedEx regarding your claim (good idea!).

 The claim payment will be sent to the seller, so it's up to the seller to make restitution with the buyer. The result should be as it is in the sidebar "A couple of claim stories" — as soon as the claim is approved, a refund should be made.

Part VII

Working the eBay Community

The 5th Wave   By Rich Tennant

"Same old story – he won a lava lamp at eBay, she sniped 500 Jackie O. pillbox hats on closeout, he won a Dutch auction of Nehru jackets, they bagged a whole collection of Corvette hubcaps, and they just found a missile silo in Kansas with LOTS of room..."

Opening an eBay Store

Save Time By

✔ Knowing what you need to get started

✔ Understanding the fees involved

✔ Setting up your eBay Store

O pening an eBay Store can expand your business. The more that savvy buyers learn about eBay Stores, the more popular they become. The more popular they become, the more people buy from them. Simple. An eBay Store provides you with your own little corner of eBay in which you can leverage your good relationships with your customers to promote your auctions and to sell directly to them. But eBay Stores are not a total solution, and having an eBay Store isn't a one-way ticket to easy street.

I get emails all the time from people who open an eBay Store and are not successful in moving merchandise. Why? Because running an eBay Store takes an extra level of effort. The more energy you invest in your eBay business, the more work you have to do. Simple. No matter how many "money-back guarantees" you receive from online spammers promising magical success on eBay, the only magic is putting your nose (and shoulder) to the grindstone and exerting the effort necessary to bring customers to your store.

eBay wants you to succeed as well. Although I'm sure they like getting the monthly fee for the store, they'd much rather see your sales grow. After all, the more you sell, the more eBay earns in Final Value Fees.

If you're just beginning on eBay, the best advice I can give is to hold off on opening an eBay Store until your feedback rating is over 100. Participating in transactions on eBay is a natural teacher because you'll see mistakes that sellers make when they sell to you. You'll get emails from sellers that are plain unfriendly, and you'll have a true understanding of how quality customer service will help you build your business. You'll also learn from your own mistakes and be able to provide better service to your customers.

The purpose of expanding your eBay business is to make more money, not to start losing money. Big businesses expand in order to make more money, even though their costs may increase. There's *always* a risk involved in *any* business venture, but with experience on the site and what you learn in this book, hopefully you can minimize the risk.

Making the "Store" Decision

So you think it's time to open a store, eh? If you feel it in your gut and you're ready to take the leap, here's what you need to know. eBay has very few requirements when it comes to opening an eBay Store:

- ✔ **Registered User:** You need to be a Registered User on the eBay site.

- ✔ **Feedback rating:** You must have a feedback rating of 20 or more or be ID verified.

It doesn't get much easier than that! Personally, I like to add these additional prerequisites to back you up for success:

- ✔ **PayPal Account:** You need to have a Business or Premier (personal) PayPal account to accept credit cards. Accepting credit cards is a necessity for building sales, and PayPal is integrated directly into the site, as well as being widely accepted by buyers.

  Be sure you understand how a PayPal account works so you can decide on the types of payments you will accept — and from which countries you intend to do business. (See Part V for in-depth discussions on PayPal.)

- ✔ **Sales Experience:** Having selling (and buying) experience over and above the 20 transactions required by eBay is a big plus. The best teacher (aside from this book) is the school of hard knocks.

- ✔ **Merchandise:** Opening an eBay Store with ten items that you only have one each of isn't a good idea. You need to have enough merchandise to support consistent sales in your store.

- ✔ **Devotion:** You need to have the time to check into your eBay business *at least* once a day, and the time to handle shipping the purchased merchandise in a prompt manner.

 The items listed as store inventory will not come up in an eBay search. The only ways new buyers can find your store inventory is by clicking the search Stores tab in eBay search by searching items on the store hub page, or by clicking from one of your auction pages to see what else you have on sale.

Choosing between store types

Different real estate has different costs. Just like opening a store on Rodeo Drive in Beverly Hills is going to cost more than a store in Dipstick, North Dakota; opening an eBay Store has different start up costs. But the best part is, that the old real estate adage "location, location, location" counts only in real estate — when you're on eBay, you have an excellent chance to get new customers.

All eBay Stores are on a level playing field. You can be right up there with the big guys and compete. The only cost differential is the type of store you wish to open. They're all equally searchable for the eBay Stores hub page, as pictured in Figure 41-1.

• **Figure 41-1: The eBay Stores landing page.**

All eBay stores share these features:

- ✔ **Listings:** All of your eBay listings, whether auction, fixed price or store inventory, will appear in your eBay Store.

- ✔ **Custom URL:** Your eBay Store will have its own Internet address that you can use in links in promotional material — even to promote your store on the Internet (see Part IX).

- ✔ **Store Search:** When customers visit your eBay Store, they will be able to search within your listings for their desired item — with your own personal search engine.

- ✔ **Cross-Promotions:** You have the ability to insert thumbnail promotions for your store items within each of your items for sale on the regular eBay site.

- ✔ **Seller Reports:** You'll receive monthly reports on your store sales via e-mail.

Although you will need to pay a small fee for each listing, eBay Store rental is available on three levels:

- ✔ **Basic Store:** For $9.95 a month, you get your own eBay Store with all the benefits.

- ✔ **Featured Store:** You get all the benefits of a Basic Store, plus there will be a link to your store from the store category page and randomly on the eBay Stores hub page (refer to Figure 41-1). You also get more advanced sales reports. This type of store will set you back $49.95 per month.

- ✔ **Anchor Store:** This is a top-of-the-line store on eBay. For $499.95 a month, your store logo rotates with others on the home hub page of eBay stores. Your logo also randomly appears on eBay's home page. When prospective buyers are browsing eBay Store categories, your logo will show up at the top of the pages.

 There is no limit to the number of items you put up for sale in the Basic Store. An Anchor Store can have as few or as many items as the Basic Store.

For the independent seller, a Basic Store will do the trick. Many high-level PowerSellers find that the basic eBay Store fulfills their needs.

Knowing the fee structure

There are other fees involved (are you surprised?). There are listing fees, options fees, and Final Value Fees, as shown in Tables 41-1, 41-2, and 41-3.

TABLE 41-1: STORE INVENTORY LISTING FEES

Time Period	Listing	Surcharge	Total
30 days	$.02	$.00	$.02
60 days	$.02	$.02	$.04
90 days	$.02	$.04	$.06
120 days	$.02	$.06	$.08
Good 'Til Cancelled	$.02 per 30 days	N/A	$.02 per 30 days

 Listing your items for a looong time may be a tempting way to automate your listings — and it's a good strategy. Remember, though, that once someone makes a purchase from an item listing, you can no longer make massive changes — you can only update inventory. If you have a new picture or new ideas for a title or description, you must close that listing and relist the item with the new information. But heck, it's only 2¢!

TABLE 41-2: STORE INVENTORY LISTING UPGRADES

Upgrade	Cost per 30 Days of Listing Duration
Gallery	$.01
Item Subtitle	$.02
Listing Designer	$.10 (same as auctions)
Bold	$1.00 (same as auctions)
Highlight	$5.00 (same as auctions)
Featured in Search	$19.95 (same as auctions)

TABLE 41-3: STORE FINAL VALUE FEES

Final Item Price	Final Value Fee
$.01 to $25.00	5.25 percent of the selling price
$25.01 to $1,000.00	5.25 percent on the first $25, plus 2.75 percent on selling prices of $25.01 to $1,000
$1,000 and up	5.25 percent on the first $25, plus 2.75 percent on selling prices of $25.01 to $1,000, plus another 1.5 percent on selling prices over $1,000

Store Final Value Fees are the same as the Final Value Fees for eBay auctions. For a more detailed description on how to calculate fees and set profitable price points, see Part II.

 When someone visits your eBay Store, there's no way they will know whether you're a Basic, Featured, or Anchor Store. The design of your store is up to you – you can make it as fancy as you wish.

How to save 50 percent on your Store Final Value Fees

Yes! The honchos at eBay are really smart. By promoting your eBay Store on your Web site and linking to your eBay Store, you can save 50 percent of your Final Value Fees on the items you sell though the referral link. It's a win-win situation. You draw people to your eBay Store, where you can have a more robust layout and features and save on fees — and eBay gets more visitors coming to the site!

In order to get the referral bonus, you must set up a special link. The link consists of your eBay Store URL, and some code. Here's my referral link with the referral code in bold face text:

```
http://stores.ebay.com/marshacolliers
    fabulousfinds?refid=store
```

This code can also be used in promotional e-mail that you send out. The only bad thing is that buyers have to purchase the item during the same browser session as when they enter your store.

Definitely worth a try! Check out the figure below to see a part of one of my eBay invoices; it shows how the savings can stack up!

	Jan-11-04					
6648010000	11:41:16 PST	Final value fee	2964392864		-US $7.03	-US $48.71
		gleamcity Final price: $232.99 (Store)				
	Jan-11-04					
6648010010	11:41:16 PST	Store Referral Credit	2964392864	US $3.53		-US $45.18
		2964392864 Final price: $232.99 (Store)				

Setting Up Your Store

If you're up to the task of opening a store, read on to find out about the things you need to have ready *before* you open your eBay Store.

It's best to sit down during some uninterrupted quiet time to plan your store. Opening a store properly involves adding additional store information (such as the name and description of your store), and writing it out first really helps you to gather your thoughts.

To open a store, go to the eBay home page and click the link in the upper-left corner (under Specialty Sites, as shown in Figure 41-2) for eBay Stores. You can also go there directly by typing the URL

```
http://stores.ebay.com
```

 Although eBay may change the step-by-step procedure for opening a store, you'll still need to have all the information in the Setting Up your Store Content area.

• **Figure 41-2:** Click the eBay Stores link from the eBay home page.

Setting up your store content

To set up your store, you have to go through several steps. The first is the basic store content.

1. Click the Open Store Now bar (and you also get the first 30 days free) to begin.

2. Enter your initial Store Content. This entails:

▶ **The name of your eBay Store.** I hope you've thought of something catchy, and perhaps something that's a bit general. If you name your store Patti's Video Shop and someday choose to also sell clothing, your store name won't properly reflect your merchandise. You can always change your store name, but the Internet address for your store includes the store name — any links you've sent out with the old URL won't work to bring repeat buyers back to your store.

▶ **Your payment information:** Your payment information includes the name to which you'd like your payments addressed.

▶ **Address:** Enter the address to which you want payments sent.

▶ **Phone number (optional):** If you want buyers to be able to see your phone number when checking out after a purchase.

▶ **Store description:** This is important. The text you type in here will appear in the header box of all your store pages. It should be short, but full of descriptive keywords. You have only 250 characters for your Store Description.

 Keywords work for you in the Store Description in two ways. First, people searching only store names and descriptions from an eBay Store search with keywords will find your item easily. It will also work to bring buyers from the Internet as Web Search engine spiders may pick up your keywords.

▶ **Store Specialties:** Here you have 200 characters to list your store's specialties. You can modify this description at any time.

Counting characters the easy way

If you want to type out this information in advance (a good idea), use Microsoft Word. To count the characters in text for areas where a segment of text allows a limited character count:

✔ Type out your idea of the text you'd like to use.

✔ Highlight the text.

✔ Click Tools⇨Word Count.

✔ Your total count will be found in the line *Characters (with spaces)*.

As long as you're in Word, use the spell checker before copying your text onto the Store Content page.

▶ **Categories:** Giving the items in your store custom categories are a great idea. They will be displayed on the left side of your store home page and will help buyers find their way to the specific types of items they're looking for. You may add up to 20 different categories. They will only show up in your store directory if you list an item in them.

3. **Indicate your Store subscription level.**

   This is where you decide (by putting a check mark in the check box) which type of store you wish to open.

4. **Add About Your Store information.**

   This information will show up on your Store Policies Page, as shown in Figure 41-3.

Description of Business	I'm the author of "eBay for Dummies" and "Starting an eBay Business for Dummies." Here's where I sell to all my eBay friends. You'll find items to help you sell on eBay, as well as fun and absolutely fabulous gifts!	
Terms and Conditions Payment and shipment terms may vary on individual items.	**Payment methods**	**PayPal** VISA CHECK Money Order/Cashiers Check. All credit Card payments are graciously accepted through PayPal only.
	Store ship-to locations	the United States only. Please email if you'd like an item shipped out of the US. I will try to accomodate your needs. For United States shipments, we use Priority Mail. THANK YOU!
	Shipping & Handling	Buyer Pays Shipping.
	Sales tax	8.25% if shipped to CA. Resale numbers accepted please email after auction.
	Customer service & return policy	All items are guaranteed to be exactly as stated in the auction description.
Additional Store Information	Aside from many fun items, I try to sell items for eBay sellers: items that will help them run their business more efficiently!	

• **Figure 41-3: Store Policies page from my eBay Store.**

▶ **Payment Methods:** You need to indicate which payment methods you'll accept in your store.

▶ **Store Ship-To Locations and Shipping & Handling:** Designate which countries you will ship to if you ship internationally. If you ship only to the United States, you must specify that here.

There is also a 200-character area where you may optionally input additional shipping information.

▶ **Sales Tax:** Input your state here and the sales tax as a percentage. eBay will automatically calculate sales tax when items are shipped within your home state.

There is also a 200-character text box to input additional tax information. If you accept a resale number from buyers within your own state that are buying to resell, you might indicate that here. If you've nothing extra to say, just pass the text box by.

▶ **Customer Service & Return Policy:** If you have a return policy or additional information, you have a 90-character space to spell it out here.

▶ **Additional Store Information:** If you've just got oodles more to say about your store, you can say it here (okay, *oodles* means 200 more characters in this case).

Designing your store's "look"

Now comes the fun part. Here's where you can customize the look of your eBay Store. The choices you make here will design the way your store looks — it's your opportunity to make your store stand out.

1. **Select a color scheme.**

   Since not everyone is an HTML color expert, eBay graciously has quite a few pretested color combinations that you can use for your store. Click the drop-down box to select a color combination by name. If you want to view the colors prior to selecting them (an excellent idea), click the link on this page that says Preview Colors Below.

   You also have the option of selecting your own Hexadecimal colors. Huh? Yes, that's what I said. Click the little color box next to the text boxes here, and get a teeny color chart. If you roll your mouse over the teeny boxes, you'll see the HTML hexadecimal numbers for that color as in Figure 41-4.

If the teeny boxes don't give you enough of a taste of the colors, you can go to my Web site `www.coolebaytools.com` and find a link in the Tips area to a very large sampling of hundreds of colors and their hexadecimal numbers.

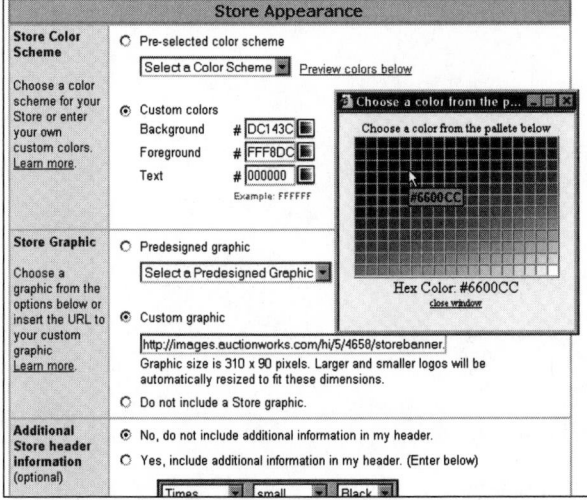

• **Figure 41-4: Selecting your Store Appearance colors.**

2. Choose your store graphic.

eBay has a bunch of clean looking banners available here for your store's home page. You can use one of those if you want your store looking like everyone else's.

 To get a reasonably priced custom graphic for your eBay Store, search eBay for `eBay (banner, banners)`. I just did and found 86 buy-it-now listings for people who are willing to design a custom banner for under $20. Be sure you like the samples of the seller's designs and are comfortable with their terms before you buy.

Do yourself a favor and get a custom-designed banner just for your store. You can always change it if you want, but it will go a long way to add professionalism to your store.

3. Add additional store header information.

Here you can input even more information about your store. eBay gives you an HTML generator to accomplish this here. If you have time to do this, fine. If not, don't make yourself crazy — just put up good items and sell them.

4. Choose the item default display.

Select the way you'd like your items to appear. They can appear as a list, just like regular eBay listings, or you can select the Gallery View, as shown in Figure 41-5.

• **Figure 41-5: My store with Gallery view layout.**

5. Choose the item display order.

You can select the order in which your items will appear in your store:

▶ Highest prices first

▶ Lowest prices first

▶ Ending soonest first

▶ Ending latest first

Designing a custom store home page

If you want your eBay Store to be totally customized and you're comfortable with writing HTML, you can design a custom home page for your store in this area.

If you don't want a custom home page, just check the box that says No, do not include a custom home page.

Don't feel bad if you don't want to devote the time and effort into designing a custom page. I opted not to. I would rather err on the side of caution — my HTML talent really isn't up to snuff. I'll let my items do the talking!

When you finish with these steps, press the button that says Save Changes and Publish. Your new store should be ready for action within the hour.

Technique 42

Building Your Reputation by Becoming a PowerSeller

Save Time By

- ✔ Identifying what eBay PowerSeller status entails
- ✔ Knowing the qualifications
- ✔ Understanding the benefits

When you browse through the items on eBay, you're bound to notice a PowerSeller icon next to another member's user ID. To the uninitiated, this may look like an award given to a used car salesman for bullying hundreds of people into expensive car leases — but it's not. The eBay PowerSeller status is given only to those sellers who uphold the highest levels of professionalism on the site.

eBay refers to them as "pillars of the community." I say they're smart businesspeople. PowerSellers have to maintain certain monthly levels of Gross Merchandise Sales (total dollar amount of eBay sales — GMS in eBayspeak), and they get there by providing good items for sale and excellent customer service.

You may notice that many sellers on the site with feedback ratings in the tens of thousands do not have the PowerSeller embellishment on their auctions. That's not because they're not good people, it's just that some of their transactions may have gone awry. In this case, be sure to check the seller's feedback and thoughtfully evaluate it. Many times buyers do not read the seller's policies before they buy and then give negative feedback (as in the case of buyers not reading the seller's warnings when buying liquidation merchandise).

To become a PowerSeller on eBay, you must fulfill the following requirements:

- ✔ Be an active seller for at least 90 days
- ✔ Sell a minimum of 4 items on the site per month for the past 3 months
- ✔ Have a minimum of a 100 feedback rating
- ✔ Maintain a feedback percentage of at least 98 percent
- ✔ Keep your eBay account current
- ✔ Comply with all eBay listing policies
- ✔ Run your business by upholding eBay's community values (see sidebar)
- ✔ Sell a minimum average of $1,000 a month in GMS

PowerSeller Tiers

Being a PowerSeller provides membership in an exclusive club, and there are five different levels of membership. Members of the different tiers must sell to a certain level every month.

Each PowerSeller tier gives the Seller more privileges from eBay. One of the most valuable benefits is that when an issue needs to be addressed with eBay, the PowerSellers can access priority customer service support (see Table 42-1).

TABLE 42-1: POWERSELLER LEVELS AND SUPPORT BENEFITS

Tier	Monthly Average GMS	E-mail Support	Toll-free Phone	Manager Support
Bronze	$1,000	✔		
Silver	$3,000	✔	✔	
Gold	$10,000	✔	✔	✔
Platinum	$25,000	✔	✔	✔
Titanium	$150,000	✔	✔	✔

Benefiting from the Program

In addition to receiving premium support, eBay PowerSellers also have other benefits.

- ✔ **VIP status at eBay events:** They get invitations to special eBay events including eBay University and eBay Live.

- ✔ **Co-op advertising:** eBay will also contribute to off-eBay print or media advertising. (For full details, see Technique 58.)

- ✔ **Health care:** PowerSellers and their immediate family have the opportunity to purchase exclusive health insurance.

- ✔ **Approved use of PowerSeller logo:** eBay supplies PowerSellers with business card and stationery templates so they may print custom stationery and business cards that include the official PowerSeller logo.

- ✔ **Discounts:** eBay partners offer special discounts off services to eBay PowerSellers.

Becoming an eBay PowerSeller is an important step to eBay professionalism. It's something worth aspiring to!

eBay community values

The set of eBay community values aren't taken lightly by the eBay community and eBay employees. The values were set out early on by the company's founder, Pierre Omidyar.

- ✔ We believe people are basically good.

- ✔ We believe everyone has something to contribute.

- ✔ We believe that an honest, open environment can bring out the best in people.

- ✔ We recognize and respect everyone as a unique individual.

- ✔ We encourage you to treat others the way that you want to be treated.

All eBay sellers are expected to uphold these tenets in all their dealings on the site.

Okay, no snickering from the peanut gallery, we all know that there are quite a few sellers who don't follow these precepts. But then, they're not PowerSellers, are they?

Technique 43

Becoming an eBay Trading Assistant

What is an eBay Trading Assistant? Simply, an eBay Trading Assistant sells merchandise for people on eBay. A more complex definition is that a Trading Assistant sells items on consignment for those who are not familiar with the eBay site or are simply too lazy to learn the ropes. Several chains have opened up across the country with retail locations accepting merchandise from the general public to do just this. By becoming an official Trading Assistant, you can compete with the big boys in your own area.

The best part is that if you are running your eBay business out of your home, from a garage, or from a low-rent industrial office, you're a step ahead of the big guys who have to pay high rents in fancy neighborhoods to get their "drop in" business. They also have to hire people who are familiar with setting up auctions on eBay — aren't you already set up for that?

eBay will help the individual Trading Assistants with many things. Most importantly, you're listed in a searchable directory with other eBay selling professionals for all the world to find at www.eBay.com/ tradingassistants.

Becoming a Trading Assistant

The first thing to take into consideration before becoming a Trading Assistant is to be sure you're familiar with the eBay site, the rules and regulations, and most of all — experienced in selling items at a profit. To be a successful Trading Assistant, you need to be savvy about how to research items on eBay (see Part I) and also know how to parlay keywords into winning auction titles (Part II).

The Trading Assistant directory appears on the eBay site at www.eBay.com/ tradingassistants, as shown in Figure 43-1. From the directory page, potential customers can search for a Trading Assistant to sell their items by ZIP code, telephone area code, or by country. I just ran a search and at this moment there seem to be no Trading Assistants in Jamaica or the Bahamas (*they* might be a nice place to do business from)!

Trading Assistants Program

Let an experienced seller on eBay sell or buy for you.

Trading Assistants are eBay sellers who can sell your items on eBay for a fee. Discover how to sell the easy way.

Trading Assistants
Members Helping Others

Find a Trading Assistant in your area:

Zip / Postal Code [   ] [All Categories ▼] [Search]

Example 95125 or 95*
U.S. and Canada ONLY

Or expand your search for a Trading Assistant.

Area Code [   ]
U.S. & Canada ONLY   **OR**
[Search]

Country [Select country ▼]
[Search]

• **Figure 43-1: The Trading Assistants directory page.**

This page is promoted on the eBay site to new users and in eBay Promotions. Being listed on this page will help your customers find you.

eBay makes it very clear that whether you fulfill the requirements for Trading Assistant or not, being a Trading Assistant is a privilege. If eBay receives complaints about your services, they have the right to remove you from the Trading Assistant directory. eBay's requirements are:

✔ **Listings:** You must have sold at least 4 items in the last 30 days.

✔ **Feedback Rating:** You must have a minimum rating of 50 or higher, while maintaining a minimum of 97 percent positive comments.

As a Trading Assistant, you will acquire merchandise and sell it on eBay on consignment. You will also be responsible for

✔ Consulting with consignors about their items.

✔ Researching the value of the item. Many non-eBay users may have unreasonable expectations of the price their items will sell for. It's your duty

to check this out beforehand and explain the realities to them.

✔ Coordinating the listing. Take digital photos and write a complete and accurate description of the item.

✔ Keeping a close accounting of fees and money collection.

That's not much in the way of requirements, but you need to get some things together *before* you sign up.

> Becoming a Trading Assistant does not make you an employee, agent, or independent contractor of eBay. You should be careful to refer to yourself as an independent business.

When you sign up as a Trading Assistant, you have to fill out a form describing your business to prospective customers. Think through the things you have to say before posting them. Your information here works like an ad for you. Here are the things you have to put on your Trading Assistant listing page.

✔ **Personal information:** This includes your eBay User ID, your real name, address, and languages spoken.

✔ **Category Specialty:** If you specialize in a particular category, be sure to mention it. You may indicate up to three eBay home page categories.

✔ **Service Description:** In this area, you can say as little or as much as you like about your eBay experience and the services you provide. Remember that the more you communicate in advance, the more successful you'll be.

Here is a sample Service Description:

> I've been active on the site since 1996 and am an eBay PowerSeller. I specialize in selling all types of eBay items and am particularly familiar with the fashion category. I can handle large numbers of listings. Please contact me so that we can discuss your particular needs and time availability.

I can visit your home within 15 miles from my place of business to inventory the items. I will list, ship, and provide you with an itemized list of all items sold with the sale price and my fees.

✔ **Policy Description:** Ensure that the consignees understand your policies. A sample description looks like this:

I will list your items for two listing cycles, spread up to 30 days. If items do not sell, they will be returned to you. Items must be in my possession to be submitted to eBay unless prior contractual arrangements are made in advance. I handle all correspondence and shipping. A consignment contract is required. I also do independent consulting specializing in Internet auctions and their application to your business.

✔ **Fee Description:** This is where you need to do some research. Search your own telephone area code on the Trading Assistant directory page and see what other fees are being charged in your area. After you have an idea of what you want to charge, you can put that information here.

 You can provide incentives for higher-value items by charging lower commissions (such as 40 percent if an item sells for less than $50, 30 percent if the item sells for more). Also, charging a higher percentage and including fees allows an easier fee discussion with the client (for example, "40 percent, all fees included" is generally simpler than "30 percent and you pay all the fees, which include. . . .")

Many Trading Assistants also use transaction fees for listing with a reserve (knowing it probably won't sell because the consignor doesn't have a fair guess at market valuation).

When you've decided everything you need to list, click the link on the Trading Assistant homepage that says Become a Trading Assistant. Fill out

the forms and, just like magic, you've become a Trading Assistant!

Promoting Your Business

When I was working in the newspaper advertising business, we had a saying about someone who opened a new store: If all the advertising they do is their Grand Opening ad and nothing after; it won't be long before you'll be seeing the Going Out-of-Business Sale ad.

The same is true with your Trading Assistant business. Although you may not go out of business if you don't promote it, you'll probably have no business at all.

eBay gives you many tools to help you grow your consignment business, even a co-op advertising program. For more information on co-op advertising, visit Technique 58.

Adding the Trading Assistant logo to your eBay listings

Your best customers may come from people who see your existing items when browsing eBay. Why not show all viewers that you're a Trading Assistant? Put the Trading Assistant logo into your listings, as shown in Figure 43-2. When a prospective customer clicks on the link, they will be sent to your Trading Assistant Information page (just as if they searched you out in the directory).

• **Figure 43-2: The eBay Trading Assistant link.**

 Insert the Trading Assistants logo when your regular eBay business is slow, and take it out when you're overly busy. That way you can control the amount of work you have.

To add the link to your listings, you have to use a little HTML. Don't panic though, because I supply the code for you below. To get the code for your personal Trading Assistant link, follow these steps:

1. **Find out your Trading Assistant number.**

Go to your listing in the directory. Take a look at the top of your Internet browser, and you will see your Trading Assistant number (this is also your eBay account number) at the end of that Web page's URL. The Web address looks like this: `http://contact.ebay.com/aw-cgi/eBayISAPI.dll?ShowMemberToMemberDetails&member=000000`

In this example, your number would be 000000.

2. **Add code to your listing description.**

Add the following HTML code at the end of your listing description (be sure to replace `000000` with your own eBay number):

```
<center>
<a href="http://contact.ebay.com/aw-cgi/eBayISAPI.dll?ShowMemberToMemberDetails&member=000000">
<b>I am a Trading Assistant - I can sell items for you!</b>
<br>
<img src="http://pics.ebaystatic.com/aw/pics/Trading_Assistant2_88x33.gif" vspace="5" border="0" height="33" width="88"></a>
<br>
```

After you insert this code in your listings, a link and button appear in your eBay sales (refer to Figure 43-2).

Posting flyers

eBay has designed a nifty flyer that you can customize and print out on your own printer. Put it up at the supermarket, the car wash, the cleaner — anywhere and everywhere flyers are allowed.

Even if you don't see flyers in a retail location, ask the owner of the business if you can put one up — maybe even offer a discount to the business owner for selling their items on eBay in exchange!

To get to the eBay collateral materials (flyers and posters) go to `http://pages.eBay.com/TradingAssistants/collateral/index.html`. On this page, you can find the current graphical offerings from eBay.

The posters and window signs are in Microsoft Word format so that you can customize them with your own business information. The flyer/poster, shown in Figure 43-3, includes small tear-off strips where you can place your contact information. When people see your promotion, they can just snip off your phone number (or e-mail address) and contact you when they get home.

• **Figure 43-3: The Trading Assistants Flyer.**

Handling Your Business Professionally

Handling merchandise that's not yours takes responsibility, and how you conduct your business can demonstrate to your customers that you're a responsible person. You need to present a professional appearance when you meet your client, and you should have a professional attitude in your dealings.

Being professional also means anticipating possible problems. In addition to being very clear about financial issues with your clients (especially fees and the realistic selling value of your clients' merchandise), you may want to consider getting additional insurance to cover the merchandise you are holding in your home.

You may also want to consider designing a few forms to reinforce with your clients that this is your business and that you know it well, for example:

Inventory form: This form lists the entire inventory you receive from the client and should include as detailed a description of the item as your client can supply. Also, include the minimum amount (if any) the client will accept for the item — this will be your reserve price if necessary.

Sales Agreement: Professional Trading Assistants have their clients sign a Sales Contract. Read the sidebar following for some good suggestions on what to put in your contract. Since I'm not an attorney, you should have a lawyer take a look at your contract before you use it.

Important items for your Trading Assistant contract

The information below was graciously supplied by one of eBay's successful Trading Assistants, *LikePhate* (Kate & Phil Bowyer). It includes quotes from their own Trading Assistant contract that cover many things that you might overlook when you put together your own contract. This, of course,

is not a full agreement, but it provides some of the salient points not to forget.

Be sure to include an explanation of the consignment process:

- The Consignor will bring item(s) to the Seller, who, upon both parties signing this contract, will take possession of the items for the duration of the auction.

- Acceptance of any item consigned will be at the Seller's sole discretion.

- The Seller will inspect the item(s) for quality and clean if necessary (a fee may apply).

- The Seller will take quality photographs and write an accurate description of item(s).

- The Seller will research eBay® for similar items to assure proper pricing.

- The Seller will start the auction(s) and handle all aspects of the sale including correspondence with bidders.

- The Seller will collect payment from the winning bidder ("Buyer") at the end of the auction and will ship the item(s) in a timely manner, once funds have cleared.

- The Seller will follow-up the sale by contacting the Buyer to make sure they are satisfied with the transaction.

- Once the Seller and Buyer are satisfied with the transaction, payment will be made to the Consignor.

- The Seller will keep the Consignor aware of the auction progress either by telephone, or e-mail and by supplying the Consignor the auction number(s) to track the item(s) themselves.

- The Seller will return unsold item(s) to the Consignor upon payment of outstanding fees.

It's also a good idea to provide the consignor with a statement of items sold, summarizing the total purchase price, all fees, and the amount the consignor receives.

Outline your fees. "The Consignor will be billed the actual rates and fees as incurred for all services, to include the Seller's *00%* Commission. Any services or upgrades requested by the Consignor will carry the exact fee and will be deducted from payment, or after three (3) failed auction listings, will be due to the Seller payable in cash. If the auction sells, these fees will be subtracted from the winning bid before the Consignor receives payment."

Be sure to include a copy of current eBay fees: Listing, Options, Reserves, PayPal, and Final Value Fees.

Outline the terms of your commission. "The Seller's commission for this service is a percentage based on the auction's winning bid. If the auction does not sell, the Consignor is only responsible to pay the applicable insertion and reserve price auction fees. An Unsold Reserve fee of *$0.00* will be due to the Seller for a reserve price auction that does not sell."

Be sure you don't guarantee the item will sell. "If an item does not sell, the Seller will re-list it two additional times. The Seller may contact the Consignor to discuss combining individual items into lots to attract buyers. The Consignor's verbal consent, or e-mail consent, will be documented in the Consignor's file and will serve as a revision to this contract. After a third unsuccessful listing, the Consignor will be billed for the fees associated with all three auctions, plus a $5.00 surcharge. Items will be returned to consignor upon payment of those fees. Items not claimed within 14 days from the end of the final listing will become the property of the Seller."

Protect yourself and your eBay reputation. "The Consignor of said item(s) consents to the sale of said item(s) based on the terms described in this agreement. The Consignor also attests that said item(s) are fully owned by the Consignor and are not stolen, borrowed, misrepresented, bogus, etc."

You might also mention that you will only sell it if eBay policies allow the item to be sold.

"The Seller will do everything possible to secure the safety of the Consignor's item(s), however, the Seller is not responsible for any damage to the item, including fire, theft, flood, accidental damage or breakage, and acts of God. The Consignor releases the Seller of any such responsibility for any unforeseen or accidental damage."

I choose to protect myself additionally, because reputation on eBay is paramount. I have a small business rider on my homeowner's insurance with Allstate that covers merchandise in my home up to $5,000. It's an inexpensive addition to your policy — *definitely* worth looking into.

Ending a sale prematurely. "If such an instance arises that the Consignor demands the item(s) to be pulled, the Consignor will pay a cancellation fee of $75. Items will not be surrendered to Consignor until this fee is paid in cash."

Protect yourself from possible shill bidding. An important line you should add protects you from possible shill bidding. How about: The Consignor also agrees not to place a bid on an auction that the Seller has listed for the Consignor (hereafter "Shill Bid") on eBay, nor to arrange for a Shill Bid to be made on the behalf of the Consignor by a third party. If the Consignor or an agent of the Consignor submits a Shill Bid on an auction listed by the Seller, then the Consignor agrees to pay all fees, commissions, and penalties associated with that auction, PLUS a $75.00 fine, and the Seller may refuse to grant auction services to the Consignor in the future.

Again, I *strongly* suggest that you get professional advice before putting together your own contract or agreement.

Technique 44

Getting the Stamp of Approval from SquareTrade

Save Time By

✔ Getting the scoop on the SquareTrade service

✔ Tracking potential buyers with seal activity reports

✔ Becoming a SquareTrade seal holder

Okay, SquareTrade doesn't give you a *stamp* of approval; it's technically a *seal*. But whether stamp or seal, having this small icon associated with your items can boost your sales quite a bit. The SquareTrade Seal is a known commodity in the eBay community with buyers and sellers alike. When buyers see the SquareTrade Seal in an auction, it's an immediate tip off that they're doing business with a reliable, honest seller. (See Technique 4 for more information on how the seal works for the buyer.) This seal is the most widely recognized symbol of trust on eBay, and you can view it in about two million listings a day.

This technique is concerned with getting the SquareTrade Seal with its associated services and reports to work for you, the seller. One of the best benefits is that showing the seal lowers the occurrence of negative feedback. When people view the seal on your auctions, they feel more trusting and at ease with buying from you. So if there's a glitch in the transaction, they're far less apt to fly off the handle and leave you a negative feedback comment without contacting you.

SquareTrade conducted a survey, which included a study of 130,000 feedback ratings among 600 of its seal members, and found an astounding result. The average seller noticed a remarkable 43 percent decrease in negative feedback received after becoming a member. That's pretty amazing. Although there's no guarantee that you won't get negatives (and you still need to watch your Ps & Qs), the SquareTrade Seal certainly seems to calm buyers' nerves.

SquareTrade Stretches Beyond eBay

SquareTrade began operations in 1999 to service eBay sellers and to help them handle disputes in transactions. The company grew steadily over the years and established itself as an international leader in online dispute resolution. SquareTrade has acted as key presenter on the issue of global online consumer protection to the Federal Trade Commission, the European Union, and the United Nations Economic Commission for Europe.

 It's nice to know that a company working for eBay members is so well respected worldwide. For eBay sellers who subscribe to *the seal,* SquareTrade offers many worthwhile tools to help build their reputations and their businesses on eBay.

Making SquareTrade Work for You

The best part about subscribing to SquareTrade (and the main reason most sellers join) is that members get to show off the seal and so become *seal holders.* That ubiquitous lime-green-and-navy-blue seal builds business. When potential buyers view your eBay listings, they see a seal marked with the current date. SquareTrade updates the seal daily and roots out those sellers who have possibly joined the dark side.

SquareTrade runs 40 automated compliance checks on seal holders daily. Anytime there's an automated alert, a human being (specifically, a SquareTrade employee) checks to see what's occurring with the seal holder's account and may then contact the seal holder for further information. Figure 44-1 shows my SquareTrade seal.

• **Figure 44-1: My SquareTrade seal.**

Notice that a clickable link appears on the left of the seal. When the buyer clicks it, your SquareTrade profile opens up in another window, as shown in Figure 44-2.

 Sellers can customize the look of the SquareTrade seal and can choose whether it appears on the top or the bottom of their item descriptions. I like to have the seal appear at the top of my listings so that buyers readily see the seal as they read the item listing.

• **Figure 44-2: My SquareTrade profile.**

In addition to the handy seal, SquareTrade offers sellers some other good tools and services:

- **Automatic seal posting:** If you don't want to mess with HTML every time you list an item (and who does?), you can set your seal preferences to automatically post. Then once a day, SquareTrade autoposts the seal to any new listings you've placed on eBay.

- **Seal Activity Reports:** If you like the idea of putting counters in your auctions to see how many visitors you get, the Seal Activity Reports give you totals (for a time period) of how many people have looked at your auctions. Figure 44-3 shows a segment of my current Seal Activity Reports. I find it amazing that so many people have viewed my auctions during these time periods. (I don't keep many items listed when I'm writing a book.) These totals are quite a testament to the number of people who visit eBay every day.

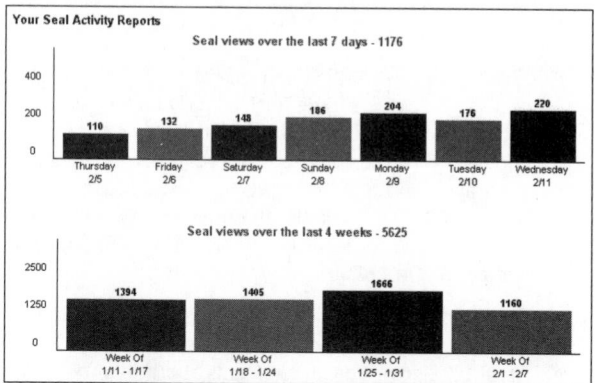

• **Figure 44-3:** Can you believe this many people visited my auctions?

✔ **eBay Sales Reports:** As a seal holder, you'll be able to log on to your account on the SquareTrade Web site and view a large array of reports reflecting your eBay business.

Basic-level seal holders can view reports with the following information:

▶ Average selling price

▶ Price comparison, sold versus unsold

▶ Percent of listings that sold successfully

▶ Monthly sales

▶ Number of listings sold

▶ Average number of bids per sold listings

▶ Bids-per-auction pie chart

▶ Feedback growth summary

Figure 44-4 shows a couple of sample reports from my Business Reporting Center.

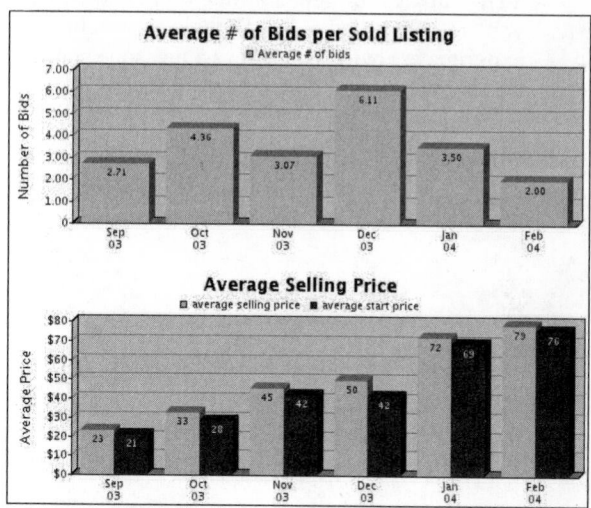

• **Figure 44-4:** From my SquareTrade business reports.

✔ **Seal Rewards:** If another eBay member signs up as a SquareTrade member through the seal link to your listings, you receive $5.00 for the referral. This is redeemable in auction services, gift certificates, and more. If people sign up through your link on a regular basis, the rewards can pay for your SquareTrade membership in no time!

✔ **Negative Feedback Notification:** You have the option of having SquareTrade notify you whenever (horrors!) negative feedback is posted to your account. SquareTrade then works with you and the other party through mediation — to hopefully get the premature negative feedback removed or withdrawn.

✔ **Buyer Protection program:** When you're a seal holder, your buyers are covered under an additional Buyer Protection program. (For more about this program, see Technique 3).

✔ **Buyer Alert e-mails**. If you opt for the Buyer Alert service, SquareTrade sends your bidders an e-mail on your behalf letting them know that you are committed to giving them a good buying experience. Figure 44-5 shows a message sent to one of my bidders.

• **Figure 44-5:** SquareTrade bidder alert e-mail.

Getting Your Own Seal

Having a SquareTrade Seal sounds like a pretty sweet deal. And sweet deals usually have a catch or two. With SquareTrade, the catches are

✔ You have to qualify for the seal

✔ You have to pay for your seal subscription

Internet seals of safety

When you travel the Internet, you see many seals. You hope that the seals you see legitimately stand for something and that the Web sites using them follow standards that ensure some level of quality. Two of the most trusted seals are

✔ **BBBOnLine:** The BBBOnLine seal qualifying process, as with the SquareTrade Seal, actually investigates candidate seal holders to make sure they're who they say they are. Seal members also agree to participate in arbitration and to accept visits from BBB (Better Business Bureau) officials. The seal loosely costs about $400 to $500 for small businesses and up to $5,000 for larger corporations.

✔ **Trust-e:** Web sites may post a Trust-e seal provided that the site posts a privacy statement and sticks to it. Trust-e will investigate complaints about member sites and yank the site's seal if necessary. For Trust-e members with annual sales below $1,000,000, the Trust-e seal costs around $250. The price goes up to $5,000 for larger firms.

Although posting a well-known seal costs you money, doing so has proven to be a business tactic that makes customers feel at ease. Sometimes such expenditures just make good business sense.

To qualify for the SquareTrade Seal, you must go through an approval process that takes two to five days. From any seal holder's profile, click the See If You Qualify link and take advantage of the 30-day free trial to get the ball rolling. You start by supplying information to SquareTrade, and SquareTrade investigates your info in two areas:

✔ **Personal Information:** Most seal applicants are verified through Equifax, a prominent identity verification service. SquareTrade checks your information against Equifax's consumer and business databases for consistency.

✔ **eBay Selling History:** SquareTrade runs 20 different checks on your eBay transaction history through systems developed to identify at-risk sellers from their feedback information, as well as from the products bought and sold.

After SquareTrade notifies you (through e-mail) that you're approved, you have to pay SquareTrade for the right to become a seal holder. As of this writing, the basic seal holder gets an initial 30-day free trial and then pays $7.50 per month for all the services described in the section "Making SquareTrade Work for You." You can also choose a Premium level of services that offers more reports at a higher monthly fee.

Technique 45

Meeting Other eBayers

Save Time By

- ✔ Connecting with the community through Groups
- ✔ Learning about your specialty from chat
- ✔ Understanding how the boards work

There was a time when I would tell you that the eBay boards and chat rooms were pretty much a waste of time. They're great, I used to say, if you only use eBay part time and enjoy the social aspect of chatting with others online. But if you have a busy life, minutes can become hours in the chats and boards, and you can burn through your valuable time before you know it.

Today, however, I also see a bright side to the eBay community. It allows you to make contact with others in your own situation — stay-at-home moms and dads, coin collectors, guys into fishing gear, and people just into socializing. There's a vast group of people just like you in the eBay community from every part of the world. Through the eBay community, you can make contact with them and maybe even make a new friend or two.

On the other hand, beware of getting caught up in heated discussions that accomplish nothing except raising your blood pressure. In some of the chat areas, differing opinions often rise up and people (being only human) can get carried away. Although it may seem that your comments are inconsequential, they may affect other people seriously. Giving advice on things that you're truly not an expert on may cause problems down the road for other community members reading your posts. Remember that everything you post in the eBay community is etched in granite (okay, etched in cyberspace), and your User ID is attached to your statements.

Navigating the eBay Community

The beginning of your journey into the world of personalized eBay-ing starts at the eBay navigation bar, as shown in Figure 45-1. Click the word *Community* and a drop-down subnavigation bar appears with links to the overview page (that's the page you're currently on), talk, news, events, and people.

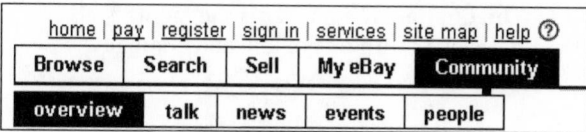

• **Figure 45-1:** The eBay navigation bar with the
Community sub-bar.

Scroll down the page and take a look at how eBay
divvies up these various areas. Below the Welcome
to eBay Community headline, you'll see the four different areas and their links, as shown in Figure 45-2.

• **Figure 45-2:** The eBay Community hub page.

Participating in talk

Although the methods of communication are different, the Talk area is where you can converse directly
with other members of the community. Talk covers
several areas:

✔ **Discussion boards:** In discussion boards, you'll
find community help boards, category-specific
discussion boards, general discussion boards,
workshops, and Giving Works boards.

Covered in the discussion area:

▶ **Community help:** About 25 boards are topi-
cally organized to provide help on eBay tasks,
such as bidding, shipping, technical issues,
and so on.

▶ **Category-specific discussion boards:**
Discussion regarding close to 40 different eBay
categories, such as Collectibles, eBay Motors,
Clothing, Shoes & Accessories, and more.

▶ **General discussion boards:** Discuss whatever
tickles your fancy here. Boards with neighbor-
hood-sounding names where you can stop in
and visit. Lots of free association chatter and
fun topics in these boards!

▶ **Workshops board:** This is the spot to find
"deirdre the pink" who hosts workshops on
various topics regarding eBay. She invites spe-
cialists in various areas to give online workshops. You can sign in and watch the posts as
the workshops happen, or sign on later and
read all the posts.

▶ **Giving Works (charity) board.** Here's where
you go to talk to others regarding charitable
auctions on eBay.

 "Pinks" are eBay employees who dart in and
out of the chat rooms and boards. They occasionally answer questions and sometimes jump
in on the action. You can spot them easily, as
their posts are shaded with a light pink bar.

✔ **Chat rooms:** Here's where things can get hot and
heavy. People love the chat area for posting opinions on eBay!

In the Chat area you'll find:

▶ **General chat rooms:** The classic eBay Café is
here, as well as the AOL Café, Emergency
Board, and others.

▶ **Category-specific chat rooms:** I just checked
them out; there's even one for Furby collectors! Lots of fun and lots of friends make this
an active area. It's fun to check these boards

and see what's hot and what's not in the various categories.

✔ **Question and answer boards:** The Q&A Boards are where you can post a question about all things eBay — and hopefully someone will post an answer to you quickly.

Topics cover all eBay services and tasks.

 The most important part about the Talk area is that no business is allowed! The chats are there for discussion and comments, but not for posting items to sell or buy.

Checking out what's news

The eBay News area has some of the most important links. From here you can go to the announcements area that helps you stay on top of changes in the eBay system.

✔ **General Announcements:** Here's where eBay first posts announcements about new changes to the system (as in Figure 45-3). If something looks a little different to you one day while performing a task on eBay, check here to see what's up.

✔ **System Announcements:** If something's not working on the site, eBay will generally post information about the temporary glitches. That way you can check to see whether it's your computer or eBay that's messing up!

• **Figure 45-3: The General Announcement board for February 14, 2004.**

✔ **The Chatter:** *The Chatter* is the monthly eBay newsletter with bits of info and company messages.

Understanding the differences in posting between the boards

There's quite a bit of difference among the methods of posting and reading posts. The individual posts are handled very differently in the various areas.

The Booksellers Discussion Board in the Boards area is pictured in Figure 45-4.

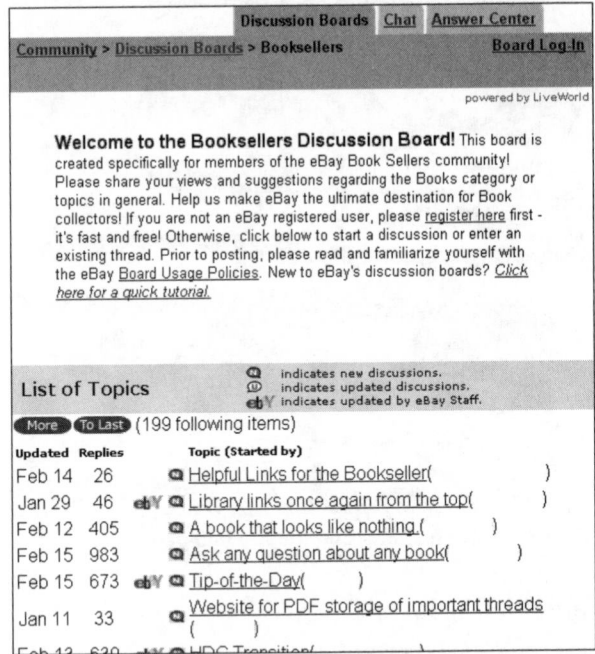

• **Figure 45-4: The Bookseller's Discussion Board in action.**

To post on the board, follow these steps:

1. **Post a question or comment by logging into the boards at the top of the page.**

2. **Click the Board Log-In link, and you'll be transferred to the Sign In area.**

3. **Type in your User ID and password and press Sign In.**

You'll be returned to the Board with the option to post in a blank text box at the end of the posts.

4. **Type your query into the text box and click the Post Message button.**

The query is listed on the site for other interested parties to reply.

To reply to a post or to see what responses you have to your own post, just return to the area and click on the post. The number of responses will be listed next to it in the Replies column.

eBay Chat rooms are for real-time (kind-of) chatting as shown in Figure 45-5. Users type in their comments and other users populating the particular chat area can see their posts when they press reload. If you find an interesting thread of conversation in the chatter, you can reload your page showing the last 200 messages posted up to 24 hours prior by using the drop-down menu. When the boards are busy, however, the 200-message limit may cover only an hour's time.

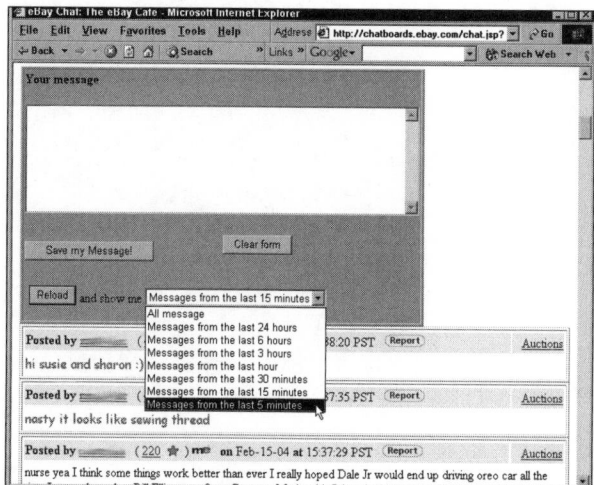

• **Figure 45-5:** Chatting and reloading by time increment.

The Answer Center runs things on a slightly different format. When you click on a subject you wish to view, you will be presented with a list of questions, as shown in Figure 45-6. You can post your own question, or get the answer to a question you see.

To read all answers, click the View Answers link at the bottom of the question.

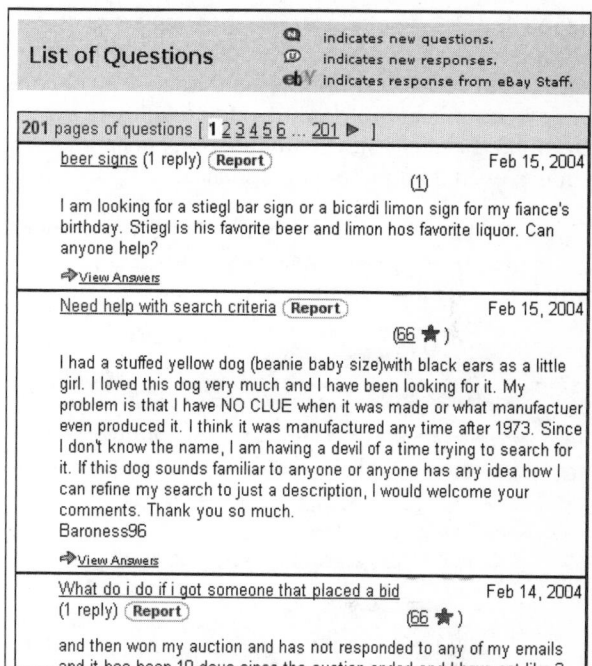

• **Figure 45-6:** List of Questions from the eBay Answer Center, Search questions.

Visiting the events

Here's where you can find out what events are planned for the eBay Community.

- ✔ **Calendar:** Click the calendar link to see what eBay is doing around the country. The calendar links are clickable so that you can find out more details on the various events.

- ✔ **Workshops/Events List:** Click Workshops to go directly to the Workshops Board — or better yet, click the link on the Event List and see the details on upcoming events.

- ✔ **Charity:** This link takes you to the eBay Giving Works hub page where you can search and check out the charity auctions currently on the site. (See Technique 59 for more on raising money for nonprofits on eBay.)

Joining a Group

People hub is one of the fastest-growing areas on eBay. Here's where people start clubs or "groups" with people of similar hobbies and ideas. I'm a member of a couple of groups and enjoy reading the discussions (because they're about subjects I care about), even if I don't post responses.

Figure 45-7 shows you the Groups home page, where you can search new groups or sign into groups in which you're already a member.

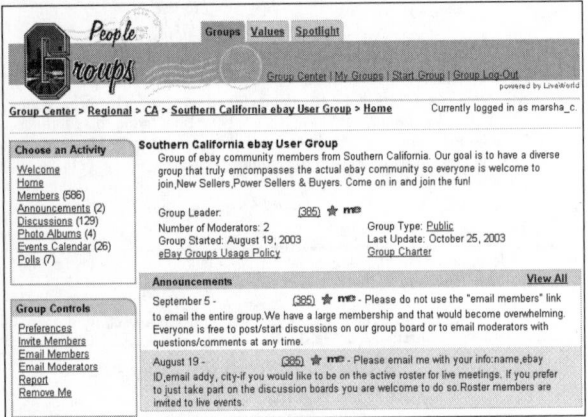

• **Figure 45-7:** An eBay Groups home page. Note the links to the different areas of the group at left.

The groups give you the opportunity to join like-minded people online (or even in person) and share your eBay adventures.

How the community works for you

While writing this technique, I went to all the areas of the community. I saw a post from another community member saying that her mom's WebTV unit had quit working and she didn't know what to do. Her mom was stuck on that particular system and wanted nothing else.

I emailed her, letting her know that my mom was also a WebTV user, but had recently passed away. I offered her my mom's WebTV setup (including printer) for minimal cost plus shipping.

That's what community can be all about!

Part VIII

Running an Efficient Back Office

The 5th Wave   By Rich Tennant

"Oh, we're doing just great. Philip and I are selling decorative jelly jars on eBay. I run the auctions, and Philip sort of controls the inventory."

Technique 46

Going Legit with Your Business

Save Time By

✔ Getting your business straight

✔ Deciding on your structure

✔ Contacting your state for licenses

If you've played around on eBay, had some fun, and made a few dollars, then good for you — enjoy yourself! Once you start making serious money, however, your business is no longer a hobby. Before you know it, it's time to consider some serious issues like business structure, tax planning, and licenses. I say this because when you're concentrating on fulfilling multiple orders and keeping your customers happy, the last thing you need is a G-man breathing down your neck. Worst-case scenario: How about getting audited in December when you haven't been keeping good records all year?

In short, *getting serious* means making some decisions. It means getting licenses that cost something, and, possibly, collecting and paying sales tax. I know this sounds like stripping the fun out of doing business on eBay, but taking a bit of time and effort now can save you a ton of trouble later on.

Giving Your Business a Name

In most states in the U.S., you can find funny liner ads in the classified section of the local newspaper. They're called fictitious name statements, and they need to be registered with your state before you can open a bank account in a business's name. They let the state know who owns and operates a business. In California, you must file a fictitious name statement within 40 days of the commencement of your business. (Other state laws vary, so check the Web sites listed at the end of this technique for more information on your state's requirements.) Your statement must also include a physical address where the business is operated — not a mailbox address.

 Before you assume registering a name isn't required in your state, be sure to check with your state's business code (links to all 50 states are at the end of this technique). Some states, such as Indiana, require that a business's assumed name be registered with the secretary of state.

In the states requiring publication, your fictitious name statement must be published in an adjudicated (officially approved) newspaper for a certain amount of time. Ostensibly, this is to let the community know that a business is starting and who owns it. The newspaper will supply you with a proof of publication, which you keep in your files as a record of your filing. You generally have to renew the statement after a prescribed number of years.

Don't waste your money!

There are all kinds of very expensive services on the Internet that prey on the inexperienced; they'd be more than willing to handle all the work for you — for a fat fee. Don't waste your money. If newspaper publication is required, look in the phone book for a small community newspaper and call them to see if they handle these type of legal ads. Most small newspapers are 90 percent supported by the money they make on filing legal ads. They're the experts on these types of filings — plus, you get to help out another small business. Every 5 years, I file my company's DBA (Doing Business As) with the nice gray-haired lady at the newspaper with a single-room office.

After you have your proof of publication, you can bring that to the bank and open an account in your business's name, which is a very important step in separating your personal living expenses from the business.

Deciding Your Business Structure

I know that this may seem like a leap, but bear with me. You need to decide in what form to set up your business. You're going to have to live with this decision for quite a long time, so I suggest you consult with a tax professional or an attorney who's familiar with your situation. If you don't know such a professional personally, ask around. Getting a personal referral is far better than picking a name blindly from the phone book. You might even get a good referral from another eBay seller in your area.

You have four choices, and each has different tax and legal ramifications. I'll give you the highlights here.

Sole proprietorship

A sole proprietorship is the simplest form of business. No other form of business is easier to manage or cheaper to run. A sole proprietorship is the form of business that most business owners use when they're first starting out. Many people often graduate to a more formal business format when bigger money comes in.

Keeping track of all expenses related to your eBay business is crucial, even in a sole proprietorship. (Especially as they act as tax deductions against your profits.) Be sure to check Technique 47 for information on what you need to keep records for.

A few highlights of sole proprietorships include:

- Profits and expenses of the business appear on the individual's personal tax return on Schedule C.

- *Sole proprietors* (the owners of sole proprietorships) are in complete control of the money and are personally liable for paying all taxes.

- Some benefits (such as health insurance) are not directly deductible from business income.

- Liability is all on the person owning the business. If you're acting as a Trading Assistant and something seriously goes wrong with an item you've sold for another, you are liable for any damages.

Sole proprietorships are also the easiest businesses to dissolve if you choose to end an enterprise.

Partnership

A *partnership* comprises two or more people. It's a slightly more complicated business format, in which everything — profit, decision-making, liability, and so on — is shared between the partners according to terms governed by a partnership agreement.

A partnership should be formed by a written agreement, which is a legal document. Each person in the partnership contributes capital or services and both share in the partnership's profits and losses. The income of a partnership is taxed on both partners, based on the percentage of the business that they own or upon the terms of the written agreement.

Highlights:

✔ The written agreement forming the partnership should outline everything to do with the business:

▶ How to divide the profit and/or loss

▶ Compensation for each partner

▶ Restrictions of authority and spending

▶ How disputes will be settled

▶ What happens if the partnership dissolves?

▶ What happens to the partnership in case of death or disability?

✔ Profits from the business flow into the partners' personal tax returns, although a separate tax return must be filed in the partnership's name.

✔ The partners are personally equally liable for all business debts and product liability.

Business decisions must be agreed upon by both partners — sometimes that can get sticky!

 To get some intensive information on putting together your business structure, visit www. nolo.com, a Web site that gives legitimate information on do-it-yourself law.

Corporation

A corporation has a life of its own; it has its own name and tax return and is a unique and separate entity from the owners. It's chartered by the secretary of state within the state of incorporation (which is usually the state in which you do business).

Federal taxes for corporations presently range from 15 to 35 percent, based on the corporation's net profits. Employee owners of corporations may shelter income from tax by dividing the income between their personal and corporate tax returns. This is frequently called income splitting and involves setting salaries and bonuses so that any profits left in the company at the end of its tax year will only be taxed at the 15 percent rate.

Setting up a corporation doesn't have to be an expensive venture. Check out the Nolo.com site referred to in the tip above for packages to set one up in your state.

Highlights of a corporation are these:

✔ Shareholders (owners) have limited liability for the corporation's debts. You can lose only the money you invested in the business; your personal property can attach in a few situations — say, you guaranteed a loan for the business or neglected to deposit your employees' withholding taxes. Check with your attorney for more caveats.

✔ As an officer of a corporation, you are required to report to federal and state agencies.

✔ You must keep explicit records of expenses and income.

Limited liability company (LLC)

A *limited liability company* is a new, hybrid type of business that combines portions of a partnership with bits of a corporation. It's basically used when you want the limited-liability advantages of a corporation and the ease of running a partnership.

Due to the newness of this type of business, research the details at Nolo and talk to a professional to decide whether it's best for your eBay business.

Making a decision on your business format is important and can impact your business for years to come. It's best to get professional advice before setting your ideas in concrete.

Joining the Feds

If you're going to be paying anyone a salary, you'll need a Federal ID Number (FEIN). Every business has one. It's like a Social Security number for a business — the number used to identify you on government forms. You may also need one for your state.

There's no charge to get your FEIN, so why wait?

✔ A Federal Employee Tax ID number can be assigned by filing IRS form SS-4. Go to the IRS Web site at

www.irs.gov/businesses/small/article/
    0,,id=102767,00.html

to get the details and apply for your EIN online.

✔ State Employer numbers for taxes may depend on your state's requirements. Visit

www.taxadmin.org/fta/forms.ssi

for an overview of every state in the union.

City and State Business Licenses

It seems like everyone has something to say about your business, doesn't it? Yep, lots of fingers in the pie! When you're part of the business community, your business dealings will have an impact on many more people than just you.

Cities and states issue business licenses to home businesses as well as to large corporations. You're better off getting a license at the outset of an ongoing business than to be forced to pay penalties later.

Table 46-1 is a chart of URLs to individual state's business links. These links should get you all the info you need.

TABLE 46-1: LINKS TO THE INDIVIDUAL STATE'S BUSINESS REQUIREMENTS

State	Link
Alabama	www.alabama.gov/business/startbusiness.html
Alaska	www.dced.state.ak.us/occ/home.htm
Arizona	www.commerce.state.az.us/SmallBus/Default.asp
Arkansas	http://asbdc.ualr.edu/bizfacts/1006.asp or www.state.ar.us/business_res.php
California	www.calgold.ca.gov/
Colorado	www.colorado.gov/business.htm
Connecticut	www.ct-clic.com/business/business.htm
Delaware	www.state.de.us/dedo/small_business.html
District of Columbia	http://brc.dc.gov/whattodo/business/
Florida	http://sun6.dms.state.fl.us/dor/businesses/
Georgia	www.sos.state.ga.us/firststop/
Hawaii	www.hawaii.gov/dbedt/start/index.html

State	Link
Idaho	www.idoc.state.id.us/business/idahoworks/substartbusiness.htm
Illinois	www.illinoisbiz.biz/bus/step_by_step.html
Indiana	www.state.in.us/sic/owners/ia.html
Iowa	www.iowasmart.com/blic/
Kansas	www.accesskansas.org/operating/
Kentucky	www.thinkkentucky.com/kyedc/bguide01.asp
Louisiana	www.sec.state.la.us/comm/fss/fss-index.htm
Maine	www.econdevmaine.com/doing-biz.htm
Maryland	www.blis.state.md.us/BusinessStartup.aspx
Massachusetts	www.dor.state.ma.us/business/doingbus.htm
Michigan	www.michigan.gov/businessstartup
Minnesota	www.dted.state.mn.us/01x03x02f.asp
Mississippi	www.olemiss.edu/depts/mssbdc/going_intobus.html
Missouri	www.ded.mo.gov/business/startabusiness/
Montana	http://bizmt.com/bizassist/start.asp
Nebraska	www.nebraska.gov/business/html/337/index.phtml
Nevada	http://tax.state.nv.us/taxnew/forms.htm
New Hampshire	www.nhsbdc.org/startup.htm
New Jersey	www.state.nj.us/Business.shtml
New Mexico	www.edd.state.nm.us/NMBUSINESS/NEWBUSINESS/.
New York	www.gorr.state.ny.us/gorr/Startbus.html
North Carolina	www.secretary.state.nc.us/blio/startbus.asp
North Dakota	www.growingnd.com/toolkit/
Ohio	www.sos.state.oh.us/sos/busiserv/index.html
Oklahoma	www.okonestop.com
Oregon	www.filinginoregon.com/obg/index.htm
Pennsylvania	www.paopenforbusiness.state.pa.us
Rhode Island	http://www2.sec.state.ri.us/faststart/
South Carolina	www.myscgov.com/SCSGPortal/static/business_tem1.html
South Dakota	www.state.sd.us/drr2/newbusiness.htm
Tennessee	www.state.tn.us/ecd/res_guide.htm
Texas	www.tded.state.tx.us/guide/

(continued)

TABLE 46-1 *(continued)*

State	Link
Utah	www.utah.gov/business/starting.html
Vermont	www.thinkvermont.com/start/
Virginia	www.yesvirginia.org/corporate_location/vedpstart_a_business.aspx
Washington	www.dol.wa.gov/mls/startbus.htm
West Virginia	www.wv.gov/sec.aspx?pgID=1
Wisconsin	www.wisconsin.gov/state/byb/
Wyoming	http://uwadmnweb.uwyo.edu/SBDC/starting.htm

Technique

47

Simplifying Your Bookkeeping

Save Time By

- Finding a tax professional
- Getting organized with QuickBooks
- Producing reports quickly

Several e-mails come to my office every week from people who have questions about how to keep their books straight. (Incidentally, although I don't always have time to keep up with all my e-mail, rest assured that I at least *read* every message.) These folks are confused by the myriad of products and services vying for the eBay seller's dollar. Many of these products and services claim to do everything and that running a business on eBay is impossible without them. These auction services also claim to be all an eBay seller needs to achieve success, but that's not quite right. As much as auction management services do for the seller — and they can do some amazing things — they can't maintain your books in the proper bookkeeping form.

 With the advent of e-commerce, many aspects of the business world updated and changed to keep pace with the speed of the Internet. One thing that didn't change, however, is the need for methodical, rock-solid bookkeeping. Why can't you do your bookkeeping *your* way? Because the United States Tax Code demands that businesses adhere to some tried and true accounting procedures.

It's all well and good to manage your sales data in spreadsheets, note pads, and homemade ledgers (I keep my PayPal monthly sales in spreadsheets, but only as backup and customer-list documentation.) Just realize that you're making more work for yourself in the long run. Keeping your books in ways that are easy for you to understand doesn't preclude the necessity of maintaining your books in the proper format. This technique helps you save time by putting some tested procedures for eBay sellers to work for you.

Dealing with a Professional

Have you ever wondered why big businesses have CFOs (Chief Financial Officers), Vice Presidents of Finance, CPAs (Certified Public Accountants), and bookkeepers? It's because keeping the books is the backbone of a company's business.

Do you have a professional going over your books at least once a year? You really should. A paid professional experienced in business knows what to do when it comes to your taxes. Due to the complexity of the tax code, not just any paid preparer will suffice when it comes to preparing your business taxes. Here's a list of possible people who can prepare your tax returns.

✔ **Tax Preparer (or Consultant):** This is the person you visit at the local we-file-for-you tax office. Did you know that a tax preparer could be anybody? There is no licensing involved. H&R Block hires as many as 100,000 seasonal workers as tax preparers each year. Where do these people come from? I'm sure that some are experts at the tax code, but the sheer number of tax preparers and the lack of regulation can make using a we-file-for-you tax office a risky proposition for business people who want to minimize their tax liability.

 A United States General Accounting Office report estimated that, in 1998, American citizens overpaid their taxes by $945 million because they claimed the standard deduction when it would have been more beneficial to itemize. Half of those taxpayers used a paid preparer who clearly was not cognizant of the full tax law as it applied to the individuals. Scary, huh?

✔ **Volunteer IRS Certified Preparers:** The AARP (American Association of Retired Persons) does an outstanding job of assembling nearly 32,000 tax preparers to serve the needs of low- to middle-income taxpayers (special attention going to seniors). Their goal is to maximize legal deductions and credits, resulting in "tangible economic benefits" for their clients. These volunteers have to study, take a test, and become *certified by the IRS* before they can lend their services to the cause.

In 2003, AARP volunteers served a total of 1.85 million seniors in the United States. My mother was a retired corporate comptroller, and she volunteered in this program for many years. (She was disappointed when she made her lowest score on the IRS test — a 94 percent!) They staff

over 8,500 sites around the United States, and you can find if there's one near you. Call 1-888-AARP-NOW (1-888-227-7669) and select Tax-Aide Information.

✔ **Public Accountant:** A Public Accountant or PA, must complete educational, testing, and experience requirements and obtain a state license. PAs must take an annual update course to maintain their status.

✔ **Enrolled Agent:** Often called "one of the best-kept secrets in accounting," an Enrolled Agent is Federally licensed by the IRS. (CPAs and Attorneys are state-licensed.) EAs must pass an extensive annual test on tax law preparation every year to maintain their status. (They also have to pass annual background checks.) Enrolled Agents are authorized to appear in place of a taxpayer before the IRS.

Many EAs are former IRS employees. To find an Enrolled Agent near you, go to the Web site www.naea.org and enter the Taxpayer's area.

✔ **Certified Public Accountant:** A Certified Public Accountant (CPA) must complete rigorous testing and experience requirements as prescribed by the state in which they practice. Most states require a CPA to obtain a state license.

CPAs are accountants. They specialize in record keeping and reporting financial matters. Their important position is to act as an advisor regarding financial decisions for both individuals and businesses. CPAs must take an annual update course to maintain their status.

Keeping Your Books Accurately

When you meet with one of the professionals discussed in the previous section, they're going to expect you to bring a complete and accurate set of books. To prepare accurate books, you either need a bookkeeper (who will use accounting software), or you can learn how to use professional accounting software yourself.

Don't be a wussy; you *can* do this. Lots of people successfully using bookkeeping software today knew nothing about bookkeeping before they set up their own accounts. I'm one of them.

My tutor, helping me every step of the way, was *QuickBooks For Dummies* by Stephen Nelson, CPA. I met Stephen a couple of years ago. He's just as funny and smart in person as he writes. I highly recommend his books to help you with learning the program.

I highly recommend QuickBooks from Intuit for your eBay business accounting because it's tailored for business. At the end of each year, I hand my CPA a copy of my QuickBooks backup, along with the printed reports he requires. Most professionals use and accept data from QuickBooks.

When your business gets so busy that you have no time to post your bookkeeping, you can always hire a part-time bookkeeper to come in and do your posting for you.

Using QuickBooks in your eBay business

Aside from the professional reasons to use QuickBooks, there's another more basic reason, the program can give you up-to-the-minute reports about the status of your eBay business and keep track of everything in the background — including payroll and sales tax liability.

Here are a few things (among many others) that I really like about using QuickBooks to streamline an online business:

✔ **Inventory Reports:** As you purchase inventory, aside from deducting the money from your checking account and expensing your merchandise account, QuickBooks adds the purchased merchandise to your inventory. Every time you sell an item, QuickBooks deducts the item from your inventory. QuickBooks has many other reporting features for your inventory and end-of-year reporting for taxes.

Figure 47-1 shows you a part of an inventory report that I pulled out of the program today. You can see how valuable the data is. With a click of my mouse, I can see how much I have left in stock and the average number that I've sold per week.

The Collier Company, Inc.
Inventory Stock Status by Item
January 1 through March 18, 2004

Item Description	Pref Vendor	On Hand	Available	Sales/Week
Inventory				
Angled Collar	▶ Cloud Dome Angled Collar	9	9	0.1 ◀
Book Sales				
4th Dummies	eBay For Dummies 4th Edition	7	7	1.2
Business Book Sales	Starting an eBay Business for Dummies	1	1	1.6
Shopping book	eBay Bargain Shopping for Dummies	22	22	0.4
Tips booklet	eBay Tips for Dummies Booklet	19	19	2
Book Sales - Other	eBay For Dummies 3rd edition	0	0	0.2
Total Book Sales		49	49	5.4
Cloud Dome Kit	Cloud Dome Kit	5	5	1
Deluxe Cloud Dome Kit	CLOUD DOME Complete Digital Kit	-5	-5	1.3
Flip Light	Flip Light	-1	-1	0.1
Garment Rack	Rolling Garment Rack	22	22	1.1
Infiniti Board	Infiniti Board	15	15	2.3
Light Set	eBay Seller's Pro Lighting Kit	-2	-2	2.8
Spanx B	Spanx Footless Pantyhose NUDE size B	4	4	0
un-du	un-du Adhesive Remover	72	72	2.2

• **Figure 47-1:** A portion of my Inventory Tracking report.

✔ **Sales Tax Tracking:** Depending on how the program is set up (based on your own state sales tax laws), you can request a report that has all your taxable and non-taxable sales. The report calculates the amount of sales tax you owe. You can print out this report for backup information on your sales tax payments to your state.

✔ **Payroll:** Whether you use the online payroll service to prepare your payroll or input the deductions yourself, QuickBooks posts the appropriate withholdings to their own accounts. When it comes time to pay your employees' withholding taxes, QuickBooks can generate the federal reporting form (all filled in) for submitting with your payment.

✔ **Sales Reports:** QuickBooks gives you a plethora of reports with which you can analyze your sales professionally. One of my favorite reports is the *Sales by Item Summary*. This report gives you the information below for every inventoried item you sell in whatever time period you choose:

▶ Quantity sold

▶ Total dollar amount sold

▶ Percentage of sales represented by each individual item

▶ The average price the item sold for

▶ COGS (cost of goods sold) by item

▶ Average cost of goods sold by total sales per item

▶ Gross profit margin in dollar amounts

▶ Gross profit margin expressed as percentages

Depending on how you post your transactions, you can analyze your eBay sales, Web site sales, and/or brick-and-mortar sales individually or together. You can also select *any* date range for your reports.

Posting sales in QuickBooks the easy way

Some online auction management services integrate with QuickBooks. This integration means that your individual transactions can be downloaded into the QuickBooks program, setting a up a new customer for each of your sales.

Although this process is quick and easy, inputting each sale as a new customer will cause the size of the database to become huge quickly. QuickBooks is a very large program to begin with, and if you're going to use it (and update it) for several years, the database will become even larger.

If you've ever worked with large files, you know the larger the data file, the more chance there is for the data to become corrupt. That's the last thing you want. Besides, QuickBooks will max out with over 14,000 customers — very doable in several years on eBay.

To keep track of your customers, you can use an additional copy of your PayPal monthly report and combine them with cash sales into an Excel (you can also use Microsoft Works) spreadsheet to build this important data.

In the sidebar below, I show you a procedure I developed to process my PayPal sales. I've run it past several accountants and QuickBooks experts, and it's gotten rave reviews. I'm sharing it with you because I want you to be able to run your business smoothly.

Using QuickBooks the "Collier" Way

Rather than posting an invoice in my QuickBooks software for every customer (for those very few customers who need formal invoices), I can print them out on demand from eBay's Selling Manager; I input my sales into a customer Sales Receipt as shown in the figure below. Whenever I make a PayPal deposit into my business checking account, which is every few days depending on how busy sales are, I post my sales into QuickBooks. This way, the total of the Sales Receipt equals the exact amount of my PayPal deposit. (If you've ever tried to reconcile your PayPal deposits with your sales and your checking account, you know how frustrating it can be.)

In my QuickBooks account, PayPal is the customer. It makes no difference who bought what, it just matters what item is sold (to deduct from inventory) and for how much (to post to my financial data).

The program gives you the flexibility to customize forms, so the figure given here shows my customized sales receipt for PayPal sales. PayPal is a taxable customer when sales are made in the State of California, and the appropriate sales tax is applied automatically. Here are the things I have added to customize the form.

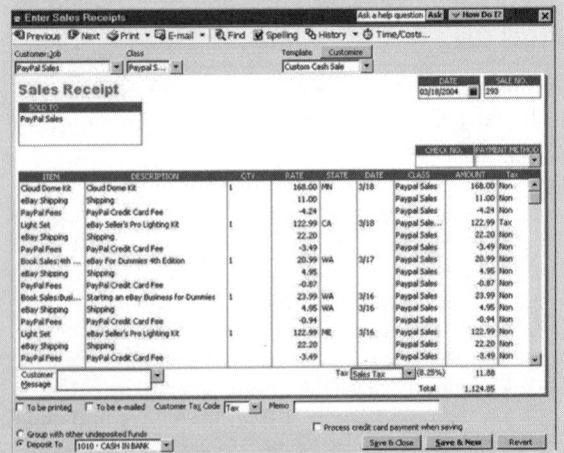

✔ **PayPal Fees:** I have set up PayPal fees as a credit against sales. (In the figure, you can see they are applied as a negative.) This helps to match the total amount of the Sales Receipt to my PayPal deposit. It also gives me a discount line in my sales reports that tracks my total paid PayPal fees. This also appears in my Costs of Goods Sold area of my financial statements.

In case you're wondering about eBay fees, they have their own line in my chart of Accounts. I charge eBay fees to my company credit card. When the credit card expenses are posted, I post the eBay expense to the eBay fees account which appears in the Costs of Goods Sold in my financial reports. In my book, *Starting an eBay Business For Dummies,* I show you how to set up QuickBooks for eBay and I include a suggested chart of expense and income accounts.

✔ **State:** I type in the two-letter state abbreviation of the shipping location with each item. This serves as backup information for my State Board of Equalization (the California sales tax board) and also allows me to run reports on what has sold in which states.

✔ **Date:** The date at the top of the Sales Receipt is the posting date. The date in the product posting indicates the date the PayPal payment was posted.

✔ **Class:** Every item posted in QuickBooks can be part of a Class to make data easier for you to isolate certain types of transactions. I have set up two classes of PayPal sales: California sales and out-of-state sales. The California sales are classified as Taxable, and the Out-of-State sales as Non-taxable. QuickBooks calculates the tax liability automatically.

✔ **Tax Classification:** When I type the first two letters into the class area (OU for out of state, and CA for in-state sales), the tax line changes automatically to Tax or Non-Tax. QuickBooks would do this whether I show this field in the Sales Receipt or not, but by having it appear, it serves as a secondary mental reminder to post the taxable Class properly.

By inputting my eBay sales data in this way, I streamline the process in several ways. I post data to only one program once. From this Sales Receipt, I get updated inventory reports, accurate Sales Tax data, accurate expense and income tracking, and easy reconciling of my checking account.

Technique

48

Monitoring Your Financial Reports

Save Time By

✔ Regularly posting your sales and inventory info

✔ Timing your reports effectively

✔ Letting your reports talk to you

After you're up and running with your eBay business, you can look forward to having lots of reports to evaluate. Of course, you get a plethora of reports from PayPal, eBay, and so on, but the most important reports are those you generate from your bookkeeping program (software such as QuickBooks). I use the QuickBooks software package to manage my business records, and it keeps several common reports (Balance Sheet, Accounts Payable, P&L, and more) in an easily assessable area. If you check out the reports tab of your bookkeeping program, I bet you'll find similar items. Before your eyes glaze over, though, check out this technique for straightforward descriptions of these reports and the information they provide.

Similar sales and financial reports are common to all businesses, and reviewing them on a monthly basis can help you stay on top of yours.

 To get your business reports when you need them, you must post your sales receipts regularly and thereby update the money in and the inventory out. Post your payments out at least weekly (especially on your company credit card — post those transactions the minute you get your statement) and reconcile your checkbook the moment your bank statement arrives.

What do your posting and reconciling tasks get you? The opportunity to hit a button and get a complete picture of your business. From the reports you generate, you find out whether your business is profitable, what products are selling, and if you're spending too much money in a particular area. Keeping your books up-to-date allows you to find problems before they become unmanageable.

 If you run your sales and financial reports quarterly rather than monthly, a problem — such as not pricing your items high enough — could be mushrooming out of control.

De-bewildering Your Balance Sheet

Your balance sheet provides the best information on your business. It pulls data from all the other reports and gives you a complete look at your business's financial condition.

Your balance sheet shows all your assets:

- ✔ **Cash in Bank:** The money in your business bank account.

- ✔ **Accounts Receivable:** If you've invoiced anyone and not received payment as yet, that amount will reflect here.

- ✔ **Inventory Assets:** This is the value of the merchandise you have purchased for resale but have not as yet sold.

- ✔ **Other Assets:** Things your business owns (not you), like furniture and vehicles. These are not considered in the Current Asset figure.

- ✔ **Accumulated Depreciation:** This is deprecation on your assets, either produced by your accounting program or given to you by your accountant.

The balance sheet also (alas) shows your liabilities:

- ✔ **Accounts Payable:** If you owe any vendors or have money due on unpaid credit cards, it will show up here.

- ✔ **Sales Tax:** The money you have collected on sales tax (that is due to your state) is a liability.

- ✔ **Payroll Liabilities:** If you haven't made a bank deposit covering the money you've withdrawn from employees (withholding taxes, Social Security, Medicare, and so on), it will show up here.

Your equity shows up in the (literal and figurative) bottom line at the bottom of the statement. It will include your initial investment in your business and the net income total from your Profit & Loss statement.

 An important business ratio — the *net working capital ratio* — is drawn from your balance sheet. Subtracting your current liabilities from your current assets gets you the dollar amount of your net working capital. But to get the net working capital ratio, divide your current assets by your current liabilities. Any value over 1.1 means that you have a positive net working capital. If you need a loan from a bank, this is the first figure the loan office will look for.

Tracking Your Accounts Payable

When bills come in, post them in your accounting program. This will generate the Accounts Payable report. Accounts payable is the area that shows how much you owe and when it's due. These are crucial dates and numbers to know so you can be sure to meet your obligations when they're due.

When you pay an outstanding bill, the bookkeeping program deducts the money from your checking account and marks the bill as paid. It will no longer appear on this report.

Knowing Your Sales Tax Liability

One of the vendors you'll owe money to is your state. In California, it's the State Board of Equalization. Every time you post an invoice or sales receipt that charges sales tax, that amount shows up in this report. You run this report on a timeframe that's determined by the state; you may be required to report monthly, quarterly, or yearly. Also, how often you report may depend on your total of in-state sales. Just make sure you match your reporting with your state's requirements for your business.

Analyzing Your Profit & Loss Statement

If your accountant asks for your income statement, she's asking for your profit-and-loss statement, or *P&L.* This report lays out clearly every penny you've spent and brought in. You can set these reports to generate by any period of time; usually eBay sellers produce them by calendar month.

A summary P&L (or Profit & Loss Statement) will itemize all your income and expense accounts individually, and total them by category. This way, you'll be able to isolate individual areas where you may notice a problem such as spending too much in the shipping expenses.

Please use the following list of income and expense accounts as a guide and not as the gospel. I am not a tax professional, and I suggest that when you set up your own income and (especially) expense accounts, you go over them with a licensed tax expert.

Here's the glimpse at the kinds of accounts and categories you see on a P&L statement:

- ✔ **Income:** Every dollar you bring in is itemized as income. For many sellers, this can break down into several individual accounts. These figures are automatically generated by your bookkeeping program from the sales receipts you input. The total of all these income areas appears at the bottom of this area as Total Income.

  - ▶ **Sales:** This totals eBay Sales and Shipping income in separate totals. These figures subtotal as Total Sales.

  - ▶ **Web-site advertising:** If you are a member of any affiliate programs or have a newsletter that takes advertising, this income posts here.

  - ▶ **Consulting:** Income from consulting or teaching others.

- ✔ **Costs of Goods Sold (COGS):** This area itemizes by category all the costs involved in your eBay (and/or Web site sales) only. (None of your business operating expenses — such as your telephone bill — show up here; they're further down on the report.) Your eBay COGS may subtotal in different accounts, such as

  - ▶ **Merchandise:** The cost of your merchandise that you bought to resell.

  - ▶ **eBay Fees:** Here's where you post your eBay fees from your credit card statement.

  - ▶ **PayPal Fees:** This figure will automatically generate from your sales receipts (as described in Technique 47 on QuickBooks).

  - ▶ **Shipping Postage:** The totals of the amounts you spend for shipping your eBay items. These also appear here from within your program from your inputting the various expenses when you pay the bills.

  - ▶ **Shipping Supplies:** The costs of the padded mailers, bubble wrap, tapes, and boxes — you get the picture. When those items are paid for, the bookkeeping program inserts the totals here.

  - ▶ **Outside Service Fees:** If you pay for your photo hosting or third-party management tools, they appear here.

 Cross-reference your Costs of Goods sold to your Sales reports. You've expensed inventory bought — but your merchandise may be sitting idle in your storage area. The COGS report works in concert with others — such as inventory reports (also generated by QuickBooks), sales reports, and P&Ls — to give you a solid picture of where your business is going.

Your Costs of Goods sold will subtotal under the heading Total COGS.

- ✔ **Gross Profit:** Your bookkeeping program magically does all the calculations, and you will be able to see in a snapshot if your basic eBay business is in good, profitable health. This is the gross profit — *before* you figure in your company expenses (often called G&A — for General and Administrative costs).

Now come your expenses. Listed in individual accounts, you have subtotals for your various business operating expenses, as follows:

- ✔ **Payroll expenses:** The total amounts you pay your employees.

- ✔ **Taxes:** Broken out by State and Federal, the taxes you have paid the regulating agencies for running your business.

- ✔ **Supplies:** Computer and office supplies. How much paper goes through your printer? Not to mention those inkjet cartridges, pens, computers, telephones, copiers, network equipment. All those expenses appear here.

- ✔ **Seminars and Education:** Did you buy this book to educate yourself on your eBay business? It counts. Have you attended a seminar to educate yourself on eBay? Going to eBay Live? Those count too.

- ✔ **Contract Labor:** This is the money you pay to anyone who is not an employee of your company.

This may include an off-site bookkeeper or a company that comes in to clean your office. The federal government has very stringent rules as to who classifies as an Independent Contractor. Check this Web site for the official rules:

```
www.irs.gov/businesses/small/article/
   0,,id=115041,00.html
```

- ✔ **Automobile expenses:** This is where you post expenses — parking, gas, repairs for an automobile that is used for your eBay business. If you have only one vehicle that you also use for personal transportation, your tax person may have you post a percentage of its use in this area.

- ✔ **Telephone:** Do you have a separate phone line for your business alone?

- ✔ **Advertising:** Expenses you incur when running campaigns in Google AdWords or in your eBay banner program.

Your expenses will come to a whopping total at the bottom, and then, at the very bottom of the page will be your net income. This is your bottom-line profit. I wish you all a very positive bottom line!

Keeping Your Records and Data Safe

Technique 49

Save Time By

- Keeping your company records organized
- Backing up your computer
- Saving documents safely

If the hazard of not backing up your computer isn't a tired subject, I don't know what is. Whenever you hear someone talking about their latest computer crash, all they can do is stare blankly into the distance and say, "I lost everything!" I admit, it's happened to me, and I'm sure that you've at least heard this cry from others (if you've not uttered it yourself): "If only I'd backed up my files!"

Even worse than a computer crash, what about a natural disaster? It can happen, you know. When I went to sleep on January 16, 1994, I didn't know that the next day, when I attempted to enter my office, everything would be in shambles. My monitors had flown across the room, filing cabinets turned over, and oh, did I mention the ceiling had collapsed? It seems that my garage office became Ground Zero for the Northridge earthquake. (I want you to picture me shoveling though the mess to find my insurance policies.) This experience taught me some solid lessons about keeping duplicate records and backed-up data copies in an off-site location.

If the ultimate computer crash (or natural disaster) has happened to you, you have my deepest and most sincere sympathy. It's a horrible thing to go through.

 What's another horrible thing? A tax audit: It can especially make you feel like jumping off a cliff if you've been filing your hard documentation with the shoebox method. (You know, one box for 2004, one for 2003, and so on.) Filing your receipts and backup documentation in an organized, easy-to-find format really can pay off in future savings of time (and nerves). Even if you're *not* going through a tax audit.

I want to tell you upfront that I don't always practice what I preach. I don't always back up my stuff on time. I have a brand new box of backup software sitting on the floor next to me, and the 2004 box of receipts is getting fuller. But in this technique, I'm gonna preach anyway about good practices for backing up your computer data and safeguarding the hard-copy documents that you inevitably will have. (I just really hope there are no disasters before I finish writing this book!)

Taking the time to organize and safeguard your data and records now may save you days, weeks, or months of work and frustration later.

Backing Up Your Data — Just Do It!

I'm not specifically suggesting that you go out and buy backup software (though I think it's a good idea). I *am* suggesting that you back up the eBay transaction records and other data on your computer *somehow*. Consider the following points when choosing how to back up the data you can't afford to lose:

- Regularly back up at least your My Documents folder onto a CD. CD burners have come way down in price (you can find external USB burners in good condition for under $50 on eBay), so there's really no excuse not to make some sort of backup.

- Backup software can make your backup chores less *chorelike*. Most such packages have features you can set to automatically run unattended backups, and you don't have to remember anything.

- Backup software doesn't have to be expensive either. I just visited one of my favorite shareware sites, www.tucows.com and searched on the term *backup Windows*. This query returned over 300 matching records!

There's no need for me to recommend a particular brand of backup software; almost any brand you buy will do a good job. When you search Tucows or Amazon, read the customer comments and let these direct you to the software that's right for you.

- Consider making monthly backups of the info from your PayPal account. You can download the data directly from the site (see Technique 30) and can archive several years' worth on one CD.

Saving Your Business Records

Business records are still mostly paper, and until such time as the entire world is electronic, you'll have some paperwork to store. You can buy manila file folders almost anywhere. A box of 100 costs you less than $10, so expense is no excuse for lack of organization.

If you don't have filing cabinets, office supply stores sell collapsible cardboard boxes that are the perfect size to hold file folders. You can buy 6 of these for around $8.

And just what do you need to file in your new organized office? Here are a few important suggestions:

- **Equipment receipts and warranties:** You never know when some important piece of your office hardware will go on the fritz, and you'll need the receipt and warranty information so you can get it fixed. Also, the receipts are backup documentation for your bookkeeping program's data.

- **Automobile expenses:** Gasoline receipts, parking receipts, repairs: anything and everything to do with your car. You use your car in your eBay business (for example, to deliver packages to the Post Office for shipping), don't you?

- **Postal receipts:** Little slips of paper that you get proving mailing from the Post Office. If you use an online postage service, print out a postage report once a month and file it in your filing cabinets or boxes as well.

- **Credit card bills:** Here in one location can be documentation on your purchases for your business. Make a folder for each credit card and file every month after you pay the bill and post the data.

- **Merchandise receipts:** Merchandise purchased for resale on eBay. Documentation of all the money you spend.

- **Licenses and legal stuff:** Important! Keep an active file of anything legal; you will no doubt have to lay hands on this information at the oddest moment. It's reassuring to know where it is!

✔ **Payroll paperwork:** Even if you print your checks and such on the computer, you should organize the state and federal filing information in one place.

✔ **Cancelled checks and bank statements:** The only ways to prove you've paid for something.

✔ **Insurance information:** Policies and proposals should all be kept at hand's reach.

I'm sure that, with a little thinking, you can come up with some more things that can benefit from a little bit of organization. When you need the information quickly and you can find it without breaking a sweat, you'll be glad you kept things organized.

Knowing How Long to Keep Your Paperwork

The possibility that one government organization (city, state, or federal) or another will want a glance at some of your business documentation at one time or another is very real.

The IRS wants you to save anything related to your tax return for three years. But take a look at Table 49-1: The IRS may want backup documentation for up to six years. So — for safety's sake — keep things for six years, if only to prove you're innocent.

TABLE 49-1: RECORDS THE IRS MAY NEED AND HOW LONG TO KEEP THEM

If You	Keep the Records for
1. Owe additional tax and items 2, 3, and 4 (below) do not apply to you	3 years
2. Do not report income that is more than 25 percent of the gross income shown on your return	6 years
3. File a fraudulent return	Forever
4. Do not file a return	Forever
5. File for credit or refund after you filed your return	3 years after tax was paid
6. File for a loss from worthless securities	7 years

Avoiding Sick Days by Staying Healthy

I've been in business, working from a home office for many years (more years than I'd like to admit to here). I've learned a few things that I've passed on to you in my books, but one thing I've never written about is the importance of keeping yourself healthy. I want you to think about this. What happens if you're too sick to handle your work? What happens if your hand is so painful from using the mouse that you can't type or even use your computer comfortably? Its not a pretty picture — I've been there, believe me. Let's not even discuss the time I sliced off a part of my finger using a box knife — and had to bandage it up myself so I could get my packages out.

 When you're a one-man (or one-woman) show the way I am, covering all the bases for your business can be difficult even when you're in the best of health. Even if you have someone to help you, you're the hub of your business. If you run an eBay business as your full-time job and you're too sick to do the work, you won't be making any money.

When I first started in business, I went to the used business furniture store and bought the cheapest chairs and desks I could get my hands on. These worked fine for a while but didn't work too well when I had to pull all-nighters getting a catalog out for an early deadline. The ill-fitting furniture made my back ache and my wrist hurt, and staring at the computer made my eyes burn. You get the picture. In this technique, I discuss the problems associated with an ergonomically challenged working environment and share solutions that help you prepare to stay healthy.

Keeping Your Eyes Clear

Ever have to rub your eyes after a long session at the computer? Eyes burn? Vision blurring? Headaches? You may never have heard about *Computer Vision Syndrome* (CVS) but it's a condition recognized by the American Optometric Association and characterized by such symptoms.

Staring at a computer screen non-stop for hours can even cause your eyes to lose the ability to focus! Here are several things you can do to help keep your vision in good working order:

✔ **Look away from your computer** and change your focal distance every 15 minutes. Look at the wall or, better yet, out the window.

✔ **Remember to blink!** That seems very basic, but often when we're concentrating, we forget to blink. That's the body's natural way to lubricate the eye.

✔ **Use a drop or two of lubricating or vitamin-based eyedrops** in your eyes to prevent dry eye. (Bausch & Lomb even makes an eyedrop solely for computer users.)

✔ **Maintain a proper monitor viewing distance** of 20-24 inches and locate the monitor slightly below eye level.

✔ **Dust off the screen every few days.**

✔ **Consider purchasing computer glasses.** These glasses are tinted and have Ultra Violet (UV) coating to prevent glare from the monitor (and the florescent light in your office). There are professionals who sell these glasses on eBay at very reasonable prices.

✔ **Get up from your computer** and walk around every hour or so. This is not only good for your eyes, but it keeps your blood moving too!

Watching Your Back

Remember those cheaper-than-cheap used chairs I told you about? Well, they weren't such a good idea. Even though I upgraded to a brand-new budget chair, I'd still get a crick in my back while working at the computer for long hours. Do yourself a favor and *don't* make your chair the cost-cutting item in your office.

I finally broke down, after reading about all those "ergonomic" chairs with the high prices, and went to a true office furniture store. Mind you, I didn't say "office supply store," I said "office *furniture* store." Real office furniture stores know all about aching backs.

I must have sat in 15 chairs, and was really tempted by the expensive-looking Aeron chair they had as well. It didn't only look expensive — it *was* expensive! The Aeron chair (by Herman Miller) comes in three sizes, and eBay Aeron sellers post the size chart (based on height and weight) with their listings. I tried all three and felt like Goldilocks: One was just right.

Strangely, according to the Herman Miller chart, I should have taken a different size, but this chair felt so cozy and comfortable (an office chair? what a concept!) that I bit the bullet and bought one. I even talked the store down on the price (if you can imagine) — it was just like shopping at eBay!

 When you decide to purchase a chair for office work, go to a store that specializes in that type of furniture. After you've found the chair you like, write down the manufacturer and the model number. Tell the store you want to think about it (which you do) and then go home and see whether you can find it on eBay for less. If not, you can always go back to the store and haggle a little!

Spending several hundred dollars for a chair seemed like a wild expense. But I'm four years into the chair's 12-year warranty and couldn't be happier. Take it from someone who sits a lot: Get the best chair you can. Your back will thank you.

Practicing Safe Mousing

I promise not to duplicate the reams of information easily available regarding Carpal Tunnel Syndrome. Anyone who uses a mouse for any length of time is going to have problems with his or her mousing hand.

Carpal Tunnel Syndrome happens when the tendons in your wrists become inflamed and enlarged so they squish the nerve in your hand. Whoa! Does that ever hurt!

Since mousing is a way of life for those who make a living with a computer, there are a few products that might prevent or solve your problems.

- **Perfit Mouse:** This Contour Design product is an ergonomically correct mouse. I bought my first one in 1996, when the pain in my hand was so great that I couldn't make a fist. They've upgraded the design, made it even more ergonomic, and it's available in both regular and optical styles. Again, just like Goldilocks, you can get this mouse to fit your hand as it comes in 8 sizes. Their Web site, www.contourdesign.com, has measuring charts and online ordering.

- **Quill Mouse:** This is an interesting mouse that has worked well for many people. When using the Quill Mouse, your hand is held vertically versus flat down. This posture allows you to relax your hand on the Quill Mouse base, and click with your fingers in the vertical position. The Quill Mouse works additionally well with the BIB "Click-Less" software sold on the site. You can get all the information at www.quillmouse.com.

- **RollerMouse:** Contour Design strikes again. I had a particularly bad bout of tennis elbow caused by mousing to the side (instead of perpendicular to my body — the proper way) and I didn't know where to turn. I tried every ergonomic gadget and gizmo I could find with no relief. My arm felt fine if I rested it in my lap. This didn't work at all for mousing until I found the RollerMouse. The RollerMouse is a platform with gel wrist rests that goes under your keyboard, and your mouse is a roller mounted on the board, as in Figure 50-1. It helped cure my arm problems, and now I go back and forth from a Perfit mouse to the RollerMouse to keep the different muscles from getting inflamed.

Its wrist rests are also useful for preventing Carpal Tunnel. You can find more about it at

www.contourdesign.com/rollermouse.

• **Figure 50-1: A RollerMouse in action.**

A few more little things

Think of other places where you have inconveniences in your office:

- **Telephone:** Did you buy the first phone you found at the office store? Or did you really research it? A good-quality telephone that has a good speakerphone (and even possibly a headset attachment) will make your office day go better.

- **Keyboard platform:** You might also find that a keyboard platform is useful. It will position your keyboard lower than your desk, allowing you to keep your arms in the proper posture.

Speaking of posture. Figure 50-2 shows the proper posture angles to stay comfortable in the office. No, she doesn't have X-ray vision (bad hair, maybe); the figure illustrates the correct angle for viewing the monitor.

• **Figure 50-2:** Proper angles make for proper posture at the computer.

Let your body talk to you when you're working (just hope that nobody's listening). If you're uncomfortable in any way, do something about it before you get an injury. That way you can continue to run your eBay business without sick time and enjoy bringing in the money!

Overcoming Accessibility Challenges

Save Time By

✔ Finding income potential online

✔ Getting support from DOUA

✔ Streamlining your online experience

Before the online community grew so pervasive (as we know it today), I bought my first computer-with-a-modem — and though there weren't a lot of uses for a modem then, you could buy a software package that hooked you up to CIS, the CompuServe Information Service. There, in some lively, real-time chat rooms, I met people from cities I'd never been to or even thought I'd visit. But there would soon be more to it — and that became obvious a few years later, when I started a business on AOL in a chat room. I ran monthly live auctions (for action figures, autographs, and other paraphernalia). I'd send invitations to people on various online bulletin boards, list the items to be auctioned, and wait for bids via e-mail. Those came in daily, and daily I'd resend the list of items with the current bids. The process ended in a chat room with a live auction where people could bid for each item. (Sometimes those auctions lasted for hours!)

I encountered some fierce competition from people who sold this way, and I liked to chat online and get to know them. It turned out that my fiercest — and very successful — competition came from a gentleman with cerebral palsy. He made many friends online, ran a nice little business, and made me realize that the Internet is a great place for the physically challenged to do business.

Fast-forward to the eBay era: Some of the most amazingly happy people selling on eBay are those who face limitations within a traditional workplace. They've found a home for their businesses on eBay, where they can — and do — work as hard and as effectively as anyone. In this technique, I tell you about the Disabled Online Users Association (DOUA), an organization that helps its members make the most of the Internet's business potential. Also, I introduce some tools designed to help with computer-related accessibility challenges.

Into a wider world on eBay

My favorite eBay PowerSeller is 78 years old and proud of it. He runs about 30 auctions a week, buys a little as well, and really enjoys his daily trip to the Post Office to drop off his packages. He's vibrant and happy — and makes a nice little income on eBay!

There's also bobal (Bob Bull), whom I met at eBay Live when he received a Community Service award from eBay CEO Meg Whitman. Bob is wheelchair-bound with MS, but always manages to find time to help other people. eBay was a turning point for Bob. He had become despondent due to his illness, and then he and his wife discovered trading on eBay. They bought, they sold — but most of all, they made friends. He's an active participant in the Images/HTML Chat Board and the Photos/HTML Discussion Board. He answers any questions when he's online — and he's been kind enough to teach me a few things. You can read his story on his Web site at `www.bulls2.com/index/bobal/mylife.html`.

These are just two stories out of hundreds I've heard. Not only can the stay-at-home mom make a living on eBay, but so can seniors and the disabled. They just occasionally need a little help.

Helping Others through DOUA

I have to tell you about one of my favorite ladies. I met her in the lobby at eBay Live in 2003, and her name is Marjie Smith. Marjie is confined to a wheelchair due to surgical complications. She's also a PowerSeller and runs a successful business on eBay (user ID is `abovethemall`), as well as on her own Web site. She's one amazing lady.

She is the founder of the Disabled Online Users Association (DOUA) — a network of disabled members interested in using the Internet to supplement their income.

"Our goal at DOUA is to help the differently-abled become self-sufficient and independent," says Marjie in her role as Founder of DOUA and moderator of the DOUA Message Board. "If you're disabled and would like to start your own online business, we can help."

The powerful message of the organization — which I include here — appears on its home page at `www.doua.info`:

> The Disabled Online Users Association (DOUA) was established as a way to bring technology to the differently-abled by means of one-on-one support, resources, motivation, and whenever possible, financial assistance. The core of DOUA consists of both differently-abled and perfectly-abled folks who just want to "give something back" and/or to assist those with disabilities that would otherwise be considered shut-ins or that live at or below the poverty level. Our main focus is to assist people in becoming financially independent — a hand up, not a handout.
>
> This is where eBay comes into the picture. It IS all about a level playing field and that's what eBay provides for us. We can work our own hours, at our own pace, as much or as little as we like. No one ever needs to know that we are differently-abled. The majority of us WANT to work — NEED to work — and LOVE to work. It's just that we don't fit into the "mainstream" and sometimes employers are afraid to hire us.

The DOUA runs a Mentor program, where eBay members who meet the qualifications — they must be legally disabled and can't have listed more than five auctions — can receive the following:

- ✔ Five products to list on eBay
- ✔ A diskette containing digital photos of the items
- ✔ Available support from an assigned mentor via telephone and e-mail

How amazing is that? Members of the DOUA come from all walks of life and all sorts of disabilities (for example, Marjie told me about an eBay seller who was blind). If you know some folks who can benefit from the DOUA, point them to the Web site `www.doua.info`.

 By the way, the DOUA does take donations.

Setting Up Windows for Easier Accessibility

When someone is operating with a disability, simple things like using a computer can be a challenge. Many companies are inventing tools to help people with online access, and these tools help eBay sellers with disabilities to become independent.

If you use Microsoft Windows, you can take advantage of Accessibility options that are built right into the Windows interface. Using the Accessibility Wizard, as pictured in Figure 51-1, you can enable several options.

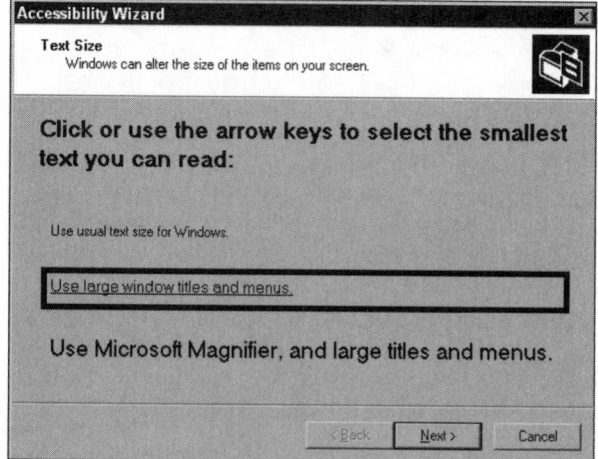

• **Figure 51-1: Using the Accessibility Wizard to set the computer's text size.**

For example, visually impaired users can set Windows to display a larger, easier-to-read interface by following either of the next two sets of steps.

 Use the Microsoft Magnifier (which you start by choosing Start⇨Programs⇨Accessories⇨ Accessibility⇨Magnifier) to read small type in Web pages or other documents. The Magnifier splits your desktop into two windows, one of which displays whatever your mouse is pointing to at magnifications levels from 1x to 9x.

Setting accessibility options with the mouse

Follow (or, as needed, have a helper follow) these steps to set up the Windows Accessibility options via mouse clicks:

1. **Click the Windows Start button.**

    A pop-up menu appears.

2. **Choose Programs⇨Accessories⇨Accessibility⇨ Accessibility Wizard.**

    The Accessibility Wizard's Welcome window appears.

3. **In the Welcome window, click Next.**

4. **Select the smallest text you can comfortably read in the display, and then click Next.**

5. **For Display Settings, be sure the Change Font Size box is checked; if it isn't, click it. If you want to use Microsoft Magnifier, check its box. Go to the next page by pressing N.**

6. **Place the mouse pointer in the box labeled *I am blind or have difficulty seeing things on screen*. Then click Next.**

7. **Click Finish to save your changes (or, if you want to cancel your selections, click No). To move back to an earlier step in the Wizard, click Back.**

Setting accessibility options with the keyboard

Follow (or, as needed, have a helper follow) these steps to set up the Windows accessibility options via the keyboard:

1. **Press the key with the Windows logo (or press Ctrl+Esc), press R, type** accwiz, **and press the Enter key.**

    The Accessibility Wizard's Welcome window appears.

2. **In the Welcome window, press N.**

    In these steps, pressing **N** does the same thing as clicking Next: It moves you to the next screen.

3. Use the Up or Down Arrow keys to select the smallest text you can read, and then press N.

4. If the Change Font Size check box is not selected, press C; if you want to use Microsoft Magnifier, press U; to move to the next page, press N.

5. Press L to select the box labeled *I am blind or have difficulty seeing things on screen.* Then press N to continue.

6. Press Enter to save your changes and exit, or, to cancel your changes, press the Tab key to move to the No button and then press Enter. To move backward in the Wizard, press B.

Windows has other Accessibility options, which are available through the Control Panel. Choose Start➪ Settings➪Control Panel and double-click Accessibility Options. Here are just a few of the options you'll find:

✔ **StickyKeys:** If you have difficulty pressing two keys at once, this program will help. (This is especially helpful if you have RSI — repetitive strain injury.) StickyKeys lets you use the Shift, Ctrl, and Alt or Windows logo key by pressing one key at a time. You can activate the program by pressing your Shift key 5 times and clicking Settings to set it up.

✔ **MouseKeys:** With MouseKeys, you can use the Num Lock calculator part of your keyboard to mimic your mouse. You can move the mouse pointer to any place on the screen by using the arrow keys; single-, right-, or double-click; and drag and drop items just as you can with your mouse.

✔ **On-Screen Keyboard:** On-Screen Keyboard displays a virtual keyboard on the screen that allows people with mobility impairments to type data by using a pointing device or joystick.

✔ **Narrator in Windows XP:** A truly amazing text-to-speech utility that resides in Windows XP for people who are visually impaired. Narrator reads what is displayed on the screen — the contents of the active window, menu options, or text that has been typed. Narrator will work with Notepad, WordPad, Control Panel programs,

Internet Explorer, the Windows desktop, and some parts of Windows Setup. To try it, press the Windows logo key, type **R**, type **narrator**, and press Enter.

Finding Tools to Meet the Challenge

I also asked Marjie if there were any special tools that DOUA members use. She suggested the ones in this list.

✔ **JAWS:** This software program, designed to be used with a speech synthesizer, is a screen reader for the vision-impaired or blind. Here's where to get it:

www.nanopac.com/JAWS.htm

✔ **ZoomText:** Screen magnifier for the visually impaired. It supports high resolution in windows and will magnify the screen 2x to 8x in steps of one, 10x to 16x in steps of two. The program enlists edge smoothing to eliminate jagged edges of magnified text. For more info, go to

www.nanopac.com/zoomtext.htm

✔ **HeadMouse:** Head-controlled computer access. A tiny sensor placed on the forehead replaces a standard mouse and keyboard. It translates movements of the user's head into movements of a mouse pointer. It can be combined with software that produces an on-screen keyboard for typing. Here's the Web site:

www.orin.com/access/headmouse

✔ **Sip/Puff Switch:** This is an over-the-ear device that is controlled by sipping and/or puffing. It can be used in concert with the HeadMouse. For more information, check out the Web site

www.orin.com/access/sip_puff/index.htm

Marjie also recommends the RollerMouse (also noted in Technique 50). This tool works well for those with limited hand or arm functionality.

Part IX

Acting Like a CEO

The 5th Wave — By Rich Tennant

"Oh yeah? Well, you might be very surprised at the number of people on eBay who would pay dearly for some decent yam-shaped headgear."

Technique 52

Building Business Buying Plans

Save Time By

- ✔ Getting your sales data together
- ✔ Evaluating your six-month merchandise plan

There are so many types of business models that sellers use on eBay. Some sellers are constantly on the prowl for new products and stock their merchandise as soon as they find a deal. Others follow the trends and try immediately to get stock of the latest and greatest gizmo that's hopefully going to sweep the country (and eBay). Plenty of sellers run their business by selling for others, and constantly beat the pavement for new customers to serve. Then there's the new eBay e-tailer.

The eBay e-tailer buys merchandise to sell on eBay. E-tailers are always looking for new wholesalers, but the e-tailers usually specialize in a particular type of stock item, such as dolls, sports cards, lighting fixtures, or apparel. Their eBay business is organized; they sell their merchandise and then buy more to replenish their stock. But is this the best way to handle things? It definitely works for most sellers, but those who actually went to school and studied retailing know there's a better way.

One of the first things you learn when studying retail buying is the use of a six-month merchandise plan. It's the ultimate tool in the arsenal of a successful retail buyer. Although it was originally designed for brick-and-mortar retailers, I've adapted it here for eBay e-tailers.

Although filling out the plan may not *seem* like a timesaving technique, after you fill it out, you'll be able to combine it with the reports generated by your bookkeeping program (I explain proper bookkeeping in Technique 47) to get a clear, concise picture of your eBay business. This is a business and not a guessing game, and handling your business in a professional manner will save you a great deal of time and money.

Understanding the Six-Month Merchandise Plan

Business means not running by the seat of your pants. I admit that running by the seat of your pants is fun and exciting, but it's really not a solid business practice. One of the reasons I started my own business is that an unorganized business format appealed to me. To my dismay, I soon learned that organization and planning really *did* make a difference in my bottom line.

Anyone who has participated in management in a corporation knows about the annual "plan." Every year, at every business, management gets together (with Ouija and dart boards) to project sales, expenses, and profits for the coming year. From this annual exercise, the "budget" for the coming year arises. These are the magic numbers that form everyone's annual raises — along with the company's plans for growth.

So, assuming that eBay sellers are online retailers, retail evaluation could help eBay sellers make sound business decisions. Making a merchandise plan is a good step in that direction. A merchandise plan covers six months at a time and sets sales goals. It also helps estimate how much money must be spent on merchandise (and when) so that a particular season's success can be replicated and magnified.

Getting the Data

There are a few numbers that you need to get your plan on paper. You should be able to get these numbers from your bookkeeping software programs Inventory Valuation report:

- ✔ **BOM:** The value, in dollars, of your beginning-of-month inventory

- ✔ **EOM:** The dollar amount of your end-of-month inventory

- ✔ **Gross sales:** Total revenue from sales (not including shipping and handling)

- ✔ **Markdowns:** Total revenue of merchandise you have sold at eBay below your target price

 The EOM figure for a specific month is the same as the BOM figure for the following month. Example: The End Of Month figure for April is the same as the Beginning Of Month figure for May.

To put together your six-month plan, you need to have sales history for a six-month period. To get a good historical picture of your sales, it's beneficial to have an entire year's worth of figures.

 Your six-month plan can be based on your total eBay sales, or only one segment of your business. For example, if you sell musical instruments, along with many other sundry items, but you want to evaluate solely your musical-instrument sales, you can use just those figures for a six-month plan for your "music" department.

What you're going to establish is your inventory turnover. You'll measure how much inventory sells out in a specified period of time. The faster you "turn over" merchandise, the sooner you can bring in new merchandise and increase your bottom line. You can also evaluate whether you need to lower your starting price to move out stale inventory to get cash to buy new inventory.

When you prepare your six-month plan (an example is provided in Table 52-1), set out the months not by the regular calendar, but by a *retail calendar*, which divides the year into the seasons of Fall/Winter (August 1 through January 31) and Spring/Summer (February 1 through July 31). This way, if you want to refer to top national performance figures in trade publications or on the Internet, you must base your figures on the same standardized retail seasons.

Formulas That Calculate Your Data

Okay, I can admit that bigger minds than mine came up with these standard formulas. Magically, they work and are used by retailers around the world. If you're not pulling the figures from a bookkeeping program, here's how you make the calculations.

You can make your calculations in dollar amounts or number of units of the item. In order to figure out how much of this item to buy, you must know how much you have left in stock.

✔ EOM Stock = BOM Stock + Purchases - Sales

✔ BOM Stock = EOM Stock from the previous month

✔ Sales + EOM - BOM = Monthly Planned Purchases

Prepare a chart for your own business, similar to the one shown in Table 52-1. Study your results and find out which months are your strongest. Let the table tell you when you might have to boost your merchandise selection in lagging months to boost sales. It will help bring your planning from Ouija board to reality.

TABLE 52-1: SAMPLE SIX-MONTH EBAY MERCHANDISE PLAN

Fall/Winter	Aug	Sept	Oct	Nov	Dec	Jan	Total
TOTAL SALES	$2,875.00	$3,320.00	$3,775.00	$4,150.00	$3,950.00	$4,350.00	$22,420.00
+ Retail EOM	$1,750.00	$3,870.00	$4,250.00	$3,985.00	$4,795.00	$4,240.00	$22,890.00
+ Reductions	$575.00	$275.00	$250.00	$175.00	$425.00	$275.00	$1,975.00
- Retail BOM	$3,150.00	$1,750.00	$3,870.00	$4,250.00	$3,985.00	$4,795.00	$21,800.00
= Retail Purchases	$2,050.00	$5,715.00	$4,405.00	$4,060.00	$5,185.00	$4,070.00	$25,485.00
Cost Purchases	$3,310.00	$3,540.00	$4,725.00	$5,150.00	$2,775.00	$3,450.00	$22,950.00
% of season's sales	12.82%	14.81%	16.84%	18.51%	17.62%	19.40%	
% of season's reductions	29.11%	13.92%	12.66%	8.86%	21.52%	13.92%	
Average stock	$3,815.00						
Average sales	$3,735.00						
Basic stock	$1,000.00						

Technique 53

Knowing Your Customers

When you're in business, you can't consider yourself only a retailer; you have to be a marketer, too. eBay enables sellers in the United States to market across a massive geographic area. I'm sure you know how large the area is, but what about the *people* you sell to? You've heard of advertising being targeted to the lucrative 18-to-49 age demographic, but what about all the other age groups? Who are *they?* If you learn about your customer, you'll know how to sell to them. It's all about targeting.

Decide who buys what you want to sell, or better yet, decide with whom you want to deal. If you don't want to deal with e-mails from teenage gamers, perhaps you shouldn't be selling items that Gen N (in the upcoming description) is gonna want.

Marketers often provide blanket definitions about the population based on their stage in life, what they are "expected" to buy, and which activities they participate in. From your eBay sales, you may find giant holes in this theory, but since everything has to have a "standard," this technique defines the demographic groups, classified by age.

Marketing to the Generations

The marketing generations are not formed truly by biological dates. It's more about their life experiences and what influenced people as they were growing up. We all know that outside influences make a big difference in how we look at things — and that affects how and why we buy things.

World War II Generation: (Or as Tom Brokaw defined it, the Greatest Generation). This is the segment of our population from the mid-70s to 90 or so. They've lived through the Great Depression and known about sacrifice. They don't like waste, purchase items in smaller quantities, and like using single-serving products.

World War II colored their lives, giving them the perspective to work together against a common enemy. The WWII generation is generally more team-oriented than other generational groups. Sadly, this group is not strongly targeted by marketers. Many people in this age group are visiting eBay looking for merchandise, and some smart eBay sellers market to them.

It's a wide-open area. Just look at the success of sellers selling glasses for the visually impaired, vitamins, and medical devices. With the growth of the Internet, many of these people are also having fun unloading their lifelong collections of "stuff" on eBay.

Post-War Generation: The largest percentage of the U.S. population, this group is aged from their mid-fifties to mid-seventies. This is an underestimated and strong market — the only people who don't underestimate their strength is the AARP (American Association for Retired Persons). Visit the AARP Web site if you think this age group is fading away at www.aarp.org. By using a little intuition, you can study this site and get a good picture of what this age group is interested in. The site suggests a wide swath of merchandise to sell.

This group has experienced the Korean War, the Civil Rights movement, and the Cold War. They moved to the suburbs with their parents, and lived through the birth of rock 'n' roll. Yes, they may be grandparents too, and that opens an entire new area of marketing. Don't you think they're shopping big-time for little ones too? Marketers know this, and many direct toy marketers target catalogs to grandparents buying for kids.

 According to the 2000 Census, the median age in the United States is getting older, at 35.3 years, up from 32.9 in 1990.

The Baby Boomers and the Leading-Edge Boomers: This is the second-largest segment of the U.S. population. It's also about time that marketers quit trying to sell them Depends, and concentrate on what they're really *doing*. They're still working 12-hour days, are into fitness and nutrition, running marathons, running businesses, and having lots of fun buying all the latest techie toys.

Aged from the mid-forties to fifties, these folks are a significant segment of the population. They've been in the work marketplace for many years and are spending big money in the market today. They grew up thinking anything was possible (they saw the first man walk on the moon), but events dulled the optimism of their youth: the Vietnam War, Cuban Missile Crisis, and the assassinations of John F. Kennedy and Martin Luther King, Jr.

 Grow your eBay business by marketing to the boomers. Earn money selling health and wellness products. They've got disposable savings to spend on technology, fashion, and travel. Talk about the market for cosmetics and age-staving potions! This group also has fun with eBay Motors!

Trailing-Edge Boomers: From the mid-thirties to late forties, this group is not the well-promoted Baby Boomers and not quite Gen Xers. Even though technically they are the same generation as the Baby Boomers, their life experience makes them feel they're in a different generation.

They don't really care about Elvis, didn't want to be hippies, and didn't serve in Vietnam. They're the first wave of Reagan-era MBAs who've had their children and are busily starting to spend on them. They're more cynical — feeling cheated by the Baby Boomers (who already had all the good jobs). They view themselves as the "best" generation.

Trailing-Edge Boomers entered their adulthood with pessimism; they were the first to enter the workforce with a lack of confidence. They also look for ways to work from home (they're the telecommuters) — think of all the things you can sell them to enhance their lives!

Gen Xers: Generation X is another difficult-to-pin-down era. The phrase "Generation X" was coined by Douglas Coupland in his 1991 novel, *Generation X: Tales for an Accelerated Culture*. (It was also the name of a group in the 1970s featuring Billy Idol.) The phrase was picked up by marketers looking to name the newest upcoming group. But who *is*

Generation X? It's a hotly debated issue. Some say the Xers were born as early as 1961, but a more accepted dateline places them in the 1965-to-1975 timeframe, when birthrates were at a new low.

Generation Xers were brought up on television and personal computers. They saw the adults around them go through incredibly selfish times, which is something they do not want to repeat. Growing up in the "me" generation, they now see that it was not all that it was cracked up to be. However, they're very concerned with financial and emotional security.

This makes them aggressive entrepreneurs, especially because they are very street-smart. They think of themselves as being "different" and are concerned with dropping the pretenses of the Baby-Boomer-dominated world.

Gen Y: The largest consumer market since the Baby Boomers grew up with the Internet. They're the 65 million Americans born between 1977 and 1995. The term was coined in 1993, by *Advertising Age,* the influential magazine for advertising, marketing and media professionals — so they're truly children of the advertising era.

During the '90s, their parents worked extra hard to strike a balance between work and family after the workaholic '80s.

Generation Y comprises the children of the Boomers — sometimes called Echo Boomers. Some sociologists even go as far as to suggest that they are attempted clones of the Boomer generation. Influenced by their parents, they value education. They've worked several part-time jobs and already know what they want from their careers once they reach the marketplace.

To Gen Y, technology is a *fait accompli.* They're aware of every up-and-coming trend and are the first to embrace (or kill) it. The spontaneity of the Internet keeps them ahead of the marketers — knowing almost before the marketers do what their favorite stars wear. Manufacturers are now giving free clothing to stars on VH1 and MTV to stay at the forefront of the market.

 They have money, and if it's hip, they want it.

Generation N: This group grew up without giving technology a second thought. They're naturally adept and have been comfortable with technology ever since they could press the buttons on a keyboard.

Dubbed "Generation Net," they're too young to have established themselves in the marketplace. They will be the force in the coming decades. They're from widely diverse ethnic groups and seem to be more social-cause–oriented than their predecessors. Only time will tell where their interests will go. The 2000 Census counted the total population under 19 as 80,473,265 — 28.6 percent of the population.

Table 53-1 below gives you the actual population figures of the United States. With this knowledge, you can better decide just how many people will be shoppers for your products in the future. The figures in the 2000 Census pegged the country at a total population of 281,421,906 — 49.1 percent male and 50.9 percent female.

TABLE 53-1: SEX AND AGE U.S. CENSUS 2000

Age Range	Population	%
20–24	18,964,001	6.7%
25–34	39,891,724	14.2%
35–44	45,148,527	16.0%
45–54	37,677,952	13.4%
55–59	13,469,237	4.8%
60–64	10,805,447	3.8%
65–74	18,390,986	6.5%
75–84	12,361,180	4.4%
85+	4,239,587	1.5%

Marketing Your eBay Listings

Selling is all about marketing, and marketing is all about promotion. eBay provides you with some awesome tools to promote your items. Face it; if you sell more, you make more money — and so does eBay. It's to their benefit to help you become a retailing mogul on the site. eBay isn't naïve either — they know that if they make it easy for you to drive sales to eBay, you'll be less likely to spend tons of time on your own retail Web site. Many successful eBay sellers sell hundreds of thousands of dollars a year in merchandise — exclusively from sales on the eBay site. The tools are easy to use, and not all eBay sellers know how to use them or where to find them. When you're finished with this technique, you'll be a savvy seller, upping your sales through eBay cross-promotions.

eBay Cross-Promotions

One of the slickest promotional tools to date is the cross-promotion. Every time you view an item for sale on eBay, you will see a filmstrip featuring four other items currently up for sale by the seller, as shown in Figure 54-1.

• **Figure 54-1: eBay cross-promotion for one of my auctions.**

Another filmstrip with four items will be presented after you bid on an item or make a purchase from the seller. If the seller is smart and has an eBay Store, he'll have preselected the items you'll see when viewing or bidding on an item.

Smart cross-promoting

Cross-promoting can work to the *nth* degree for you if you think about what buyers want. If you're selling a man's size Large shirt and you have ties or similar shirts in the same size, why not list those items in the cross-promotions area? Promoting a jackhammer along with the search, on the other hand, may be a bit more of a stretch. And you might be slipping farther from reality if you chose to promote an eye makeup kit along with the man's shirt. Get it? Promote items that relate to each other, and catch the prospective buyer's eye.

In Figure 54-1, the items pictured appeared in a listing cross-promotion from my other book, *Starting an eBay Business For Dummies*. I felt if someone is interested in starting a business on eBay, they might be interested in buying some tools to make their selling easier.

You can also change your promotions if you have a hot item that appeals to everyone. You can switch that item into one of the boxes by visiting the cross-promotions area.

Setting up cross-promotions

The first step toward cross-promotional bliss is to agree that you want to use the eBay cross-promotion tool. Follow these steps:

1. **Go to your My eBay Preferences page, scroll to the bottom to the heading Personal Information, and click the *Participate in eBay Merchandising* link.**

2. **Sign in again (you have to retype your password for security).**

   You're whisked off to the Cross Promotion Program Participation page. This is where you

agree to cross-promotions and set up your initial preferences.

3. **Click to select the Cross Promote My Items radio button.**

   Now, you're ready to create your default Display Settings further down the page.

The next step along the way to cross-promotion nirvana deals with choosing the default merchandising settings to use when a user views one of your items. In an area similar to the one shown in Figure 54-2, you have to decide on several things, including these:

- ✔ **Selling Format:** This is where you decide which types of items you'd like to show with other types of items. You can also select Show Any Item.

- ✔ **Gallery Items:** Select in which order you'd like your items with gallery pictures to appear.

- ✔ **Item Sort:** Select how you want to display your items: Ending Soonest, Ending Last, Newly Listed, Highest Price, or Lowest Price.

Cross-Promotions Display Settings - When a user **Views** my items:
eBay selects and arranges your items to cross-promote based on the settings below. Learn more about how eBay automatically selects items.

Selling Format:	● Show only Store Inventory items
	○ Show only items with a Buy It Now price
	◉ Show items with a Buy It Now first
	○ Show any item
Gallery Items:	○ Show only items with Gallery images
	● Show items with Gallery images first
	○ Show any item
Show my items sorted by:	● Ending soonest
	○ Ending last
	○ Newly listed
	○ Highest price
	○ Lowest price

• **Figure 54-2:** Your choices for item display in cross-promotions.

After making your choices, you next select the settings for when someone bids on or wins one of your items. These options are the same as the ones listed above for viewing.

After you finish, click Save My Changes.

 No matter what your settings, you can always access your cross-promotions and make changes as to what will show with individual items. So don't feel locked in when making the selections above.

Checking the status of your cross-promotions

If you're not using Selling Manager, you will have a link on the top of your Items I'm Selling page that reads `Cross-Promotions`. Click there, and you'll be taken to your cross-promotions status area, as shown in Figure 54-3.

Status of Your Cross-Promotions

All your current listings are below. You can view or change the items being cross-promoted from a listing by clicking the **Edit** link. Learn more about how cross-promotions work.

Status

⚠ **6 items** have had their ended cross-promotions replaced

✔ **4 items** have manual cross-promotions specified

❤ **12 items** have automatic cross-promotions, based on your default category settings

Item #	Item Title	Qty	End Date	Cross-Promotion Status	Action
2983653213	CLOUD DOME Complete Digital Kit ALL YOU NEED	1	Feb-08-04	❤	Edit
2983684043	eBay Sellers Steel Rolling Garment Rack NEW	1	Feb-08-04	❤	Edit
2983687785	~ FREE SHIP ~ CLOUD DOME w 7" Ext Collar Kit	1	Feb-08-04	❤	Edit
2983688199	CLOUD DOME Angled Extension Collar NEW!	1	Feb-08-04	❤	Edit
2964357159	CLOUD DOME Angled Extension Collar NEW!	12	Feb-19-04	❤	Edit
2964392864	CLOUD DOME Complete Digital Kit ALL YOU NEED	6	Feb-19-04	❤	Edit
2850637051	Spanx Footless Body Shaping Pantyhose B NUDE	19	Feb-23-04	❤	Edit
2946682895	NEW eBay Bargain Shopping for Dummies SIGNED	11	Feb-24-04	❤	Edit
2870991030	Spanx Footless Body Shaping Pantyhose A NUDE	12	Feb-26-04	❤	Edit
2966720670	eBay TIPS for Dummies AUTHOR SIGNED 2003	8	Feb-29-04	❤	Edit
3568178559	EASY French Normandy Original Classic Recipes	48	Feb-29-04	❤	Edit
2931822191	un-du Adhesive Remover	14	Mar-03-04	❤	Edit
3584877631	eBay Bargain Shopping for Dummies SIGNED 2U	1	Feb-08-04	✔	Edit
3585592139	Starting an Ebay Business for Dummies SIGNED	1	Feb-11-04	✔	Edit
2985415422	Photography Photo Lights NIB Lighting Kit	1	Feb-12-04	✔	Edit
2985928696	Cloud Dome Background PORTABLE BOARD STAGE	1	Feb-14-04	✔	Edit
2374768623	Andy Warhol Art MARILYN MONROE Cup & Saucer	6	Feb-21-04	⚠	Edit
2982848688	Cloud Dome Background PORTABLE PHOTO STAGE	12	Feb-25-04	⚠	Edit
2983419208	eBay Sellers Steel Rolling Garment Rack NEW	6	Feb-27-04	⚠	Edit
2983845520	Photography Photo Lights Flood Lighting Kit	12	Mar-10-04	⚠	Edit
2983852467	CLOUD DOME KIT for Digital Macro Image Photos	12	Mar-10-04	⚠	Edit
3584342433	Starting an Ebay Business for Dummies SIGNED	10	Mar-10-04	⚠	Edit

• **Figure 54-3: My eBay Items I'm Selling cross-promotions status area.**

eBay uses three icons to communicate the status of the promotions for your items:

✔ **Green check mark with a blue circle:** Cross-promotions have been automatically selected for you by eBay based on your preferences.

✔ **Green check mark:** This refers to items you've selected individually for cross-promotions and that are still active on the page. (Meaning that none of your cross-promotions have expired, causing the system to substitute another for you.)

✔ **Yellow shield with an exclamation point:** This means that one of the items you previously manually set up needs attention. One of the manually selected cross-promotion items has ended and has been automatically replaced within the parameters of your default settings.

If you use Selling Manager, you'll have an alert area on your Summary page as shown in Figure 54-4.

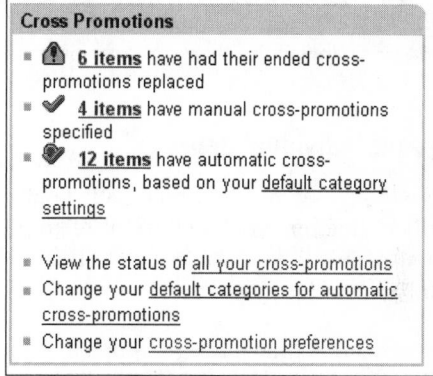

Cross Promotions

- ⚠ **6 items** have had their ended cross-promotions replaced
- ✔ **4 items** have manual cross-promotions specified
- ❤ **12 items** have automatic cross-promotions, based on your default category settings

- View the status of all your cross-promotions
- Change your default categories for automatic cross-promotions
- Change your cross-promotion preferences

• **Figure 54-4: Selling Manager Summary page Cross Promotions alerts.**

To edit your cross-promotions from here, you can make changes to your merchandising.

1. Click on the link to view the status of All Your Cross-Promotions.

Clicking that link will take you to a page exactly like the one pictured in Figure 54-3.

2. Click the link to change your Default Categories for Automatic Cross-Promotions.

You're taken to a page where you can change cross-promotions by category, as shown in Figure 54-5.

Default Categories for Automatic Cross-Promotions	
The settings below are used by default to cross-promote your items to buyers. When someone views, bids on, or wins one of your items, your other items from a particular category will be automatically promoted. You can change which categories are cross-promoted to maximize your sales. Learn more about how default settings are used.	
For items in **Seller's Tools**: (17 items)	change default categories
when someone **views an item**, promote item from...	Seller's Tools (17 items)
when someone **bids** or **wins**, promote item from...	Seller's Tools (17 items)
For items in **Dummies Books**: (0 items)	change default categories
when someone **views an item**, promote item from...	Seller's Tools (17 items)
when someone **bids** or **wins**, promote item from...	Seller's Tools (17 items)
For items in **Vintage Barbie**: (0 items)	change default categories
when someone **views an item**, promote item from...	Vintage Barbie (0 items)
when someone **bids** or **wins**, promote item from...	Vintage Barbie (0 items)
For items in **Star Trek**: (0 items)	change default categories
when someone **views an item**, promote item from...	Star Trek (0 items)
when someone **bids** or **wins**, promote item from...	Star Trek (0 items)
For items in **Girly Things**: (2 items)	change default categories
when someone **views an item**, promote item from...	Fun Stuff (2 items)
when someone **bids** or **wins**, promote item from...	Seller's Tools (17 items)
For items in **Fun Stuff**: (2 items)	change default categories
when someone **views an item**, promote item from...	Fun Stuff (2 items)
when someone **bids** or **wins**, promote item from...	Fun Stuff (2 items)
For items in **Designer Clothing**: (0 items)	change default categories
when someone **views an item**, promote item from...	Designer Clothing (0 items)
when someone **bids** or **wins**, promote item from...	Designer Clothing (0 items)
For items in **Fancy Food**: (1 item)	change default categories

• **Figure 54-5: Changing the category cross-promotions default page.**

Editing your individual items

When you look at eBay alerts on a daily basis, you'll eventually notice that you need to make some adjustments. To edit your cross-promotions, follow these steps:

1. **From your Selling Manager Summary page click the link to view the Status of Your Cross-Promotions.**

Or from an individual eBay listing click the Change Your Cross-Promoted Items link below the cross-promotion merchandising panel. Go to the Cross-Promotions status page (refer to Figure 54-3).

2. **Click the Edit link next to the item in which you wish to edit the cross-promotion.**

You see an area similar to Figure 54-6. On the top of the page are the items currently being shown when someone views an item, and on the bottom of the page are the items the bidder views when they bid on or win the item.

A red notation indicates that eBay has replaced items based on your default preferences due to another item being sold.

• **Figure 54-6: Viewing the current merchandising of your item.**

To change an item cross-promotion to better suit your marketing for the item, follow these steps:

1. **Click the Add Item or Change Item button.**

You land softly on the Select Item page. On the top of this page, you can find a tool that permits you to search your own listings by keyword. I've filled in the form in Figure 54-7.

2. **Search with the tool for related items by keyword, your store category, or by listing format.**

3. **After you make your selections, press Update Search.**

Select by Searching

Use the following options to refine your list of items to cross-promote. Select the item by clicking the **Add** button next to the title, or cancel

eBay Store Custom Category
All My Items

Keywords in item titles
dummies

Listing Format
Store Inventory

Price Range
From: US $ ___ To: US $ ___

Update Search   Start a new search

• **Figure 54-7: Selecting a replacement promotion by searching my sales.**

On the next page that appears, you can view the results of the search, as shown in Figure 54-8.

4. **Press the Add button next to your desired item, and the item will replace (or add) the indicated item in your promotion.**

Select	Picture	Item#	Current Price	Qty	Item Format	(PST) End Date ▲
Add		NEW eBay Bargain Shopping for Dummies SIGNED 2946682895	US $14.99	11	🖼	Feb-24-04
Add		eBay TIPS for Dummies AUTHOR SIGNED 2003 2966720670	US $4.50	8	🖼	Feb-29-04
Add		Starting an Ebay Business for Dummies SIGNED 3584342433	US $21.99	10	🖼	Mar-10-04
Add		New 2004 EBAY FOR DUMMIES 4th Author Signed 3586544879	US $20.99	11	🖼	Mar-19-04

• **Figure 54-8:** The results of finding replacement promotions by using the Search tool.

Below the Select by Searching function is a long (depending on how many items you have up for sale) list of every item in your listings. It may be faster to quickly scroll down the page and click the Add button from the visual list.

Using an eBay Marketplace

If you don't want to set up a separate Web site for your items for sale, eBay has a super alternative idea. Why not install an eBay Marketplace on your Web site? Even if your Web site isn't commercial and just has pictures of the baby or your dog, people will stop by — why not show off your eBay listings! (Just be careful when selling the ugly lamp that Aunt Lizzie gave you for Christmas!)

Figure 54-9 shows a portion of my eBay Marketplace on one of my Web sites.

eBay updates your eBay Marketplace every 20 minutes and shows all your listings, including Gallery pictures. Best of all — the service is free!

• **Figure 54-9:** My off-eBay, An eBay Marketplace page.

eBay will generate a "sniplet" of HTML for you to insert on your Web page. That's all there is to it! Your eBay listings will then automatically display on your Web page, with no effort from you. eBay's API does all the work.

To get your own Marketplace, go to `pages.eBay.com/api/merchantkit.html`. When you follow this link, know that you are going into the deepest recesses of eBay — you are accessing their API (Application Program Interface). Those are the tools that the big guys use for their eBay sales — and now these are available to you!

On the eBay Marketplace API page, you can read all about how now you can "showcase your merchandise on two channels simultaneously" — don't you feel cool now?

Scroll down the page and click the link that says Get Merchant Kit Now. To create your HTML "sniplet," you'll have to answer a few questions.

- ✔ **Choose the items you want to show:** Your choices will be to show all your items from all categories, selected items from a particular eBay category, or items from your personal store categories.

- ✔ **Choose the number of items ending first to show:** You may select from the first 25 or 50 items from your listings.

- ✔ **Sort items displayed by:** Do you want the items ending first to show first? Lowest prices? Highest prices? Items ending last? You make that selection here.

- ✔ **Font Face:** If you want a specific font face, you may enter it here. The default is Verdana (one of

my favorite online fonts) which was developed for Internet use.

- ✔ **Font size:** How big do you want the text to appear? The default is size 2 — and that's what I use.

After you make your choices, press Preview Sniplet. You will now be able to see what your eBay Marketplace looks like. If you like what you see, copy the provided HTML code and paste it on your Web site.

If you don't like the looks of it, press the Edit/Create New Sniplet button. Change the font sizes and such until you are happy with the results. After you're happy and have pasted the code in a safe place, click the Logout button.

Congratulations, now you have your own eBay Marketplace to put on your Web site!

Using Google to Build Your Business

55

Technique

Save Time By

✔ Getting the buzz from Google

✔ Listing your eBay Store or Web site on Google

✔ Promoting your business with Google AdWords

Originally, this technique was to tell you all about Google AdWords, a fantastic Web-based promotion product. But as I learned more about the service, I found that Google itself is way more than a mere search engine. Google can help you find data, keep abreast of marketing trends, make you laugh, and give you more information than you ever thought possible. The best part about it is that it's pure. You're not barraged with pop-up ads on every page.

What Google means is information: marketing information about your customers for you and information about your eBay Store for your customers. In this technique, I show you how to make Google your silent eBay marketing partner. Google works for you while you're busy with your sales. Also check out the Cheat Sheet in the front of this book; it lists even more short tricks that you can accomplish with the Google toolbar.

Finding Out What the Zeitgeist Is

It's all about the *zeitgeist*. And what the heck, you may wonder, is a *zeitgeist?* The term comes from the German (originally *Geist der Zeit*) words *"Zeit"* meaning time and *"Geist"* meaning spirit. It's the all-embracing intellectual atmosphere of a distinct time period. In today's terms? It's the buzz.

Similar to the Yahoo! Buzz mentioned in Technique 8, the Google *Zeitgeist* feature keeps current and historic data on the site. It's based on the total number of queries on a particular subject in a succinct period of time. It's updated on a weekly, monthly, and — when called for — on a daily basis, and can be found at www.google.com/press/zeitgeist.html.

From that page, you can also see the Zeitgeist (what's hot and what's not) in other countries (invaluable information if you are selling on eBay internationally); in the United Kingdom, Canada, Germany, Spain, France, Italy, the Netherlands, Australia, and Japan. This page also links to historical Zeitgeist data.

The Zeitgeist page is where you can get the nuggets of thought for your marketing and selling plans. Figure 55-1 shows data from the week ending March 8, 2004.

Google Zeitgeist - Search patterns, trends, and surprises according to Google

For both breaking news and obscure information alike, people around the world search on Google at www.google.com. With a bit of analysis, this flurry of searches often exposes interesting trends, patterns, and surprises.

Top 10 Gaining Queries Week Ending Mar. 8, 2004	Top 10 Declining Queries Week Ending Mar. 8, 2004
1. martha stewart	1. leap year
2. ford	2. mardi gras
3. john kerry	3. the passion of the christ
4. circuit city	4. oscars
5. average joe hawaii	5. fafsa
6. spalding gray	6. ash wednesday
7. disney	7. haiti
8. sopranos	8. diego luna
9. dr. seuss	9. charlize theron
10. pokemon	10. howard stern

• **Figure 55-1: Top 10 Queries week ending March 8, 2004.**

If you come to this page and see this data, you can *know* for sure that it's time to start selling old Martha Stewart Living Omnimedia stock certificates, brochures of vintage Ford vehicles, and Tony Soprano T-shirts. It also tells me to start gathering up all the free John Kerry campaign memorabilia that I can get my hands on for future selling. I also know its time to pack up any Oscar stuff I have to sell and wait to put it up next year!

The Zeitgeist also has information for previous periods. If you take a look at Figure 55-2, you'll find some obvious data (hindsight *is* 20/20). If you were selling items based on any of the popular queries or brands in 2003, it's fair to say you did very well.

Check out the Zeitgeist. It *could* be your crystal ball into stocking your store.

Popular Queries 2003	Popular Brands 2003
1. britney spears	1. ferrari
2. harry potter	2. sony
3. matrix	3. bmw
4. shakira	4. disney
5. david beckham	5. ryanair
6. 50 cent	6. hp
7. iraq	7. dell
8. lord of the rings	8. easyjet
9. kobe bryant	9. last minute
10. tour de france	10. walmart

• **Figure 55-2: The Google Zeitgeist summary for 2003.**

The roots of Google

The word *Google* is a malformation of *googol*, a word coined by mathematician Edward Kasner signifying a number of immense proportions — a one followed by 100 zeros. It's a number that signifies near-infinity. That's where Google got its name. The company was originated to make sense of the seemingly infinite amount of information on the Internet.

The company was founded (as you can imagine) by a couple of brainy guys. Larry Page and Sergy Brin met in graduate school at Stanford (majoring in Computer Science, what else?). Then and now they are a pair of uniquely brilliant guys. Larry even once built a working, programmable plotter and inkjet printer out of Lego™!

Google was born from their first enterprise, BackRub, an ever-growing network of low-end PCs (they couldn't afford big-time servers). Its goal was to provide a "back-link" to data on the Internet so that students could more easily find data. In 1998 they founded Google in a rented house, honing their technology with a terabyte (a thousand billion bytes or a thousand gigabytes) of storage on miscellaneous disks purchased at discount. (If they would have had eBay they probably could have saved even more — but who could even conceive of a terabyte in 1998? These guys, I guess.) They shopped their new project to big-time money men and silicon valley big wigs to no avail. Yahoo! founder, David Filo, told them to call back when it's fully developed. Others just blew them off inconsequentially. Their angel came in the form of Andy Bechtolsheim, one of the founders of Sun Microsystems. After seeing an abbreviated version of the guys' demo (being a leader of industry, he had places to go and people to see), he did see potential in the product and said, "why don't I just give you $100,000?" He made the check out to Google, Inc.

Oops, there was no Google, Inc. The check had to hang around in a desk drawer for a couple of weeks before they got a corporation together. (See why I tell you to plan ahead? You never know when someone will drop $100K in your lap!) From their small start with a staff of three, Google now reigns supreme in the Zeitgeist (read on) of the computer era, operating with 1,000 employees from their offices at GooglePlex.

Today, the average Google search takes about a half second, driven by 10,000 interconnected computers. It can be searched in 46 different languages and is considered the #1 B2B Web site and #5 in any medium: online or off. Although I'll be teaching you a taste of Google in this technique, I highly recommend *Google For Dummies* by Brad Hill. It'll give you even more insight to this amazing enterprise.

Catching Attention for Your eBay Store on Google

Have you ever Googled (that's part of the new vernacular, a new verb meaning to search the Google engine for something) your eBay Store? I did; I searched the name of my store and included the word eBay in the search parameters. Figure 55-3 shows you the results. Google your store; is it listed?

• **Figure 55-3: Wow! My eBay Store is listed!**

If it isn't, you're missing out on a huge opportunity for free promotion. Google runs "spiders" (just picture the way a spider runs — swiftly and all over the place), automated robots that scour the Internet on a monthly basis looking for data to become part of the Google index. The robot is named Googlebot.

Thousands of sites (and you do know that since your eBay Store has a unique URL, it's considered to be a Web site) are added to the Google index every time their spiders crawl the Web. If, for some unknown reason, your eBay Store *isn't* listed, go to www.google.com/addurl.html, as pictured in Figure 55-4.

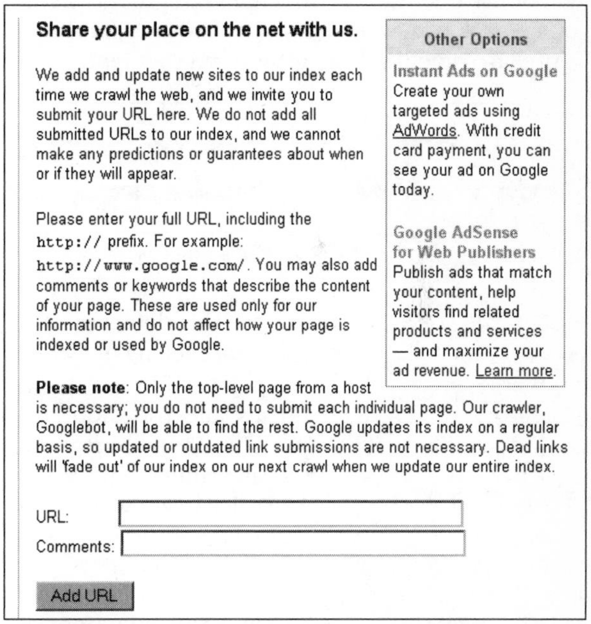

Share your place on the net with us.

We add and update new sites to our index each time we crawl the web, and we invite you to submit your URL here. We do not add all submitted URLs to our index, and we cannot make any predictions or guarantees about when or if they will appear.

Please enter your full URL, including the http:// prefix. For example: http://www.google.com/. You may also add comments or keywords that describe the content of your page. These are used only for our information and do not affect how your page is indexed or used by Google.

Please note: Only the top-level page from a host is necessary; you do not need to submit each individual page. Our crawler, Googlebot, will be able to find the rest. Google updates its index on a regular basis, so updated or outdated link submissions are not necessary. Dead links will 'fade out' of our index on our next crawl when we update our entire index.

URL:

Comments:

Add URL

Other Options

Instant Ads on Google Create your own targeted ads using AdWords. With credit card payment, you can see your ad on Google today.

Google AdSense for Web Publishers Publish ads that match your content, help visitors find related products and services — and maximize your ad revenue. Learn more.

• **Figure 55-4: Get your free shot at the big time.**

When you get to this page, type in your eBay Store URL. Just click on the store red tag icon next to your eBay user ID to get to your store. Copy and paste the URL in the address line of your browser into the URL line on the form. When I went to my eBay Store, I got the URL, http://stores.ebay.com/Marsha-Colliers-Fabulous-Finds. (That's the URL you should use in your email and printed propaganda to promote your store.)

In the second line, add a comment if you wish, describing your store merchandise and click Submit. There are no guarantees here, but odds are you'll find your little shop up on Google within a few weeks.

Get Found in a Hurry with AdWords

Being a regular user of the Google index, I began to notice small ads in the right-hand side of my searches under a headline called Sponsored Links. I definitely figured they were expensive links from high-dollar operations until I found out the truth. If you take a look at the results of a Google search in Figure 55-5, you'll see my little ad on the right.

• **Figure 55-5:** OK, I Googled myself.

People use Google more than 200 million times a day. Google AdWords allow you to create these profitable little ads. You choose keywords to let Google know where to place your ads. Certainly you can come up with some relevant keywords to promote your eBay Store! (If you're stumped, try the 30-day free trial of Sellathon mentioned in Technique 14.)

The coolest part of the deal is that you only have to pay for the ad when someone clicks on it (very much like eBay Banners talked about in Technique 57). Wanna know more? Go over to www.adwords.com.

Once you're there, you can go over the details and set up your own campaign.

For your campaign, there are a few things to keep in mind.

✔ **Keywords and Keyword phrases:** Come up with a list of keywords that would best describe your merchandise. Google allows you to estimate, based on current search data, how often your selected keyword will come up every day. They will also estimate your daily cost based on the current amount of clicks on that word. That can be a shocking number. Don't worry, not everyone who sees your ad will click on it — but if they did, eeyow!

✔ **CPC (Cost Per Click):** You determine how much you'll pay for each click on your keywords. You can pay as little as $.05 or as much as $50 a click. The dollar amount you place on your clicks makes the basis for how often your ad appears.

✔ **CTR (Click Through Rate):** This is a statistic that reflects how many people click on your ad when they see it. If your CTR falls below .5 percent after 1,000 impressions, AdWords may slow, or even discontinue, your ad views. When one of your keywords isn't passing muster, it will be indicated on your reports as Moderate or less.

Without showing my keywords, Figure 55-6 shows you a month's worth of keyword analysis for my account. You can see clearly that some keywords are doing their jobs and others aren't. To keep my account current, I evaluate my CTR every month and delete the laggers.

✔ **Daily Budget:** You can set the cap in dollars on how much you'll spend a day. Going back to the theory that if you have some really hot keywords, you could spend thousands on clicks!

Setting up your AdWords account will take a while and some thinking. So wait until your mind is clear (Saturday morning?) and sit down at the AdWords site with a cup of coffee and expect to take a while.

Status	Clicks	Impr.	CTR ▼	Avg. CPC	Cost	Avg. Pos
	657	37,770	1.7%	$0.08	$46.21	3.7
	272	726,644	0.0%	$0.08	$19.10	3.1
Strong	**34**	111	30.6%	$0.05	$1.70	1.0
Strong	**13**	256	5.0%	$0.09	$1.10	1.2
Strong	**22**	434	5.0%	$0.09	$1.89	5.1
Strong	**221**	9,712	2.2%	$0.08	$17.61	4.2
Strong	**40**	1,853	2.1%	$0.06	$2.12	1.2
Strong	**106**	6,138	1.7%	$0.06	$5.79	1.3
Strong	**156**	10,423	1.4%	$0.07	$10.87	1.5
Strong	**28**	3,199	0.8%	$0.08	$2.13	3.4
Strong	**5**	649	0.7%	$0.06	$0.28	1.9
Moderate	**9**	1,191	0.7%	$0.10	$0.84	14.2
Strong	**23**	3,247	0.7%	$0.09	$1.88	7.1
Moderate	**0**	161	0.0%	-	-	6.4
Moderate	**0**	158	0.0%	-	-	33.9
Moderate	**0**	99	0.0%	-	-	103.1

• **Figure 55-6: AdWords Keyword statistics.**

Google gives you excellent step-by-step instructions once you've signed in at www.adwords.com. This is the general process you will follow.

1. **Decide if you want to target your ads geographically.**

You can pinpoint your market if you'd like, or you can blast the entire world. Choose from a list of 14 languages, 250 countries, or as far down as 200 United States regions.

2. **Create your ad.**

This is not as easy as I thought! You can only create three lines of ad text with a total of 95 characters. Be as concise as possible. Don't throw in useless adjectives. Figure out the perfect 95 characters that will sell your site to the world. (I told you that this might not be an easy task.) You must also supply your Web site or eBay Store URL.

3. **Select your keywords.**

Write out your keywords and key phrases in the box provided. You can use Google's Keyword Suggestion tool to help you out. Since this is your initial pass and won't be etched in granite, take some wild stabs and see what happens.

4. **Choose you maximum CPC (cost-per-click) and then press *Calculate Estimates*.**

Here's where the sticker shock gets you. The data in front of you will let you know which keywords you can afford to keep and which ones must be discarded. If you want to change your CPC amount, do so and press Recalculate Estimates. The Traffic Estimator calculates how much, on average, you'll end up spending in a day.

5. **Specify your daily budget.**

There will be a prefilled in amount that would ensure your ad stays on top and gets full exposure every day. No Mr. Google, I do not want to spend $50 a day on my keywords. Set a cap on your budget and Google will never exceed it. You may make it as low as you wish, there's no minimum spending amount.

6. **Enter your e-mail address and agree to terms.**

After you verify your e-mail address, you can put in your billing information and you'll be minutes away from your ads going live on the Google index.

Interestingly, your ads may also appear on other places on the Internet through Google's Webmaster's program. Take a look at Figure 55-7; my ad ended up on my book's listing page on Amazon since one of my key phrases is *eBay For Dummies* (and my targeting is considered relevant).

Customers interested in eBay for Dummies may also be interested in:
Sponsored Links (What's this?) Feedback

• Cool eBay Tools
eBay For Dummies author's tips Marsha Collier's Free newsletter
www.coolebaytools.com

• **Figure 55-7: My AdWords campaign on Amazon.**

Technique 56

Bonding Your Sales: Raising Bids and GSM

Save Time By
- ✔ Learning about bonding
- ✔ Bonding your eBay sales

When it comes to high-dollar transactions on eBay, in the past the only thing a seller could do to provide security for the buyer was to throw in an escrow. Escrow is a great way to protect the buyer, but it ties up the seller's money for considerably longer than necessary. The best legitimate company currently for escrow on eBay is escrow.com.

Lately, there have been many scandals in the online escrow arena. Fraudsters have put up bogus Web sites, offered expensive items for sale online, and then run the escrow through their bogus site. The buyer, thinking everything to be legit, sends their money. After the money arrives, however, the Web site is taken down and the bad guys make off with the loot.

There's even a Web site called www.sos4auctions.com. They have a database of fraudulent escrow Web sites and a discussion area where people discuss and report ongoing frauds. Escrow has gotten a bad reputation with buyers. As a matter of fact, the issue is so serious that if you go to the escrow.com Web site area (at https://escrow.com/fic/), you'll find a very helpful zone about how to recognize escrow fraud.

There's finally a viable alternative to escrow, something that will make the customer feel good about spending buckets of money on your site: Bonding. It's all about potato chips, beer, and Monday Night Football. No, wait, that's *male* bonding. The bonding I'm talking about here refers to guaranteeing that a seller will perform *as advertised*.

Bonding isn't just for high-dollar transactions, either. Originally I was thinking this was good just for expensive items, but not so! I've heard from small-time sellers that their total number of bids and their final selling price increased by one-third after bonding *all* their items with the buySAFE seal (even the $5 sales!).

Learning About Bonding

I'm sure you've heard about bonding. In ads on TV maybe you've heard that a contractor is "licensed and bonded." On large projects in the entertainment or graphic design business, the person doing the job might be bonded to guarantee that the job will be completed on time. A *bond* warrants that the person (or business) performing the task will complete their part of the deal as contracted.

 A bond is *not* insurance. Insurance assumes that a loss is a possibility. When there is a bond, it guarantees that a buyer will not suffer a financial loss.

There's a new company, buySAFE, (an eBay certified developer), who has come up with a traditional bonding plan exclusively for eBay sellers. buySAFE procures surety bonds through The Hartford Financial Services Group (they've been around for 193 years and are one of America's largest financial services provider) to bond eBay sellers' transactions.

The bond provides that The Hartford will refund the item sale price or replace the item in the event the seller does not perform as promised in the item listing.

The bond can protect buyers when:

✔ The bonded seller fails to deliver the item.

✔ The seller delivers an item different from the one described and pictured in the item listing.

✔ The seller offers a return or refund policy but refuses to honor it.

✔ The seller fails to use the shipping method as described in the item listing and the item arrives damaged (as when the buyer pays for insurance but the seller fails to insure the package).

✔ The seller refuses to follow the payment policy described in the item listing.

✔ The seller experiences financial setbacks and does not fulfill the conditions of the sale.

A bond basically guarantees that the seller will perform, period. Bonding your auctions tells your prospective bidders that you care about the buyer, and that you're a professional seller. This assurance easily can translate into more bids and higher final selling prices.

The best part? The seller receives their money through regular channels and doesn't have to ship the item until paid. No waiting around for weeks to get your money, because, as is the case with an escrow, you're at the mercy of the system.

When one of your items is bonded, it displays a seal (as shown in Figure 56-1). If the prospective buyer clicks on it, they will see the details of what the seal represents.

• **Figure 56-1: This item is bonded!**

Seller Bonding on eBay

You may be wondering if it's some sort of big deal to get your items bonded on eBay. Not really. Here's how it works.

Your auctions can get bonded up to a total maximum of a prescribed dollar amount. The total amount of bonded auctions cannot exceed this figure. Think of the maximum like a line of credit, you can only draw against it until you've maxed out your line.

To become bonded, you must meet at least some minimum requirements:

✔ $1,000 a month in eBay sales

✔ 100 eBay feedback rating

✔ 98 percent positive eBay feedback

✔ Your eBay business is based in the United States (but not in the state of Hawaii)

If you fulfill those requirements, you then need to fill out a form on the buySAFE Web site, which will ask you information about yourself and your business. After applying, you undergo a thorough qualification process, which evaluates your online sales experience and reputation; verifies your identity; and analyzes your financial stability. Then you must also legally commit to either honoring their terms of sale or repaying any losses that they cause.

 Yes, you may have great feedback, but bonding is not about the people who are already buying from you — the point is to attract new buyers with a signal that *proves* you're professional and rock solid.

Bonding items

After you receive approval and know your total bonding amount (based on how you were qualified), you may choose which of your auctions to bond and which not to bond.

The auctions you choose to bond cost you 1 percent of the final selling price. You pay nothing in advance, and there's no hidden fees or commitments. You also don't have to pay if a bonded item doesn't sell. With this plan there's *no* minimum fee either. If the bonded item sells for $3 (shipping, handling fees, and taxes are not included in the bonded total) your fee will be $.03.

Take a look at Figure 56-2 to see a sample Bonded Seller's Log In page at buySAFE. Here, at a glance, you can see any of your items that aren't yet bonded as well as your total bonding limit, bonds outstanding (bonds on a sold item are kept open for 30 days), and the total of your bonded transactions.

Note that there's also Live Help, should you have a question during business hours.

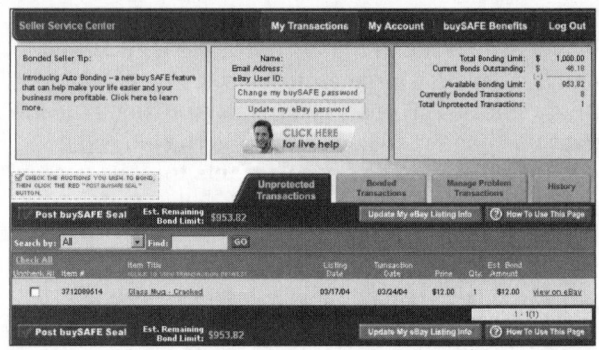

• **Figure 56-2: buySAFE Seller Services area.**

To take a look at your bonded transactions, click the tab to go to that page as in Figure 56-3. Here you can see any open items with bonds and view any problems that may have arisen.

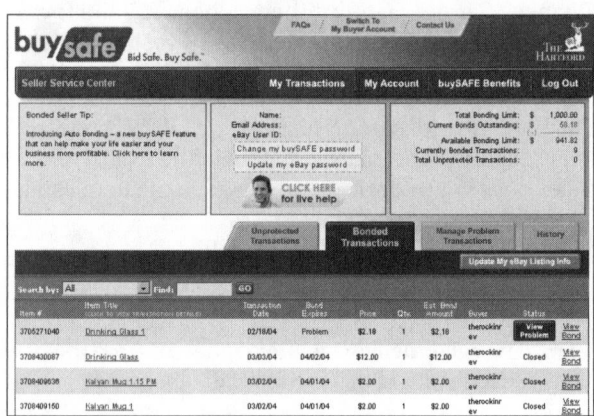

• **Figure 56-3: Your Bonded Transactions.**

If you click the item title, you can see the details of an open auction, as shown in Figure 56-4.

• **Figure 56-4: Details of an open auction.**

What happens when something goes wrong?

When a buyer feels slighted in a transaction, that customer is still yours to solve the problem with. If unhappy buyers contact buySAFE, they will be sent directly back to you.

If, for some reason, they still insist they need help resolving the issue, they may fill in a Problem Transaction report on the buySAFE Web site, stating the problem and saying what the seller can do to resolve the issue. This will appear on your Seller Services page; you will see a red button that reads View Problem, indicating a problem. By clicking the button, you'll come to the Problem Summary page (as shown in Figure 56-5).

You can see the buyer's comments when you click the Problem bar, as shown in Figure 56-5.

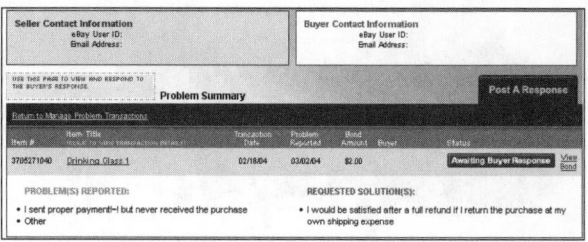

• **Figure 56-5: See the status of a transaction's problem.**

An e-mail is sent to you, and your response is recorded. If, after two e-mail exchanges pass, nothing has been solved, a professional mediator (a claims representative) joins in to solve the problem.

There is no charge for the mediation. The mediator may contact both the buyer and seller via phone to get both sides of the story. A bond from a surety company, such as The Hartford, has a legal obligation to protect both parties. It *protects the seller from false allegations* and the buyer from losing their money.

If no compromise is made, the mediator will make a binding decision, based on the evidence provided, in favor of one party or the other.

The Hartford is *regulated* by each state's Insurance Department and is held accountable by them for adequately investigating each claim. Bonding is the only licensed and regulated form of seller guarantee.

Bonding, as I have said, may be new to eBay, but it's proved successful with many of the sellers who have tried it. If you'd like to give it a whirl, go to www.buysafe.com/coolebaytools and you'll get a special introductory offer.

57 Technique

Flying Your Banner on eBay

Save Time By

- ✔ Bidding for click-throughs
- ✔ Designing a banner to rival the big guys
- ✔ Setting up your banner with eBay

Sitting on your hands doing nothing is no way to increase business, but checking out every available opportunity is. While browsing on eBay, I noticed banner ads at the top of the Search pages. What surprised me most was that the banners did not always advertise some huge, mega-corporation like Home and Garden TV, Toyota, or Stanley Tools — but instead, they highlighted little guys with eBay stores like mine!

Just as I assumed that these banner ads were reserved for the high and mighty, I also assumed that they must be very expensive. But they're quite reasonable and easily within the eBay seller's budget! Remember this is "advertising." It's something the big guy will never go without. So eBay opened the floodgates for eBay sellers to promote their items to eBay buyers right on the site.

These banners, just as with Google AdWords, are based on keyword searches, and link to your eBay store (or to particular items in your store). The name of the game here is *click-throughs*. How many people can you get to click your banner and buy your goods? Read this technique and find out how easy it is to become a "big guy" with your banner flying on eBay.

Getting the Click-Throughs

Probably close to a hundred million people use eBay's search engine every day — and hope the search terms they use help them find the goods they want. When you have listings in the same genre that the search terms describe, your items get matched with the search. But even better, you can direct searchers to your listings by paying eBay to display your advertising banner at the top of the matching search page.

This magic is performed with keywords — the same keywords that I discuss in Technique 14. This type of advertising works out financially only if you're selling several items that fall under the same group of keywords. For example, suppose you have several related items with keywords such as For Dummies. Your ad is served to the eBay page in response to search terms such as *eBay Timesaving Techniques For Dummies* that match your keywords or keyword phrases.

eBay's adMarketplace (which controls the banner ads) is a cost-per-click network, just as is Google AdWords (see Technique 55). But placing a banner ad for eBay keyword advertising isn't as expensive as you might think:

✔ You pay nothing for the banner to appear. Remember, you pay only if your ad gets clicked.

✔ You control how much you pay for a banner chick-through by placing a bid on the amount you want to pay.

 Here's the trick to keyword advertising. Those who bid the highest tend to have their ads prioritized first. So the higher your bid for the ad, the higher you're ranked in the ad rotation for the specified keywords. This means that your banner ad will potentially appear on the search results page more often than will the ad for your competitor who bid less.

Bidding for placement starts at $.10, and increases by increments of 1 cent. In the section, "Setting Up Your Banner Campaign," I show you how the bidding works.

Making Your Banner

So that you don't put the cart before the horse, it's best to decide what you would like your banner to say to potential buyers.

 If you're spending time and money on a banner ad, make sure you target a specific item. A general banner relaying only the message "Shop from Me" isn't going to get you a lot of clicks. A specific banner telling readers that you offer "The Wildest Widgets on the Web" has a better chance of getting a little mouse action. The whole idea of the campaign is to get people to click your banner and thereby find your sales.

On a sheet of paper, write down all the words you can think of that relate to your item. Also, do you have an image you'd like in the banner? Pull together all the resources you have so you can decide on your banner's look as well. With everything assembled, you can start reviewing the options for creating your banner.

Making your own

eBay's keyword advertising program has a simple online tool for creating banners, and I'm sure you've seen the resulting banners on eBay. They all look much the same and thereby lack a polished, professional image. If you're trying to develop your own "brand" and be in business for real, you need to create a custom banner.

If you're one of those creative sorts and have some extra time, you can easily create your own custom banner. (For some people, designing a banner would be a relaxing time!) There are plenty of graphics programs that will do the trick.

 If you're looking for a graphics program to try your hand at banner making, consider Corel R.A.V.E. This program is very reasonably priced, and you can get a super deal on eBay.

Finding someone to make it

When you don't have the time or inclination to sit down and design your own banner, getting a custom banner designed for you needn't be an expensive proposition.

Plenty of sharp graphic designers sell custom designed banners on eBay. These designers work from the information you assembled and produce a banner within a few days, so it's not long before you can start your campaign.

All you have to do is search the eBay site (see the upcoming search term list) and take a look at the designers' listings. See which artist creates the type of banners you like. Be sure you're happy with his or her terms of sale (but I don't think I really have to tell *you* that!) and verify that the artist's time schedule will meet yours. Of course, read the feedback. On a graphic artist's work, the feedback will be especially telling. Here are some search terms to use.

- ✔ animated banner
- ✔ eBay banner
- ✔ banner design

Designing to eBay style

Banner graphics are designed in many different sizes (yes, I know they all look the same, but they're not). Whether you're designing your own or contracting with a designer, be sure to match these specifications:

- ✔ **Banner Size:** 468 × 60 pixels.
- ✔ **Format:** GIF.
- ✔ **Animation:** No aggressive animation. It should not be excessively fast, long, or strobe-like. (These traits make for an annoying, unproductive banner anyway!)
- ✔ **Maximum file size:** 12 KB.
- ✔ **Border:** Must be non-white.
- ✔ **Banner text:** Must be relevant to what you're selling. No keyword spamming! Banner text also may not contain phone numbers, URLs or e-mail information.

Setting Up Your Banner Campaign

When you go to set up your campaign, be prepared with some keywords. The keywords you use for your advertising need not be as precise as the keywords you use to search on eBay. Actually, your preliminary keyword list can be more hit and miss. After

your program starts, you'll be able to see which searches net you the most hits. Write down all possible keywords that might possibly relate to your item; you're allowed a long list. Later in the section ("Targeting with keywords and phrases"), I show you how to narrow it down.

Keep to these guidelines when making up your list:

- ✔ **Use "key phrases" versus keywords.** Key phrases can be made up of two or three words, like "Craftsman hammer" or "eBay For Dummies." By using multiple word key phrases, your banner ad can achieve a closer match to the prospective buyer's search.
- ✔ **Be sure the keywords relate to your item.**
- ✔ **Avoid overused and over-general keywords.** eBay will reject your keywords if you choose to use the ever-popular title words; *Wow, Cool, Super, Nice,* or *New.*
- ✔ **Don't use apostrophes, special characters or repeated periods.**

Signing up

To get moving with your campaign, click the Service link on the eBay navigation bar and scroll down the page to the Advanced Seller Recommendations area. Click the Keywords on eBay link. Alternatively, you can go directly to www.eBayKeywords.com.

 Scout around the page you land on and look for any *First-Time User* or *Introductory* discount. I always hate it when I sign up for something and *later* find out I could have gotten a discount! They just may have a discount that will cover the cost of your first ad flight!

After you've secured any discount or promo code, click the New Users button and enter the site. You'll need to go through several steps to begin your campaign ad, as shown in Figure 57-1.

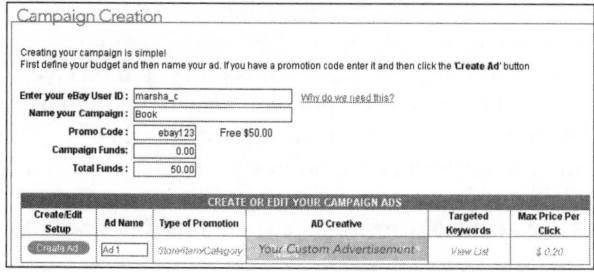

• **Figure 57-1: The beginnings of your Campaign Creation.**

1. **Type your eBay User ID as prompted.**

This is how the eBay Keywords people can match you up with your listings or your eBay store.

2. **Type the promotional code you found on the front page in the Promo Code box.**

If you found a promo code, a dollar amount automatically appears in the Total Funds text box. If you didn't find one, go to the next step and invest as little cash as you want.

3. **Type the amount you want to invest in your banner campaign in the Campaign Funds box.**

4. **Click Create Ad to get going!**

 You can pause your campaign anytime you want and pick it up again when you want. You can also change your banner at any time during the campaign.

Playing the links

In the Create New Campaign screen, you choose where your banner ad takes potential buyers when they click it. Figure 57-2 shows your choices. Click the appropriate link if you want your banner to link to:

✔ **My Store:** This will link to your eBay Store.

✔ **Store Category:** A category you've set up in your store.

✔ **Search Within Your Store:** This sets up a link that will search for preset search terms in your store.

✔ **All Items List:** This links to a list of all your items, as they appear when a Seller Search is performed.

✔ **Items List:** This will set up a link to a particular item that you sell.

✔ **Selected Link:** You may also insert a link of your choice, as long as it links to your eBay items.

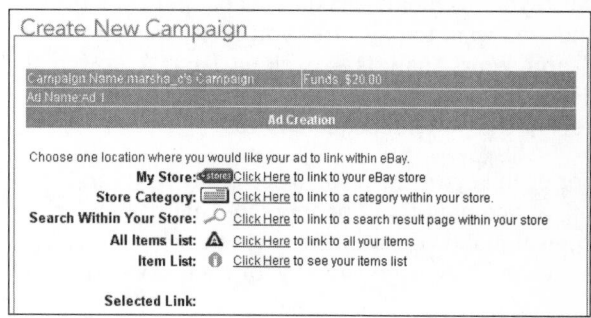

• **Figure 57-2: Selecting your link.**

Targeting with keywords and phrases

Next, you type your keyword (or key phrase) list. Figure 57-3 shows you a keyword list for a banner campaign for my books. You may also upload a CSV text file, but why bother? Just cut and paste from your list, separating each word or phrase by a comma.

• **Figure 57-3: Inputting my keywords.**

When you're finished typing, click Submit. Your keywords are uploaded and reviewed for "editorial correctness." Click OK when you see the confirmation screen and continue to a fully populated keyword page.

Bidding for exposure

Next, you decide the maximum cost per click (CPC) that you want to pay. After you click Proceed to Search Word Analysis — exciting, isn't it? Wow, real analysis! — you can enter your maximum bid and review the potential effectiveness.

For each keyword, you also see teeny tiny versions of your competition's banners for that particular keyword, and you see how much they bid. You may adjust your bids individually for each keyword.

 The higher bid amount gets viewing priority, so if a keyword is especially important to you, you might want to up your bid. Just remember to click `Calculate Ranking` to evaluate your changes at each step.

 You don't always have to be in the number one (highest bidder) slot. I'm ranked number 3 for one of my keywords. It's a very popular one, and my little banner still gets close to 15,000 views per month. Remember that a zillion people are browsing eBay. You're charged only when they click your banner. Holding the number one for all your keywords, that will burn up your budget in a hurry!

Bidding is handled as with eBay auctions, on a proxy basis. Even if you select $.20 as your high bid, eBay keywords will increase your bid by only enough to put you $.01 ahead of the competition.

 You will not always be paying the maximum you bid per click — just enough to outbid the competition. eBay Keywords will let you know about your ranking as you indicate your bid.

Each time a user clicks your banner, the bid amount is deducted from your campaign fund. When the campaign money runs out, you'll receive an e-mail notifying you that you need to add funds. You may also choose an auto-renew option, but that can easily get away from you. If you're like me, you like to know how much you're spending and want to control when things are charged to your account.

If a particular budget gets used up too quickly, consider waiting a week or so before infusing more money. That is, of course, unless your sales are going through the roof, and then the expenditure is well worth the cost.

I can honestly say that several keyword campaigns that I've used (and am using) have successfully worked to increase my sales.

Uploading your banner

Uploading your banner is the easiest part of this long process. When you arrive at the screen that specifies the banner size, follow these steps:

1. **Click the Browse button to find the GIF file that is your banner on your computer's hard drive.**

2. **Click the file, and your banner appears in the box on the screen.**

3. **Click the Proceed to banner upload link.**

   Your banner is uploaded to the Keywords server.

Now all you have to do is view your campaign summary. When you're done, your keywords will be marked with a red *Pending approval*. Don't have a cow; this usually takes less than a day to be cleared. If the keywords are not approved for any reason, you'll receive an e-mail explaining why.

Paying for your campaign

Paying for your banner ad campaign is also easy. If you've entered a promotion code, you have nothing to pay. But when you have to ante up, eBay accepts all credit cards as well as PayPal.

I recommend you use the credit card you have set aside for your eBay business. The charge will clearly show up on your credit card bill as eBay Keywords advertising. If you allow eBay to debit your PayPal account instead, there's a chance it can cause problems with keeping track of your accounting. (See Techniques 47 and 48 for more about keeping your accounting records intact.)

Co-oping with eBay to Lower Advertising Costs

Technique 58

Save Time By

- ✔ Checking out co-op advertising
- ✔ Placing your ads
- ✔ Getting your money from eBay

When you consider placing advertising for your business, budget is always an issue. This is the case whether you're in a brick-and-mortar store, on your own Web site, or selling on eBay. When I was in the advertising business, one of the biggest challenges we had was convincing a startup to spend money on advertising. It's simple arithmetic; you spend money on advertising, and it attracts more people to your store. When you've got a prospective customer's attention, it's up to you to close the sale.

The ace-in-the-hole for any retailer is *co-op advertising,* which puts advertising dollars contributed by a manufacturer (or other interested party) into the company's advertising campaign. The manufacturer benefits by getting its name out to potential buyers, and the retailer attracts more buyers (and ideally increases sales revenue) by more vigorously advertising the manufacturer's product.

Many manufacturers have co-op advertising programs available based on the dollar amount that the retailer purchases from them. Even if you buy your merchandise for eBay sales from a wholesaler instead of the manufacturer, you may still be able to share some of the co-op funds available to your wholesaler. Just ask — the worst you'll hear is "No," and maybe your wholesaler will say "Absolutely!"

Because sharing the advertising costs is such a good idea, I wrote this technique to tell you how to co-op with eBay. And once you have the co-op advertising dollars, where do you spend them? Almost any traditional media will do, but in the case of eBay, print media is the target. You can get co-op advertising dollars if you advertise in your local newspapers, magazines, catalogs, specialty collectors' publications, or any publication with a circulation figure of 10,000 or more. As a coin collector, I've noticed several eBay co-op ads in my monthly coin magazine, and I've seen these ads in other publications, too. Sound like a good deal? In this technique, I give you some hints on finding the right places for advertising your business.

Getting In on the Gold

What could be better than advertising your business and having someone else help pay for it? To get your little mitts on some of eBay's co-op cash stash, you must qualify by being one of the following:

- ✔ **An eBay PowerSeller who operates an eBay store:** This is almost a given. If you're a PowerSeller, you no doubt already have an eBay store.

- ✔ **An eBay PowerSeller who is a registered Trading Assistant:** Again, if you're a PowerSeller, I don't doubt that you've sold items for others in the past. If you're not a registered Trading Assistant, check Technique 43 for more info.

I think you've noticed the constant in this list. You have to be a PowerSeller to qualify for the co-op dollars. And if you think about it — this requirement makes sense. eBay would logically choose to put this kind of investment into those sellers with experience selling on the site and with a high GMS (Gross Merchandise Sales). For qualifications and direction on becoming a PowerSeller, see Technique 42.

How much will eBay pay?

eBay will pay up to 25 percent of your advertising bill as long as your ad has been approved before printing. You can get an extra discount through some publications, which smartly court eBay PowerSeller advertising. These publications are members of eBay's Preferred Publisher Program. Table 58-1 gives you a current list.

These discounts are in addition to your 25-percent eBay reimbursement. In some cases you can save 50 percent off the price of an ad. To check to see if more publications have joined eBay's Preferred Publisher program, visit www.ebaycoopadvertising. com/preferredpublisher.aspx.

 When approaching any publication for advertising, don't forget to ask for a discount. Discounts are available to many people for many reasons, and perhaps you can tailor your ad (a certain size or theme) to get the deal. Maybe you'll get one, maybe you won't. Just be sure to ask.

eBay gives sellers a budget, and that budget is based on your PowerSeller level (which is based on your GMS). The budget renews ever calendar quarter, and you can only spend to the limit assigned to your level within one quarter. Amounts that are not used *cannot* be carried over to the next quarter. Table 58-2 shows you the reimbursement budgets.

TABLE 58-1: PREFERRED PUBLISHERS THAT GIVE DISCOUNTS TO EBAY POWERSELLERS

Publication Name	URL	Discount Off Advertising Rates
AntiqueWeek	www.antiqueweek.com/eBay_pp.html	10 percent
AntiqueWest	www.antiqueweek.com/eBay_pp.html	10 percent
Collector Editions Magazine	www.collector-editions.com/PowerSellersCE.html	25 percent off ¼ page or smaller
Collector's News	www.collectors-news.com/PowerSellersCN.html	25 percent off ¼ page or larger
Southeastern Antiquing & Collecting	www.go-star.com/antiquing/ebaydiscount.htm	10 percent

TABLE 58-2: CO-OP ADVERTISING QUARTERLY BUDGETS

PowerSeller Level	Maximum Quarterly Reimbursement
Bronze	$500
Silver	$800
Gold	$1,200
Platinum	$3,000
Titanium	$8,000

How do you get your money?

Claims for reimbursement may be submitted to eBay at any time during the time your ad runs, but must be received no later than 60 days after the initial insertion date.

As long as your claim is qualified (you have to get it approved before you run the ad), you'll be paid via PayPal within 45 days of eBay's receipt of your claim.

By now I'll bet you're convinced that this is a good deal, and if you're qualified, why not sign up now? To get your piece of the pie, here's the condensed version of the procedure:

1. Go to www.ebaycoopadvertising.com and click the key to Register.

2. After you've registered, click the link for the Ad Creation Wizard to get your template set up.

3. Upload your ad for pre-approval. When it's approved you will receive a Pre-Approval Authorization Number.

4. Run your ad.

5. Once the ad appears, go to www.ebaycoop advertising.com/Common/ReimbursementForm.pdf and print out the reimbursement form.

6. Put the following documentation into one envelope:

   ▶ Your completed reimbursement form

   ▶ A full tearsheet from the publication running your ad (the entire page, not just a cut-out of your ad)

▶ A copy of the invoice from the publisher

▶ The publication's rate card stating confirmed circulation of 10,000 or more

7. Mail the whole shebang to the address at the bottom of the reimbursement form.

Advertising Basics: Choosing Where to Run Your Ad

Here's another reason why I say, "Know what you sell." If you're selling collectible coins, you know which trade (or special interest) publications you like to read. Why don't you give those a shot first?

If you're not really sure, or perhaps you'd like to see what other publications are available, go over to Google and search the words *magazine, publication,* and *news* along with the keyword that describes the items you sell.

When you go to your chosen publication's Web site, check it out: Find the link that goes to the advertising department and read the information.

 Planning an ad campaign should be done several months in advance of when you'd like the ads to appear. Many publications have a long lead-time between booking and final publishing.

Following are a few more tips about advertising your business that you can take to heart:

✔ **Preview the publication:** If you've never seen the publication before, e-mail (or call the 800 number) and ask for a sample along with the rate card. They'll be more than willing to send you a back issue!

After you get a copy of the magazine, newspaper, or whatever, take a hard look at it and answer these questions: Would people that read this publication be likely to shop at your eBay store?

Do you like the magazine? Does it fit your perception of your customers' lifestyles? Do the advertisers seem legitimate?

✔ **Check out the ad rates:** With publications, cheap doesn't always mean best. Figure out what your cost per thousand readers will be and keep that in mind. When the ad runs, use your eBay statistics (more about getting stats from eBay in Technique 14) to see how much of an increase you get in visitors.

✔ **Consider running your ad more than once:** A one-time ad rarely pulls enough to pay for itself. A consistent advertising campaign of repeated ads (even every other issue) will get the attention of the publication's readership and build confidence in you and increase visits to your store. A consistent campaign works much better than scattered ads here and there with no direction.

✔ **Start out small with a single publication:** That will make it easier for you to track the success of your campaign.

eBay maintains a list of qualified newspapers and magazines. It's a rather long and ever-changing list, so go to `www.ebaycoopadvertising.com/QualifiedPublisher.aspx` for the most up-to-date list.

Creating Your Ad

Because these ads have to be approved by eBay, it might behoove you to follow the distinctive guidelines. There are rules as to which logos you can use, as well as in what size and color they can appear.

If you choose to use eBay's online Ad Creation Wizard, it has templates in different sizes — as well as themed templates for eBay Stores or Trading Assistants.

Figure 58-1 shows an ad I've started designing with the Ad Creation Wizard. You can select from different typefaces, sizes, and colors for each area of your ad.

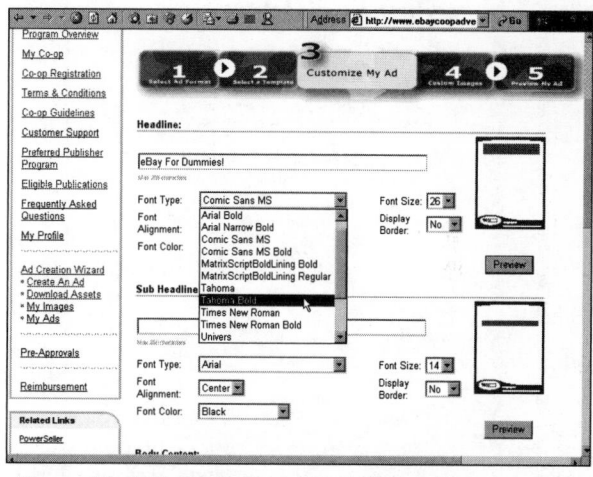

• **Figure 58-1: Designing an ad in the Wizard.**

The only problem I have with the wizard is that it's not very flexible. For example, it doesn't allow you to vary your type size within an area, and you can't make bulleted lists or italics. Still, the wizard works quickly, and within a few minutes, I put together the ad in Figure 58-2.

But since business is business, if you have the talent, you should take some time and download the templates and logos from the `Download Assets` area and create an ad that suits your style.

 When designing your own ad, remember: The eBay portion must occupy at least ⅛ of the overall ad size to be eligible for reimbursement.

• **Figure 58-2:** My quick-and-easy (but not too attractive) Ad Creation Wizard ad.

To be sure that your ad will qualify for reimbursement under the co-op advertising plan, be sure to upload an electronic copy of it through the My Ads area. After you upload it, you simply click the Submit button to submit the ad for approval. Along with your ad approval, you receive your Pre-Approval Authorization Number. The length of time for which this number is active depends on the ad itself:

- ✔ If you design your ad with eBay's Ad Creation Wizard, you can continue to use the same Pre-Approval Authorization Number until eBay redesigns the templates. When a template redesign happens, eBay lets you know by e-mail.

- ✔ If you design the ad yourself, the number expires within 90 days. After that, you need to resubmit the ad and get a new Pre-Approval Authorization Number.

All your approved ads will be held (with details of approval) in an area called My Pre-Approvals on the www.ebaycoopadvertising.com site.

Part X

The Scary (or Fun) Stuff

The 5th Wave

By Rich Tennant

"Found it on eBay under Space Toys. Took it forever to get here—and now I can't find its little astronaut."

Technique 59

Raising Money for Your Favorite Charity

Save Time By

- Finding out about eBay Giving Works
- Shopping for charity
- Raising money for your favorite charity

One of my favorite places to shop on eBay is the Charity area. Charities as small as the local pet rescue and as large as the National Multiple Sclerosis Society run auctions for super items to raise money for their good works.

When charities receive donations of merchandise rather than cash, the merchandise is called *gifts-in-kind*. Many manufacturers donate excess inventory to charities for a full-value tax deduction. The charity can either use the merchandise in their charitable works or sell the items to raise money. (You mean you've *never* shopped at the Salvation Army store?) In the past, charities had to rent retail locations to turn their gifts-in-kind into cash. Now they've got eBay; and eBay supplies the Giving Works area for all qualified charities.

 All groups that run auctions in the eBay Charity area are registered charities. When you have a hankering for unique items, consider buying them from the charity auctions on eBay where your money will do good.

This technique tells you not only how to shop the charity auctions, but also how to take advantage of eBay's programs for your favorite charity. Also, you find out about the opportunities for individual sellers to participate in the fund raising by donating proceeds from their own auctions to qualified charities on eBay.

Finding Out About Giving Works

Are you involved in a charitable organization that you'd like to raise money for? If you think your organization is too small, think again. Perhaps you just want to sell an item to benefit your favorite charity; you can do that, too. If you're a larger charity and you don't think you have enough people to handle the sales — eBay has a program that can help you!

The formal Giving Works area was launched in November, 2003, and within the first month had signed up over 2000 nonprofits. eBay ran charity auctions prior to the launching of Giving Works, but these auctions were mostly for high profile organizations with an IRS 501 (c) (3) designation.

eBay Giving Works is now open to *any* IRS-approved nonprofit. This could include your high school band booster club, local volunteer fire fighters, or cat rescue organization.

Fishing for donations

eBay has partnered with MissionFish, an organization based in Washington, D.C., that has been raising money through online auctions since 2000. They're a forward-thinking, great group of people who founded this company with the purpose of doing good for others. Now, MissionFish is a service of the Points of Light Foundation and operates their Web site at www.missionfish.org.

MissionFish operates as the hub for nonprofits selling on eBay. They qualify the nonprofits, by verifying their eligibility before they can begin to raise money online with eBay. Aside from verification they also provide other service and support activities including donation collection and disbursement, tax receipting, and online contribution tracking.

Starting Small and Buying

Suppose you enjoy visiting eBay and would like to buy items from a charity. (I do this all the time.) Your first stop should be the eBay Home page where you scroll down past the long list of categories to the Charity link at the bottom. Click this link and you arrive at the Giving Works hub page shown in Figure 59-1. Should things (like link names or locations) change at eBay (and they often do), you can always access the eBay nonprofit area directly at

www.ebay.com/givingworks

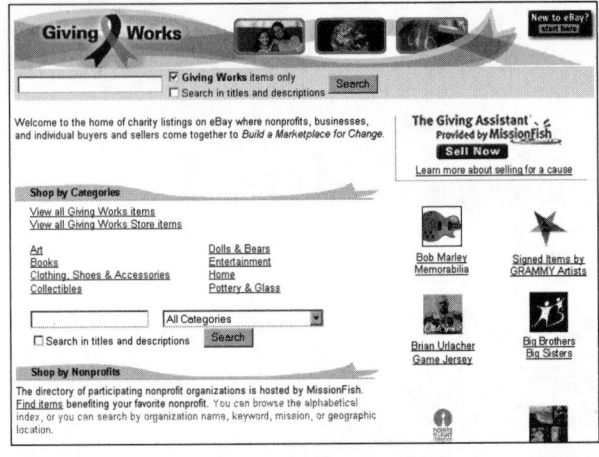

• **Figure 59-1: The eBay Giving Works hub page.**

To browse all items being sold to benefit nonprofits, click the link View All Giving Works Items. There will also be nonprofit items listed in eBay store, so to view them click the link View All Giving Works Store Items.

You may also search Giving Works items with the search box on the top of the page — although I find that browsing charity auctions is more fun — you just might find something you didn't even know you needed!

When you arrive at the item page, above the item description, you'll find the MissionFish information box, similar to the one shown in Figure 59-2, which indicates what percent of the auction proceeds are donated and the name of the receiving charity.

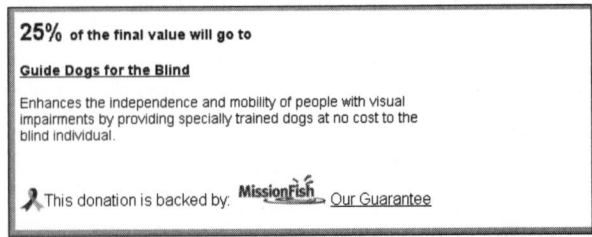

• **Figure 59-2: Charitable information on the item page.**

Also on the Giving Works page you find a postage stamp icon of featured charitable auctions. These icons generally signal major promotions for a particular nonprofit, with many auctions running at once.

Raising Money for the Little Guy

If you're currently an eBay seller, and you'd like to sell some items to benefit a nonprofit, eBay will do most of the work for you. You must select a nonprofit from the directory (shown in Figure 59-3) and you can contribute from 10 percent to 100 percent of the final bid at the end of the auction.

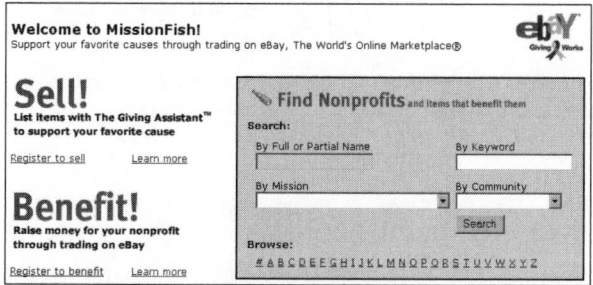

• **Figure 59-3: The Nonprofit directory.**

After an item is sold, it's your job to collect the money from the buyer and to ship the item. You'll receive an e-mail confirming the dollar amount of the final sales price and the percentage that you agreed to donate. After you verify these figures, MissionFish charges your credit card for that amount.

MissionFish sends your donation to the nonprofit, and you receive a receipt for your contribution.

To participate in the program, you must register at MissionFish. Go to the Web site at

    www.missionfish.org

and click the Seller Registration link.

1. **Type your eBay User ID and password and click Continue.**

   After MissionFish confirms that you are registered at eBay, you proceed to the next page (a SLL secure connection), which is populated with your mailing address from eBay's records.

2. **Check over your information and correct it if necessary.**

3. **Type your credit card information.**

   This information is used to send the money to your selected nonprofit when your auction is over.

4. **Create a MissionFish user ID and password for accessing your information at MissionFish. (I used my eBay User ID.)**

Now you're ready to sell. See if your chosen nonprofit is listed in the directory, by typing in their name — or keywords relating to the charity. You can also find a nonprofit by browsing through the alphabetic directory.

Select your nonprofit and then listing your item is the same as listing any other item on eBay — only this time you'll have a Giving Works gold and blue ribbon next to your item title (indicating to the eBay community that your auction is for a nonprofit).

Getting Your Nonprofit on the List

If you are involved in a small organization that's not listed in the Giving Works directory, it's easy for you to become listed. And after your organization appears in the directory, any eBay member can select it to receive auction proceeds.

 Whenever an eBay member chooses your nonprofit for an auction, you have the opportunity to accept or decline the beneficial listing.

From the MissionFish home page, click the For Non Profits link. From there you may register your organization to participate. You must have a few things ready, including a fax machine to get the required documentation to MissionFish:

✔ Contact Information (in case they need to call you).

✔ The nonprofit's Federal Employees Number (EIN).

✔ A copy of the logo in GIF or JPG format, with a maximum size of 50KB.

✔ Your prepared Mission Statement in about 40 words (512 characters maximum).

✔ A copy of your nonprofit status letter.

✔ A voided organization check with authorized signature (to verify your banking information for deposits).

✔ Web site information. If you have a Web site, supply the URL, so that a link can be made from beneficial eBay listings to your Web site.

✔ Acceptance setting. You'll have to indicate what's best for you:

▶ **Accept all, don't notify me.** This means that anytime anyone selects you as a benefiting nonprofit, the item will go up for sale on eBay without prior authorization from you. You will still be able to view all items you are benefiting from in your my MissionFish account.

▶ **Notify me, one-day auto accept.** You'll be notified by e-mail every time someone wants to list an item for you. If you don't approve or disapprove within one business day, the listing will go live automatically.

▶ **Notify me, one-day auto decline.** You'll receive an e-mail notifying you of someone's intent. If you don't approve or decline within one business day, the item will be declined automatically.

Check out Table 59-1 for the timeline of activities for running a Giving Works auction on eBay.

TABLE 59-1: TIMELINE FOR A GIVING WORKS AUCTION

Action	Time Interval
Nonprofit accepts or declines item	1 business day after the item is listed (1 to 3 days is the usual reality)
Listing on eBay	3, 5, 7 or 10 days, depending on the selling format
Seller pays donation	1 to 7 days after listing ends
Donation is automatically collected	2nd Monday after listing ends (from 8 to 13 days)
Refund request period	Until the end of the month when the listing ends, plus one month and 15 days
Donation delivered to the nonprofit; tax receipt available to the seller	End of the month when the listing ends, plus one month, plus 20 days.

Planning a big auction?

If you're with a charitable organization and you'd like to plan a really big auction, you may not want to handle all the details yourself. You want to get the highest prices for your items, and when the bidding gets into the thousands per item, getting help from someone who knows the ropes can really help.

Kompolt & Company, an auction management agency founded by two marketing wizards, Jenny Kompolt and Melissa James, runs some of the top auctions on eBay for nonprofits. They've run charitable auctions for The Today Show, The Grammys, Lifetime Television, British Airways, Bon Jovi and Britney Spears (just to drop a few names). Their client list is a who's who in the giving community.

They handle everything for the charity including: registration, pricing strategies, photography, custom design of the listing pages (as well as the About Me page), bidder pre-qualification (payment assurance and protection against bogus or fraudulent bidding), payment collection and item fulfillment, and full closing reports and analysis.

Check out their Web site at www.kompolt.com.

 There are no additional fees when a nonprofit sells direct (other than eBay listing and Final Value Fees). But when an eBay seller sells on behalf of a non-profit, there is a $3.00 MissionFish transaction fee and a 2.9% (of the donation) credit card fee. The seller also has to pay eBay standard fees.

Technique 60

Organizing with Auction Management Tools

Save Time By

✔ Evaluating your activity level

✔ Deciding among the available tools

✔ Managing your listings with software

✔ Checking out auction management services

When you get to the point of running 20 or so auctions a week, I highly recommend that you begin to use a management tool. At this level of activity, using eBay's Selling Manager will suit you nicely, and I go over how Selling Manager works in Technique 12. But when your eBay business begins to push 60 or 70 listings a week, I even more highly recommend that you get some additional help in the form of an auction management service or software.

 Whether you use an online service or software based on your own computer is a personal decision. You may find it easier to use an online system because you can log on to your selling information at any time from any computer. But if you have a slow Internet connection or pay usage fees by the hour, managing your eBay business online can become impractical.

Most desktop-based software packages have features that enable you to do your work on your desktop computer and then upload (or download) your data when you go online. If having multiple locations to work from is not important and you run your eBay business from a single computer in your office, you may feel more comfortable with a desktop-based software product.

In either case, if your business has reached the level where you need an auction management tool, congratulations! With this technique, I want to save you some time finding the service or software that's right for you. I'll outline some of the specific tasks that you can expect an auction management product to provide. At the end, I include two tables that compare pricing on various services.

Choosing Your Auction Management Tools

There's a huge difference between auction *listing* software and sites and auction *management* products. For a small to medium seller (approximately 20 to 60ish listings per week), listing software like eBay's Turbo Lister (see Technique 11) may just do the trick. Combine that with eBay's

Selling Manager (a *management* program) and your eBay business will be humming along just fine.

When your business activity level increases and you turn to an auction management solution for your eBay business, there are certain standard features that you should look for when you evaluate software and services. Also consider what information management features you currently have through your bookkeeping program (see Technique 48). You have the data there, regardless of whether you use it in a management solution.

Because many of the products listed have several product pricing tiers, Table 60-1 gives you the link directly to the product's pricing page. I've also listed the minimum price for each company's *management* products. Some offer less expensive options for listing your auctions (with templates and all kinds of swell bells and whistles), but the price shown in the table is for the minimum management product.

 Never choose auction management tools based solely on price. Go to the various Web sites and take a look at everything they offer for the price stated. You may find out that a service charging a bit more may just be worth it because of all the extra tools offered.

Looking for the Essential Features

Here are some of the must-have features to look for when you evaluate the offerings of auction management services and products:

✔ **Image hosting:** Some Web sites dazzle you with high-megabyte storage numbers. Keep one thing in mind. If your average eBay image is around 40KB (that's kilobytes, not megabytes — see Technique 15 for more on the details of eBay images) then in a 5 MB storage space you could store 128 pictures. In a 100 MB storage space you could hold around 2,500 images.

Unless you're a big-time seller, you really don't need that much space. Your eBay images should

be archived on your computer (how about in a folder called eBay Images?). Images for current listings should only be on the hosted site while the transaction is in progress. When the buyer has the item, and all is well, you can remove it from the remote server.

 You most likely already have free image hosting on your ISP's Web site, as noted in Technique 19.

✔ **Designing listings:** The basis of most of these products is a good listing function. You'll be able to select from supplied templates or be able to design your own and store them for future use. An important feature now coming into use is a spell checker. There's nothing worse than a misspelling in a listing!

✔ **Uploading listings:** Most of these products have a feature that launches a group of listings to eBay all at once. They may also allow you to schedule auctions to get underway at a prescribed time.

You can also expect to be able to put together your listings at your leisure offline and upload them to your service. They will usually archive your past listings so that you can relist at any time.

Many services also offer bulk relisting (relisting many items at once).

✔ **E-mail management:** You can expect to be able to be provided with sample e-mail letters (templates) that you can customize with your own look and feel. The services will also offer auto generated end-of-auction, payment received, and/or shipping e-mail service.

✔ **Feedback automation:** Post feedback in bulk to a number of your completed listings, or leave predesigned feedback one by one. Some products support automatic feedback when a buyer leaves you a positive message.

✔ **Sales reports:** Some services (even the least expensive) will offer you some sort of sales analysis. Be sure to take into account how much you really need these, based on data that you may already receive from QuickBooks, PayPal, eBay Stores, and SquareTrade.

Exploring the Advanced Features

Depending upon the type of business you run, you may need some of the more advanced features offered by management products:

✔ **Inventory tools:** Management products may allow you to create inventory records for your different products, permitting you to click a bunch to automatically list. When an item is sold, they will deduct the items from your inventory.

✔ **Sales-tax tracking and invoicing:** With full management, you can expect your sales tax to be calculated into your invoices, and complete line-item invoices to be sent automatically. Multiple items, when purchased by the same buyer will be combined.

✔ **Consignment tracking:** If you are a Trading Assistant (described in Technique 43), be sure to look for a product that enables you to to separately track the merchandise you sell for different clients. You should also be able to produce reports of consignment sale by customer.

✔ **Shipping:** Most of the services will give you the option to print your packing lists and shipping labels directly from the product. Some of the larger services integrate with the major shippers, allowing you to go directly to his or her site and ship from within their software.

Tables 60-1 and 60-2 give you the dollars and cents of subscribing to various online and offline services. To put together these tables, I disregarded lower subscription levels where companies offered only listing products. These are the lowest prices for products that are truly management tools.

TABLE 60-1: REPRESENTATIVE DESKTOP AUCTION MANAGEMENT SOFTWARE

Name	URL	Prices Start at	Number of Closings	Image Hosting?
AAA Seller	http://www.aaaseller.com/fees.asp	$9.95/month	Unlimited	YES
AuctionHawk	www.auctionhawk.com/help/?s=pricing	$12.99/month	50	YES
AuctionTamer	www.auctiontamer.com/auction/purchase.asp	$39.75/3 months	Unlimited	NO
Auction Wizard 2000	www.auctionwizard2000.com/Purchase.htm	$75 first year $50 renewal	Unlimited	NO
Auctiva	www.auctiva.com/products/default.aspx	Pro Pass $19.95	Unlimited	YES
DEK Auction Manager	www.dekauctionmanager.com/FEES.ASP	$9.95 + 2% GMS/month	Unlimited	YES
Shooting Star	www.foodogsoftware.com	$49.95 Flat Fee	Unlimited	NO
Spoonfeeder	www.spoonfeeder.com/pricing.php	$49.95 + $4.99/month	40	YES
Zoovy	www.zoovy.com	$49.95 ($399.95 setup fee)	Up to 1,000 listings	YES

TABLE 60-2: REPRESENTATIVE ONLINE AUCTION MANAGEMENT SOLUTIONS

Name	URL	Prices Start at	Number of Closings	Image Hosting?
AuctionHelper	http://www.auctionhelper.com/ah/info/fees.asp	1.95% GMS + .02 (min $10/month)	Unlimited	YES
AuctionWorks	http://www.auctionworks.com/pricing.asp	2% GMS/month (minimum $14.95)	Unlimited	YES
ChannelAdvisor	pro.channeladvisor.com/pro	$29.95/month	500/month	YES
InkFrog	www.inkfrog.com/index.php?file=pricing	$12.95/month	Unlimited	YES
Meridian	www.noblespirit.com/products-pricing.html	$9.95/month	500/month	YES
SpareDollar	www.sparedollar.com/corp/pricing.asp	$4.95/month	Unlimited	YES
Vendio	www.vendio.com/pricing.html	$.10 per listing	Up to 50 listings	YES

Technique 61

Networking Your Office

Save Time By

✔ Evaluating the need for a network

✔ Setting up your network

The first time I spoke to my editors about putting information in my books about networking, they scoffed at me. Bah! People who work at home don't need networks (as if networks were solely for the big companies with lots of cubicles). The more I spoke to the eBay community, the more I saw the need for networks — and the more people asked me about them.

I started writing about eBay in 1999, and now it's 2004. A lot of technology has washed under the bridge, and many advances have been made. Setting up a network in 1999 meant spending hours (maybe days) changing settings, testing, and checking computers; and it involved a lot of cursing. That was if you were lucky enough to finally get it right. Otherwise, as in the case of most home users — including me — you'd give up and take the whole thing as a loss and go on with your life.

Lucky for us non-techie types, Microsoft has made Windows considerably more home-network-friendly than in the old days. Also, more pleasant modes of networking (other than having miles of Ethernet cables going around the walls of your house) came to the fore of technology.

By networking your home (or eBay office) you'll save time by having the flexibility to work from different rooms or locations. (City dwellers, don't hate me for this.) You can also list auctions out by the pool (or in your backyard) in summer!

Using a Powerline Network

When I tell you how simple to install and inexpensive a Powerline network is, you'll be shocked. Considering that I'm someone who likes to tinker with things, I was upset that setting it up was so easy!

All you need to have to share a high-speed Internet connection, files, and printers are:

✔ **Electrical outlets:** I'll bet you have more than one in each room of your house.

✔ **An Ethernet card for each computer:** If your computer doesn't already have one (and many new computers do), you can get inexpensive Ethernet cards for around $10.

✔ **A wall-plugged Ethernet bridge for each computer:** The basis for the setup is a small box, about the size of a pack of cigarettes, that plugs into any two- or three-pronged electrical outlet. Take a look at one in Figure 61-1.

• **Figure 61-1: Netgear's wall-plugged Ethernet bridge.**

✔ **A router:** You only need this higher-end bit of gear if you intend to connect a high-speed Internet connection throughout your home or office (and isn't that really the point of all this?).

The benefits of this nifty little system are various:

✔ **It's inexpensive.** The requisite magic box costs around $40. You need one for each computer.

✔ **It's fast — as fast, or faster than, other types of network connection.** You could stream DVD movies from one room to another.

✔ **The networking connection is made through your existing electrical wiring.** It doesn't consume extra electricity.

✔ **Installation is easy.** Just plug a cable into your computer, and connect it to the Powerline box. Plug in Powerline box.

✔ **If your computer comes with an Ethernet jack, (most new computers do) you don't need to open up your computer and touch things you shouldn't be touching.**

If you have a high-speed Internet connection, no doubt you received a modem when you signed up. Since it's not sensible to connect the modem directly to your computer (a router does the work for you — see Tip below), you may already have a router.

 A *router* allows you to share a single Internet IP address among multiple computers. A router does exactly what its name implies; it routes signals and data to the different computers on your network. If you have one computer, the router can act as a firewall, or even a network device leading to a print sharer. But basically, to hook up more than one computer, you do need a router.

The integration works like this:

✔ The high-speed connection comes in through your DSL or cable line.

✔ The cable line plugs into your modem.

✔ An Ethernet cable goes from your modem into a router.

✔ One "out" Ethernet cable connection from the router goes to a local computer.

✔ Another "out" Ethernet cable goes to the Powerline adapter.

✔ The Powerline box is plugged into a convenient wall outlet.

Take a look at Figure 61-2 for a graphic display.

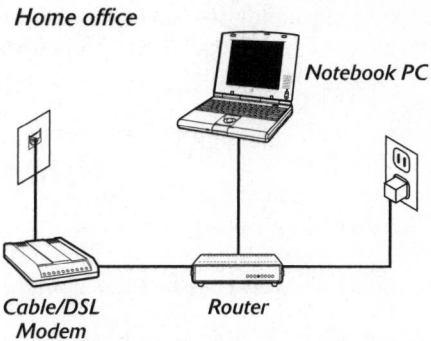

Home office

Notebook PC

Cable/DSL Modem

Router

• **Figure 61-2: A typical base setup for the Powerline network.**

When you want to connect the computers in other rooms to the network, just plug in a magic box.

So many networks, so little time

The best part of networking today is that you can combine more than one type of network to form a fully functional, professional data transfer medium with Internet access throughout the house. In my house, I have my own bizarre hybrid. I've got an Ethernet/home phone line/wireless combination. Home phone line networks (10 Mbps networks operating over existing phone lines without the need for additional wiring, routers, or hubs) didn't end up becoming real popular with the consumers. It's not that they didn't work flawlessly; they did. It's just that it seems that I'm the only one in the United States with enough free phone jacks in their home and office to make it work.

After the downfall of Phoneline architecture, the geniuses began to think, "What does that average home have lots of outlets for?" Hmmmm, how about *electricity?* Duh . . . and the Powerline network was born, running a network through the electric outlets in homes and apartments.

Now we have wireless networks too — and they're life-changing when they work. It's funny to see a whole new generation of people moving around antennas to try to get a good signal. It reminds me of television when I was a kid (maybe I should put some tin foil around the wireless antenna?).

Going Wireless

Wireless networking, also known as WiFi, or to the more technically inclined, IEEE 802.11 networking, is the hot new technology for all kinds of networks. It's a very impressive system when it works, with no cables or connectors to bog you down.

As a matter of fact, I was in New York recently, staying on the 16th floor of a hotel. I turned on my travel laptop to check e-mail and my laptop found signals for nine different wireless networks! I had to call the front desk to find out which one was the hotel connection. The whole world seems to be going wireless.

Just so you know, I wouldn't have been able to connect to the other networks. Wireless networks are protected by their own brand of security, called WEP (or Wired Equivalent Privacy). WEP will encrypt

your wireless transmissions and prevent others from getting into your network. Although super-hackers have cracked this system, it's the best possible until a new security system is invented.

To link your laptop or desktop to a wireless network with WEP encryption, you will need to have the key code from the wireless access point. Just enter it into your wireless card software onto every computer that uses the network and you should be good to go.

 The WiFi hotspots you may come to may not have any encryption, and they are free for all to use.

The types of wireless

If you've ever used a wireless telephone at home, you've used a technology similar to a wireless network. Most home wireless phones transmit to each other on the radio frequency band of 2.4 GHz, and they have the option to choose from several channels automatically to give you the best connection.

The two prevalent forms of wireless networks also work on the 2.4GHz band, and you will need to pre-set the channel when you set up the system. But there are three kinds:

- ✔ **802.11a:** This is a wireless format that works really well — fast with good connectivity. It's used when you have to serve up a wireless connection to a large group of people, as in a convention center or dormitory. It's fast, delivering data at speeds as high as 54 Mbps (megabits per second). It also runs at the 5GHz band (hence its nickname WiFi5), so it doesn't have any competition for bandwidth with wireless phones or microwave ovens. It's also very expensive.

- ✔ **802.11b:** My laptop has a built-in 802.11b card, so I can connect to the ever-popular "HotSpots" in Starbucks and airports. It's the most common wireless type, and it's used on the most platforms right now. The B version is slower than the A version, only capable of transferring data at 11 Mbps. It's a solid, low-cost solution when you have no more than 32 users per access point.

The lower frequency of 2.4 GHz drains less power from laptops and other portable devices. If you're using a laptop, the battery will last longer. Also, 2.4GHz signals travel farther — and can work through walls and floors more effectively — than 5GHz signals.

✔ **802.11g:** This is the newest flavor based on the 2.4GHz band. It speeds data up to a possible 54 Mbps, and it's backward compatible to work where the 802.11b service is available.

Setting up your wireless network

With a wireless network, you'll have to hook your computer (a laptop works best) to the Wireless Access Point (the access point is the gizmo with the antenna that broadcasts your signal throughout your home or office) to perform some beginning setup tasks like choosing your channel and setting up your WEP code. (The wireless access point will come with instructions for your particular brand.)

After you complete the setup and you turn your Wireless Access Point on, you will have a WiFi hotspot in your home or office. Typically, your new hotspot will provide coverage for about 100 feet in all directions, although walls and floors definitely cut down on the range. Even so, you should get good coverage throughout a typical home. For a large home, you can buy signal boosters to increase the range of your hotspot.

Simplified, this is how your network will be configured:

1. **Run a cable from your DSL line to your modem.**

2. **Connect an Ethernet cable from your modem to your router.**

3. **Connect the Ethernet cable to your Wireless Access Point.**

Take a look at this network diagram from Netgear in Figure 61-3.

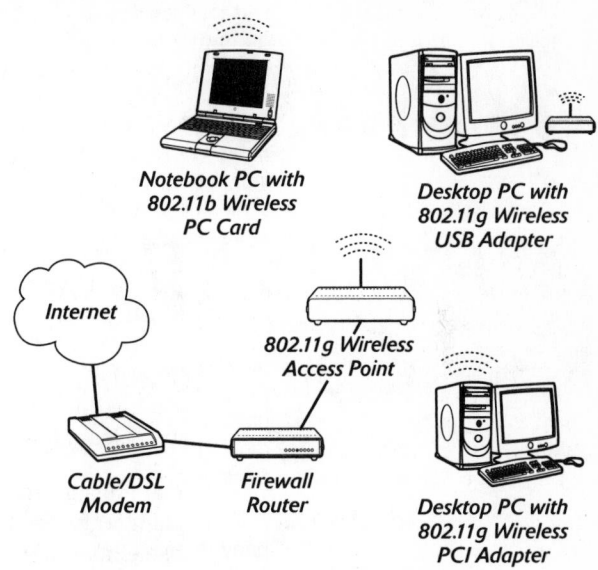

• **Figure 61-3: A typical home wireless network.**

Using a Hybrid Network

You may find that a wireless network may not work throughout your home. That's easy to fix. You can combine different networks together, allowing you to have wireless connectivity in some rooms of your house and in your backyard, and a wired network inside the house.

At my house, I have an old-fashioned home phoneline network coming from my router, along with a wireless Access point. They're all the same brand, Netgear, so there are no compatibility problems. This way, no matter where I go (or if my family wants to log on to the Internet), we can hook up with ease.

Technique 62

Keeping Kosher: Staying Away from Spam

Every morning when I get to my computer, I have to allow about five minutes to clear the spam out of my e-mail. It used to take up to a half hour, considering that I flip on my computer and am greeted by close to 200 e-mails every day. It used to be a terrifying time when I clicked my Send/Receive button in Outlook. I never knew what would be coming down the pike or wires. Read further on to see how I've cut my spam-scanning time!

Spam has gotten so sneaky. Everyone is scurrying to get the latest in anti-spam software, but I've found that antispam software was causing me to lose e-mail that I needed (because it seems that the word "eBay" is a favorite of spammers). These programs, because of my liberal use of the word eBay, often bounce the newsletter I send out to my readers from my Web site. Sometimes, I do a spot check with a reader, and they say they want the newsletter; the problem is that their spam protection refuses it. There's not much I can do!

I want *news* on eBay — but I don't want to get those make-a-fortune-on-eBay e-mails. Nor do I want to help out dear Mr. Felix Kamala, son of the late Mr. A.Y. Kamala. It seems his family lost millions in Zimbabwe to a scammer in the government, and he wanted me to help him get his secret stash of "Fifteen million five hundred thousand united state dollars." He was going to give me 20 percent just for helping him — how thoughtful! (In case you didn't know, this e-mail is part of what the FBI calls the *Nigerian e-mail scam* — also called the *419 scam* — named after the African Penal code violated with this crime.)

 A fine member of the Internet community collects these e-mails and posts them on his Web site, www.potifos.com/fraud. **Check out the page when you have a minute — it's quite funny!**

For the record, I'm also very comfortable with the size of my body parts; I don't want to buy drugs from some stranger over the Internet; and I don't need another mortgage.

Some scams aren't so amusing. They're the ones who pretend to be from eBay, PayPal, Citibank, and others, and try to bilk you out of your personal information. I show you a foolproof way to recognize them as well.

In this technique, I'm also going to show you how spammers get your e-mail address. Even if you never give it out, they have ways of getting it from you. I hope to teach you how to be a little more savvy about which e-mails you open and how to fight back.

Keeping Your E-mail Address Quiet

Have you ever signed up for anything on the Internet? Before you signed up, did you check to see if the site had a posted Privacy Policy page? You probably didn't. After you type your name in a box on the Internet on a site with no spam or privacy policy, you're basically giving your privacy away, because you're considered an "opt in" customer. *Opt In* means that you asked to be on a list, and the site that now has your e-mail address can sell it to spammers.

Take a look at Figure 62-1. It's a portion of an ad that should really scare you. It's an eBay auction for a CD containing 140,000,000 opt-in e-mail addresses. Yes, and you can buy all fourteen-million potential suckers for only $5.

The possibilities with this HUGE email list are outragious!

If you send an email to 140 million customers with only a 10% response, that's 14 million people! If only 1% of them respond, that's 1.4 million people! If only .1% respond, that's 140,000 people! And even if only .01% respond, that sill 14,000 sales!

• **Figure 62-1: A tempting offer to violate people's privacy.**

Just opening your e-mail can give you away as well. Spammers will often (as you can tell by some of the To addresses) make up return e-mail addresses to mask their true location. If you open and view their e-mail, the e-mail sends a notice to the spammer's server and then they know that your e-mail address is valid. This can be masked in the HTML to occur when the e-mail consists of merely a picture — when it goes back to grab the picture for your e-mail, it reports your e-mail address is good.

Recognizing Spam

I guess this isn't rocket science. Much of the spam you get can be recognized by the subject line. I used to check my e-mail once I downloaded it to my computer. That's a pretty dangerous procedure, though, considering that some e-mails do their job without your even having to respond.

Finding spam before it finds you

Now I'm using a program called MailWasher Pro. When I flip on my computer in the morning I open MailWasher and see the giant barrage of trash in my mailbox as in Figure 62-2.

• **Figure 62-2: MailWasher (the Free version).**

MailWasher lists your e-mail directly from your ISP's server. It does NOT download the e-mail to your computer. By using MailWasher, you can delete the offending e-mails from your mailbox, and then bring only the ones you want into your e-mail program.

As you can see from the figure, I can find out all the following:

✔ **Who sent the e-mail:** I'm not really acquainted with Lavonne N. Bingham (note that her e-mail address ends in .be — that's Belgium). I'm also not familiar with Viola Cantu, who strangely has *jsavcxy* as her e-mail ID at Yahoo!. Not to mention my buddy, chun-she (otherwise known as carrie@t-online.de). Hmmm, Germany? Nope. Don't know anyone there either.

✔ **E-mail subject:** Just in case Chun-she really does know me, they should know that I don't read Cyrillic, and, as the subject line is *Ilocemume семинар,* I'm pretty sure I can delete that one. And although Velma sent me an e-mail letting me know how much I'd enjoy something, I'm really too busy to enjoy anything just now, so I guess I'll delete that e-mail too.

✔ **To:** Notice that the To line can be a definite tip-off. If someone has e-mailed to a name other than my own or to an e-mail box at my Web site (with news about mortgages), I can fairly assume that the e-mail wasn't sent by someone I know. For example, one e-mail was sent to Yvette. I have no Yvette at this e-mail address! There are no dummies here either.

✔ **Attachments:** Yes or none. If there's an attachment from someone I don't know, I delete the entire e-mail. As a matter of fact, I delete most e-mails with attachments. If a friend wants to send me something, they can always resend if I delete it accidentally (or on purpose).

MailWasher allows you to put check marks next to suspect e-mails. You can merely delete them, or you can bounce them back to whence they came and blacklist them (so they'll always be marked for deletion if they e-mail you again).

My e-mail program is set to only get e-mail from the server when I ask it to, so after I delete all the spam, I can click Send/Receive and feel considerably safer.

Also, although I use the Pro version (see my Web site for more details), which can scan more than one e-mail account, you should download the free version for one e-mail account and see if you like it before paying $29.95 for the Pro version. You can download the free version at www.mailwasher.net.

Checking out nefarious e-mail

What? It seems I've gotten an e-mail from PayPal. They say my account needs to be renewed. Oh my!

I certainly don't want to lose my PayPal account, so I'd better click the link and give them the information they need.

Or how about an e-mail from PayPal that says: We recently reviewed your account and suspect that your PayPal account may have been accessed by an unauthorized third party. Protecting the security of your account and of the PayPal network is our primary concern. Therefore, as a preventative measure, we have temporarily limited access to sensitive PayPal account features.

Click below in order to regain access to your account:

STOP RIGHT THERE!

 Take a good look at the e-mail. Who is it addressed to? When PayPal sends you an e-mail, the opening line says Dear (your registered name). In my case, a real e-mail from PayPal would only address the opening as "Dear Marsha Collier." These spam e-mails are usually addressed to "Dear Valued User" or "Dear youre-mailaddress.com." PayPal will *never* address an e-mail to your e-mail address!

Responding to these e-mails is tantamount to giving away your information to a stranger. Let me give you a tip on another way to double-check these e-mails.

Open the e-mail, as I have in Figure 62-3. Right-click your mouse and find the option to View Source.

With the menu open, click View Source with your left mouse button. Text will open up on your computer in notepad. You will now see the e-mail in HTML text.

Scroll to the bottom, in this case, to the line that says Please follow the link below... followed by a URL, as shown in Figure 62-4.

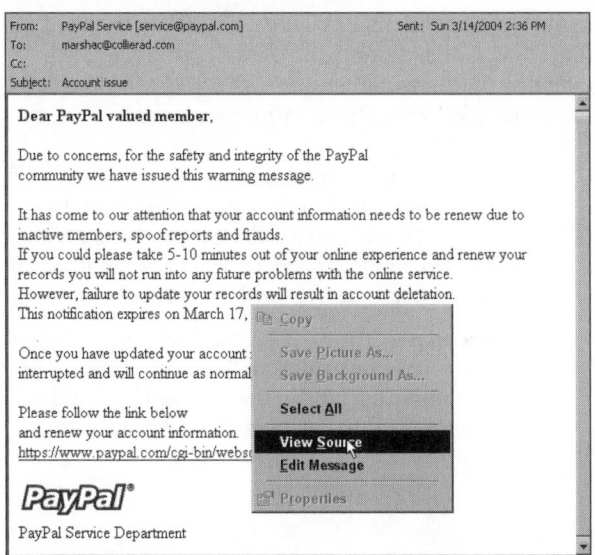

• **Figure 62-3:** Checking to View Source on an e-mail.

```
<br>Please follow the link below <br>
<i></i> and
renew your account information.
<br><a
href="http://66.223.44.203/cgi/index.htm"onMouseOver="status
='https://www.paypal.com/cgi-bin/webscr?cmd=login-run';
return true"
onMouseOut="status='';return
true">https://www.paypal.com/cgi-bin/webscr?cmd=login-run</a
>
```

• **Figure 62-4:** The HTML coding for the link URL address.

Take a good long look at the figure. You'll see the link to the URL in the e-mail. But look just before it in the source code and you can see that you're really being redirected to `http://66.223.44.203/cgi/index.htm` — not to the PayPal secure URL!

When I click the link, I come to an *exact duplicate* of the PayPal Log In page — or is it? A quick glance at the Address bar of my browser confirms I've been misdirected, as shown in Figure 62-5. If I were at PayPal, the URL address would read

```
https://www.paypal.com/cgi-bin/
    webscr?cmd=_login-run
```

(Note that the real PayPal URL begins with https, not an http URL; `https` stands for *secure*.)

 Even checking the URL may be misleading if you're using Internet Explorer as your browser. A vulnerability has been identified, which can be exploited by bad deed doers to display a fake URL in the address and status bars. To avoid these Microsoft glitches, be sure to keep your Windows critical updates, er, up to date. Visit `http://windowsupdate.microsoft.com` regularly and allow critical security updates to be installed.

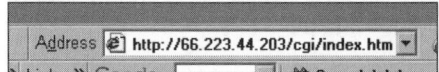

• **Figure 62-5:** My address bar with the misdirected URL.

 You can use the right-click and View Source trick on any HTML e-mail, and HTML e-mail is what fraudsters use to hide the misdirected address.

If you still question whether your PayPal or eBay account has a problem, close the e-mail and go directly to the site and log in at the real URL. If there is a problem with your account, believe me, they'll let you know after you properly log in.

Fighting Back!

There's quite a bit that you can do to help stop this flood. Spam comes in many forms and eventually, if things keep going the way they do, cleaning spam will be a full-time proposition.

Have you ever clicked the link at the bottom of some spam you've received to have your name removed from their list? I have — at least I used to — until I found out that's the gold standard for spammers to collect valid e-mail addresses! If you respond to the spam in any way, shape, or form, they know they have found a valid address — and watch the spam to your mailbox increase!

Never, I repeat, *never* click one of those links again.

When signing up for some sort of newsletter with an organization you're new to or unsure of, be sure to use an anonymous Yahoo! or HotMail address. It's easy enough to sign up for one, and if spammers get hold of that address, they will not be privy to your private address.

Also, no matter how curious you are about enlarging certain parts of your anatomy, don't even open the e-mails. But in any case, don't respond. You're only encouraging the vicious cycle.

Last, report spammers. There are several legitimate sites that take reports and forward them to the appropriate authorities. Don't bother trying to forward the spam to the sender's ISP. These days they're mostly forged with aliases, and all you'll do is succeed in clogging up the e-mail system. The following is a list of places you can go to report spammers:

- ✔ **Federal Trade Commission:** Yes, your tax dollars are at work. You can forward spam to uce@ftc.gov, where it will become available for law enforcement. (Especially in the case of e-mail trying to get your personal information.)

- ✔ **spamcop.net:** They've been around since 1988 and report spam e-mails to ISPs and mailers. They have a reporting link on their home page, and they work hard to get spamsters out of the loop.

Technique

63

Keeping Password Accounts Secure

Save Time By

✔ Accepting responsibility for security

✔ Knowing how to report stolen info to eBay

✔ Making your passwords harder to crack

When was the last time you changed your passwords? I mean the whole enchilada: eBay, PayPal, your online bank account? Hey, I'm not the keeper of the *shoulds*, but you *should* change your critical passwords every 60 days — rain or shine. That's not just me saying that. It's all the security experts who know this kind of stuff. The world is full of bad-deed-doers just waiting to get their hands on your precious personal information. Password theft can lead to your bank account being emptied, your credit cards being pushed to the max, and worst of all, someone out there posing as you.

You've seen the commercials on TV poking fun at the very real problem of identity theft. If you ask around your circle of friends, no doubt you'll find someone who knows someone who's been in this pickle. It can take years to undo the damage caused by identity theft, so a better plan is to stay vigilant and protect yourself from becoming a victim.

In this technique, I give you tips for selecting good passwords and other personal security information. I also show you the sort of passwords to stay away from and what to do if (heaven forbid!) your personal information is compromised.

Reporting Messed-Up Accounts

If someone gets hold of your personal information, the most important thing to do is report it immediately. If you see any items that aren't yours on the Items I'm Bidding On or the Items I'm Selling areas of your My eBay page, it's time to make a report — and *fast*!

Okay, you know that something hinky is going on with your eBay account because *you* never placed a bid on the Britney Spears stage-worn T-shirt (did you?). And you can't imagine that your husband did either (but double-check with him just to be sure). Here's what to do immediately:

✔ **Change your personal e-mail account password with your ISP:** Go to your ISP's home page (for example www.earthlink.net) and look for an area called Member Center or something similar. In the Member Center, access your personal account information — probably through a link called something like My Account. You should be able to change your password there.

✔ **Change the e-mail account password on your home computer:** Don't forget to change the password on your computer's e-mail software as well (Outlook, Eudora, and the like) so you can continue to download your e-mail from the server.

Perhaps you discover that your private information has been compromised when you suddenly can't log in to your eBay or PayPal account. If this happens on eBay, follow these steps to request a new password:

1. **Go to the eBay Sign In page.**

Don't type your password. You just tried that and it doesn't work.

2. **Click the Forgot Your Password link, as shown in Figure 63-1.**

Doing this takes you to `http://cgi3.ebay.com/aw-cgi/eBayISAPI.dll?ForgotYourPasswordShow`.

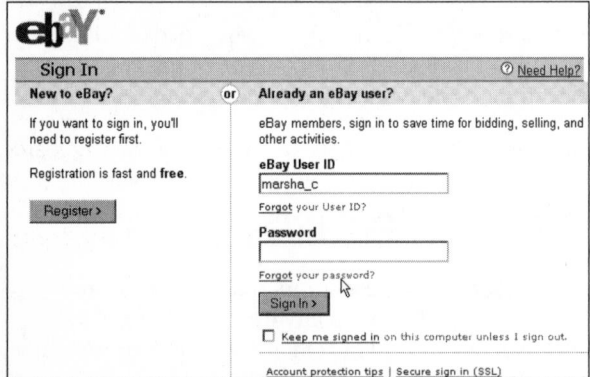

• **Figure 63-1: The Forgot My Password link on the Sign In page.**

Those silly security questions that you answered when you registered for eBay become very important now.

3. **Answer at least one of the questions you see on the page along with your registered phone number and ZIP code and click Continue.**

eBay will e-mail you instructions for resetting your password.

4. **When the e-mail arrives, follow the steps and change your password.**

 If you *don't* get eBay's e-mail telling you how to change your password, that means some fraudster may have changed the contact information in your eBay account. See the sidebar "Freaking out is not a good thing" for instructions on what to do.

5. **If all goes well and you can change your password, go to the link pictured in Figure 63-2 to change your secret question.**

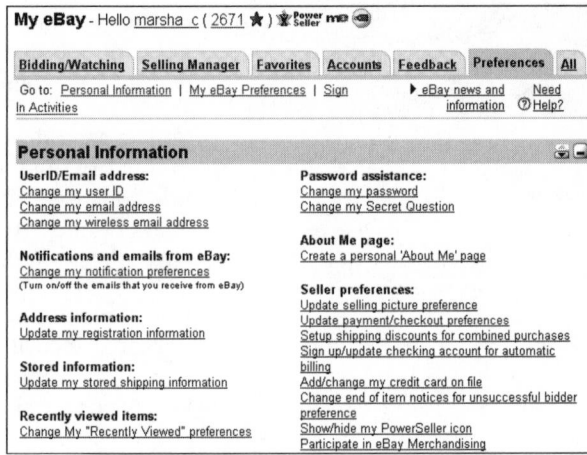

• **Figure 63-2: Your My eBay Preferences page with all the security links.**

Freaking out is not a good thing

If you can't seem to get a new password for your eBay account, and you're unsuccessful at finding a Live Chat link, there's still hope. Remain calm, follow these steps, and take notes as you go:

1. **Go to any eBay page, scroll all the way to the bottom, and click the Security Center link shown in the following figure.**

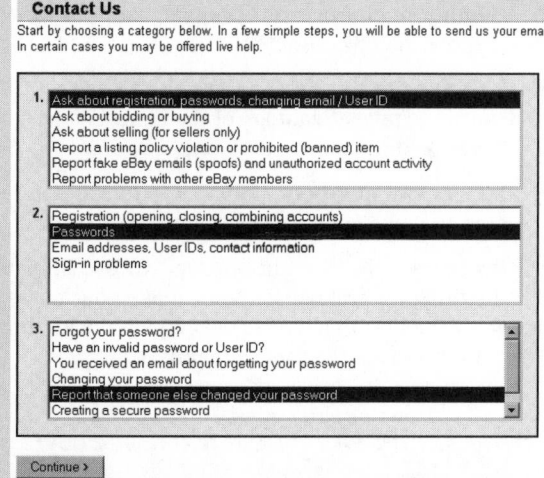

2. When you get to the Security Center, click the green bar labeled *Report a problem*.

The *Contact Us* form appears.

3. Highlight the parameters of your problem, as pictured here.

Box 1: Highlight *Ask about registration, passwords, changing email/User ID.*

Box 2: Highlight Passwords.

Box 3: Highlight *Report that someone else changed your password.*

4. Click Continue.

5. Click the link on the next page that reads "Securing Your Account and Reporting Account Theft."

6. On the following page, find the boldface headline that reads *Contacting eBay*. Click the link labeled "E-mail us to report that you cannot sign in to your account."

An e-mail form appears.

7. Fill in the e-mail form and send it.

Be sure to tell eBay who you are (name, address, phone number) along with your User ID and e-mail address and a brief summary of the situation.

Choosing a Good Secret Question

If you read the harrowing procedure in the "Freaking out is not a good thing" sidebar, you know that having someone sabotage your eBay account is something you never want to go through. But if your secret question is easy to figure out, a hacker can find it even easier to wreak havoc on your account.

 Your password is only as secure as the secret question, so *don't relate your password and secret question in any way.* For example, do not make your secret question a clue to your password — and *especially* don't make your password answer the secret question. Better yet, think of your secret question as a completely separate, auxiliary security device for your account.

Figure 63-3 shows eBay's Create a Secret Question and Answer page, which you can access from your My eBay Preferences page. It shows several suggested questions.

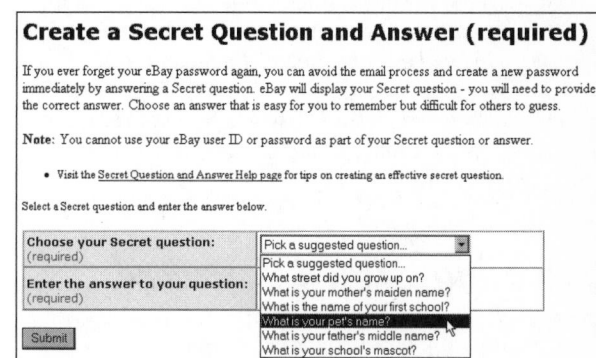

• **Figure 63-3:** Create a Secret Question page.

Here are some tips for setting a secure secret question:

- ✔ **Never use your mother's maiden name.** That is most likely the *secret* that your bank uses as your challenge question. (They usually ask when you open the account.) So that is definitely out — you don't want to give *anybody* that word.

- ✔ **Select a question and provide a creative answer.**

  - ▶ **What is your Pet's name?** Give an answer like Ralph the Rhino or Graak the Pterodactyl or something *creative*. Don't give your actual pet's name (or species). Anyone who knows you is likely to know your pet's name.

  - ▶ **What street did you grow up on?** Name an unusual landmark from your hometown. Don't use a street name.

  - ▶ **What is the name of your first school?** Make up a good one — perhaps Elementary Penguin Academy? School of Hard Knox?

 It should go without saying, but what the heck: Don't use any of the sample passwords shown here. It's safe to say that lots of people will be reading this book, and anything seen by lots of people isn't secret. (I know you know that, but still. . .)

  - ▶ **What is your father's middle name?** Make up a goodie or skip it.

  - ▶ **What is your school's mascot?** There's a lot of creativity that can go on here. How about *Red-and-white-striped zebra? Pink elephant?*

Your bylaws for selecting answers to a secret question are two: Be creative *and* be sure you remember the darned thing!

Selecting a Good Password

Poorly chosen passwords are the number-one loophole for hackers. If you think that hackers are just a small group of hypercaffeinated teenagers, think again. It's now also the domain of small- and big-time crooks who hack into an account, spend a few thousand dollars that belong to someone else, and move on.

I searched Google for hacking software and came up with over two million matches. Many of these Web sites offer an arsenal of free hacking tools. They also provide step-by-step instructions for beginners on how to crack passwords. The Internet can be its own worst enemy.

Any password can be cracked by the right person in a matter of seconds. Your goal is to set a password that takes too much of the hackers' time. With the number of available users on eBay or PayPal, odds are they'll go to the next potential victim's password rather than spending many minutes (or even hours) trying to crack yours.

Here are some industrial-strength tips for setting a secure password.

- ✔ **Number of characters:** Compose your password of more than 8 characters.

- ✔ **Case sensitivity:** Since passwords are case-sensitive, take advantage of the feature. Mix lower- and uppercase in your passwords.

- ✔ **Letters and numbers:** Combine letters and numbers to make your passwords harder to crack.

- ✔ **Proper words:** Don't use proper words. Think of the title of your favorite book. Make your password the first two letters of each word with numbers in the middle (*not* sequential).

Stay Smart: Don't be a Make-It-Easy!

Any beginning hacker (or tech-smart teenager) can figure out your password if it falls into the following categories. Don't use 'em! They are pathetically easy!

- ✔ **The obvious:** The word *Password*. D'oh!

- ✔ **Birthdays:** Don't use your birthday, your friend's birthday, John F. Kennedy's birthday. Not only are these dates common knowledge, but so is this truism: A series of numbers is easy to crack.

✔ **Names:** Don't use your first name, last name, your dog's name, or anyone's name. Again, it's common knowledge and easy to find out. (Most people know my husband's name; it's been in many of my books!)

✔ **Contact numbers:** Social Security (if they get hold of *that* one — watch out!), phone numbers, your e-mail address, or street address (got a White Pages? So do they . . .).

✔ **Any of the lousy passwords in Table 63-1:** These have been gleaned from the millions of password dictionaries available from hackers. Note that this is *not a complete list* by any means; there are thousands of common (lousy) passwords, and unprintable ones are more common than you may think. If you really care to scare yourself, Google the phrase *common passwords*.

TABLE 63-1: LOUSY (EASILY CRACKED AND MOST FREQUENTLY USED) PASSWORDS

!@#$%	!@#$%^&	!@#$%^&*(	0	0000	00000000	0007	007	01234
123456	02468	24680	1	1101	111	11111	111111	1234
12345	1234qwer	123abc	123go	12	131313	212	310	2003
2004	54321	654321	888888	a	aaa	abc	abc123	action
absolut	access	admin	admin123	access	administrator	alpha	asdf	animal
biteme	computer	eBay	enable	foobar	home	internet	login	love
mypass	mypc	owner	pass	password	passwrd	papa	peace	penny
pepsi	qwerty	secret	supeman	temp	temp123	test	test123	whatever
whatnot	winter	windows	xp	xxx	yoda	mypc123	powerseller	sexy

Technique 64

Letting the World Know All About You, er, Me

The About Me page is a really fun and helpful tool on eBay — and it's free to every registered eBay user. Having an About Me page shows the community you're jumping in with both feet. Prospective customers can use your About Me page to get to know a little more about you — to get a sense of your personality and your dedication. You can use your About Me page as a tool to direct customers to your eBay Store (or to your own Web site — About Me is the only place on eBay that it's legal to post an off-eBay commerce Web site).

eBay members like to check out both sellers and buyers on the site. By learning about your potential trading partner, you get information — and information is key to preventing fraud. From an eBay member's About Me page, you can see just how involved they are in the eBay business world.

The About Me page can also be a deal maker, or a deal breaker. Once I was looking around eBay for some extra long printer cables, and I found several sellers selling just what I wanted. One of the lower-priced sellers had a low feedback rating — he was new at eBay. But, he had an About Me page, so I clicked. I found out that the seller was a computer technician by trade and that he and his son made these computer cables together as a family business at home in the evenings. The money they made went to pay for their father-son trips to see their favorite baseball team play. What a great family enterprise! Better yet, he guaranteed the cables. As you might have guessed, I bought the cables, and we both got positive feedback.

You can tell whether someone else has an About Me page because you'll see a small icon with a blue lowercase *m* and a red lowercase *e*. In this technique, you find out how to put together your own About Me page (in three minutes) and get to see some examples from longtime eBay sellers.

Getting Your About Me Page

Putting together your About Me page takes no time at all. Most of the time you spend will be in the planning. (Check out some of the examples of About Me pages toward the end of this technique for inspiration.)

The page can be as simple or as complex as you want. You may use one of eBay's templates as presented, or you may gussy up the page with lots of pictures and varied text using HTML. (See Technique 20.)

There are several things you must think about ahead of time:

✔ **Title:** Come up with a title for your page. It can be as simple as a welcome greeting.

✔ **Subtitle:** Decide on a few words to go below your page title that elaborate on your page theme.

✔ **Introductory paragraph:** Structure this paragraph to tell a little about you and your hobbies or interests. You can also talk about the items you sell on eBay, but most of all, it should reflect your personality.

 In the paragraphs of the About Me page, you can use HTML to add images or fancy text. The titles, however, are standard and won't permit HTML coding.

✔ **Second subtitle and paragraph:** Elaborate on your interests and your business on eBay. Add more information. Pictures are good, too!

✔ **eBay activity:** Decide what you'd like to show on the page — like how many of your most recent feedback comments — and whether you'd like to show your current listings.

 Don't get carried away by showing your last 100 feedback messages; doing so takes up too much space. Display either 10 or 25 and leave it at that. If visitors want to know more about your feedback rating, they can click your feedback number. (After all, they clicked your ME icon to get here, and that's next to your feedback number.)

✔ **Web-site links:** Think of some of your favorite Web sites; also include yours or a friend's (ask first). You may legally put these links on your page.

If you've been an advanced user on eBay for a while, consider adding the following to your existing My eBay page:

✔ **Your logo:** If you've designed a logo for your eBay business, be sure to put it on the page.

✔ **Returns policy:** Outline your standard returns policy on the page for your customers.

✔ **Shipping policy:** Explain how you ship and when you ship. Offer discounts on shipping for multiple purchases through your eBay Store.

✔ **Searchable index to your eBay Store:** Let your customers search your store by apparel size, brand name, or item. You can accomplish this by HTML coding.

✔ **Payment methods:** Let the customer know what payment methods you accept.

Setting up the page

To set up your About Me page, follow these steps:

1. **Go to your My eBay Preferences tab, as shown in Figure 64-1. Scroll down the page to find the link under the About Me page heading.**

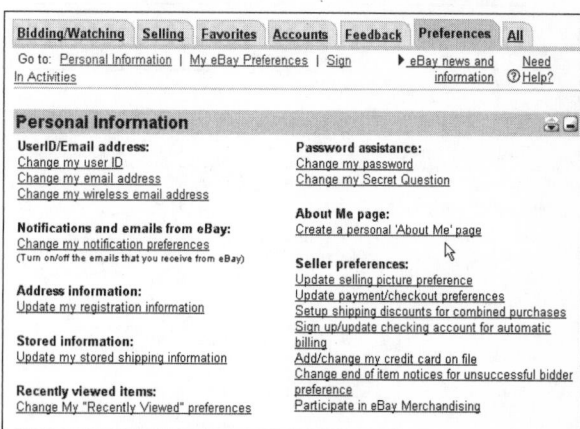

• **Figure 64-1: Step one in setting up your page.**

2. **On the About Me hub page (where you end up), click the Create or Edit Your Page button to proceed, as shown in Figure 64-2.**

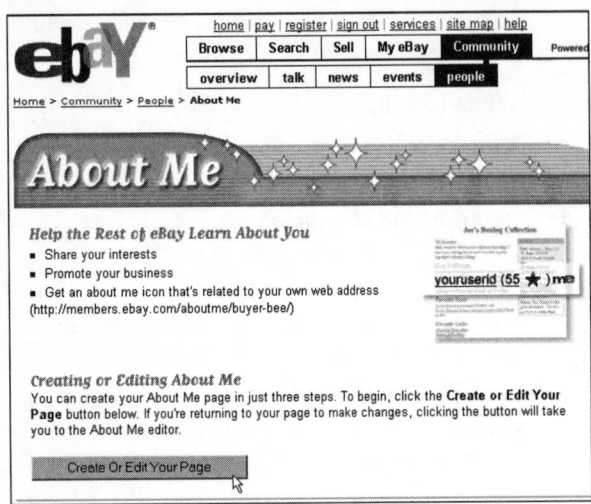

• **Figure 64-2:** The About Me hub page.

3. On the Choose a Layout page, decide whether you want a centered, two-column, or multi-column layout for your page.

eBay will show you examples, as shown in Figure 64-3.

4. Fill in the form with the information I describe earlier in this technique.

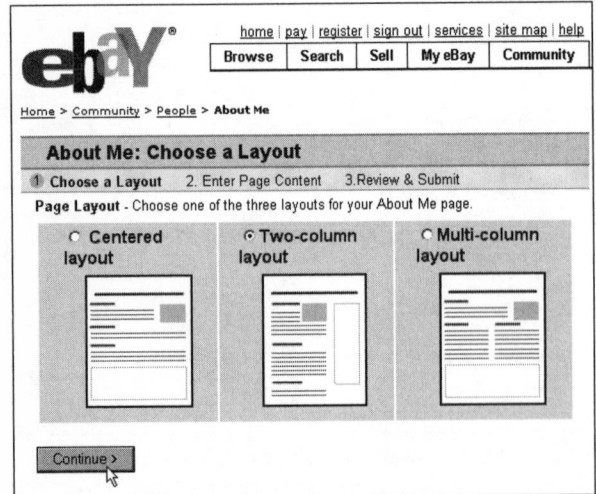

• **Figure 64-3:** Deciding on your layout.

You can preview your page at any time by clicking the Continue button at the bottom of the page. If you don't like what you see, click Back, and you can continue to edit your page.

I put together the page in Figure 64-4 for a friend in about three minutes. It's not the perfect About Me page — but a simple page like this certainly tells something about the seller. It will do until you have time to put together a more professional look.

• **Figure 64-4:** A three-minute About Me page!

 When you have an eBay Store, your About Me page is also the About the Store page. Your eBay Store's graphic header will appear at the top of your About Me page.

Using little-known, eBay-unique HTML tags

It's not a highly publicized deal, but you can use some special *unique-to-eBay* HTML codes that give your About Me page a custom look. Some of these codes can be combined with others (such as those for bold and color). Play around with them and see what you come up with! (See Technique 20 for more HTML for your page.)

Table 64-1 gives you the secret codes (sorry, no decoder rings) and shows you what they can do.

TABLE 64-1: EBAY HTML TAGS

Tag	What It Does
`<eBayUserID>`	Displays your User ID and real-time feedback rating
`<eBayUserID BOLD>`	Displays your User ID and feedback rating in boldface
`<eBayUserID NOLINK>`	Displays your User ID with no clickable link (useful if you plan to change your ID soon)
`<eBayUserID NOFEEDBACK>`	Displays your User ID with no feedback number after it
`<eBayUserID BOLD NOFEEDBACK>`	Combines two of the above tags into one
`<eBayFeedback>`	Shows your up-to-the-minute feedback comments
`<eBayFeedback COLOR="red">`	Changes the color of the second line on your feedback comment table to red
`<eBayFeedback TABLEWIDTH="75%">`	Changes the width of your feedback comment table as a percentage of the allowed space (the default value is 90%)
`<eBayItemList>`	Automatically inserts a list of the items you currently have up for sale
`<eBayItemList BIDS>`	Displays everything you're currently bidding on
`<eBayTime>`	Inserts the official eBay time into your text
`<eBayMemberSince>`	Inputs the exact date and time of your initial eBay registration

Checking Out Some Pros!

Okay, maybe they're not *all* pros, but the About Me eBay pages pictured in this section are from some new, some longtime, and some very professional sellers. Take a look at each one and see how they used their About Me page to their best advantage.

Due to page constraints, I couldn't show you the entire About Me pages, but just look them up in seller's search and click their ME icons. You'll get the full picture there.

I show you the pages in order from part-time sellers, to full-time sellers, to full-on eBay professionals.

marsha_c

Figure 64-5 shows my lowly About Me page. Since I'm part-time on eBay (even though I'm a PowerSeller), I chose to make my page personal. I talk about a little eBay history, mention my books, and basically introduce myself to the reader.

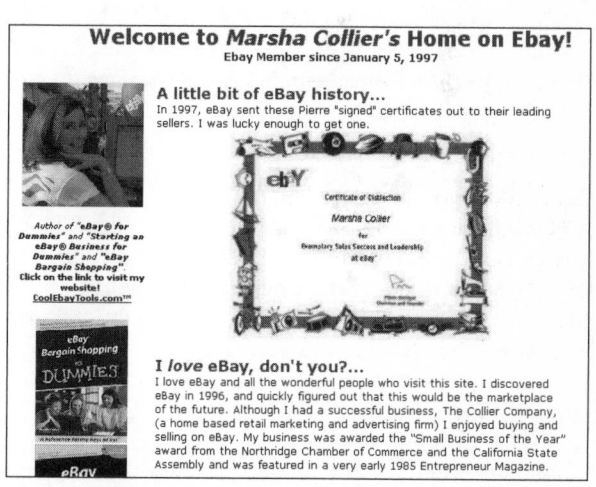

• **Figure 64-5:** The marsha_c About Me page.

cosmiquemuffin

Dorothy Nelson is the self-appointed "Queen of Goofy Toys." It says so right on her page. She sells on eBay part-time and has lots of fun with it. I love her auctions because she gets very creative with her description text, just as she does here on her About Me page. You can learn a lot about Dorothy by looking at her page, which you see a bit of in Figure 64-6.

Notice her store's banner at the top, "Cosmique's Tchotchke Barn." (Now you know how *tchotchke* is spelled!)

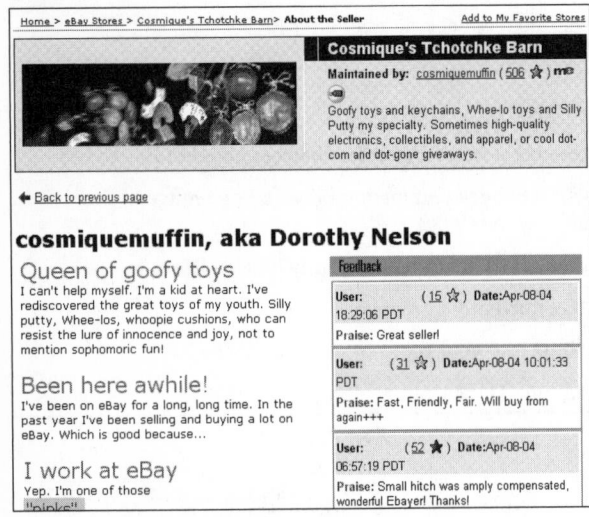

• **Figure 64-6: The cosmiquemuffin About Me page.**

preservationpublishing

Figure 64-7 shows an excellent example of using your page to show your business and hobbies. Jillian Cline sells her custom dog-imprinted items and has published several books about dogs. She also works against breed-specific legislation and talks about it on her page.

listingrover

I think Steve Lindhorst changed his User ID from *greenfuz* to *listingrover* because that's what he does. Steve specializes in selling big-ticket items like cars at eBay Motors and also acts as a Trading Assistant for auto dealers. The reason he has nothing listed just now is that he's been busy teaching at eBay University. (I took the picture of him on his page shown in Figure 64-8 when we were teaching together.)

• **Figure 64-7: The preservationpublishing About Me page.**

Steve also has an amazing sense of humor. His humor definitely comes through when you see his About Me page!

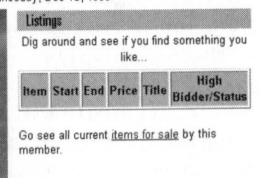
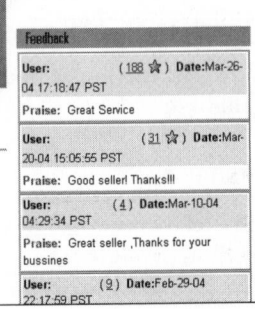

• **Figure 64-8: The listingrover About Me page.**

aunt*patti

Meet Patti (Louise) Ruby (the technical editor for this book), the strawberry wacko. True, Patti sells lots of different items on eBay, but you can bet when it comes to buying, she's scouting out the strawberry gear!

Patti's a long-time eBay seller, and as you can see by the banner at the top of the page in Figure 64-9, she has an eBay Store.

• **Figure 64-9:** The aunt•patti About Me page.

Shoetime

Shoetime sells (duh) *shoes* on eBay. I've bought from them often because their merchandise is so easy to sort through. On the Shoetime About Me page, you find a list of links on the left side that allows you to search the auctions by style, type, or size — pretty convenient!

Shelly Hudson of Shoetime really knows her shoes, and her enthusiasm comes across on this page, as shown in Figure 64-10.

noblespirit

Joe Cortese of noblespirit is one of eBay's top sellers. Just by looking at this About Me page (in

Figure 64-11), you immediately get an idea of what the seller is about and what he sells. Not only does he describe his merchandise, he also tells the story of how he got started on eBay.

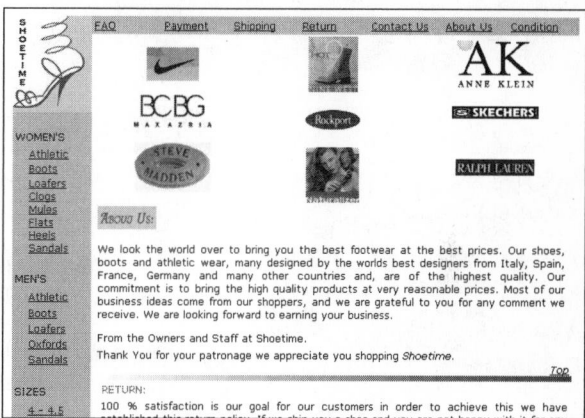

• **Figure 64-10:** The Shoetime About Me page.

Each of the images in the center of the page links to related ongoing eBay sales. What a marketing tool!

This section shows examples of About Me pages for all levels of sellers. You can keep the ideas they illustrate in mind when you post your own About Me page!

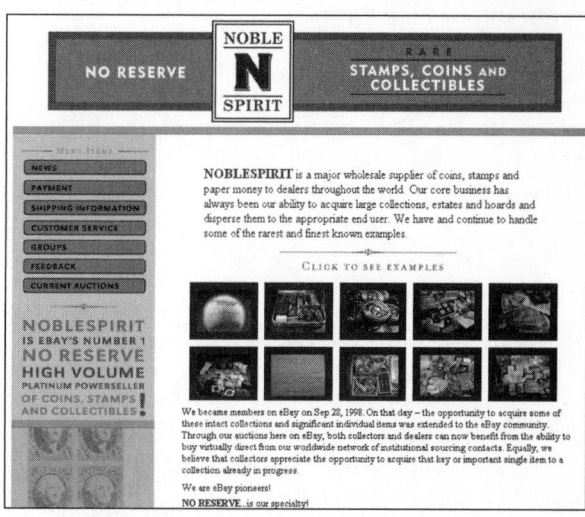

• **Figure 64-11:** The noblespirit About Me page.

Technique 65

Glossary of eBay Sellers' Business Terms

Save Time By

✔ Knowing the e-tailing jargon (with a little practice, you can translate instantly)

About Me page: The free Web page given to every eBay user. It's an excellent promotional tool. (See Technique 64.)

Accounts payable: Expenses that have been charged but not paid for. (See Technique 48.)

Accounts receivable: The pending amount due from a sale to the seller. Merchandise has been sold, but money has not been collected. (See Technique 48.)

Advance order: An order placed for merchandise to be delivered on a future date.

Advertising budget: The amount of money you set aside for advertising your items in any media (newspaper, radio, ad banner, and so on).

API: Application Program Interface. An application program that is created to interface with another computer.

Apparel/merchandise mart: A single building or complex filled with many wholesale sources where vendors lease space to provide buyers one-stop-shopping. Visiting one gives you the opportunity of checking out many wholesale sources in one area.

Archive: Moving an inactive file to another area for storage. (See Techniques 13, 26, 30, and 49.)

B2B: Business to business. Businesses targeted to other businesses rather than to consumers, such as shipping supplies (B2B) versus fishing supplies (B2C).

B2C: Business to consumer. Businesses targeting the consumer market with their goods (versus the business market as in B2B).

Back order: (Something you don't want to hear if you're buying from a drop-shipper.) The merchandise you ordered is not available for delivery. Your vendor will usually supply you with a date if and when they'll be able to ship.

Barcode: A set of lines and spaces of different widths that can be scanned (read) by a barcode reader to identify the product.

Basic stock method: A method of stock planning where you maintain a basic dollar amount of merchandise on hand. It remains constant from season to season.

Black Friday: The day after Thanksgiving when American retailers go from "in the red" to "in the black." Considered by many the heaviest brick-and-mortar shopping day of the year, but not on eBay.

BOM: Beginning-of-month stock or dollar-sales figure.

Bonding: A surety bond can be issued by a third party (usually an insurance company) to guarantee a seller's performance within a transaction. (See Technique 56.)

Business formulas: Standard formulas to produce math calculations relating to sales.

- ✔ Specific amount = `Total amount × percentage`

- ✔ Percentage = `Specific amount ÷ total amount`

- ✔ Percent of increase (or decrease) = `Difference between figures ÷ original amount`

- ✔ Total Amount = `Specific amount ÷ percentage`

Buyer's premium: A percentage added to an auction's final bid that goes to the auctioneer. Used in brick and mortar and eBay Live auctions.

Buy It Now: An auction format on eBay that offers a buyout price that ends the listing.

Cannibalization: When you buy new products to resell that outdate your existing inventory.

COD: Collect On Delivery. When you ship an order to a buyer and they have to pay the shipping company upon receipt. Not recommended for eBay sellers.

Consignment selling: Accepting merchandise to sell where the vendor is paid only when the merchandise sells. The seller takes a commission on the sale. (See Technique 43.)

Co-op advertising: Allowances offered to sellers by some vendors and third-party sources — for example, by eBay to Power Sellers (as described in Technique 58) — toward advertising in print or other media. The third party shares the cost of pre-approved advertising based on your dollar volume.

Cost of goods: The cost of goods takes into account the actual cost of the merchandise plus shipping costs to get the item to you.

Cost of goods sold: A figure from the Profit and Loss statement (see Technique 48) for your business — it totals the full amount of all expenses involved in selling your items.

CTR (Click-Through Ratio): The number of times an online advertisement is clicked, divided by the times the ad is viewed or served to the page. This ratio helps you calculate whether your online ads are effective. The ratio of the number of times an ad is shown to the number of times it is clicked on. For example if the click-through ratio is 50:1, it means one in fifty people (or 2 percent) clicked the ad. (See Techniques 55 and 57.)

Demographic data: Data that outlines the characteristics of your customers. It can include age, marital status, income, education, and more. (See Technique 53.)

Domain name: Your address on the Internet, as in `www.coolebaytools.com`.

Double Opt In: The best way to assure that your newsletter customers are "opt-in." When a customer requests to be on your e-mail list, you send a confirmation response asking the customer to verify their desire to receive your e-mails.

Drop-shipments: Shipments sent by a drop-shipping source directly to your customer. (See Technique 6.)

Dumpster diving: Acquiring the castoffs of others to resell on eBay. (Not necessarily accomplished by being held by the ankles headfirst into a garbage dumpster — but it *has* been done sometimes. Don't ask!)

Duty: A tax you may have to pay if you purchase merchandise from another country.

EAN: European Article Number. The international version of the UPC.

Early adopters: Consumers who seek out the newest trends in fashion or electronics in the earliest stages of the product cycle.

Emotional buying motive: Trigger this motive in your description by plying the customers' emotions (that they have to have the product) versus selling with logic.

EOM: End-of-month stock or sales figure. The end of one month is the same figure as the *BOM* of the next month.

Escrow: A payment system to protect the buyer from fraudulent sales. The buyer's money is held by a third party until the buyer receives and approves of the item, then the payment is released to the seller. (See Technique 56.)

Even pricing: A merchandise pricing strategy to create an upscale image for your item by pricing the item in even numbers, $25.00 instead of $24.99.

Export: Goods shipped outside of the United States to other countries.

Expos/trade shows: Shows generally held at large convention centers where manufacturers introduce their latest merchandise. These shows may be general merchandise or only from a particular category.

Fad: A short-lived fashion trend that comes and goes quickly.

Fashion followers: Those who look for apparel only after the trend has fully caught on and the general populace has accepted the style. Perfect eBay apparel customers!

Feedback: eBay's User-to-User rating system. (See Technique 4.)

FIFO: First In First Out. An inventory control method, where merchandise that's first in is the first sold.

Fixed-price sale: Selling an item (or a number of items) on eBay at a set price with no option for auction.

FOB (Free On Board) shipping: The seller has title to the goods until the merchandise reaches a certain point in the shipping process. From that point, the buyer takes title and is responsible for all further shipping charges. As in FOB Miami — buyer pays all shipping charges from a Miami location.

FTC (Federal Trade Commission) Mail Order Rule: Also known as the "30-day" rule, this states that if you cannot ship a customer's order within the time you originally stated *or within 30 days,* you must obtain the customer's permission to delay the transaction. If you do not get permission, or you get no reply from the customer, you must refund all money paid to you for the unshipped merchandise. (See Technique 7.)

FTP: File Transfer Protocol. The online communications protocol used to transfer files from one computer to another.

Global marketplace: An open marketplace (like eBay) where buyers can purchase from sources worldwide.

GMS: Gross Merchandise Sales. In dollars, your total merchandise sales figure.

Gross: A quantity of twelve dozen, or 144, of a single item. *Also:* Finding a hair in your fried eggs.

Growth stage: In the life cycle of a product, this is the stage at which the product or service is past the innovator's initial input and grows through consumer acceptance.

Hammer fee: See *Buyer's premium.*

Hard Goods: All merchandise other than apparel and accessories or home fashions. Hard goods would encompass furniture, appliances, high-tech goods, sporting goods, and so on.

Hot item: An item that's nearly impossible to keep in stock due to customer demand. This is the stuff you can generally sell for over *MSRP.*

Imports: Merchandise purchased from foreign countries and sources and brought into the United States for resale.

Impression: One of a number of times an online ad is served to be viewed. One impression means there was one opportunity to see the ad. (See Techniques 55 and 57.)

Initial markup percentage: The percentage you're comfortable tacking onto an item to sell in a Buy-It-Now transaction.

Introduction stage: When merchandise is first introduced and has made it past the early adopters, but is new to the general merchandise scene.

Invoice: A bill that outlines the items in a specific transaction — who the item is sold to and all costs involved.

Irregulars: Merchandise that is not first quality and contains imperfections that may not be visible to the naked eye.

ISBN: International Standard Book Number. Just like the UPC on a can of beans, the ISBN identifies the book by a universal number.

Job lots: A varied assortment of merchandise that's left over at the end of a season. Usually sold to a buyer at a discounted price off the normal wholesale cost.

Keystone: Marking up your merchandise the amount that you paid for the item. Cost 50%, Markup 50% = 100% Keystone markup.

Layaway: Allowing someone to purchase an item and pay for it over time. You ship the item when the final payment is made.

LIFO: Last In First Out. An inventory control method that assumes that merchandise that was received last should be first out.

List Price: See *MSRP.*

Logo: A graphic symbol to identify a business. It may be an icon, or the business name in a distinctive type or graphic style.

Loss leader: Items you choose to sell (or to start the bidding) at a price lower than the going rate. You may sell at a loss, but the goal is to sell other items from your eBay store to make up for the loss.

Mannequin: A representation of the human form made of wood, fiberglass, or plastic to model clothing for your eBay apparel sales. (See Technique 16.)

Markdown: Reduction in selling price below your predetermined target price.

Markup based on cost: Pricing an item based on the price you paid for the items to be resold, rather than the "retail" price. The most common markup method used by eBay sellers.

Markup based on retail: Pricing your item to full retail price.

Maturity stage: This is toward the end of product life when prices and sales reach the maximum level. The item is no longer hard-to-find.

Merchandise plan: Sales goals in dollar amounts planned out for a prescribed period of time. (See Technique 52.)

Merchant account: A bank account that enables a business to accept credit cards for payment — in PayPal, a higher level account for larger sellers. (See Technique 28.)

Middleman: The person between you and the manufacturer, if you're not buying direct. (See Technique 5.)

MSRP: Manufacturer's Suggested Retail Price. The price (suggested by the manufacturer) that hardly anybody is willing to pay.

Odd-cent pricing: Pricing your item with odd cents. A technique that creates the impression that the buyer will be getting a bargain.

Off-price merchandise: Manufacturers' excess merchandise that's available to retailers at a considerable discount for resale.

Open to buy: In dollars, the amount left for acquiring merchandise within a specific season or time period.

Opt in: When a customer requests to be put on a mailing list. (See *Double Opt In.*)

Penetration pricing: Cutting your profits to generate more sales. Penetrate the market by gaining market share to overthrow the competition.

Physical inventory: The actual physical count of your merchandise versus what your bookkeeping or management program says you have.

Plagiarism: When another seller steals your description and/or images and uses those materials in their own sales. Report this eBay policy violation as *Image or description theft* in the Security center. (See Technique 6.)

Price skimming: Charging the highest price you can for merchandise resulting in lower transactions total, but a higher profit margin on the sales that are completed.

Price war: When two or more competitive sellers lower their product price to undercut their competitive sellers, thereby gaining market share.

Product life cycle: A chart depicting expected selling cycles of a product over its life.

Purchase order: A business form outlining the details of a merchandise purchase, usually from a retailer to a vendor.

Returns: Merchandise that has been accepted as a return in a retail transaction. Often returns are resold to eBay sellers as part of liquidation-lot merchandise. (See Technique 5.)

Seconds: Merchandise that clearly contains damage or imperfections. A step in quality below *Irregulars*. (See Technique 5.)

SKU (Stock Keeping Unit): A number assigned to each piece of inventory for identification and/or tracking purposes. It may be your own number or it may relate to the item's UPC.

Sniping: The act (or fine art) of bidding at the very last possible second of an auction. (See Technique 3.)

Spam: Unrequested and unwanted e-mail. (See Technique 62.)

Staple merchandise: Items that people buy regardless of season, year in and year out.

Steamer: An electrical appliance used to remove wrinkles from fabric. (See Technique 16.)

Stock-to-sales ratio: A planning tool that shows the relationship between stock on hand and monthly sales. This shows the amount of inventory required to generate planned sales. Ideally it should be about 3:1, so you can have a three-month supply of inventory. (See Techniques 25 and 52.)

Street price: The price that merchandise can be purchased for at brick-and-mortar or online discounters.

Turnover: The number of times your average amount of stock sells during a given period. Turning merchandise into cash.

UPC (Universal Product Code): The number that is part of the barcode that is used to identify almost any product. (You can also type a UPC into Google for identification.)

UVM (Universal Vendor Marking): This is the practice of premarking items so their origin may be identified. Many eBay sellers use a UV pen to mark their merchandise to prevent fraudulent returns. The marks of these pens can only be seen with a UV light.

Warranty: A written guarantee of the seller's or manufacturer's responsibility toward the workability of the product sold. It outlines the terms of return or repair.

Index

FOR DUMMIES®

The easy way to get more done and have more fun

PERSONAL FINANCE

0-7645-5231-7

0-7645-2431-3

0-7645-5331-3

Also available:

Estate Planning For Dummies
(0-7645-5501-4)

401(k)s For Dummies
(0-7645-5468-9)

Frugal Living For Dummies
(0-7645-5403-4)

Microsoft Money "X" For Dummies
(0-7645-1689-2)

Mutual Funds For Dummies
(0-7645-5329-1)

Personal Bankruptcy For Dummies
(0-7645-5498-0)

Quicken "X" For Dummies
(0-7645-1666-3)

Stock Investing For Dummies
(0-7645-5411-5)

Taxes For Dummies 2003
(0-7645-5475-1)

BUSINESS & CAREERS

0-7645-5314-3

0-7645-5307-0

0-7645-5471-9

Also available:

Business Plans Kit For Dummies
(0-7645-5365-8)

Consulting For Dummies
(0-7645-5034-9)

Cool Careers For Dummies
(0-7645-5345-3)

Human Resources Kit For Dummies
(0-7645-5131-0)

Managing For Dummies
(1-5688-4858-7)

QuickBooks All-in-One Desk Reference For Dummies
(0-7645-1963-8)

Selling For Dummies
(0-7645-5363-1)

Small Business Kit For Dummies
(0-7645-5093-4)

Starting an eBay Business For Dummies
(0-7645-1547-0)

HEALTH, SPORTS & FITNESS

0-7645-5167-1

0-7645-5146-9

0-7645-5154-X

Also available:

Controlling Cholesterol For Dummies
(0-7645-5440-9)

Dieting For Dummies
(0-7645-5126-4)

High Blood Pressure For Dummies
(0-7645-5424-7)

Martial Arts For Dummies
(0-7645-5358-5)

Menopause For Dummies
(0-7645-5458-1)

Nutrition For Dummies
(0-7645-5180-9)

Power Yoga For Dummies
(0-7645-5342-9)

Thyroid For Dummies
(0-7645-5385-2)

Weight Training For Dummies
(0-7645-5168-X)

Yoga For Dummies
(0-7645-5117-5)

ailable wherever books are sold.
to www.dummies.com or call 1-877-762-2974 to order direct.

WILEY

FOR DUMMIES®

A world of resources to help you grow

HOME, GARDEN & HOBBIES

Feng Shui
0-7645-5295-3

Gardening
0-7645-5130-2

Guitar
0-7645-5106-X

Also available:

Auto Repair For Dummies
(0-7645-5089-6)

Chess For Dummies
(0-7645-5003-9)

Home Maintenance For Dummies
(0-7645-5215-5)

Organizing For Dummies
(0-7645-5300-3)

Piano For Dummies
(0-7645-5105-1)

Poker For Dummies
(0-7645-5232-5)

Quilting For Dummies
(0-7645-5118-3)

Rock Guitar For Dummies
(0-7645-5356-9)

Roses For Dummies
(0-7645-5202-3)

Sewing For Dummies
(0-7645-5137-X)

FOOD & WINE

Cooking
0-7645-5250-3

Cookies
0-7645-5390-9

Wine
0-7645-5114-0

Also available:

Bartending For Dummies
(0-7645-5051-9)

Chinese Cooking For Dummies
(0-7645-5247-3)

Christmas Cooking For Dummies
(0-7645-5407-7)

Diabetes Cookbook For Dummies
(0-7645-5230-9)

Grilling For Dummies
(0-7645-5076-4)

Low-Fat Cooking For Dummies
(0-7645-5035-7)

Slow Cookers For Dummies
(0-7645-5240-6)

TRAVEL

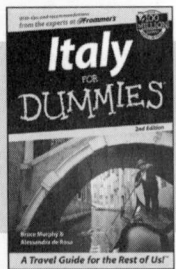

Italy
0-7645-5453-0

Hawaii
0-7645-5438-7

Las Vegas
0-7645-5448-4

Also available:

America's National Parks For Dummies
(0-7645-6204-5)

Caribbean For Dummies
(0-7645-5445-X)

Cruise Vacations For Dummies 2003
(0-7645-5459-X)

Europe For Dummies
(0-7645-5456-5)

Ireland For Dummies
(0-7645-6199-5)

France For Dummies
(0-7645-6292-4)

London For Dummies
(0-7645-5416-6)

Mexico's Beach Resorts For Dummies
(0-7645-6262-2)

Paris For Dummies
(0-7645-5494-8)

RV Vacations For Dummies
(0-7645-5443-3)

Walt Disney World & Orlando For Dummies
(0-7645-5444-1)

Available wherever books are sold. Go to www.dummies.com or call 1-877-762-2974 to order direct.

FOR DUMMIES®

Helping you expand your horizons and realize your potential

INTERNET

0-7645-0894-6

0-7645-1659-0

0-7645-1642-6

Also available:

America Online 7.0 For Dummies
(0-7645-1624-8)

Genealogy Online For Dummies
(0-7645-0807-5)

The Internet All-in-One Desk Reference For Dummies
(0-7645-1659-0)

Internet Explorer 6 For Dummies
(0-7645-1344-3)

The Internet For Dummies Quick Reference
(0-7645-1645-0)

Internet Privacy For Dummies
(0-7645-0846-6)

Researching Online For Dummies
(0-7645-0546-7)

Starting an Online Business For Dummies
(0-7645-1655-8)

DIGITAL MEDIA

0-7645-1664-7

0-7645-1675-2

0-7645-0806-7

Also available:

CD and DVD Recording For Dummies
(0-7645-1627-2)

Digital Photography All-in-One Desk Reference For Dummies
(0-7645-1800-3)

Digital Photography For Dummies Quick Reference
(0-7645-0750-8)

Home Recording for Musicians For Dummies
(0-7645-1634-5)

MP3 For Dummies
(0-7645-0858-X)

Paint Shop Pro "X" For Dummies
(0-7645-2440-2)

Photo Retouching & Restoration For Dummies
(0-7645-1662-0)

Scanners For Dummies
(0-7645-0783-4)

GRAPHICS

0-7645-0817-2

0-7645-1651-5

0-7645-0895-4

Also available:

Adobe Acrobat 5 PDF For Dummies
(0-7645-1652-3)

Fireworks 4 For Dummies
(0-7645-0804-0)

Illustrator 10 For Dummies
(0-7645-3636-2)

QuarkXPress 5 For Dummies
(0-7645-0643-9)

Visio 2000 For Dummies
(0-7645-0635-8)

FOR DUMMIES®

The advice and explanations you need to succeed

SELF-HELP, SPIRITUALITY & RELIGION

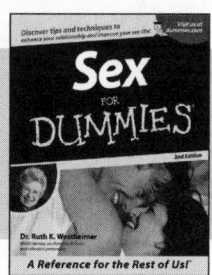
0-7645-5302-X

0-7645-5418-2

0-7645-5264-3

Also available:

The Bible For Dummies
(0-7645-5296-1)

Buddhism For Dummies
(0-7645-5359-3)

Christian Prayer For Dummies
(0-7645-5500-6)

Dating For Dummies
(0-7645-5072-1)

Judaism For Dummies
(0-7645-5299-6)

Potty Training For Dummies
(0-7645-5417-4)

Pregnancy For Dummies
(0-7645-5074-8)

Rekindling Romance For Dummies
(0-7645-5303-8)

Spirituality For Dummies
(0-7645-5298-8)

Weddings For Dummies
(0-7645-5055-1)

PETS

0-7645-5255-4

0-7645-5286-4

0-7645-5275-9

Also available:

Labrador Retrievers For Dummies
(0-7645-5281-3)

Aquariums For Dummies
(0-7645-5156-6)

Birds For Dummies
(0-7645-5139-6)

Dogs For Dummies
(0-7645-5274-0)

Ferrets For Dummies
(0-7645-5259-7)

German Shepherds For Dummies
(0-7645-5280-5)

Golden Retrievers For Dummies
(0-7645-5267-8)

Horses For Dummies
(0-7645-5138-8)

Jack Russell Terriers For Dummies
(0-7645-5268-6)

Puppies Raising & Training Diary For Dummies
(0-7645-0876-8)

EDUCATION & TEST PREPARATION

0-7645-5194-9

0-7645-5325-9

0-7645-5210-4

Also available:

Chemistry For Dummies
(0-7645-5430-1)

English Grammar For Dummies
(0-7645-5322-4)

French For Dummies
(0-7645-5193-0)

The GMAT For Dummies
(0-7645-5251-1)

Inglés Para Dummies
(0-7645-5427-1)

Italian For Dummies
(0-7645-5196-5)

Research Papers For Dummies
(0-7645-5426-3)

The SAT I For Dummies
(0-7645-5472-7)

U.S. History For Dummies
(0-7645-5249-X)

World History For Dummies
(0-7645-5242-2)